Southeast Asia's Best Dive Sites

120° 135°

La Union
Luzon

Philippine Sea

500 km

250 miles

Subic Bay

□ **MANILA**

Nasugbu

Anilao Batangas Verde

Puerto Galera

Apo Reef *Mindoro*

Coron Bay *Panay*

Cuyo Is.

El Nido

Jessie Beazley

Palawan Sumilon *Bohol* Cabilao,
Apo Panglao,
Balicasag

Tubbataha Reef

Mindanao

PHILIPPINES

Moal Negros

CIFIC OCEAN

P a c i f i c T r e n c h

Davao

Basilan I. *Davao Gulf*

Soronsol Is. **PALAU**

nabalu *Jolo I.*

Tawi Tawi *Karakelong*

Sulu Archipelago Pulo Anna

Sipadan Merir

Celebes Sea Tobi

Sangihe Is. *Talaud Is.* Helen

Sangalaki *Morotai*

Tanjungredeb **Manado**

Manado *Molucca Sea* *Halmahera Is.* *Halmahera* *Halmahera Sea*

Togian Is. *Goraici* Weda Bay *Waigeo*

Bacan Kri Island

ikpapan *Obi* Raja Ampat Biak

Banggai Is. *Talibu* *Mangole* *Misool* Misool Eco Numfoor
Resort Marine Yapen
Park

Sulawesi *Seram Sea* *Seram* *Centrawasih Gulf*

Gulf of Bone *Buru* **Ambon Bay** **Papua**

N E S I A **Banda**

il Is. **Makassar** *Buton* Wakatobi *Banda Sea* *Kai Is.* Kobroor

Selayar *Aru Is.*
Selayar Dive Resort *Trangan* *Workai*

Flores Sea Alor Archipelago *Yamdena*

Komodo Maumere *Wetar* *Tanimbar Is.*

eluk *Flores* *Adonara* *Alor* *Selaru*

Sumbawa *Lomblen* **DILI**

di Dasa, **TIMOR LESTE** *Arafura Sea*
a Lembongan **Kupang**
usa Penida *Sumba* *Timor*

Savu Sea *Timor Sea*

Rote

Savu

T0151259

ABOUT TUTTLE
"Books to Span the East and West"

Our core mission at Tuttle Publishing is to create books which bring people together one page at a time. Tuttle was founded in 1832 in the small New England town of Rutland, Vermont (USA). Our fundamental values remain as strong today as they were then—to publish best-in-class books informing the English-speaking world about the countries and peoples of Asia. The world has become a smaller place today and Asia's economic, cultural and political influence has expanded, yet the need for meaningful dialogue and information about this diverse region has never been greater. Since 1948, Tuttle has been a leader in publishing books on the cultures, arts, cuisines, languages and literatures of Asia. Our authors and photographers have won numerous awards and Tuttle has published thousands of books on subjects ranging from martial arts to paper crafts. We welcome you to explore the wealth of information available on Asia at **www.tuttlepublishing.com**.

Published by Tuttle Publishing,
an imprint of Periplus Editions (HK) Ltd

www.tuttlepublishing.com

Text and maps copyright © 2016
Periplus Editions (HK) Ltd
See Photo Credits page for © photographs

Distributed by
North America, Latin America & Europe
Tuttle Publishing
364 Innovation Drive
North Clarendon, VT 05759-9436 U.S.A.
Tel: 1 (802) 773-8930
Fax: 1 (802) 773-6993
info@tuttlepublishing.com
www.tuttlepublishing.com

Asia Pacific
Berkeley Books Pte. Ltd.
61 Tai Seng Avenue, #02-12
Singapore 534167
Tel: (65) 6280-1330
Fax: (65) 6280-6290
inquiries@periplus.com.sg
www.periplus.com

Indonesia
PT Java Books Indonesia
Kawasan Industri Pulogadung
Jl. Rawa Gelam IV No. 9, Jakarta 13930
Tel: (62) 21 4682-1088
Fax: (62) 21 461-0206
crm@periplus.co.id
www.periplus.com

ISBN 978-0-8048-4594-6

18 17 16   10 9 8 7 6 5 4 3 2 1

Printed in Malaysia   1611TW

TUTTLE PUBLISHING® is a registered trademark of Tuttle Publishing, a division of Periplus Editions (HK) Ltd.

DIVING IN
SOUTHEAST
ASIA

The Best Dive Sites in Malaysia, Indonesia, the Philippines and Thailand

**Texts by Sarah Ann Wormald,
David Espinosa, Heneage Mitchell, Kal Muller,
Fiona Nichols and John Williams**

TUTTLE Publishing

Tokyo | Rutland, Vermont | Singapore

CONTENTS

INDONESIA

THE PHILIPPINES

Diving in Southeast Asia
A Bounty of Reefs, Wrecks and Coral Gardens

Whatever extraordinary notion possesses us that first time to strap on our backs a metal tank full of compressed air, fit fins to our feet, stuff an uncomfortable contraption in our mouth and a tight-fitting piece of glass across our eyes? Uncomfortable and inept, struggling and sweating, we lurch in our new uniform, wondering whether the effort is worthwhile. But our gracelessness soon vanishes as we tumble below the surface and move weightless through the water, drift with currents and have the chance to observe, often at close quarters, creatures large and small that we would never otherwise have imagined. It is quite simply a magical world and one which invariably seduces the novice diver. He is hooked on scuba diving.

Fifteen years ago, while snorkeling from a dive boat in the gin-clear waters of the Similan Islands, a divemaster friend suggested I don a tank and regulator and drop below the water to see what diving was all about. With little more comment, he told me to stick by his side, descend slowly and remember to breathe out. Within minutes of descending, I was amidst a school of sweetlips, then visited by Moorish idols, and was enthralled by the pink soft corals sprouting from the reef like some exotic cotton wool. For some, that might have been enough, but when I caught sight of a black tip shark (shark!), admittedly at the edge of the 20-meter visibility, I, too, was hooked.

Southeast Asia's reefs lie in the heart of the coral triangle and have the biggest diversity of corals on the planet.

Within two months I had crawled the length of a public swimming pool where second-hand Band Aids were the only novelty to spot, had learned to control buoyancy somewhere under the diving board and was finally rewarded with a PADI open water certificate. Armed with this little plastic card, the real diving experience was about to begin.

For many a novice diver, education takes place after work in public swimming pools in the cold northern latitudes. Dive tables seem like just another bit of school maths and the idea of search and rescue in a swimming pool appears totally absurd. The promise of warm water and subtropical species is a lure but rarely a reality.

In Asia, one of the most species-rich areas in the world, diving is a whole different ball game. Water that hovers around the 25° C mark, a tropical climate that is tempered by sea breezes, more species than most books cover, and a wealth of different marine environ-

The bodies of anemone fish are covered in a mucus that prevents them from being stung by their host anemones.

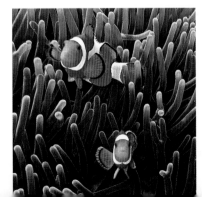

ments—not to mention idyllic sandy shores for surface interval picnics—make diving a special pleasure. Imagine learning in this particular environment!

PIONEER DIVERS

The sport evolved radically in Southeast Asia from the 1960s to the early 2000s largely due to the Vietnam War and the oil industry. The former brought Americans who were used to recreational diving in the New World and who sought to enjoy their hobby when on R&R, notably in Pattaya, while the latter brought expatriates from the United States, Europe and Australia to work in the fast developing oil business. Amid the personnel who came to work in the industry—in Thailand, Indonesia and Malaysia—there were plenty of professional divers and, often

Southeast Asia's coral reefs are excellent habitats for gorgonian fans, which can grow up to 3 meters across.

benefiting from periods of long leave and a fat salary, many of these people explored the region diving recreationally.

Twenty years ago, it was not unusual to come across divemasters whose first experience of diving in Asia was at the bottom of the Gulf of Thailand, off platforms in the South China Sea, or from some deserted island in Indonesia. Working at depths that were measured more often in fathoms than feet, diving was not always a pleasure. But armed with the skills to withstand the most taxing conditions, recreational diving in more shallow waters, on reefs that were in pristine condition, was a real pleasure even if the infrastructure for diving was largely missing. These pioneers of sports diving lugged their tanks from far-flung compressors, bartered with local fishermen and *bêche-de-mer* and pearl divers for a boat ride, and picked the brains of local mariners for reefs and shoals in a bid to find good diving. The rest was easy. Life on shore in Southeast Asia was (and still is to some extent) inexpensive and they had no need of fancy hotels. Nipa thatched huts and simple meals in the local cafes were good enough.

This striped triplefin (Helcogramma striata) is resting on a ball of tunicates and soft corals, Tulamben, Bali.

But what about their buddies who were envious of their travels and fun? In the early 1970s, there were precious few places to learn to dive in Asia (Pattaya was one of them), and it was not until the last few years of the decade, with easier air travel and greater awareness of the sport, that the bulk of dive shops and operators finally began to open their doors to novices.

It was then that a number of saturated professional divers took a look at the area they had grown to love and decided to turn their skills to teaching recreational diving. All it took was a little capital and some formal qualification from one of the professional dive associations.

GROWING PROFESSIONALISM

The debate as to which of the professional dive associations is the best is one that continues without respite but all training agencies follow the guidelines set out by the Recreational Scuba Training Council (RSTC). This means there is little difference in the content of each of the agencies' courses but the materials and the teaching systems and methodologies do vary. PADI has by far the greatest foothold in Southeast Asia (and worldwide), followed by SSI. You'll find that the majority of dive operators are either PADI or SSI affiliated and follow the standards set out by these two major agencies. Affiliations with other training bodies are also found, such as with CMAS, BSAC or other smaller agencies. All are equally acceptable but PADI and SSI are the two largest internationally recognized training agencies globally. It is not necessary to have training qualifications from the same agency that your chosen dive center is affiliated to. For example, SSI trained divers are welcome in PADI (or any other) affiliated dive center. It is, however, important to dive with a center that does

have an affiliation, a good reputation and decent equipment for hire if you are not traveling with your own. There are literally hundreds of affiliated dive centers in Southeast Asia who employ thousands of accredited instructors and divemasters so it is not necessary (or recommended) to dive with operators who are lacking in properly trained staff or facilities.

Entry level courses, such as the open water course, are widely available and usually take between 3 and 4 days. Be aware of operators offering cheaper and shorter courses as you may not be receiving proper instruction and be sure to check that your instructor is up to date with their registration. You can ask to see their certification card. The instructor's name on your certification card and paperwork should match the name of the instructor who conducted your course. Dive courses in Southeast Asia can be considerably cheaper than those offered in Europe, the United States and Australia and the standard of teaching (generally) is good. If you are short of time during your trip, it is possible (with PADI and SSI) to complete the theory components of your course online before leaving home.

A green turtle resting on a hard coral outcrop in Sipadan, Sabah.

Mandarin fish are one of Southeast Asia's most colorful marine species. They are a shy species during day time and hide away amidst the base of corals.

It is even possible to complete the pool training dives with a dive center in your home country beforehand and to just make the open water dives during your trip. This makes your training during your holiday considerably shorter.

Southeast Asia is also a great destination for continuing your diver training. Advanced open water courses are common as arespecialty courses and rescue courses. For those seeking training beyond recreational levels, Southeast Asia is home to a booming industry in professional level courses with divemaster courses and internships widely available and instructor level courses available in most major diving regions. The prices for professional level courses compare very favorably to prices in Western countries.

ECO-SENSITIVITY

Another improvement in the dive scene over the last three decades is the growing awareness of environmental con-cerns which touch not only the experiences of recreational divers but the lives of locals and the flora and fauna. Deforestation, discharge of sewage, oil and refuse in the sea, destructive fishing methods as well as coral and shell collection have also all come under the environmental spotlight in Asia.

While lifestyles have not radically changed, some of the destructive practices have been curtailed and local governments have begun to set up marine reserves to encourage the regeneration of the marine environment. Of course, mangrove swamps that have been suffocated by silt do not recover overnight, nor do coral reefs that have been blasted by dynamite or repeatedly broken up by anchors and fins. But recover they do, albeit more slowly than from the blanket damage inflicted by natural disasters, and the results are encouraging. The marine environment rarely returns to what it was before damage but it does recover and proliferate.

WHERE TO DIVE AND WHY

So where do divers head for and what can they expect to find in Southeast Asia?

In Malaysia, most diving has been centered from the east coast and Sabah, in Indonesia from Bali and Manado, across to Flores and beyond to West Papua, in the Philippines from Batangas and the Visayas, and on the Gulf of Thailand and Phuket.

MALAYSIA In Malaysia, the development of an infrastructure on a number of east coast islands has made it easy for dive enthusiasts to enjoy some of the best coral reefs, while the country's premier dive spot in the deep waters off Sabah has developed into a real dive destination. Off Sabah too, the oceanic reef Layang-Layang has developed into a world-class destination for dive enthusiasts.

INDONESIA With far-flung islands, Indonesia has developed resorts in tandem with the establishment of regular air connections, and in many of these diving and snorkeling are given priority. An improving network of domestic air carriers has made many areas more accessible and liveaboard boats have also made an impact, offering divers the chance to explore really remote areas like the Banda Sea, Raja Ampat and West Papua and numerous other small island chains across the archipelago.

THE PHILIPPINES The diving fraternity in the Philippines has benefited from a burgeoning infrastructure in the smaller island destinations and a proliferation of liveaboard boats that explore the Sulu Sea. The retreat of the US military opened once off-limits areas to the public along with some fantastic wreck diving.

THAILAND In the search for pristine locations and big pelagics, Phuket-based

Juvenile round-faced batfish (Platax orbicularis) can be quite inquisitive.

operators have pushed out into the Andaman Sea as far as the Andaman Islands themselves, which are in Indian waters, and to the Mergui Archipelago in Burmese waters (Myanmar). They have also forged southward, toward the Malaysian border, where they have discovered, like their pioneering colleagues from Pattaya, untouched coral reefs and forgotten wrecks.

DIVE TOPOGRAPHY

Most Southeast Asian reefs are **fringing reefs**, and most diving will be along the outer reef edge, often quite close to shore. The profile is sometimes gently sloping, and sometimes full of bommies and coral heads. But the region is perhaps most famous for its steep **drop-offs**, particularly in Indonesia and the Philippines. The wall at Bunaken near Manado is world famous, and Menjangan, Komodo, Kupang, the Bandas, Selayar Island, Weda Bay in Halmahera and Sangalaki also feature steep drop-offs.

The Philippines offers plenty of good **walls**—at Verde, Anilao, Nasugbu and Apo as well as a dozen more places. Malaysia offers fabulous walls at Sipadan

The Seven Seas liveaboard is a traditional Indonesian-style phinisi vessel that operates in both Komodo and Raja Ampat, Indonesia.

and Layang-Layang, and even tiny Tenggol off Peninsular Malaysia offers a good one.

While not particularly widespread, Southeast Asia also has its fair share of **wrecks**. There are numerous war graves and vessels lost during World War II off Pattaya in Thailand and in the bay at Coron in the Philippines, and there are easily dived wrecks off Manado and Bali in Indonesia. There are also fishing vessels that have met an untimely end and even the odd dive boat or two.

In some places, artificial wrecks (tires, old buses and broken boats) have been sunk to encourage regeneration of reefs and their associated fauna. Singapore has done this outside its harbor waters. The Philippines and Thailand have also adopted this method.

You'll find that diving in Southeast Asia is generally on the continental shelf but **oceanic diving** is possible too. This inevitably entails a trip on a liveaboard.

LIVEABOARD DIVING

Liveaboard dive boats have made a big impact on the scope and range of diving. In Indonesia, liveaboard operations take divers to the Banda Sea, the islands north of Manado, the Raja Ampat Islands of West Papua, and Komodo and other islands in the Nusa Tenggara provinces. Yacht chartering is becoming popular in Bali with holidaymakers who also enjoy diving. In the Philippines, the fabulous reefs at Apo and those of Tubbataha, Jessie Beazley and Basterra are only accessible by liveaboards while other liveaboards and chartered yachts ply the small islands of the Visayas and Palawan. So do yachts and dive vessels in Sabah, Malaysia, that offer diving in remote offshore areas, while yachts and small motor boats (often converted fishing vessels) offer diving trips in Malaysian and the northern Indonesian waters from Singapore. Phuket, especially, has developed this industry, building new marinas to accommodate charter yachts and dive vessels. And, if you want to, you can dive in the Mergui Archipelago from Thailand, discover the reefs off the southeast coast by the Cambodian border in the Gulf of Thailand, or head for the almost virgin territory of the Andaman Islands. Well-equipped liveaboards are the only answer to reaching these remote areas.

When diving first started in the region, it was a cheap hobby once you had bought a regulator and other basic gear. Today, the relationship between learning to dive, buying the gear and getting going has changed. The gear is getting more sophisticated but less costly, dive courses are becoming more competitively priced and the cost of diving itself is getting more expensive, mainly because today's diver is a more sophisticated animal and not the hardy aficionado of yesteryear. In the Practicalities section at the end of this book you will be able to see how the cost of diving compares through the region.

Best of all, there are still many areas in Asia to be charted, let alone developed as dive destinations—areas that have, up to now, discouraged tourism and development, places that were off-limits for political or commercial reasons, and spots where transport was almost non-existent. But it is only a matter of time before these virgin areas open up to enthusiastic divers.

—*Fiona Nichols/Sarah Ann Wormald*

Indonesian reefs are so rich that on a single spot one can find soft corals, sponges, hydroids, four species of algae and five species of tunicates.

THAILAND
Songkhla
Hat Yai
Pattani
Yala
Langkawi
Narathiwat
Alor Setar
Pulau Payar
Kota
Bharu
Perhentian
Sungai Petani
Redang
Butterworth
Georgetown
Kuala
Terengganu
Kapas
Taiping
Tenggol
Ipoh
MALAYSIA
Teluk Intan
(Teluk Anson)
Pangkor
Kuantan
Klang
KUALA LUMPUR
Petaling Jaya
Tioman
Tanjungbalai
P. Tioman
Seremban
Melaka
Muar
Aur
P. Tinggi
Keluang
P. Selat
Kering
Batu Pahat
Johor Bahru
SUMATRA
SINGAPORE
P. Rangsan
Batam
INDONESIA
P. Karimun
Bintan

200 km
100 miles

MALAYSIA
INDONESIA

Kepulauan Natuna Utara

P. Natuna
Besar

Kepulauan Anambas

Kepulauan Natuna Selat

Serosan

Singka

Strait of Malacca

MALAYSIA
INDONESIA

Diving in Malaysia
Where Rainforest Meets Reef

Up to the late 1980s, those adventurous travelers who made their way to Malaysia were rewarded with a rich culture and a lifestyle that had changed little over the centuries. Occasionally, they snorkeled the island coral reefs and even more occasionally dived the offshore waters. The attractions that the country advertised overseas were, however, largely on *terra firma*. Much of that has changed in recent times and scuba professionals have set up operations in a number of places in the country offering a good variety of services and dive options. With the help of some individuals in the private sector, the tourism arm of the government has made a conscious effort to attract overseas visitors to Malaysia's marine attractions, with some success.

Malaysia lies entirely within the tropics and is divided into two main geographical areas. Peninsular Malaysia joins, on its northern boundary, Thailand, and on its southern shore the Republic of Singapore through a causeway linking the two countries. Some 650 km away, on the huge island of Borneo across the South China Sea, lie two more Malaysian states, the vast states of Sabah and Sarawak, separated by the independently ruled Sultanate of Brunei. The two states on Borneo complete the 13 states of Malaysia, ruled under a federal system from Kuala Lumpur on the Malay Peninsula.

Since the 1990s, like many of its Asian neighbors, Malaysia has made tremendous economic progress resulting in a large growth in population and a huge

Layang Layang 🛬

P. Blambangan P. Banggi

PHILIPPINES MALAYSIA

P. Jambongan

Tunku Abdul Rahman Park 🛬 Kota Kinabalu

Sandakan

BRUNEI DARUSSALAM 🛬 Labuan

Lahad Datu

BANDAR SERI BEGAWAN ▢

Kuala Belait

Miri

MALAYSIA INDONESIA

Tawau Sipadan 🛬

P. Sebatik

Sirik Cape

MALAYSIA

Bintulu

Sipang Cape

Sibu

Tanjungredeb

Kuching

MALAYSIA INDONESIA

INDONESIA

A hard coral reef top around Sipadan Island, Sabah, where you will find an excellent selection of dive spots.

Located some 25 minutes north of Sipadan Island, Sipadan Water Village Resort in Mabul offers macro diving around Mabul and the Kapalai Islands and safaris to Sipadan Island.

increase in urban development on both a commercial and domestic level.

The capital, Kuala Lumpur, has expanded both laterally and skyward, while Johor Bahru, the country's second largest town and Singapore's nearest neighbor, has similarly grown in size and population. Shopping malls, office buildings and international class hotels now decorate these skylines that once carried a silhouette of palm trees and thatched roofs.

Malaysia has two distinctive seasons, dividing the country climatically, though the temperatures at sea level do not vary radically with either season. You can expect a high that rarely exceeds 31° C on the coast, and a low that rarely drops below 22° C. Of course, in the highland areas temperatures are quite different. While the northeast monsoon lashes the eastern shores, dumping heavy rain from November to late February, the western parts of the country—and that includes the dive sites around Langkawi—enjoy

drier, sunny tropical weather. Conversely, when the southwest monsoon picks up from May to October, it is time for the east coast dive sites, and those in Borneo, to enjoy sunny dry days—while the western shores get their torrential downpours.

Of the estimated 30 million inhabitants in the 13 states comprising Malaysia, 7 percent are ethnically Indian, 22 percent are of Chinese origin while the majority, approximately 60 percent, are Malays and aborigines. A number of minority groups make up the remainder.

The Malays, a Muslim population, have always been fishermen though perhaps not sailors. They know their coastal waters and have fished them for centuries. Unfortunately, with a growing population to feed, an active tourism industry and a worldwide interest in tropical fish for aquaria, their fishing techniques became more radical in the 1960s and 1970s. Dynamite and cyanide might bring more fish into their nets, but it also killed and maimed many more and did irreparable damage to the country's coral reefs.

CREATION OF MARINE PARKS

In the mid-1970s, Sabah gazetted one of the first marine parks in the country, the Tunku Abdul Rahman Park. Then, in the 1980s, answering a call from concerned environmentalists and divers, four further marine reserves were gazetted to protect the fauna and flora off Peninsular Malaysia's coasts. These included Pulau Payar in Kedah and the three areas off the east coast of Malaysia. These last three marine parks together cover thousands of square kilometers of water and embrace some of the most picturesque islands and coral reefs anywhere, among them Redang, Tenggol, Kapas, Rawa, Tioman and Aur. It was no accident that Pulau Tioman was chosen as one of the sites for filming part of the movie *South Pacific*, an island that breathed the ingredients of a tropical paradise.

All of the east coast islands are reefed with coral and host a marine ecology that enthralls snorkelers and provides plenty of interest for divers. In addition, the outer islands are sufficiently far away from the effects of the mainland and deep enough into the South China Sea to boast a variety of large pelagics, although in recent years their numbers have been dropping.

These islands and the shores of the east coast generally are also, interestingly, one of the main breeding grounds for leatherback, green and hawksbill turtles. Traditionally, turtle eggs have been collected in Malaysia as they are believed, in some instances, to have aphrodisiacal qualities. This, and the killing of turtles for their flesh, has led to a huge decline in numbers. In an effort to conserve these harmless creatures, wardens and volunteers search nightly during the

Hawksbill turtles are commonly seen resting on the reefs of eastern Borneo.

summer laying season for nests containing turtle eggs, incubating them in the safety of government hatcheries and releasing the young turtles into the sea. Similar schemes to ensure turtle survival operate on the three islands comprising Turtle Island Park off Sandakan, around the tiny isle of Sipadan, Sabah, and on Pulau Besar, near Melaka, off the west coast of Peninsular Malaysia.

LOCATING MALAYSIA'S CORAL REEFS

On Peninsular Malaysia's east coast, the best coral reefs are to be found in the nine islands that comprise Pulau Redang which, until the boom in tourism, were only inhabited by fisher folk. Redang's natural beauty inevitably caught the eye of developers who created a golf course on the island and a hotel with scuba diving facilities. Nowadays, there is a choice of places to stay and dive. Fine corals, too, are to be found at fairly shallow depths around the two Perhentian islands and at Lang Tengah.

To the south, Pulau Tenggol has good coral formations in excellent condition and the only real wall diving in Peninsular Malaysia, while Kapas, with its exquisite white sandy beaches, offers shallow and pretty coral reefs.

Tioman, despite its beauty, is not the best place for corals. Overfishing, dynamite fishing and human influence have done much to destroy the nearby corals. Offshore and on submerged reefs the conditions are better. But because it is served by a small airport with daily flights to and from Kuala Lumpur and Singapore, and excellent sea connections, Tioman is a very popular resort for holidaymakers and divers, particularly over

Nazri's Beach on idyllic Tioman Island.

weekends. In the southern waters of the east coast lies the small island of Aur, which boasts good corals and some fine diving. Because of its proximity to Singapore, Aur also attracts plenty of weekend divers from the republic.

Although the formation of marine parks has helped limit the damage caused by illegal fishing, it can do nothing to prevent the run-off from the peninsula itself (deforestation has not been kind to the rivers and offshore waters), which has had disastrous effects on the mangrove swamps as well as inshore corals.

If you see a cloud of juvenile fish or small cardinalfish like this one, look closely as there could be a frogfish lurking somewhere on the outcrop.

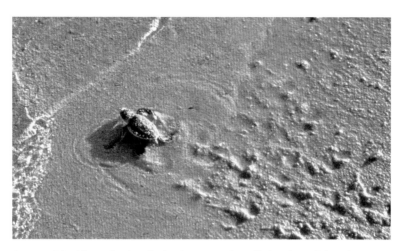

A green turtle hatchling reaches the surf, only to face many predators. The best place in Malaysia for sea turtle watchers is Sipadan Island.

The best areas for coral on the west side of Peninsular Malaysia are around the three islands that form the Pulau Payar Marine Park just south of Langkawi. Even though the visibility is not as good as that on the east coast of the peninsula, divers report that there is good coral and marine life.

In Borneo, the situation is far better. With the gazetting of Tunku Abdul Rahman Park, the reefs around the five small islands off Kota Kinabalu's shore have benefited enormously from the park's protection over recent decades. Visibility is not always as clear as it might be, but the shallow reefs are a major attraction to holidaymakers in the area. Snorkeling and diving facilities are widely available to visitors.

But the best reefs lie, without a doubt, at Sipadan, a small mushroom-shaped island rising from the ocean floor situated some 25 km off the coast from Tawau. The reefs are in excellent condition, with

Hammerhead shark sightings are the number one attraction in Layan-Layang.

a rating amongst the best in Asia, and when the waters are not filled with plankton the visibility can be good. Sharks are common as are large schools of fish. Dive permits (with limited availability) are required for diving around Sipadan and so booking in advance is essential.

The more remotely positioned Layang-Layang, some 240 km north of Kota Kinabalu, offers reefs that are in fine condition and provide divers with some fabulous encounters not only with reef life but with large pelagics.

MALAYSIAN LIVEABOARDS

For those who are not seeking a shore-based experience in Malaysia, divers have found that liveaboard dive boats offer an excellent alternative to land-based diving. Divers can also enjoy Sipadan and the Kunak group of islands north of Sipadan from the comfort of a liveaboard dive boat. Lastly, many dive trips to Malaysia, in particular those to the islands off the east coast, can also be organized from neighboring Singapore.

—*Fiona Nichols/Sarah Ann Wormald*

Sipadan

Memorable Diving from an Oceanic Isle East of Borneo

The diving is always good at Sipadan and occasionally it can be superb. Good-sized pelagics and large schools of fish generally represent Sipadan's main attraction to divers. While nothing is guaranteed, it's not unusual for dives around Sipadan to be highlighted by one or more of the following: hammerhead and leopard shark sightings, barracudas in shoals of several hundred, a rumbling herd of many bumphead parrotfish, a manta or two, countless turtles and perhaps half a dozen white tip sharks.

Reef fish are present in fair numbers and variety, and perhaps most impressive are the quantities of medium-sized fish—between 25 and 40 cm—in relatively shallow waters. This is especially the case for groups of up to a dozen harlequin sweetlips, but also snappers, emperorfish, triggerfish, long fin batfish and a couple of species of unicornfish.

These sweetlips are accompanied by a swarm of tiny glassfish.

Access	Boat times vary from Mabul, Kapalai and Semporna
Current	Variable, 10–22 meters
Reef type	Light, occasionally more
Highlights	Generally good variety
Visibility	Slopes and walls, cave
Coral	Generally good numbers of big fish at best sites
Fish	Hammerheads; Turtle Cave; turtles galore

Macro lens wielders and those with acute powers of observation could spot an unusual crinoid, shrimp and tiny fish combination, all matching the host's coloration, or a golden spotted shrimp on a very flattened carpet anemone. Some divers have found a patch of relatively tame spotted garden eels, elsewhere requiring the patience of Job to photograph outside of their burrow. Sharp eyes can also reveal a pink sailfin leaffish or a scorpionfish and nudibranchs.

It has been said that the reefs of Sipadan are less colorful than elsewhere in Southeast Asia. This is possibly due to the restricted visibility in the shallows (often of pea-soup quality) but also to far less aggregations of fairy basslets and other small fry. However, sponges are there in various shapes, especially enormous barrel sponges.

We find the dive spots live up to their names: **White Tip Avenue**, **Turtle Patch**, **Staghorn Crest**, **Lobster Lair** and **Hanging Gardens** (for soft corals).

Since 2005, when Sabah National Parks made huge efforts to protect the

Barracuda Point

Turtle Cave   Coral Gardens

North Point   Drop-off   White Tip Avenue

Resting House   Turtle Hatchery

Sipadan Island

West Ridge   Mid Reef

Hanging Gardens

Turtle Patch

Lobster Lairs   500 m   1000 ft

Sipadan Dive Sites

StaghornCrest

South Point

area, fish numbers have remained relatively stable and large numbers of fish are seen on most dives around Sipadan. There are no longer resorts based on the island. Divers must either stay at neighboring Mabul or the Kapalai Islands which are home to most of the upmarket dive resorts that offer trips to the park. For those on a tighter budget, accommodation is available in the cheaper area of Semporna and day boats also leave the harbor from there for day dive trips to Sipadan.

Diving in the Sipadan area is strictly regulated and operated on a permit basis. Only 120 divers per day are allowed to the island and dives must take place between 6am and 4pm. No night diving is permitted. Due to the limited number of permits available per day, booking in advance is essential. Permits are sold to operators who then, in turn, allocate them to guests. It is not recommended to arrive in the area without a prior booking. It may be that if you can wait around for a few days an operator may be able to free up a pass for you but it could take longer. In peak season, it may not be possible at all.

South Point On one trip we saw a school of 50 hammerhead sharks at South Point, a solid wall of barracudas stretching over 10 meters high, almost

Water bungalow-style accommodation gives guests direct access to the water for snorkeling at any time and certainly makes it easy to check the tides!

motionless in the current and relatively undisturbed by the gazes of fellow divers, and several dozen bumphead parrotfish in a herd, lazing just under the surface in dappled sunlight. These highlights require a touch of luck. But on every one of our 18 dives we saw green turtles—up to a dozen in a single dive—along with reef white tip sharks and always a fair variety of reef fishes.

Barracuda Point There is one good reason to dive this spot—barracuda. Time after time they turn up in their hundreds, a shoal that turns the water into a glinting wall of fish. There are also sharks accompanying almost every dive, along with a shoal of bumphead parrotfish.

Hanging Gardens Coral lovers will be in awe at this beautiful dive spot. The soft corals hang like dripping wax from can-

Turtle Cave is one of Sipadan's most famed sites.

dles in a profusion of colors that can hardly be matched elsewhere. We have rarely had good visibility here (diving in the morning without sunlight is not the best) but the beauty of the sights compensates.

Turtles While you tend to become blasé about green turtles, this is the one guaranteed highlight on Sipadan. It is claimed that these waters have the largest turtle population found anywhere. Just swimming close to one is thrilling. Or watching them tearing and chewing a chunk of soft coral. And almost nothing disturbs a mating pair, not even other males climbing on top hoping to get in on the action.

TURTLE FACTS

A large population of green turtles (*Chelonia mydas*) call Sipadan home. Their name comes not so much from their overall color, an olive brown, as from their greenish fat. We saw some of these turtles on every dive, with an occasional individual close to the species' maximum size (140 kg) and a carapace length of over 1 meter. Turtles are one of the main reasons for Sipadan's popularity.

Schooling anthias are often found around hard coral heads in Sipadan.

The animals are almost exclusively vegetarian, feeding on sea grasses, algae, occasionally sponges and soft corals. While they are protected on Sipadan, elsewhere green turtles are killed for their meat, hide and oil. Turtles take their time copulating, and because of this some believe the eggs can increase male potency, especially if the first three of any batch are eaten raw. The slow rate at which turtles mature combined with low infant survival rates and pressures from illegal egg hunting and poaching have led to a general worldwide decline in their numbers.

Schooling fish are another reason for diving Sipadan. Barracuda and South Point are particularly good in this respect and we sometimes drifted down through four good-sized schools at the start of the dive. Anemones and their guest fish can be spotted on almost every dive, along with hefty sized solitary barracuda (usually in the shallows) and an occasional imperturbable crocodilefish, alias longsnout flathead. Moorish idols, often in pairs, usually accompany every dive.

The pier at Pulau Sipadan where most tourists arrive.

DIVING BASICS

Sipadan diving is not for everyone. Currents are often present and shift during the course of a dive. At Barracuda Point, in particular, there is often 2 knots of current heading away from the reef and downward. There are relatively easy dive spots, but we found the most interesting were also the ones with the strongest current: Barracuda and South Point.

Sipadan Island lies not far but in splendid isolation from the continental shelf. While it is only some 12 km to Mabul Island on the edge of the shallow Sigitan reefs, the ocean plunges to almost 1,000 meters before rising abruptly.

The 15-hectare island, with its lush vegetation and white sand beaches, is but the tip of a marine outcrop. To walk the surrounding beach would take around 30 minutes, and there is much nature to observe along the shoreline.

On the north east coast, where the reef top extends less than 10 meters from the shore, the turquoise waters abruptly turn dark blue at the edge of a vertical wall. Elsewhere, the shallow reef extends as an irregular fringe, over 500 meters off South Point. A dozen or so dive spots dot the edge of the reef, all above vertical walls.

The discovery of Sipadan only goes back to 1984. While on a commercial job on a nearby grounded ship, Borneo Divers checked out the island and liked very much what they saw. After obtaining all the necessary permits, the company started bringing clients to the island in 1985. Divers were initially put up in tents until a small resort was constructed. Following this, two more resorts opened up in the same area. However, the three resorts were only open until 2005 when Sabah Parks recognized the need to protect and conserve an area of such outstanding natural beauty. Since 2005, the resorts have been closed and staying on the island is not permitted, and diving is restricted in order to allow the area to continue to flourish.

Mabul Island has crystal clear waters surrounding its picturesque pier.

Prior to 2005, the island received a boost at international level when Jacques Cousteau spent several weeks there to shoot his film, *Ghost of the Sea Turtles*. While Cousteau claimed the discovery of **Turtle Cave**, he and his team were allegedly taken there by Borneo Divers, who had already surveyed the site.

MABUL AND KAPALAI

If you are staying in either Mabul or Kapalai, the highlight of your trip will be diving around Sipadan Island. However, due to the permit system, you should not expect to be doing so every day. If you purchase a diving package for less than a week it may be that only one day of this is on Sipadan (a day trip to Sipadan usually includes 3-4 dives, depending on the operator). Check when booking how many Sipadan days versus non-Sipadan days are included in your package.

Most Mabul and Kapalai operators will strongly suggest that you first dive the sites around the island on which you are based. This gives the operator the opportunity to access your skills prior to venturing over to Sipadan, which is renowned for having currents.

Mabul offers some fantastic muck diving with critters galore and plenty of macro life ranging from blue ringed octopus, ghost pipefish and seahorses to a range of nudibranchs. Like Sipadan, Mabul also has a healthy turtle population and eagle rays are also known to pass through the area.

Kapalai offers relatively easy diving and a range of sloping sandy reefs that are home to numerous creatures and critters, including pipefish, stonefish, crocodilefish, cuttlefish, mandarinfish, frogfish, ribbon eels and nudibranchs.

—Kal Muller/Sarah Ann Wormald

Layang-Layang and Kota Kinabalu
Diving off Sabah's Northwestern Coast

Two world-class possibilities exist for diving from the East Malaysian state of Sabah on the island of Borneo. About 300 km northwest of Kota Kinabalu (KK), in the midst of the South China Sea, lies the Layang-Layang Atoll, which translates literally as "Swallows Reef", part of the group of atolls that make up the Borneo Banks. **Layang Layang Island Resort** is the only diving operator and hotel accommodation available, so booking well in advance is highly recommended.

The majority of the atoll here lies underwater with the exception of rocks that are exposed at low tide. The reefs drop in walls on all sides to depths of up to 2,000 meters. There are some excellent dives at all depths with healthy corals and good diversity. Without a doubt, though, the main reason for visiting Layang-Layang is the opportunity to see schools of scalloped hammerheads.

A GATHERING OF PELAGICS

Layang-Layang's diving season is from March until September. It is, above all, famous for schooling hammerhead sharks, and they are there in abundance until

Access	5–15 minutes by boat
Current	Good, 10–25 meters
Reef type	Light to moderate
Highlights	Excellent condition
Visibility	Walls and reef crests
Coral	Good numbers and variety of big pelagics
Fish	Hammerhead sharks, dog tooth tuna, mantas, turtles

July, but as the water warms up the sharks go deeper. The best diving is around the northeastern end of the atoll, followed closely by the southwestern end.

The eastern point of the atoll is called **Dogtooth Lair**, and in addition to the tuna that the site is named after, this seems to be the spot for hammerheads. Normally swimming at depths of 40 meters or more, we once encountered a school of sharks in the 10-meter-deep waters of the coral gardens. Schools of barracuda populate the reef and wall. A huge school of jackfish hang out at 10–15 meters and manta rays are also frequent visitors here.

Layang-Layang Dive Sites

The **Gorgonian Forest** is a continuation of the wall at Dogtooth Lair, so it is not uncommon to see schooling hammerheads on this dive either. But this site is famous for its sea fans. From 20 meters down, the wall is covered in multicolored sea fans (gorgonians) of impressive size—great for wide-angle photography.

Navigator's Lane, next along the wall, is where sea fans give way to an impressive display of soft corals. The site was visited by hammerheads during our dives, and invariably there were grey and white tip sharks circling around off the wall. Tuna cruise up and down the drop-off in search of any unwary reef fish among the schools along the wall.

At the southwestern end of the atoll is a site called **D-Wall**, a wall so impressive because it is so sheer and so deep. Even at 50 meters there seems to be no end to its vertical drop. The wall is festooned with colorful soft corals that entice the diver deeper. On one dive, while photographing soft corals at some 35 meters, a school of 40 hammerheads swam by. Although not sighted as often in this area, they were here! White tip sharks,

Despite their formidable teeth, pufferfish are docile.

tuna and clouds of reef fishes populate the wall to make a great dive site.

At the end of D-Wall is a site aptly named **Shark Cave**, for at 20–25 meters there is a deep cave extending under the reef where a group of white tips can often be found sleeping. Here we found 10 sharks piled up like logs on the left side of the cave and a school of about 50 snappers hanging around the entrance on the right side of the cave. Down current, the reef is flatter with rolling terrain. This area is generally swept by currents, and consequently is often favored by large fishes.

Yellow snappers in Layang-Layang.

TUNKU ABDUL RAHMAN PARK

If sharks are not your idea of fun diving, Kota Kinabalu, capital of Sabah, has an alternative. Twenty minutes by boat from the center of KK lie five islands that make up the Tunku Abdul Rahman Park, offering secluded beaches and reefs just offshore, which are perfect for snorkeling and diving.

Mid Reef near Manukan Island is a good site. The reef is generally round and slopes off on all sides from 5 to 20 meters. The top of the reef has good hard corals. Dropping down to 15-29 meters, you encounter a garden of black coral trees. A small school of yellow fin barracuda are frequently present on most

dives and juvenile leopard sharks can often be seen here on night dives.

Clement Reef, closer to Sapi Island, is also a sloping reef that ranges from 12 to 18 meters, with the exception of a small finger that juts out from the reef and reaches 25 meters in depth. This finger is covered with sea fans, sponges and soft coral, attracting schools of snappers and abundant reef fish. In February and March, whale sharks migrate through the area and are sometimes seen.

Mamutik Island is home to the Borneo Divers dive center, which offers dive trips and PADI courses from introductory to instructor levels.

—*Bob Bowdey/Sarah Ann Wormald*

Kota Kinabalu Dive Sites

1 km
1 mile

N

Bulijong Bay
Mt. Sayang
Wrasse Point
Agill Reef
Police Bay
Gaya Garden
Merangis Reef
Gaya East Reef
Clement Reef Seafans
Ribbon Reef North
Ribbon Reef South
Macro Corner
Gaya I.
EV Garden
Extention
Turtle House
Fan Corner
Whell House
Sapi I.
Beach Reef
Sapi Slope
Sapi Reef
Ron's Reef
GPS Point
Nudi Garden
Padang Point
Patch North
Water Village
Patch South
Water Village
Mangrove Corner
Patch Small
Land Slide North
Manukan Slope
Kota Kinabalu
and Slide West
Mid Reef
Manukan I.
Mid Reef Wreck
Black Coral Reef
Manukan Reef
Mamutik North
The Rock
Mamutik I.
North Reef
Mamutik East
The Tyres
Sulug I.
South Reef
Sulug Reef

Terengganu
The Best Diving in Peninsular Malaysia

From its northern borders near the small coastal town of Kuala Besut to the sandy shores of Kemaman in the south, the Malaysian east coast state of Terengganu boasts 225 km of nearly uninterrupted coastline and a score or so offshore islands, many offering excellent coral reefs that form part of a marine park.

The state of Terengganu is a traditional Muslim one with a pretty capital town, Kuala

Nemanthus annamensis, more commonly known as the gorgonian wrapper or whip coral anemone, on a gorgonian host.

Access By bumboat from coastal towns and from island resorts

Current Fair, 8–20 meters

Reef type Usually negligible to light

Highlights Good condition, fine variety in most places

Visibility Usually coral gardens

Coral Schools, reef fish, pelagics

Fish Occasional whale shark and manta ray sightings; wall at Tenggol

Terengganu, at the mouth of the river. Fishing, palm oil and agriculture were traditionally the mainstay of the economy. When oil was discovered offshore, the fortunes of this state changed radically, and it became one of the wealthiest in the federation. Today, tourism now plays a major role in the state's economy for its beaches and offshore islands have been discovered by sun lovers and divers. Divers flock to the Perhentian Islands (Besar and Kecil) for the beaches and reefs. Redang Island also offers good diving opportunities and some more upmarket accommodation.

Kuala Terengganu airport (Sultan Mahmud) has a few daily flights from Kuala Lumpur and from there it is around a 2-3 hour drive to Kuala Besut, the main entry point to the Perhentian Islands. However, transit through Kota Bharu in Kelantan offers better conections to Kuala Besut by both train and air. If you are planning to stay on Redang Island, then Merang is the main ferry point.

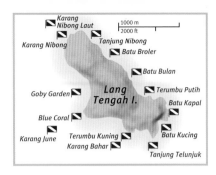

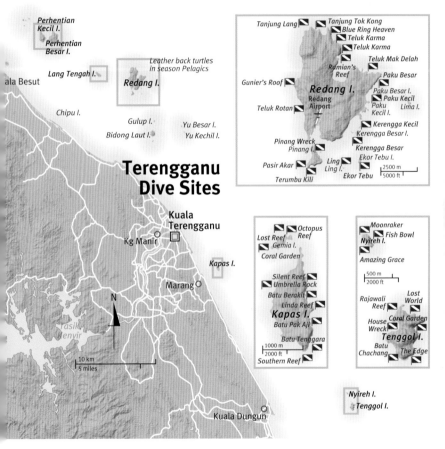

PERHENTIAN ISLANDS

The two islands of Perhentian lie some 23 km offshore from Terengganu and are accessible by ferry from Kuala Besut. **Perhentian Kecil** (the smaller island) has a range of accommodation and dive centers for every budget and is a popular choice with young backpackers.

Perhentian Besar, with its beautiful white sandy beaches, also has numerous places to stay and dive operators but is generally a little more upmarket.

Perhentian Island is accessible by ferry and has accommodation and dive centers for every budget.

In the dry season (May to September), diving from Perhentian can be excellent, and the waters on the South China Sea side of the island are quite clear. The reefs are generally fairly shallow, although they extend deeper on the northern sides of the islands. There are some hard corals, though not that many, plenty of beautiful soft corals and some impressive gorgonians on the outer reefs.

On a good dive you can expect to come across schools of trevallies, jacks, glasseyes and rainbow runners. There are some black tip reef sharks in the area as well as a good population of green turtles. Visibility here averages 12 meters, though it can fall. Among the pelagics often encountered around the Susu Dara group of isles just northwest of Perhentian— probably the best dive location—are several species of sharks, but barracudas and large groupers are also common.

LANG TENGAH

Some 15 km south of Perhentian lies the 120 ha island of Pulau Lang Tengah, another good spot for diving. Whilst accommodation is available on the island, it is not yet as developed as the neighboring Perhentian Islands.

Because of the surrounding deep waters and its isolation, Lang Tengah has good corals, both hard and soft, hosting a proliferation of marine life. There are a number of good dive sites in the area, including one with prolific *Dendronephthya* and another of table corals. On a regular 15-meter dive, you should find schools of jacks and trevallies, yellowtails and rainbow runners. Late afternoon is a particularly good time for diving and turtles. Shovelnose rays and bamboo sharks have been known to frequent the area on occasions. For macro photographers, there are some great nudibranchs and the night diving around the island offers a range of crustaceans and critters. The best time to dive here is in the dry season, from May to October.

REDANG

The premier dive spot on the east coast, Redang comprises nine islands. It is accessible from all the coastal towns mentioned earlier, with Merang Jetty being the most popular departure point. Check with your operator if transfers are included and where they depart from. Once home to a few fishing families, Redang is now one of the country's best known tourist destinations. Its powdery white sandy beaches and excellent coral reefs are a powerful magnet, and divers who want to explore the nearby reefs and islands further afield should book for at least five days to do the area justice.

The reefs around Redang have suffered the least amount of damage over the years because of their relative distance from the mainland. Thus, the reefs offer a fine variety of both hard and soft corals that host a wealth of marine life.

Around the southeastern end of the main island there are some small off-shore isles, **Kerengga Kecil** and **Kerengga Besar**, **Pulau Ekor Tebu** and the large rock known as **Ling**. The reefs here are shallow in depth and you'll encounter a veritable forest of mushroom corals on the southwestern tip of Kerengga Besar. A huge area of finger coral, rising over 5 meters from the sea-bed, is a favorite dive site around Ling,

while staghorn corals are also predomi-nant. The main island has some good shallow patches of coral, ideal for snorkel-ing or a repeat dive, which drop to deeper levels on the east coast.

There are several decent dive sites amongst the reefs off the northeastern part of the main island and also around **Pulau Paku Besar** and **Pulau Paku Kecil**. A bit further eastwards, **Pulau Lima** has deep coral reefs, while the reefs around **Pulau Pinang** are very shallow and suffer from the run-off from the Redang River.

In season (April to November, before the monsoons arrive), you can expect to see schools of jackfish, golden trevally, grouper, coral trout, snapper and barra-cuda. Macro photographers should keep their eyes open for Spanish dancers— pink, purple and orange delights. The seabed is the place to find stingrays (there are plenty), while pelagic high-

Redang Island is home to numerous friendly species of small reef fishes, notably sergeant majors, butterflyfish and silver monos.

lights include several species of shark. Another highlight of the diving in Pulau Redang is an encounter with turtles. Huge, lumbering leatherbacks often lay their eggs on the beaches of the islands, and can also be spotted swimming offshore. It's worth looking out for them at night, too, when they come ashore to lay their eggs in the sand. As mentioned elsewhere, turtles are a protected species in Asia and any encounter is a truly fascinating experience.

Although the diving is good in Redang throughout the summer months, it can be especially good in early November and in late April. Visibility averages 10–15 meters, occasionally to 18 meters.

KAPAS
Accessible from Kuala Dungun, the beautiful island of Kapas is better known for its white, sandy beaches than for its diving opportunities. However, it does have pretty corals in the shallows and this appeals particularly to snorkelers. The reef shelves gradually from 3 to 12 meters but it is symptomatic of the reef's condition that you'll find plenty of sea

The yellow barred parrotfish is one of a number of parrotfish species found around Perhentian Kecil.

The Clark's anemone is a host of clownfish, which are recognizable by their two white bands, finely outlined in iridescent blue.

urchins! Look out for clownfish and their host anemones, small nudibranchs, damselfish and sergeant majors.

TENGGOL
The island of Tenggol is situated further south from Redang and some 20 km offshore. It comprises one main island with a beautiful sandy beach of fine white sand and two small isles. On the western side of the island lies a sheltered bay.

However, the big attraction at Tenggol is wall diving, for the island has steep rocky cliffs on its eastern South China Sea side, which drop dramatically to the seabed. In addition, there are some pristine coral formations and a number of submerged rocks with excellent coral growth on them. Diving at Tenggol goes down to 48 meters, to the seabed, and divers who are more interested in fish than in corals and tunicates will find bumphead parrotfish, lizardfish, large schools of jacks and even the possibility of some white tip sharks. Occasionally, a whale shark or manta ray has been known to pass through and ghost pipefish are among some of the smaller fish known to make their homes here.

—*Fiona Nichols/Sarah Ann Wormald*

Tioman and Aur
A Playground for Divers and Holidaymakers

From the very first glimpse of its white sandy beaches, azure waters and often mist shrouded mountains, the island of Tioman exerts an almost mystical pull. Since the late 1950s, it has delighted film-goers, especially fans of *South Pacific*, and it continues to delight romantics today. Tioman has become renowned as a great place to holiday. Indeed, during the late April to September season, visitors arrive from Kuala Lumpur, Johor and Singapore, so it is essential to book in advance.

Tioman is not a divers' paradise, but rather a paradise in where divers can dabble in their favorite sport. The once pristine corals show evidence in places of previous illicit dynamite fishing. The general effects of being a popular resort are also visible. Rubbish can be an issue although projects are now underway to deal with this.

Access By bumboat from Tioman or liveaboard boats from Mersing and Singapore Fair, average of 9 meters; Aur averages 12 meters

Current Variable

Reef type Fair in Tioman; good in Aur

Highlights Coral gardens

Visibility Schooling fish, corals

Coral Good numbers, fair variety

Fish Beautiful beaches; corals around Aur

In 1985, however, the waters around Pulau Tioman were designated part of a large marine park where sustainable fishing is permitted but dynamiting, cyanide poisoning and spear fishing are outlawed. Similarly, the islands off the coast of Johor—Rawa, Tinggi, Besar, Sibu and Aur—at the bottom of the peninsula were put under protection.

Tioman is known mainly for its white sand beaches although there are a number of good dive sites offshore within an hour's ride by boat.

Although the visibility is usually in the region of 8–9 meters, it can very occasionally reach 30 meters. On an average dive, you'll meet schools of jacks, trevally, coral trout, pufferfish, a few stingrays and a number of moray eels. The crown-of-thorns starfish, which has caused much damage to the reef in the past, seems to be less prolific nowadays. We've heard stories about meeting a dozen hammerheads on one dive, but such sightings are unusual. There are sharks—black tip reef sharks usually—but nurse sharks are also not uncommon.

There are numerous dive spots around Tioman, most accessed in less than an hour via converted fishing boats.

Magician Rock is the place for schooling fish to hang out but currents here can be strong so it is best suited to experienced divers. There are also plenty of large fans for the photographers. Off the east coast, **Juara** is a good spot to see barracudas, snappers and stingrays, and to enjoy the hard corals. There is a submerged pinnacle here that attracts plenty of fish. Off the northeast, **Sri Buat** is renowned for its beautiful hard corals and some exceptionally tall soft corals.

Adjacent islands with good coral include **Labas** and **Tulai**. Check out the Napoleon wrasses at Tulai Island (it has a beautiful beach, too), and look out for the schools of trevally and barracuda. There are angelfish and coral trouts for the keen eyed. Labas is also a favorite due to its rock formations, swim-throughs and passing barracudas, stingrays and reef sharks.

Tiger Reef has two huge pinnacles where there are schools of yellowtails, angelfish and snappers. Nurse sharks are often sighted here. There are also some impressive sea fans and lovely soft corals. Diving is also good on the **Jubilee Shoals**, but as they are further away many operators do not journey out this far or will only do so with a minimum number of divers.

AUR

This small island, located 65 km from the Malaysian coast, was traditionally home to a small fishing community. Together with the neighboring islands of **Dayang** and **Lang**, Pulau Aur is a great favorite with divers as the distance from the mainland has ensured its corals remain

Tioman offers interesting rocks and swim-throughs such as this one.

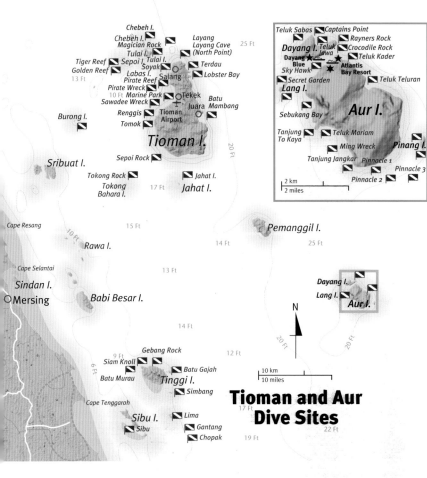

Chebeh I.
Chebeh I.
Magician Rock
Tulai I.
Tiger Reef   Sepoi I. Tulai I.
Golden Reef   Soyak
13 Ft   Labas I.
Pirate Reef
Pirate Wreck
10 Ft   Marine Park
Sawadee Wreck
Burong I.   Renggis
Tomok

Layang
Layang Cave
(North Point)   25 Ft
Terdau
Lobster Bay
Salang

Tekek
Juara
Batu
Mambang

Tioman
Airport

Tioman I.

20 Ft

Sepoi Rock

Sribuat I.

Tokong Rock
Tokong
Bahara I.   17 Ft   Jahat I.
Jahat I.

Teluk Sabas   Captains Point
Dayang I.   Teluk
Jawa
Dayang
Blue
Sky Hawk
Secret Garden
Lang I.

Rayners Rock
Crocodile Rock
Teluk Kader
Atlantis
Bay Resort
Teluk Teluran

Aur I.

Sebukang Bay

Tanjung
To Kaya
Teluk Mariam
Ming Wreck
Pinang I.
Tanjung Jangkar   Pinnacle 1
Pinnacle 3
Pinnacle 2   Pinnacle 3

2 km
2 miles

Cape Resang   15 Ft
10 Ft   Rawa I.

Pemanggil I.
14 Ft   25 Ft

Cape Selantai   13 Ft
Sindan I.
Mersing   Babi Besar I.

Dayang I.
Lang I.   Aur I.

N

14 Ft

20 Ft   20 Ft

9 Ft   Gebang Rock
Siam Knoll
Batu Murau   Batu Gajah
Tinggi I.
Simbang

12 Ft

10 km
10 miles

Cape Tenggaroh

Sibu I.   Lima
Sibu   Gantang
Chopak

17 Ft

19 Ft

Tioman and Aur
Dive Sites

22 Ft

*This nudibranch (Nembrotha kubaryana) is one of
many colorful species found in this area.*

in good condition while its relative remoteness contributes to a better-than-
average visibility for this part of the
coast. Accommodation is available on
both Pulau Dayang and Aur and access
is usually via the town of Mersing.

Expect to find trevallies, sweetlips,
coral trout, wrasses, plenty of parrotfish,
anemones and a wide variety of nudibranchs. Night diving in the main bay is
also fun. Further from the shelter of the
island, currents can be strong, especially
on the surface, but as a compensation
there are more big fish and the possibility of larger schools.

—*Fiona Nichols/Sarah Ann Wormald*

Langkawi
The Marine Reserve at Pulau Payar

This marine park encompasses four islands, Pulau Payar, Pulau Kaca, Pulau Lembu and Pulau Segantang, and is located 30 km south of the island of Langkawi and 65 km north of Penang. The park's pride lies in its wide variety of habitats and the largest number of coral species in the country, including the most colorful soft corals.

The Marine Park was conceived to protect the natural marine wealth, while specific zones have been marked for research and educational activities as well as for recreation.

Access 5 minutes to upwards of 1 hour to more distant sites

Current Fair, 2–10 meters

Reef type Negligible

Highlights Best variety in Malaysia

Visibility Coral gardens, artificial reef

Coral Fair variety

Fish Ease of access; great for snorkelers

Coral Garden At the southwestern tip of Pulau Payar, this site offers a scenic dive with multicolored soft corals, mainly *Dendronephthya*. The panorama is one with steep gullies and crevices that hide plenty of jacks, titan triggers, moray eels, blue ringed angelfish, lionfish, porcupinefish and many barrel sponges. Don't expect gin-clear visibility—it's around 10 meters usually, but can extend up to 16–20 meters.

Grouper Farm This is a reef that bottoms out at around 15 meters. It is named after the large number of groupers that dwell here. This nearby site also provides a home to mangrove snappers (*Lutjanus*

The anemone fish Amphiprion perideraion in the magnificent anemone Heteractis magnifica. The larger fish of an anemone fish pair is the female.

Pulau Payar Dive Sites

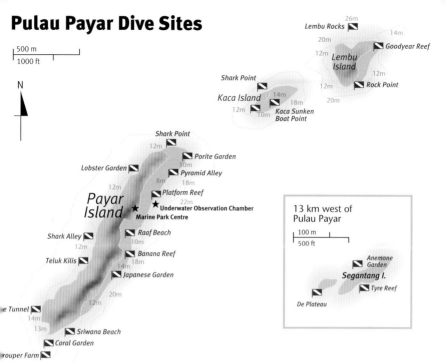

500 m
1000 ft

N

Lembu Rocks 🏴 26m
14m
20m
12m 🏴 Goodyear Reef
Lembu
Island
12m 🏴 12m
Shark Point 20m 🏴 Rock Point
Kaca Island 🏴 14m
🏴 18m
12m 🏴 10m
Kaca Sunken
Boat Point

Shark Point
🏴 12m
🏴 Porite Garden
Lobster Garden 🏴 10m
🏴 Pyramid Alley
8m 18m
12m 🏴 Platform Reef
Payar 22m
Island ★ ★ Underwater Observation Chamber
Marine Park Centre
Shark Alley 🏴 🏴 Raaf Beach
12m 10m
🏴 Banana Reef
Teluk Kilis 🏴 18m
14m 🏴 Japanese Garden
20m
12m
e Tunnel 🏴
14m
13m 🏴 Sriwana Beach
🏴 Coral Garden
rouper Farm 🏴
20m

13 km west of
Pulau Payar

100 m
500 ft

🏴 Anemone
Garden
Segantang I.
🏴 Tyre Reef
🏴
De Plateau

---

argentinaculatus) and barracudas.
Visibility, unfortunately, is usually very
poor and only reaches 10 meters on a
good day. However, the groupers, and the
small schooling fish, are worth coming
to see.

Sriwana Beach At the southeastern
side of Pulau Payar, a shallow coral reef
at a depth of between 6 and 8 meters is
a great place for a snorkeler or diver to
explore coral. Look out for the staghorns
(*Acropora nobilis, formosa and florida*),
brain and *Montipora* corals. There are
also sponges, anemones with their associated anemone fish, jacks, black tipped
fusiliers, groupers and Moorish idols.
Keep an eye open also for young black tip
sharks. The fish life here is more abundant than at the other sites nearby.

Kaca Sunken Boat Point An artificial
reef has been created off the southern tip

This leaf scorpionfish is a master of camouflage!

Apart from the anemonefish living in anemones, it is not unusual to find porcelain crabs as well.

of Pulau Kaca by the sinking of confiscated fishing boats. These have proved a haven for hard corals and fish life. Japanese jacks, lionfish, mangrove snappers (*Lutjanus argentimaculatus*) and giant groupers are all frequently encountered, while you'll also come across nudibranchs and a range of critters and crustaceans.

Tyre Reef The steep vertical walls at Tyre Reef extend down to 20 meters before sloping down gently to a sandy bottom depth of 26 meters. Fish life is plentiful, with large shoals of barracudas, sergeant majors, red snappers, mangrove snappers, jacks and rabbitfish. Sea fans, black corals, and wire and whip corals are common in the deeper waters.

Anemone Garden Sea anemones cover the surface of most of the rocks and boulders on the northern side of the island. Helmet shells, spiny lobsters, a range of critters and moray eels are all common.

Fish feeding still occurs in parts of Malaysia, pictured here on Payar Island.

Pulau Segantang Two rocky outcroppings rise up out of the sandy bottom from around 20 meters. This site boasts some decent hard coral as well as sea fans at around 15 meters. Visibility here is usually slightly better than that around Langkawai and Pulau Payar, which makes for nice scenic diving. On good days here, nurse sharks are known to pass through as well as barracudas, and amongst the corals look out for moray eels, nudibranchs and other critters.

—Danny Lim/Sarah Ann Wormald

A wide range of transfer and dive boats are available around Langkawi, including speedboats such as this one.

Diving in **Indonesia**
A Vast and Incredible Archipelago for Divers

An archipelago of over 17,000 islands, stretching more than 5,000 km from west to east, with a coastline of more than 80,000 km washed by tropical waters, Indonesia has some phenomenal dive sites. Indeed, the world's fourth largest country contains 10–20 percent of the world's coral reefs.

Over the course of the last 20 years, Indonesia has become firmly established on the map as home to some of the world's best dive sites with new sites and new areas still being explored and discovered to this day. Major tourist areas such as Bali offer a range of dive sites

as well as accommodation, dive courses and dive safaris, whilst traveling further east in Indonesia reveals remote islands and promises of discovery.

Diving in Indonesia has some great advantages as well as some challenges. The advantages of diving the clear rich waters of an uncrowded site, or better still, the virgin waters of an unexplored corner of the archipelago, need hardly be mentioned. Ask anyone who has dived in Indonesia. But these advantageous are also the country's drawback. Distances and remoteness can make trips to certain areas financially demanding, but

Indonesia's Best Dive Sites

1000 km
500 miles

Celebes Sea

Basilan I.
Jolo I.
Tawi Tawi I.
Sulu Archipelago
Davao Gulf
ngalaki
Sangihe Is.
Talaud Is.
Karakelong
Molucca Sea
Manado
Manado
Halmahera Is.
Morotai
Halmahera
Halmahera Sea
Togean Is.
Goraici
Weda Bay
Bacan
Obi
Mangole
Banggai Is.
Talibu
Gulf of Bone
Buru
Seram
Ambon Bay
Sulawesi
I
E
S
A
assar
kassar
Buton
Wakatobi
Selayar
Selayar Dive Resort
Komodo
Flores Sea
Maumere
Adongra
Lomblen
Alor
Wetar
wa
Flores
Sumba
Savu Sea
Savu
Rote
Kupang
Timor
DILI
TIMOR LESTE
Timor Sea
Waigeo
Kri Island
Raja Ampat
Misool
Misool Eco Resort Marine Park
Seram Sea
Maluku Islands
Banda
Banda Sea
Kai Is.
Aru Is.
Kobroor
Trangan
Workai
Yamdena
Tanimbar Is.
Selaru
Arafura Sea
Alor Archipelago
Biak
Numfoor
Yapen
Cendrawasih Gulf
Papua
Yos Sudarso

120°
135°

for those with deep enough pockets and a taste for adventure there are definite opportunities to sample some of the most exciting diving in the world.

Bali is Indonesia's most popular tourist destination, catering for millions of tour-

Snorkeling in Indonesia's remote eastern waters is a special treat.

ists each year. The diving here is still superb, offering a splendid wreck, critter diving, some phenomenal drift dives, manta rays and the oceanic sunfish or mola mola. There is a vast range of operators catering for all abilities (and pockets), prices are competitive and logistics can be easily managed. Many operators offer diving in a number of regions, giving divers the chance to experience a taste of everything on offer.

TO THE BACK OF BEYOND

As more and more diver operations have opened their doors, levels of professionalism have increased. However, some logistical stumbling blocks still need to be overcome. Aside from a few international airports being located in diving areas, such as Denpasar in Bali and Manado in North Sulawesi, most trips will require

an international flight from your home country into Indonesia and then onward domestic flights to transfer you to your chosen destination. The majority of international flights arrive in either Bali or Jakarta but Makassar is also serviced internationally, as are Manado and Lombok. Whilst there are numerous domestic carriers such as Lion Air, Sri Wijaya Air, Wings, Merpati Nusantara, Xpress, Trans Nusa and, of course, Garuda, the country's national carrier, efficiency and reliability levels are not always on par with international airline and airport services. That being said, prices are considerably lower, with domestic flights costing very little. The further you travel from major cities or from tourist areas (and in general the further you head east), the greater the problems can be. The biggest problems are delayed or cancelled flights. Also, the aircrafts servicing some of the smaller islands and more remote areas are often much smaller crafts and divers can find themselves limited to as little as 15 kg of baggage allowance. Fortunately, excess baggage fees tend to be more reasonably priced than those for international travelers.

That is not to say that everything falls foul. But travelers should be aware that business does not always run as smoothly as one would like, and some margin of time should be allowed for travel to and from the more remote parts of the archipelago. Patience, tolerance and a strong sense of humor are indispensable for travel in this country, even when you are opting for high end operators who organize transfers and travel for you. They also suffer from localized logistical problems often outside of their control.

Colorful soft coral on the walls around Bunaken in northern Sulawesi.

A huge manta ray near Nusa Penida, Bali.

Once at the dive destination, there can be a range of ways to travel to and from dive sites. Divers can still find themselves aboard anything from a well maintained, spacious and swift speedboat to a local fishing outrigger boat just about wide enough for one!

DIVE OPERATORS

The caliber of dive guides in Indonesia has certainly improved over the last 20 years and many of the local guides employed in tourist areas and in remote western-owned resorts have excellent English and vast knowledge about the marine life of Indonesia. Plus, they have excellent eyes for spotting some of the most bizarre, miniscule and rare creatures and fish. The best local guides are able to locate the most popular and sought after species with an accuracy and speed that is truly startling.

The dive training industry in Indonesia is now booming, particularly in the main tourist areas such as Bali, the Gili Islands, Labuan Bajo and North Sulawesi. The

Komodo National Park is a paradise for diving and exploring and home to the Komodo dragon, the world's largest species of monitor lizard.

majority of dive centers are accredited with PADI, and the PADI open water course is the entry level course that is most commonly available. Other entry level courses include SSI open water and CMAS certifications. New divers should opt for an accredited dive operator that employs qualified instructors. You can ask to see an instructor's card if you have any doubt about their credentials and they should be able to produce it. Continuing education courses are also widely available. When taking any dive course, you should make sure that the instructor's name on the paperwork matches that of the instructor who conducted your training.

Most dive guides in tourist areas are fully certified divemasters. In other areas the level of training can vary. Do not be afraid to ask your operator what experience the guides at their operation have.

Again, in the tourist areas, such as those listed above, equipment hire is readily available and if you are diving with a reputable operator (advised) the equipment is usually in good (serviced) condition. However, as you travel increasingly east across the archipelago, the availability of equipment hire decreases. Some operators in South Sulawesi and Raja Ampat, for example, will expect you to have your own gear, and on liveaboards it is generally required that you bring your own gear. If you are considering any of these options, check with your chosen operator at the time of booking what is and what is not required for you to bring. Equipment can be purchased and serviced in Bali and Jakarta but it is best to buy in advance of travel to avoid any disappointment.

Indonesia is a not a place, either, to push the dive tables or argue with dive computers. There are recompression chambers in Bali and Manado that meet international standards. There are other chambers in several other locations but they are not internationally approved. If you become symptomatic of decompression sickness in a more remote part of Indonesia, you cannot count on immediate emergency assistance or evacuation. It is simply not always possible given the distances and logistics involved. Liveaboards and operators in remote locations have emergency procedures in place, but an extraction from an island in Komodo or Raja Ampat, for example, can still be expensive and rely on crucial timing. For these reasons, divers are advised to have fully comprehensive dive insurance and to be familiar with any limitations of their policy, such as depth limits. Insurance coverage aside, it is better to simply err on the side of caution.

Generally, the best practise is to dive conservatively, even to the point of extreme caution, and safely, always making safety stops at the end of each dive, even shallow dives, and ascend slowly to the surface. The reefs are rich enough that you will never be bored spending a few extra minutes at the end of a dive exploring the shallows.

WHEN AND WHERE TO VISIT

Because of the size of Indonesia, diving is possible all year round if you plan your trip according to seasonal and regional optimal times. Some areas are only dived from September to June, such as parts of West Papua. Others are best dived from June to October, and in some areas diving is available for 12 months of the year. In general, the busiest time for tourists is from July to September and over the Christmas and New Year Holidays.

The areas included in this dive guide all have compressors, equipment and other professional facilities for diving. Some areas offer the visitor a great place to holiday and have the added bonus of well-organized diving as a diversion. Others have great diving but only modest accommodation. As mentioned earlier, there are numerous liveaboard boats in Indonesia. These can range from high end and luxury vessels to more backpacker oriented boats, but generally a reputable liveaboard will be at least fairly well equipped.

Indonesia is home to some of the world's most stunning coral reefs and divers of all levels should remember that these reefs are fragile ecosystems. Always dive carefully and maintain good buoyancy control, keep fins and hands away from the corals, minimize contact with the reef and marine life and wherever possible opt for operators who have marine conservation initiatives and procedures in place.

—*Fiona Nichols/Sarah Ann Wormald*

Mandarinfish (Synchiropus splendidus) are most commonly seen at dusk, Lembeh Strait, North Sulawesi.

East Kalimantan
Mantas, Turtles and a Mysterious Lake

Because of their proximity to both Indonesia and Malaysia, the islands of Derawan and Sangalaki in eastern Borneo have long been the subject of a heated territorial dispute. But divers can all agree on one thing: the diving here is world-class and features turtles on virtually every dive, cruising manta rays and a wealth of macro life. There are only limited operators in the area, but both Sangalaki Island and Derawan Island are home to land-based resorts.

The dive sites around Derawan offer some drift diving and muck diving, with a good range of critters, which makes it a popular choice for photographers. There are also good shore dives to be made. Due to the proximity of the islands, boat dives also operate daily to sites around the neighboring islands.

Access 10 minutes–1.5 hours by boat, depending on location

Current 5–25 meters

Reef type Variable, 0–2 knots

Highlights Good

Visibility Walls and coral slopes

Coral Good variety

Fish Mantas; diving in marine lake

SANGALAKI

For divers, the major attraction around Sangalaki is the resident population of manta rays, of which there are reliable sightings year round. During the rainy season (November through March), the visibility is poor (5–8 meters), but there is plenty to see. As mantas tend to feed

Remote Derawan Island in the Sangalaki Archipelago in East Kalimantan, offers the chance to see manta rays, groupers and even the odd beach wreck.

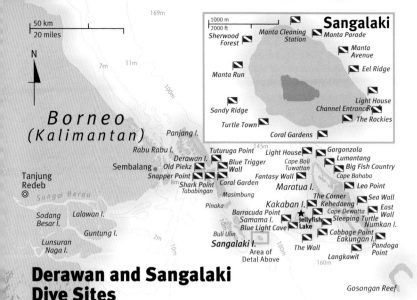

Derawan and Sangalaki Dive Sites

near the surface and in light currents, divers need only descend a few meters underwater to enjoy the show. The rays are even accustomed to human presence.

The other dives at Sangalaki are worthwhile, as the corals are healthy, the currents are mild and the visibility is stellar. There are huge groupers and bountiful reef fish at a bommie near **Coral Gardens**, and **Stingray Patch** is famous for regular sightings of blue spotted rays, eagle rays and, what else, mantas.

Green turtles live, breed and lay eggs on several of the small islands off the northeast coast of Kalimantan. Derawan and Sangalaki are the islands of choice.

KAKABAN ISLAND

Kakaban offers an excellent wall, which drops to 50 meters, pocked by caves and crevices and covered in an array of hard corals. The wall is thronged by surgeonfish and snappers but sharks are often encountered. There is typically a mild to strong current here, but experienced divers should have no troubles. The **Blue Light Cave** is another excellent site. At

low tide, guests swim over the top of the reef to a small hole that opens inside into a large cathedral. Blue Light Cave is for experienced divers only.

But Kakaban lays claim to a much more unusual fame. A lake fills much of the central part of the island, slightly above sea level, and with a salt concen-

The non-stinging species of Kakaban jellyfish is endemic to an inland lake on Kakaban Island.

tration about two-thirds that of the ocean. The lake holds a variety of marine life, including thousands of stingless jellyfish.

Other marine life observed includes tunicates, small colonial bivalves, nudibranchs, pure white anemone-like animals, a variety of species of holothurian sea cucumbers, sponges of two distinct growth forms and various crabs.

The lake is ringed by thickly encrusted mangrove roots, and the slopes at the lake edge are covered in lush vegetation.

Manta rays can be viewed close up in Sangalaki.

MARATUA

The horseshoe-shaped island of Maratua lays further to the east of Sangalaki and Derawan but boat diving options are available.

The best place to dive at Maratua is at **The Channel**, also known as Big Fish Country, on the eastern rim where, as the name suggests, divers hope to see pelagic fish in abundance. The channel's mouth is where the best action occurs. On an incoming or slack tide, it is swarmed by separate schools of chevron and yellow tail barracuda, gigantic bus-sized groupers, schools of surgeons, trevally and tuna. Visibility is nearly always gin-clear.

Below the lip, a vertical wall drops to 60 plus meters, where eagle rays, grey, white tip and black tip sharks are frequent visitors. If the current is running, it's best to sit at the edge to watch the show, then drift into the shallow lagoon.

—*David Espinosa/Kal Muller/*
Sarah Ann Wormald

Even though this magnificent sea anemone is closing up, the clownfish that inhabit it stay within the tentacles for protection.

Sulawesi
World-class Walls and Outstanding Fish Life

NORTH SULAWESI

Divers have nothing but praise for the reefs surrounding the small islands in Manado Bay. These are sheer walls covered with an incredible amount and variety of hard corals and invertebrate life. Visibility is usually very good—in the 20-30 meter range, sometimes even better—though periodic plankton-rich upwellings can reduce the visibility to 10-15 meters.

In 1989, thanks to the collective efforts of Dr Hanny and Ineke Batuna, Loky Herlambang and Ricky Lasut, 75,265 hectares of area underwater around Bunaken, Manado Tua, Siladen, Montehage and Nain islands became a national marine reserve, **Bunaken National Park**, and the corals and reefs have remained in admirable condition.

Access 5 minutes–1.5 hours by boat

Current Fair to very good, 12–25 meters

Reef type Usually gentle; at some sites to 2 knots or more

Highlights Excellent condition and variety, particularly soft corals

Visibility Steep coral walls

Coral Good numbers and excellent variety

Fish Excellent walls and muck diving; Selayar and Wakatobi—exceptional house reefs

North Sulawesi and the islands in the Bunaken group face the Sulawesi Sea, which plummets down to more than 6,000 meters. Nutrient-rich water from these depths sweeps across the reefs.

This green sea turtle (Chelonia mydas) has a sucker fish attached to its carapace. The two species live in symbiosis, with the turtle being cleaned and the sucker fish being fed!

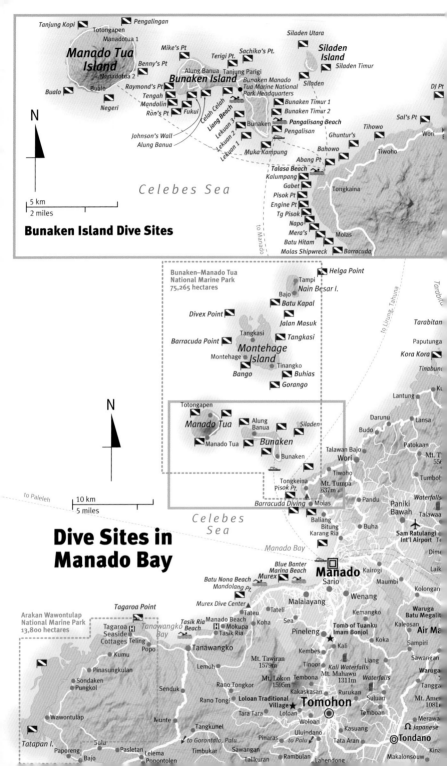

The variety of marine life here is excellent. The surfaces of the walls are crowded with hard and soft corals, whip corals, sponges and clinging filter feeders like crinoids and basket stars.

Huge schools of pyramid butterflyfish, black triggerfish and clouds of anthias swarm around the reef edge and the upper part of the wall. Scorpionfish, a vast array of nudibranchs, moray eels and sea snakes—particularly the black and grey banded colubrine sea snake—are common here and larger pelagics such as sharks and rays are well known to pass through.

The Bunaken-Manado Tua reserve features easily over 20 dives sites without counting those situated off Manado on the mainland. Most are concentrated off the south and west coasts of Bunaken, a low, crescent-shaped coral island surrounded by a steep fringing reef. Adjacent to Manado Tua (Old Manado) is a volcano, a well-shaped cone reaching 822 meters. Three other islands complete

A successful turtle sanctuary on Siladen Island has helped turtle numbers in the Bunaken marine reserve and now green turtles are seen on almost every dive.

the group: tiny Siladen, a stone's throw northeast of Bunaken; Montehage, the largest of the islands, north of Bunaken; and Nain, a tiny island north of Montehage surrounded by a large barrier reef.

The reef tops of the majority of Bunaken's walls are mainly made up of staghorn corals that host schools of damselfish, such as those pictured here.

BUNAKEN ISLAND

Bunaken is the centerpiece of the reserve with the majority of the dive sites being situated around its southern coastline.

Most of the sites offer similar topographies in that they feature steep walls of coral with small caves buzzing with reef fish. Good coral growth usually extends down to 40–50 meters, and on a good day, in the deeper parts of the wall, it is possible to see sharks, eagle rays and Napoleon wrasse.

The most popular sites in the park are along this spectacular three-pronged coral wall that can keep any diver enthralled for dive after dive after dive. Check out the turtles (some of which are of exceptional proportions), occasional Napoleon wrasse and a wealth of macro and critter life adorning the walls. **Bunaken Timur** offers shelter from the occasional storms that come out of the west, so the coral gardens remain some of the best in the park, though the fish density is much less than the other popular sites. **Sachiko's Point** offers good soft coral growth and, like any of the current-swept points around the island, possible shark and pelagic action. The entire west side of Bunaken is a fine 2-km stretch of wall that can see troublesome down currents on a falling tide. But on a rising tide it's a superb drift running in a northerly direction with plenty to behold: excellent coral growth along **Mandolin** as schools of fusiliers wash past you in waves, forests of whip corals along **Tengah** and extending into **Raymond's Point**, which also boasts lovely soft corals. Common inhabitants include turtles, colubrine sea snakes, the occasional passing eagle ray, Napoleon wrasse, dog tooth tuna or reef sharks, and when the current is light enough to allow closer inspection along the wall, numerous scorpionfish, soft coral candy

Green sea turtles around Bunaken are not bothered by divers and close-up encounters are not uncommon.

crabs and other macro riches. **Fukui** is the exception to the walls of Bunaken: a gentle slope offering fish life ranging from ghost pipefish to Napoleon wrasse, an impressive bed of garden eels, a collection of giant Tridacna clams that's a popular photo stop and a nearby sea mount that comes to within 10 meters of the surface, which is frequented by schools of batfish, midnight snappers, big eyed jacks, giant trevally, barracuda and occasionally reef sharks.

MANADO TUA

"Old Manado" is a dormant volcano jutting up just west of Bunaken. The two best sites are wall dives on the west coast: **Muka Gereja** and **Negeri** offer good coral growth and macro life with plenty of caves and cracks to peer into, but don't expect any pelagic action. **Tanjung Kopi** is where to go if you are hoping for bigger fish, but the currents dictate that this site is not for beginners and can only be dived properly at slack tide. The reef profile is a steep wall to about 40 meters.

SILADEN, MONTEHAGE AND NAIN

These three islands see fewer divers than the main two islands but they do offer some fine dives. The west side of Siladen has an exquisite reef that starts right off the best beach in the park and has fine macro attractions. Montehage is a large, flat, mangrove-dominated island with a wide fringing reef flat that has sustained some damage. For big fish, **Barracuda Point** is the best bet, though a bit of a gamble. Divers here usually see almost nothing or have their best dives, with possible sightings including schools of chevron barracuda, eagle rays, schools of jacks, trevally, bumphead parrotfish and a variety of reef sharks. The furthest island in the park from Manado is Nain,

Manado's house reefs are a treasure trove for the bizarre and colorful, like this free-swimming male ribbon eel.

located in a large lagoon surrounded by a barrier reef offering good hard coral growth in places. **Batu Kapal** is an interesting dive, but it's for the very experienced only.

MANADO BAY

Though the coral growth can't compete with the splendor of Bunaken-Manado Tua, and the visibility is usually in the 8–15 meter range, Manado Bay has plenty to offer. The area has some excellent muck diving sites which make a super break from wall diving. The most popular site is the ***Molas* Wreck** (or Manado Wreck), an intact, steel-hulled, 60-meter merchant ship that sits upright on a sandy slope at 25–40 meters, with the bow and roof reaching up to 17 meters to greet divers descending the mooring line. After a tour of the ship, divers follow the slope up into the shallows, which, like the entire Molas coastline, offers critter hunting equal or even better than Bunaken, with ribbon eels, cuttlefish, ghost pipefish and more. Following the bay, some resorts have interesting house reefs, with the reef off **Tasik Ria** hosting seasonal pygmy seahorses.

LEMBEH STRAIT

Over the course of the last 20 years, no one area has truly come to exemplify the ocean's strange and bizarre outcasts quite like the Lembeh Strait. When the first resort opened its doors in the mid-1990s on this sheltered stretch of water east of Manado, it was designed and marketed as a relaxing upscale retreat that also offered diving.

Under the auspices of the late renowned divemaster Larry Smith, the Kungkungan Bay Resort quickly became the Mecca for macro photographers and marine biologists. As Larry and his team of highly trained guides developed more and more sites, featuring frogfish in all sizes and colors, a veritable rainbow of

Many of Lembeh's resorts have excellent facilities, including pools with views over the strait.

Tiny critters like the diminutive pygmy seahorse (Hippo-campus bargibanti) abound in Sulawesi's waters. The trick is finding them!

countless nudibranch species, innumerable eels, an astonishing variety of venomous fish species, octopus and cuttlefish species galore, mandarinfish by the dozens as well as myriad others, the frenzy to dive there reached astonishing heights. Some of the more notable species seen here include both the wunderpus and the mimic octopus, blue ring octopus, hairy frogfish, warty frogfish, flamboyant cuttlefish and the rhinopias and Ambon scorpionfishes. The resort nearly cornered the market on macro diving, and though Papua New Guinea's Bob Halstead coined the term "muck" diving, the impossibly rich and diverse Lembeh Strait catapulted muck into the international limelight.

In recent years, operators from nearby Manado have descended upon Lembeh—it takes only 1.5 hrs from Manado by car—servicing the boom of divers searching for muck. Though black sand sites like **Hairball** have brought most of Lembeh's fame, with over 60 dive sites covering a wide spectrum of topographies, from black sand slopes, verdant hard coral and soft coral gardens, bommies, walls, pinnacles, rubble, wrecks and mixtures of all of the above, boredom is never a problem. Indeed, when even the most seasoned of divers return from dives having spotted something they

Emperor shrimps (Periclimenes Imperator) live in symbiosis with sea cucumbers.

Traditional fishing boats with outriggers are excellent dive vessels because they offer stability in the water.

have never seen before, one begins to realize how unique this famed stretch of water truly is. It is no wonder that the Lembeh Strait has been dubbed the "critter diving capital of the world".

Lembeh is home now to over 15 dive resorts, which offer dive and full board packages ranging from budget to luxury, and the logistics of getting to the area are relatively simple, with most operators providing airport pickups from Manado.

TO THE NORTH

Atop Sulawesi sits an island group offering a sort of diving in complete contrast to Bunaken to the west and Lembeh to the east. The best dives are a number of pinnacles that rise off the east coast of **Bangka Island** and in the **Pulisan** area. The prime attractions here are the unbelievably kaleidoscopic soft coral gardens. With the clouds of antheis and other reef fish varieties schooling about, huge moray eels, occasional sharks and rays passing through, as well as great macro attractions, the area is a visual feast. Compared to Bunaken, the currents are stronger, the visibility usually reduced and the water a bit cooler, but the diving around Bangka is excellent.

Further north, a string of islands form stepping stones all the way to the Philippines. For liveaboard aficionados,

the **Sangihe-Talaud chain** offers some spectacular scenery in clear waters. Diving on volcanic flows, pinnacles and pristine coral reefs, and with no crowds, the Sangihe area also harbors one of the very few sperm whale calving grounds on earth. With deep trenches to both sides of the island chain, the currents can be wicked, but for experienced divers the region offers extraordinary adventures.

TOGEAN ISLANDS

Situated in gin-clear, millpond-calm Tomini Bay, the idyllic and alluring Togean Islands are distinguished by the simple fact that they feature all three major coral reef formations—fringing, barrier and atoll—within a small area and in a sheltered environment. This means that divers can marvel at exquisitely delicate coral growth, but only in areas where the rampant bomb fishing that has effectively destroyed much of these reefs can be avoided.

There are only a few dive operators in the area, mainly operating out of Kadidiri. Other than an intact World War II plane wreck, the inner central region of the islands doesn't offer much, but with a good guide the outer areas do. Fine dives can be had around **Kadidiri** and its smaller neighboring islands and also on the volcanic cone of **Una-Una** to the northwest. Diving is also offered by the Walea Dive Resort located near the southeastern tip of **Walea Bahi**. In that area, there are some decent reefs off the beach, which owe their continued healthy existence to the protective actions of the resort. There are also a number of nearby seamounts rising from the depths that offer superlative dives in astounding visibility, featuring possible encounters with a range of shark species as well as numerous reef fishes.

SOUTH AND SOUTHEAST SULAWESI: SELAYAR ISLAND AND WAKATOBI

Traveling further south in Sulawesi undoubtedly offers some of Indonesia's finest diving and world-class dive sites. **Bira** on the tip of South Sulawesi features some strong currents, occasional cooler temperatures but occasional passing pelagics and is now home to a handful of operators.

Christmas tree worms are found in a range of colors. These were photographed in Wakatobi.

More notably, however, is the marine park created by the Selayar Dive Resort on the east coast of Selayar Island (South Sulawesi) and Wakatobi Dive Resort situated in the Wakatobi National Marine Park (Southeast Sulawesi). Both of these resorts are blessed with exceptional house reefs that feature plunging walls pocked with caverns and crevices and covered in a profusion of healthy, untouched hard and soft corals.

Selayar Dive Resort is situated in the heart of the marine protected area, which it created in 2002. The boutique resort, which is open from October to May, has only nine bungalows that are located along a 1-km stretch of white sand beach. Diving in the marine park here is truly a delight, with no other dive boats in the region, stunning walls (such as Steps, Caves and Overhangs and Opera) adorned with a diverse mix of soft and hard coral species and huge gorgonian fans, which are awash with macro and critter life, including candy soft coral crabs, ghost pipefish, pygmy seahorses, innumerable species of nudibranchs and shrimps, eels, leaffish and scorpionfish, to name but a few. The deeper sites in the park, such as **Shark Point** and **Karl's Corner**, offer the possibility of numerous shark sightings in one dive, including grey reef sharks and black and white tips. Mobula rays, eagle rays, huge tuna, giant trevallies, Napoleon wrasse, schooling jacks and a number of barracuda species are also amongst the residents here. Green turtles also thrive within the park and a handful of sightings on each dive are not unusual. In short, diving within the Selayar Dive Resort marine protected area offers something for everyone and should not be overlooked if you are seeking some of the best diving that Sulawesi has to offer.

Wakatobi Dive Resort (Wakatobi being an acronym for the four main islands of the Tukangbesi Archipelago— **WA**-ngi- Wangi, **KA**ledupa, **TO**mia and **BI**nongko) is located in the vast Tukangbesi National Marine Park. This high-end eco resort boasts two types of accommodation across over 20 bungalows in addition to a handful of luxury villas, all complete with impeccable service and transfers from Bali by private plane.

Diving in the Wakatobi National Park gives divers the opportunity to dive world-class pristine reefs, stunning wall dives and abundant marine life, particularly in the Tomia area. Turtles, rays, sharks and a whole host of critters are common, and when coupled with quiet dive sites and good visibility, it makes for some phenomenal diving.

The islands of Wakatobi are stereotypical picture perfect, with white sand, palm-fringed beaches, tropical clear water and beautifully diverse flora and fauna. There are a number of operators in the area now offering dive packages for a range of budgets, but if you are looking for tropical luxury and top-class service combined with some of the best sites within minutes of your resort, then Wakatobi Dive Resort remains the resort of choice. More than six species of seahorse have been found on their stretch of house reef alone and they are also at the forefront of marine conservation and reef protection projects in the area.

For those seeking the ultimate luxury liveaboard experience, Wakatobi Dive Resort also operate the *Pelagian Liveaboard*, a 35-meter yacht that offers an exclusive experience to the 10 guests for which it caters.

For those who have deep enough pockets, Wakatobi Dive Resort is the ultimate in luxury high-end comfort and the diving is undeniably world-class.

—*Bruce Moore/David Espinosa/ Sarah Ann Wormald*

A pink sea fan in Wakatobi is home to a school of anthias.

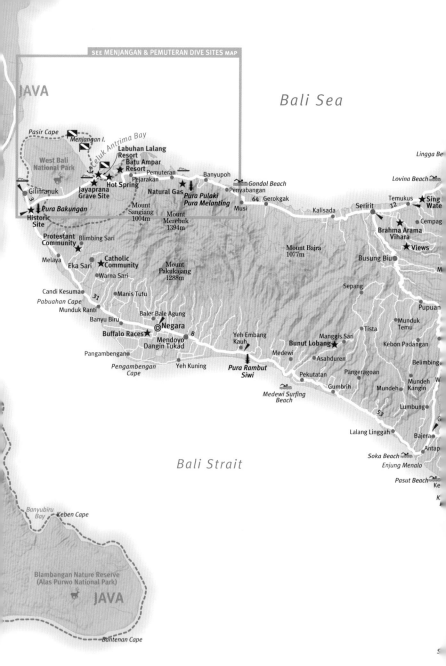

SEE MENJANGAN & PEMUTERAN DIVE SITES MAP

JAVA

Bali Sea

Lingga Be

Pasir Cape

Menjangan I.

Teluk Antrima Bay

Labuhan Lalang Resort
Batu Ampar Resort

Lovina Beach

West Bali National Park

Pemuteran

Banyupoh

Gondol Beach

Penyabangan

Temukus

Sing Wate

Gilimanuk

Jayaprana Grave Site

Pejarakan

Hot Spring

Natural Gas

Pura Pulaki
Pura Melanting

Musi

64

Gerokgak

Kalisada

Seririt

12

Cempag

Pura Bakungan

Historic Site

Mount Sangiang 1004m

Mount Merebuk 1394m

Mount Bajra 1077m

Busung Biu

Brahma Arama Vihara

Views

M

Protestant Community

Blimbing Sari

Sepang

Melaya

Eka Sari

Catholic Community

Warna Sari

Mount Pakukajang 1288m

Pupuan

Candi Kesuma

Manis Tutu

31

Munduk Temu

Tista

Manggis Sari

Kebon Padangan

Pabuahan Cape

Munduk Ranti

Banyu Biru

Baler Bale Agung

Buffalo Races

Negara

8

Yeh Embang Kauh

Bunut Lobang

Belimbing

Mendoyo Dangin Tukad

Medewi

Asahduren

Pangeragoan

Mundeh Kangin

Pangambengan

Pengambengan Cape

Yeh Kuning

Pura Rambut Siwi

Pekutatan

Gumbrih

Mundeh

Lumbung

G

53

Lalang Linggah

Bajera

Medewi Surfing Beach

Antap

Soka Beach

Enjung Menalo

Bali Strait

Pasut Beach

Ke

K

Banyubiru Bay

Keben Cape

Blambangan Nature Reserve
(Alas Purwo National Park)

JAVA

Buntenan Cape

S

INDIAN OCEAN

Dive Sites in Bali

10 km
5 miles

N

Bungkulan Point

⚓ 11
Kubu
Tambahan
araja
Jaga Raga
Bulian
Depeha
Menyali
Pacung
Tejakula
Les
Sembiran
Tembok
Madenan
Yeh Mempeh
Waterfall
Ngis Point
Siakin
kasada
Sudaji
Gitgit
aterfall
Silang Jana
Gitgit
Lemukih
Bantang
Belandingan
Tianyar
Bali Handara
Kosaido
Country Club
Catur
Daub
Kintamani
Songan
Crater Lake
Ban
Sukadana
Sukadana
Point
Mount
Batur
1412m
Trunyan
Bali Aga Village, Gede
Pancering, Jagat Temple
Kubu
SEE USS LIBERTY WRECK MAP
Botanical
Garden
bun Raya)
ake
uyan
Lake
Beratan
Belanga
Diving WW II
"The Liberty" Wreck
Mount Mangu
2020m
Batu Kaang
Batur
Selatan
Batur
Mountain
View
Hot Spring,
Volcanic Lake
Dukuh
Tulamben
Tulamben Marine
Reserve
Batu Niti Point
Puraluhur Beratan
Bukit Mungsuindah
Pura Ulun
Danu Bratan
Pelaga
Bunutin
Tengah
Buahan
Sekaan
Suter
an
Bangli
Abuan
Sekar
Dadi
Pengotan
Laba Sari
Mount Agung
2567m
Culik
Amed
uhur
aru
atiluwih
Apuan
Persiapan
Sulangai
Mekarsari
Penglumbaran
Pura
Besakih
Besakih
Pidpid
Tista
Bunutan
Pura
Lempuyang
abahan
Candi
Kuning
Petang
Taro
Kayu Buhi
Pempatan
Historic Site
Tirta Ayu
Buda Keling
Amlapura
Bukit
Spring
Yeh Gangga
Holy Spring
Tampak Siring
Tirta
Empul
Gunung
Kawi
Traditional
Village
Rendang
Selat
Sebudi
Puri Taman Ujung
(Floating Palace)
ic
Buruan
Margarana
Memorial
Melinggih
Rice Terraces
Cempaga
Undisan
Ngis
Subagan
Ujung Beach
Park
esiut
Marga
Sembung
Demulih
Abuan
Bangli
Pesaban
Sidemen
njuk
Wana Sari
Monkey Forest &
Pura Bukit Sari
Apuan
Bungbungan
Selat
Manggis
Mulu Point
aji
Gedong
Marya
Theater
Sangeh
Bunutin
Aan
Kertha
Gosa
Gegelang
Labuhanamuk
Bay
Candidasa
Padang Bai
Blahkiuh
Abian Semal
Ubud
Raksasa
Peliatan
Bedulu
Goa Gajah
Semarapura
Marine Reserve
Gili Biaj/Kambing I.
ances,
Mengwi
Sibang Kaja
Gianyar
Black Sand
Padang Bai Harbour
ongan
Tabanan
Gamelan Maker
Blahbatuh
Tulikup
13
Bona
Goa Lawah
(Bat Cave Temple)
SEE PADANG BAI DIVE SITES MAP
Kaba-kaba
Sading
Singapadu
Market
Pering
Kusamba
eraban
ric Site
Tanah Lot
Buduk
Ungan
Batu Bulan
Sukawati
Guwang
Ketewel
Lombok Strait
robokan Kaja
Kerobokan
oric Site
Denpasar
Dangin Puri
Dauh Puri
Sanur Beach
Lacerations
Surf Break
Pura Ped
Seminyak
Legian
Sanur
Sanur Kaja
Sindhu Beach
Jungutbatu
Nusa Lembongan I.
Ped
Batu Nunggal
Karang Sari
Cave
an Beach
Kuta
Sesetan
Sanur Kauh
Ceningan Reef
Surf Break
Lembongan
Nusa
Toyapakeh
Buyuk
Beach
gurah Rai
rnational
Airport
Serangan
Serangan I.
Ceningan I.
Spring
Sakti
Klumbu
Nusa Penida I.
Puseh Point
mbaran
Beach
Tuban
Tanjung Benoa
Batubelede Point
Bunga Mekar
Suana
Pura Batu Madan
Pura Batu Kuring
jimbaran
nland
Benoa
Tanjung Benoa
Beach
Sebuluh
Waterfall
Sebuluh
Tanglad
Pecatu Indah
Resort
Nusa Dua
Nusa Dua Beach
Banah Point
Wates
ngin
uhur
Ungasan
Bali Camel Safari
Maling Cape
Sekar Taji
Kuning Point
Pecatu
yang
Green Bowl
Surfing Area
Bakung Cape
SEE DIVE SITES AROUND THE NUSA ISLAND MAP

Badung Strait

Tulamben
The Legendary USS Liberty Wreck and Other Sites

At first sight, the little village of Tulamben is rather uninviting. Its beach is a rough spread of black sand, with small boulders and rubble cast here by nearby Gunung Agung's eruption in 1963. But people travel in great numbers to Tulamben to dive the predominantly black sand sloping sites, beginning, for most, with the wreck of the *Liberty*.

The wreck is Bali's most popular dive site and it does become crowded, as day-trippers from the south brave the three-hour drive just to make 2–3 dives. If you are hoping for a more exclusive experience, it is best to base yourself directly in Tulamben and make early morning or sunrise dives on the *Liberty* before the crowds arrive. The volcanic rock is a bit hard on the feet, and the waves can be

Access Beach; the ship is 30 meters offshore. Avoid midday—often crowds

Current Fair to good, 15 meters

Reef type Mild

Highlights Good growth on ship, fine growth on wall

Visibility Liberty shipwreck; wall; muck diving

Coral Excellent variety, prolific

Fish Full moon night dive

rough, but all inconveniences are soon forgotten on Bali's most famous site.

There are now numerous operators in Tulamben offering both resort facilities and diving only. Prices range from backpacker deals to more high-end dive and

The Liberty wreck at Tulamben, Bali, is completely encrusted with coral.

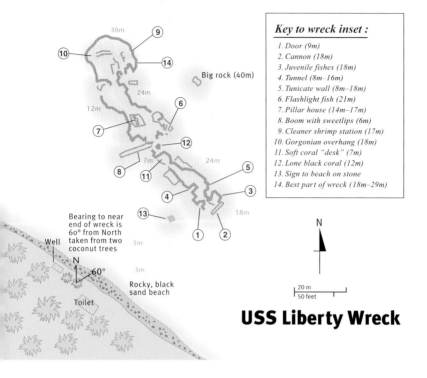

30m

⑨

⑩

⑭

Big rock (40m)

24m

12m

⑥

⑦

⑫

7m

24m

⑤

⑧

⑪

⑬

④

③

Bearing to near
end of wreck is
60° from North
taken from two
coconut trees

18m

Well

5m

N

⑴

⑵

N

60°

3m

Rocky, black
sand beach

Toilet

Key to wreck inset :

1. Door (9m)
2. Cannon (18m)
3. Juvenile fishes (18m)
4. Tunnel (8m–16m)
5. Tunicate wall (8m–18m)
6. Flashlight fish (21m)
7. Pillar house (14m–17m)
8. Boom with sweetlips (6m)
9. Cleaner shrimp station (17m)
10. Gorgonian overhang (18m)
11. Soft coral "desk" (7m)
12. Lone black coral (12m)
13. Sign to beach on stone
14. Best part of wreck (18m–29m)

20 m
50 feet

USS Liberty Wreck

stay packages. **Tauch Terminal Tulamben** offers upmarket accommodation and diving in their ideally positioned resort on the beach front next to the entry point for the wreck. A little to the south, the reputable **Markisa Resort** also offers Seraya Secret as their house reef and dive and stay packages in their boutique resort.

USS LIBERTY WRECK

Just 30 meters from the beach, the wreck lies on its starboard side, almost parallel to the shore. Parts of the superstructure are broken up and it is largely only the main frame of the ship that remains, but the wreck is still large and impressive, stretching more than 100 meters along the steeply sloping black sand. On 11 January 1942, this ship was hit by torpedoes from a Japanese submarine and was beached in Tulamben. She remained

A mixed school of butterflyfish and oriental sweetlips hang in mild current above Tulamben's Coral Garden.

Dancing shrimp in Seraya Secret. Their distinctive green eyes are quite spectacular.

there for more than 20 years until the eruption of Agung pushed the ship off the beach to its current location.

The hull, which is encrusted in hard corals and covered in soft corals of purple, red and yellow, has broken down over time and now offers divers the opportunity to swim through the ribs of the ship without the need for any penetration, as most of the wreck is open and offers direct access to the surface. The wreck is simply a wonderful place to dive, as there are hundreds of species of fish. Schooling fish are not uncommon here at quiet times and occasional reef sharks and stingrays also come to rest in the shadows cast by the vessel. Most of the medium sized fish have become semi-tame, and will literally swarm a diver in the shallows. Smaller treasures, like nudibranchs and tiny cuttlefish can be found on the wreck itself and on the black sand that surrounds it. The *Liberty* remains a wonderful place to dive, and it has recovered nicely from the El Niño bleaching, but with more divers visiting it, more than ever it is essential to be cautious.

This small spotfin frogfish is one of several frogfish species encountered around Bali.

BEYOND THE WRECK

Should you want to take a break from the wreck, the coral **Tulamben Wall/Drop-off** begins on the opposite end of the beach. Divers enter the wall from a somewhat protected nook, swim down a small sand embankment and over to the wall, which drops from 5 meters to 60 plus.

The wall does not host huge numbers of fish but has a decent variety. The wall ends in a ridge 100 meters from the starting point, and becomes a steep slope.

Further south from the Drop-off, **Seraya Secret**, which features numerous shrimps, nudibranchs and all manner of critters, is a muck diving fanatics must see site. Seraya Secret is a black sand slope around a 20-minute boat ride south from Pantai Drop-off and the entry point is just in front of the Markisa Resort (also their house reef). The slope hosts only sporadic rocks, hard corals and anemones but do not let this put you off as critters of all types can be found here, from harlequin shrimps, different species of lionfish, leaf scorpionfish, ghost pipefish and an abundance of different nudibranch species. For macro lovers and photographers with a keen eye, this can be one of Tulamben's most rewarding dives.

—David Espinosa/Kal Muller/
Sarah Ann Wormald

Nusa Penida
Abundant Pelagics and Fierce Currents

Nusa Penida, across the Badung Strait from Bali's southern tip, offers some of the best diving to be found anywhere. But conditions around Penida and its two smaller sister islands—Nusa Lembongan and Nusa Ceningan—can sometimes be difficult, with cold water and unpredictable currents reaching four or more knots.

CORAL WALLS AND PELAGICS

Most of the dive spots are along the north coast of Nusa Penida and around the channel between Nusa Penida and Nusa Ceningan, the exceptions being the two manta ray sites on the south coast of Nusa Penida. The standard reef profile here has a terrace at 8-12 meters, then a steep slope to 30-40 meters. From there the bottom slopes gently to the seabed at 600 meters plus. Pinnacles, ledges and large bommie formations are often encountered. At 35-40 meters, long antipatharian wire corals are common, spiraling outward more than 2-3 meters. Pelagics are the main attraction, and you have a good chance to see jackfish, mack-

Access 5–30 minutes from Lembongan, up to 1.5 hours from Bali

Current Good to great; 20+ meters

Reef type Moderate to very strong. Currents are unpredictable, often fierce. Seasonally cold water

Highlights Very good variety of hard corals; excellent stand of Dendronephthya

Visibility Drop-offs, steep slopes

Coral Excellent variety; many pelagics

Fish Large schools of all kinds of fish; very large hawksbill turtles. Site also hosts sharks, mantas and even oceanic sunfish

erel and tuna. Reef sharks were once common, but are now likely to be found deeper. Mantas are frequently seen feeding at **Manta Bay** and cleaning at **Manta Point**. The most unusual pelagic visitor is undeniably the bizarre, 2-meter-

Large manta rays gather at Manta Point off Nusa Penida for cleaning.

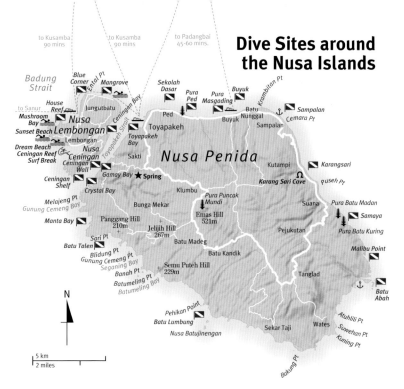

Dive Sites around the Nusa Islands

to Kusamba 90 mins

to Kusamba 90 mins

to Padangbai 45-60 mins.

Badung Strait

Blue Corner Pt

Ental Pt

Mangrove

Sekolah Dasar

Pura Ped

Pura Masgadong

Buyuk

Krambiton Pt

House Reef

to Sanur

Jungutbatu

Ceningan Bay

Ped

Batu Nunggal

Sampalan

Cemara Pt

Mushroom Bay

Nusa Lembongan

Toyapakeh

Buyuk

Sampalan

Sunset Beach

Lembongan

Toyapakeh Bay

Dream Beach

Nusa Ceningan Reef Surf Break

Nusa Ceningan

Toyopakeh Strait

Toyapakeh

Sakti

Nusa Penida

Kutampi

Karangsari

Ceningan Wall

Ceningan

Ceningan Shelf

Gamay Bay

★ Spring

Karang Sari Cave

Ω

Puseh Pt

Crystal Bay

Klumbu

Melajeng Pt

Gunung Cemeng Boy

Bunga Mekar

Pura Puncak Mundi

Suana

Pura Batu Madan

Manta Bay

Panggang Hill 210m

Emas Hill 521m

Samaya

Sari Pt

Jelijih Hill 267m

Pejukutan

Pura Batu Kuring

Batu Talen

Blidung Pt

Batu Madeg

Malibu Point

Gunung Cemeng Pt

Seganing Boy

Batu Kandik

Banah Pt

Semu Puteh Hill 229m

Tanglad

Batumeling Pt

Batumeling Boy

Batu Abah

N

Pehikan Point

Batu Lumbung

Nusa Batujinengan

Sekar Taji

Wates

Atuhlili Pt

Suwehan Pt

Kuning Pt

Bakung Pt

5 km

2 miles

long mola mola or ocean sunfish. During the late summer months, this mysterious large flattened fish with elongated dorsal and ventral fins is spotted at several sites along Nusa Penida's north coast and at Crystal Bay.

Along Nusa Penida's north coast the currents sometimes flow quickly but divers will marvel at the variety and numbers of fish and the magnificent colors of the healthy hard and soft corals, colors that are accentuated by the stunning gin-clear visibility. Guests typically enter the water over the drop-off and descend directly down the slope. Large schools of blue triggerfish and unicornfish crowd the various bommies scattered across the slope. The topography does not vary hugely from site to site, so if the current is running—and it can often top 3 knots—divers can duck behind the large bommies to wait for stray buddies or divemasters! Divers won't be

the only ones to seek shelter, as often sweetlips, fusiliers and turtles can be seen resting in the lee of these bommies.

TOYAPAKEH

One of the most commonly dived and most popular dives in Nusa Penida when conditions are right is around the corner from Sekolah Dasar, near the platform where the big *Quick Silver* daytripper boat ties up. While there are not enough superlatives to describe Toyapakeh, it can also be one of the most tricky sites to dive for the currents that rip through the strait here are sometimes fast and furious. (*Warning*: If dived at the wrong time, the currents can carry unwary divers out into the surrounding ocean.)

If judged correctly, these currents bring with them big schools of fish, sea turtles, occasionally mola molas and dozens of fusiliers and sweetlips that swarm the healthy colorful pillars in

Sunfish are seen seasonally (July–October) around Nusa Penida.

Koran angelfish (Pomacanthus Semicirculatus) aka semi-circle angelfish are found at all Nusa Penida dive sites.

various places. At rare periods of slack current, guests can make their way under the platform where large jacks feed, or sit back in 5 meters of water and watch as thousands of smaller anthias and bass- lets play. If making only one dive on Nusa Penida, Toyapakeh is an excellent choice and get ready for the ride of your life!
—*Kal Muller/David Espinosa/
Sarah Ann Wormald*

Hard corals such as these branching corals attract schools of Klein's butterflyfish on the reef tops around Nusa Penida.

Amed
Wall and Muck Diving in Northeast Bali

Jemeluk Bay, also known as Cemeluk Bay, offers gentle and calm conditions for all levels of divers. There are operators based in Amed itself and the area is also visited by dive centers traveling from both up and down the east coast of Bali. The reef features a variety of sea fans, soft corals and sponges with scattered hard formations. Whilst most of the reef is relatively shallow, upwards of 20 meters, to the right of the bay there is a wall which drops to 50 meters.

The wall is characterized by small schools of fish which gather in the gentle current out in the blue. Most commonly seen are triggerfish, butterflyfish, fusiliers and occasionally larger fish such as snapper and blue fin trevally.

If the current does pick up steam, it carries divers to a reef flat around the point. If the current gets too strong,

Access	Beach; 5 minutes by small boat
Current	Fair to good, 15–25 meters
Reef type	Mild, up to 2 knots
Highlights	Hard corals good deep
Visibility	Coastal reef; flats, slope and wall
Coral	Excellent numbers, superb variety
Fish	Density of fish on the deep wall

divers can take shelter behind the small patches of reef, large sea fans and big barrel sponges that are interspersed throughout this sandy slope.

The current typically dies out a little beyond the slope and drops divers on a second, shallower wall. The corals here have sustained some damage, but this is a popular spot for sighting parrotfish and occasionally squid.

Amed has spectacular scenery featuring incredible views of Mt Agung, Bali's highest volcano.

Leaf scorpionfish are common at Bali's east coast dive sites.

Whip corals are often home to whip coral shrimps but you have to look hard to spot them!

TO THE WEST

For those who are seeking something different to a wall or reef dive, further to the west there is a black sand slope, perfect for spotting muck critters and invertebrates. The gentle slope is littered with fish aggregation devices, typically wooden slats piled high or bundles of old tires, that attract white eyed moray eels, crabs,

lobsters and all types of colorful shrimps. With keen eyes and patience, if you comb the shallows you might be able to find Ambon scorpionfish, bizarre octopus, blue spotted rays and other sand-dwelling critters, and on lucky days even bobtail squid in the tiny patches of grass.

—*David Espinosa/David Pickell/ Sarah Ann Wormald*

Jemeluk Bay Dive Sites

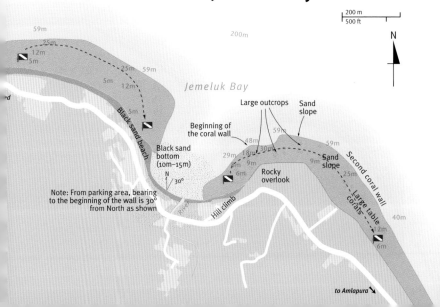

200 m
500 ft

N

59m

25m
12m
5m

25m 59m

5m 12m

Jemeluk Bay

200m

Black sand beach

5m

Large outcrops   Sand slope

Beginning of the coral wall

48m   59m

30m

Black sand bottom (10m–15m)

29m   18m
9m   9m

N
30°

6m   Rocky overlook

9m   Sand slope

59m

Second coral wall

25m

Large table corals

40m

2m

6m

Note: From parking area, bearing to the beginning of the wall is 30° from North as shown

River

Hill climb

to Amlapura

Menjangan
Clear Water and Walls off Bali's Northwestern Coast

Menjangan Island lies just offshore from Bali's mountainous northwest tip. Because the island is in a protected position, currents and wind-generated waves are rarely a bother and the reefs here offer fine, easy diving.

The reefs around Menjangan Island offer a mix of walls and slopes with some interesting caverns and formations. The reef wall is rich with life, particularly with soft corals and impressive gorgonians which play host to a range of critters. Seasonally sharks are seen here as are numerous turtles.

Diving in **Pemuteran** also offers some interesting sites, including some muck diving options and an interesting artificial reef (Bio-Rock) project, which is

Access 10 minutes from Pemuteran

Current Very good to superb, 25–50 meters

Reef type Very slight

Highlights Very good numbers and variety; abundant soft corals

Visibility Walls, particularly rugged; wreck

Coral Reasonable number, only average variety

Fish Fields of garden eels; steep walls

located just off the beach in front of the Werner Lau and Bali Diving Academy dive centers (also good for snorkeling).

The island is part of Bali Barat National Park, a protected reserve area that encompasses much of Bali's sparsely populated western end. Check with your operator if they will also provide transport as part of their packages.

CRAGGY VERTICAL WALLS

The coral walls around Menjangan are vertical and drop 30–60 meters to a sandy slope. The reef surface is rugged, and walls are cut by caves, grottoes, crevices and funnel-like chimneys. Gorgonian fans reach large sizes here, and huge barrel sponges are very common.

The variety of fish here is somewhat inferior to Bali's other dive sites, but small schools of fish can be seen out in the blue. Large batfish accompany divers, and barracuda, trevally and the occasional reef shark can be seen skimming the bottom of the wall.

Divers usually stay in Pemuteran where there is a range of accommodation, from backpacker homestays to

Menjangan has excellent wall dives and soft corals.

upmarket hotels along the beach front. The boat rides from Pemuteran are short and dive sites are easy to access. The area around Pemuteran and Menjangan Island also offer good snorkeling opportunities for non-divers.

THE NORTHWEST

Two of the most popular dives are on the island's northwest tip. The **Anchor Wreck** lies just off the reef edge in 40–50 meters. The wreck is coated with hard corals and gorgonian fans and swarmed by snappers, sweetlips and wrasse. Because it lies on a deep sand slope, few guides would take recreational divers there. Instead, most stop at the beautifully encrusted anchor before heading off along the reef.

The point itself is a magnificent dive, popular with photographers for the vast fields of garden eels. Divers enter further eastward along the wall, gently finning because there is rarely a current stronger

It is not possible to stay on Menjangan Island but it is only a 15 minute boat ride from Pemuteran village on the mainland, which is home to the majority of dive operators in the area.

than mild towards the point. The reef is healthy here, with very little damage to the table corals and hard corals. Near the point, the wall becomes enveloped in large purple gorgonian fans. Most divers choose to stay in the shallows here, where deserts of sand and extraordinarily healthy patch reefs extend southward.

—*Kal Muller/David Espinosa/ Sarah Ann Wormald*

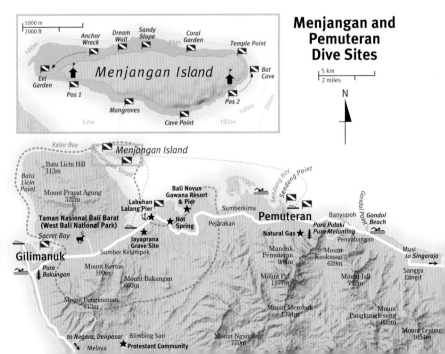

Menjangan and Pemuteran Dive Sites

Padang Bai and Candidasa
Spectacular Dives on East Bali's Offshore Reefs

Amuk Bay is 6 km across and located south of Bali's easternmost point. North of Padang Bai is the **Blue Lagoon**, a trove of marine life. Two sites—Mimpang and Tepekong—outside the bay, Biaha to the north and Gili Selang on Bali's northeast tip also offer breathtaking diving.

The small islands of Mimpang, Tepekong and Biaha are surrounded by healthy low-lying reefs and are swept at times by torrential currents that bring in nutrients, accounting for the diversity. The upwelling of very cold water from the deep basin south of Bali brings with it some stunning marine life.

The currents from the Lombok Strait require care and respect as they create unpredictable water movements. But at

Access 20–30 minutes by small outboard

Current Variable; poor to very good; 6–22 meters

Reef type Can be extremely strong—more than 5 knots and very tricky. Cold water

Highlights Excellent coverage and variety

Visibility Steep coral walls; underwater canyon

Coral Abundant and varied

Fish Tepekong's Canyon, good chance to see pelagics; Biaha's complex wall

these unprotected sites you'll find a decent number and great diversity of fish, sharks and frequent pelagic visitors set against a backdrop of craggy black walls

Padang Bai features white sand beaches and, of course, the famous Blue Lagoon.

Padang Bai Dive Sites

with beautiful healthy corals and often superb visibility.

You must have a guide who has a great deal of experience in the area. While the sites may be diveable, they are small, and if the current is too fast your dive may be finished in only five minutes.

BLUE LAGOON

Accessed usually by small *jukung* from nearby Candidasa or Padang Bai, sites here are worth the ride. While the topography is not spectacular, the variety of fish and critter life can be amazing. On any one dive, expect stonefish, moray and blue ribbon eels, nudibranchs, rays, squid and octopus and leaf scorpionfish in every hue. On lucky days, Napoleon wrasse and reef sharks are also possible.

This is a site used for courses and snorkelers because visibility in the protected bay is typically 15-20 meters. When timed correctly, conditions can be undemanding.

MIMPANG

Also known as Batu Tiga (Three Rocks), the site is part of a north-south ridge, with the richer south end (Shark Point) dropping into deeper water. **Shark Point** offers one of the best chances in Bali to see white tip sharks and, from August through October, the oceanic sunfish (mola mola).

The topography of Mimpang is diverse, with sloping reefs, craggy rocks and walls, all covered in hard and soft corals and gorgonians. Big schools of unicornfish and snappers, many blue spotted rays, Napoleon wrasse, moray eels, trumpetfish, bannerfish, butterflyfish and triggerfish swarm here.

Hawksbill turtles (Eretmochelys imbricate) are an endangered species but are still the most commonly encountered turtle species around Bali.

TEPEKONG AND THE CANYON

This island offers some of Bali's most spectacular diving: steep walls, **The Canyon**, cold water and strong currents make this a site for experienced divers. The visibility is very good.

Maximum depth at The Canyon is 40 meters, and if there is no current you can see the dramatic beauty of these stunning walls. However, in the usually swirling current, your view is somewhat obstructed by the schools of sweetlips, snapper and big eyed trevally, bumphead parrotfish, unicornfish, batfish, groupers and possible sharks and other pelagics.

EAST TEPEKONG

Enter on the right and there is an excellent wall, which plunges to depths of 40 plus meters. To the left there is a small coral reef (max. depth 24 meters) with hard, soft and table corals. The marine life is outstanding, with the occasional turtle, tuna, parrotfish, barracuda, angelfish, scorpionfish and several species of

triggerfish. Conditions are generally less difficult here than at the Canyon.

BIAHA

This crescent-shaped rocky island is 4 km from Mimpang and Tepekong and is usually a site for experienced divers. The diving is superb although both the surge and up/down currents can be very strong. Most of the awkward currents are on the northern slope.

There is a beautiful reef around the island, a rocky slope in the north, and a wall in the south, which has waves breaking from above. The inner area of the crescent, on the east side, has a cave where white tip sharks sometimes sleep.

GILI SELANG

To the northeast, the island of Gili Selang features, like all of the exposed sites on the east coast, ripping currents, suitable only for expert divers. However, take the plunge here and be rewarded with a healthy reef slope.

—Annabel Thomas/Sarah Ann Wormald

Secret Bay, Gilimanuk

Much Ado about Something

Gilimanuk is one of Bali's quieter dive spots, but despite its relatively remote location it offers some of Bali's most interesting diving. **Secret Bay** in Gilimanuk in northwest Bali is about 2 km across and very shallow, much of it less than 5 meters deep. A reef north of the bay's mouth makes the opening even narrower than it appears on a land map, and creates a channel that sweeps in and hooks around two islands in the bay's center. This strong flow, with reported speeds of up to 7 knots, through the strait is what makes the diving in Gilimanuk so interesting. The bay becomes a kind of refugium, a catch tank for larval fish and plankton.

This bay harbors a number of rare jewels for the macro photographer, including odd gobies and dragonets, and such rarities as the juvenile Batavia batfish, a beauty with zebra stripes and

Access 1 minute shore entry

Current 3–5 meters

Reef type Non-existent to light

Highlights None

Visibility Chocolate-colored sand; lots of garbage

Coral Excellent, for muck divers. Exotic and bizarre

Fish Bobbitt worms, seahorses, frogfish and so much more!

ragged fins that seems to want to make itself look like a crinoid.

MACRO HEAVEN IS MIGHTY MUCK

Gilimanuk is not a dive for everyone. Nowhere will you find a sounding of 15 meters or rich stands of coral and abundant reef fish. Secret Bay is a specialty site for photographers and for divers who

Secret Bay is home to many critters, including the hispid frogfish. This one is showing its pompom lure.

When diving north Bali, check every anemone for anemone shrimps and porcelain crabs.

Bali is home to numerous species of lionfish, including Pterois kodipungi, pictured here at Secret Bay.

are looking for something a little different. Secret Bay is best dived during a stay in Pemuteran as most Pemuteran-based dive centers offer day trips here. This caters to divers in both Gilimanuk and around Pemuteran and Menjangan. Trips are also available through the major operators in Sanur and the south of Bali but they usually require a minimum number of divers and an overnight stopover.

"I [David Espinosa] wasn't quite sure what to expect of my first dive at Secret Bay. The wall of fame in the dive center was eye opening, with pictures of multi-colored frogfish, juvenile batfish, sea-horses and the bizarre Bobbitt worm, but reports I'd heard from diving friends were mixed.

The first thing that struck me was the water's temperature. I had been warned by friends that the waters in Secret Bay could be as cold as 22° C. Though the divemaster mentioned that the temperatures are in a constant state of flux, I was overdressed in a 5mm wetsuit.

I also wasn't prepared for the nondescript landscape. The sand in Tulamben or Amed is broken by strands of coral here and there, but in Secret Bay it is

colorless and featureless, and no deeper than 9 meters. The mud-colored sand wasn't broken by so much as a coral head, though there were various bits and pieces of trash—empty cans and bottles, chip wrappers, strands of rope, entire trees, old anchors and chains and barrels.

It was on one of these rusted barrels that we uncovered our first significant find, for hiding on the inner lip of this rusted hulk the divemaster Made found a family of six red ornate ghost pipefish! After the obligatory cries of surprise, we shot our pictures and moved on.

A few feet away, hiding in a tin can, was a curious little goby being cleaned by a small orange shrimp. Inches to the left a dwarf lionfish took refuge in an empty pipe. When I looked up, Made was missing, off somewhere in the murk—visibility rarely tops 5 meters—hooting up a storm to indicate that he'd found yet another critter.

The rest of the dive was a blur of frantic activity as my buddy and I bounced from place to place as if in some large pinball machine, taking turns shooting the exotic fish Made turned up. After nearly two hours at an average depth of

7 meters I emerged, having seen Jan's pipefish, banded pipefish, mating cuttlefish, more ornate ghosties, bearded frogfish hiding amongst the branches of a dead tree and a spiny seahorse."

5-METER WORMS AND MOSSY SNAKES

"If the day dive was special, I was in for a real treat that night. For when light turns to dark, the really bizarre critters come out. With video in hand, I followed as Made swam furiously towards a predetermined site off in the distance. He halted and pointed with a knowing look in his eye at a yellow disposable Gillette razor stuck head up in the sand.

Just as rumors of a secret site in Bali had spread like wildfire, so too did the tall tales of one of its residents. According to some reports, the Bobbitt worm grew up to 3.7 meters long and lived in crevices deep in the ocean. Armed with vicious fangs, with lightning speed it lashes out from its lair to devour unwary passersby…. If that isn't the recipe for a great dive! For the entire day we pestered Made, begging him to show us this creature.

The Bobbitt worm wasn't a disappointment, though if he does grow up to 3.7 meters long the individual we saw had a long way to go. The razor was put in the sand not only to mark his burrow but also to provide a means of comparison. This little guy sported jaws a half inch wide, and he could have only been a foot long. He was playful, though, making quick feints as I switched the strobes on and off, exposing a shiny, spiny underbelly that glowed in brilliant colors of yellow, green, blue and red.

The remainder of the dive was icing on the cake. We saw different frogfish, a mossy sea snake, two more Bobbitt worms and a finger dragonet. Two hours later we emerged from the water spent, but entirely satisfied. We never once ventured deeper than 6 meters, but expended all the air in our tanks and a 60-minute videotape."

—*David Espinosa/David Pickell*

The finger dragonet (Dactylopus dactylopus) is a great find. Look out for them when diving Secret Bay.

Nusa Tenggara
Island Hopping in Style

Often passed over because divers are more anxious to arrive in Komodo, the islands east of Bali are blessed with some world-class dives. Variety is the spice of life here, and liveaboards can now offer anything from black sand dives to vertiginous walls covered in hard and soft corals.

The **Gili Islands** off Lombok's west coast are a favorite destination for young sun-seeking and party-going backpackers because of the picturesque white sand beaches and non-demanding diving. The main island of Gili Trawangan offers numerous dive schools that co-exist amongst the islands many bars and late night hangouts. Although coral rings the three islands, the diving isn't outstanding as the ravages of fish bombing and El Niño have taken their toll. Still, there is some worthwhile diving on the deeper reefs and quite an assortment of fish life that is ideal for less experienced

The green sea turtle is the second largest species of sea turtle. It survives mainly on a diet of sea grasses, sea weed and algae.

Access 5–15 minutes by speedboat from liveaboard

Current 15–50+ meters

Reef type Light, but swifter further east

Highlights Excellent variety and numbers

Visibility Walls, black sand slopes, pinnacles, submerged reefs

Coral Excellent. Large variety of reef fish and muck critters

Fish Secluded dive spots; good pelagic action

divers and for those who want pleasant, easy dives. The gentle slopes, which are swept by mild currents, feature an assortment of reef fish, occasionally including trevally, sharks, turtles and the more common angelfish and triggerfish.

Moyo Island gives divers their first taste of what can be expected in Komodo. Two submerged reefs off the island's west coast are swarmed by schools of fish, sharks and other pelagics. Though bombs have previously damaged the reef tops in some areas, the steep slopes of both reefs, which plummet to depths in excess of 80 meters, have survived and support a healthy variety of angelfish, baitfish and groupers. The smaller reef to the north is rich in nudibranchs and exotic critterss. Hairy ornate ghost pipefish have been spotted in the mossy shallows. **Satonda**, a smaller island to the east, provides another delightful half day of diving. **Painter's Pleasure**, a healthy shallow reef slope, is decorated in gorgonian fans of all sizes and coral whips, and is home to twin spot gobies, gaudy

The Komodo National Park in Nusa Tenggara was established in 1980 and was declared a World Heritage Site and a Man and Biosphere Reserve by UNESCO in 1986.

nudibranchs and dozens of mushroom corals, with the attendant pearly white pipefish. The sand patch, also in front of the main beach, has stargazers, pipefish, leaf scorpionfish and bobtail squid for a very enjoyable night dive.

The Amanwana-operated **Moyo Island Resort** offers luxury accommodation and diving on Moyo Island. For those wanting to explore further afield, then a liveaboard trip may be the best solution.

For a day diversion, bring some sturdy sandals and hike the short trail that leads to the crater's marine lake. And for a truly memorable show, sit back at dusk and watch as thousands of bats emerge from the island's southern trees and fly to the mainland in search of food.

If Komodo is Indonesia's tastiest dive spot, then **Sangeang Island** is the flavor of the day. Because guests clamored to reachKomodo, liveaboards would push on, ignoring this lush volcanic island for

the adrenaline diving at Banta, two hours to the east. In 1999, on one of his famous hunches, guide Larry Smith directed his boat to the island's southernmost point and jumped in.

At the western edge of a small beach that serves as an itinerant fishing village lies an excellent muck diving site. The

Healthy sponges and soft corals around Moyo Island.

Nusa Tenggara Dive Sites

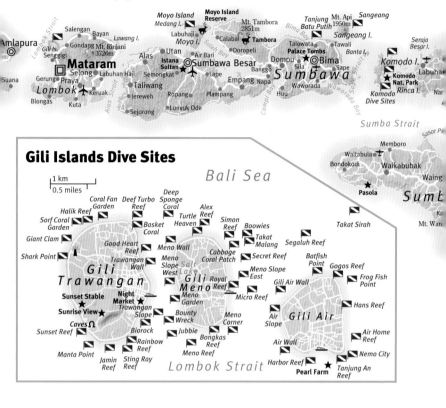

currents at **Mentjeng Wall** can be tricky due to its exposed position, but there are spots to take shelter and visibility can be good.

The wall, which bottoms out at 15–20 meters, is covered in crinoids, sponges and sea whips, some of which host colonial anemone, and while there are ghost pipefish, frogfish and saron shrimp tucked away in the crevices, the real action is at the base of the wall, where anything from boxer crabs to robust ghost pipefish make their home amongst an array of nudibranchs.

Around the corner two more rich invertebrate sites round out the diving in the south. **Tikno's Reef** and **Black Magic** are so good, some operators with the right group might avoid Banta in order to spend a full day at Sangeang.

At the mouth of the long bay that leads into Bima in **Sumbawa**, lie two sites that, although worlds apart, continue to excite ardent divers. **Diversity** on the east side has two separate walls, one that drops to 20 meters and the other to 30 meters. Though it is unprotected during the months of December to March, visibility is quite good year round, and the ribbon eels, frogfish and good reef fish make it a splendid checkout dive for trips departing from Bima. **Copycat Copycat** on the other side of the channel is the quintessential muck dive, with visibility hovering at 5–7 meters. The small patch reef at 5 meters is covered in toon shells and spiny seahorses. The vast featureless sand below the reef is punctuated by sporadic

Flores Sea

Komba I.

Sukun I.

Palue I.

Pomana I.   Larantuka   Adonara   Lembata   Alor Islands
Besar I.   Babi I.   Sagu   Balauring   Kalabahi   Taramana
Riung   Nebe   Solor I.   Lembata I.   Kabir   Tribur   Alor I.   Kolana
Dondo   Maumere   Lamakera   Pantar I.   Alor Dive Sites
Flores   Mt. Kelimutu   paga   Solor Islands   Lamaherap   Delaki   Treweng I.   Ombai Strait
aka   1640m   Maumere   Nangaroro   Ende   Wolowaru   TIMOR LESTE
ng   Bajawa   Ende I.   Ende

Batugade
Atapupu
TIMOR   Atambua
LESTE   Pantemakassar   Halilulik
Suai
Kefamenanu

Sawu   Sea   Naikliu   Mt. Mutis   Besikama
2427m
Melolo   Barate   Timor   Nikiniki
Kupang Bay   Soe
N   Kupang Dive Sites   Toineke
Haingsisi   Kupang
Semau I.   Baun
Sabu I.   Rote Strait
(Sawu I.)   Rote
Raijua I.   Seba   Bebae   Timor
Ndao, Do o,   Sea
Nuse Dive Sites   Rote I.
100 km   Nembrala   Baa
50 miles   Dana Channel Dive Sites

debris that provides homes to frogfish, pipefish and marble eyed morays. The real highlight and the main reason to dive here is the promise of the elusive mimic octopus in the surrounding desert.

Diving off southern **Sumba** is primarily by liveaboard but it is worth the trip. With nothing but water between Sumba and Australia's northern shores, this place has become a haven for surfers. However, several sites, including **Magic Mountain** and **Marlin Rock** on the offshore reefs, hold the promise of pelagic action. If the opportunity should arise, the local villages, throwbacks to a feudal time, merit a visit.

—*David Espinosa/Sarah Ann Wormald*

Feather stars vary in color according to species.

Komodo
Acclaimed as Some of the World's Best Dives

Diving Komodo is like stepping on a Jurassic gyroscope, tilting and spinning at uncontrollable speeds. There are times when guests have been perched in a 2-knot current, holding on for dear life, mouthpieces vibrating, watching a *halimeda* ghost pipefish while their buddy gesticulates wildly, trying to gain their attention to point out a hovering manta ray. Dives like this are common. It is hard to know where to look and what to focus on. Welcome to Komodo!

Komodo, as well as the other islands between Sumbawa and Flores, belongs to another time and place. Rugged, dry,

covered in scrub and borassus palms, it is just a few degrees south of the equator and represents an arid anomaly in the lushness of the monsoon-fed islands of the Indonesian archipelago. But it is the perfect habitat for one of the world's most awesome animals, the Komodo dragon.

Komodo is famous for its huge manta rays.

Komodo Dive Sites

BIOLOGICAL RICHES

The wild Komodo area offers just about every imaginable type of diving, from current-swept sea mounds patrolled by groups of sharks, tuna and other big fish to plunging walls covered in impressive corals, to calm reefs alive with invertebrates and hundreds of colorful reef fishes. The water temperature varies from a chilly 22° C to 30° C bath water. Visibility ranges from a clear 25-30 meters to a dismal 3 meters when clouds of tiny fish and plankton allow only macro photography.

Access 5–10 minutes by tender from liveaboard; 1 hour from Labuanbajo

Current Variable, from 2–50 meters

Reef type Can be extremely strong, up to 5 knots

Highlights Superb, with a good mix of hard and soft corals

Visibility Sloping reef and some walls

Coral Excellent

Fish Rugged terrain, komodo dragons, encounters with a variety of large pelagics

The variety of marine life in the Komodo area rivals the world's best. There are deep seas both north and south of the narrow straits running between the little islands. Strong currents and upwellings bring nutrients and plankton, keeping all the marine creatures well fed.

While the Komodo area is well explored and a popular liveaboard destination, because of its vastness it rarely feels crowded aside from at one or two of the most popular of its numerous dive sites. In general, there are two habitats and two seasons for diving Komodo—the winter for the cooler, temperate water southern sites, and the summer for the warmer, tropical north. The main factor in enjoying diving Komodo is visibility, and the north is the more predictable in this regard.

Komodo is a unique region because it offers divers the choice of both tropical and temperate diving within the scant space of 10 kilometers. The volcanic thrusts and limestone uplifts combined with a half meter differential between the South China Sea and the Indian Ocean have created a topography conducive to wild and unpredictable currents. Upwellings from the southern seas add to the unique mélange of planktonic life found here, hence the unimaginable, prolific and dense marine life that characterizes Komodo! If you can find shelter from the tempestuous currents, you'll discover an astounding array of rare and unusual critters to photograph and to marvel at. That's what Komodo is all about—the rare, the unique, the special, and the colors are out of this world!

DIVING THE SOUTH

South Komodo is undoubtedly a diver's dream come true and from late October through early May is when it has the most to offer. Then the sky is blue, seas are calm and there is enough of a breeze to cool sunburned bodies. Between November and January visibility (10–15 meters) is as good as it gets in such plankton-rich seas, and the soft coral, invertebrate life and fish are nothing short of spectacular. South Komodo is difficult to dive from May through September due to the southeast trade winds, which generate huge swells and howling winds. The south used to be accessed by liveaboards only, but since more land-based operators with powerful boats have opened up in Labuan Bajo, such as *Blue Marlin Komodo*, three dive day trips covering all areas of the park are now possible.

Some of the best dive sites in the south are found in the horseshoe-shaped bay between Rinca and Nusa Kode, such as Yellow Wall and Cannibal Rock.

Yellow Wall is actually two walls, one atop another, the second of which is an overhang that plunges 50 meters to the floor. The site is covered in yellow soft corals and is rich in invertebrate life—yellow pygmy seahorses, colonial blue tunicates, myriads of nudibranchs and blue ringed octopus. Yellow Wall faces west and the light is best from midday onwards.

Cannibal Rock is a more versatile site and can be dived from sunrise on through the night. The site, which is at the doorstep of a small promontory, is sloping and features mini-walls, huge boulders with valleys and giant terraces at 30 plus meters. There are 2-meter red gorgonian fans that periodically host red pygmy seahorses and ghost pipefish, typically during cold water upwellings. The rare lacy scorpionfish has been sighted nearby. Cannibal Rock is covered in sea apples, a rare and brightly colored temperate sea cucumber in hues of purple, green, blue, red and yellow, and a

Komodo is not just about big fish. There is immense diversity of all marine species, including invertebrates such as these cuttlefish.

truly fascinating sight when its feeding tentacles are extended. There are also three species of venomous urchins found on the rock, one of which hosts up to five different species of commensals. When the current runs, the fish school, and there have been sightings of mantas, large sharks and minke whales.

Other sites in Horseshoe Bay are **Crinoid Canyon**, **Boulders**, **Pipedream** and **Torpedo Point**, renowned for its torpedo rays and frogfish.

South Komodo has other distinctive dive sites off the islands of Padar and Tala. **Pillarsteen** is off south Padar and is a topographer's dream, with huge chunks of rock buckled into channels and canyons, caves, swim-throughs and chimneys. This dive is totally different from other diving in Komodo. It is fun and action-filled when the currents are running. **W Reef**, a few hundred meters to the north of Pillarsteen, is a series of four

underwater pinnacles extending perpendicularly from the island to a depth of 30 meters. This structure is covered in pristine coral and regularly buzzed by mantas and schools of bumphead parrotfish. Off northwest Tala is **The Alley**, which features large lazing schools of manta rays November through March. **Langkoi Rock** is fully exposed and so buffeted by strong current, which explains the regular presence of large pelagics. It is reputedly a mating site for grey sharks in April. **Lehoksera** is a high-voltage dive on the southeast tip. The dive begins mildly enough, with a gentle current that allows divers to get ready with reef hooks, gloves and other accouterments. The current picks up faster and faster until divers reach a slot created by the main reef and a smaller pinnacle offshore. In the middle of this slot, there is a small bommie at 30 meters, which is buzzed by large groupers, turtles, sharks and

Exploring Komodo by liveaboard opens up many hard-to-reach spots that have the best diving.

schools of every fish imaginable. The current spits divers out onto another gently sloping reef, which is very rich in soft corals and hard coral formations.

DIVING THE NORTH

Australians Ron and Valerie Taylor pioneered diving in Komodo and the site they first discovered was Pantai Merah, at the entrance to Slawi Bay. **Pantai Merah** (or **Val's Rock**) extends from the surface down to 20 plus meters and is richly adorned in all manner of colorful sea life. Pantai Merah represents a transition between tropical and temperate water habitats, north and south, and with its fabulous fish and corals is a good introduction to Komodo.

Considered by some as the best dive in the north, **GPS Point** is a submerged rock to the northwest of Banta Island's largest bay. This is one of the sites where

sharks can be regularly found, and different species can be identified in a single dive. Invariably, divers encounter strong currents here, which is why GPS Point is swarming with jackfish, tuna and schools of barracuda and surgeonfish. In addition to sharks, be prepared to scan the gorgonian fans for pygmy seahorses and the deep blue for eagle rays and even passing mantas.

If the currents are running too strong on GPS Point, operators have other options only minutes away. **Star Wars** is a gentle slope that bottoms out in a sandy floor at 30 meters. The currents, which can range from calm to raging, typically flow eastward, away from the shallow point. There are several gorgonian fans, which have been known to host the ubiquitous pygmy seahorse, invertebrates and sharks. The myriad smaller schooling fish like anthias, basslets and fusiliers that swim amongst each other look like they are playing out an outer space battle of epic proportions, hence the name. **Highway to Heaven** on the opposite point is a wild ride that must only be done on slack tide or during gentle currents. A vertiginous wall extends around

A pair of Coleman shrimp (Periclimenes colemani) living in their host fire urchin.

the point and is covered in soft corals, fans and sea whips, home to countless juvenile angelfish. But the highlight of the dive is the 40 meter plus deep bommies, around which schools of snappers, two different species of barracuda, sharks and rays are known to swarm. Continuing on to the backside, mantas and eagle rays play off in the blue. For end of the day muck dives with no current, **It's a Small World**, a sand slope fringed by a healthy reef, has resident stargazers, frogfish, leaf scorpionfish and a host of invertebrate life. It is no small wonder that Banta is a must stop for liveaboards visiting Komodo.

Sabolan Kecil, north of Labuanbajo, is a site regularly visited by land-based operators. To the east of the island are two sea mounds at 20 meters, a site called **Shark Bank**. The hard coral cover is minimal but the soft corals and large gorgonians are excellent. The fish life, particularly sharks, makes this site well worth visiting. Work your way down the valley between the two mounds as you pause to view the pelagics.

Tatawa Kecil and **Batu Bolong** are two bare rocks in close proximity that

Nusa Tenggara dive sites are famous for their diversity of both hard and soft corals and sheer biomass of fish.

Diving around Komodo offers seasonal exceptional visibility and an abundance of Moorish idols at all sites.

are exposed to the full force of the currents that rage through the Linta Strait. On a high slack tide, when currents abate and the diving is less stressful, these are two more popular sites for land-based operators. Giant trevally, mantas and dugongs have been encountered here.

There are three great dives to the north of the island of Gili Lawa Laut: **Crystal Bommie**, **Castle Rock** and **Lighthouse**. All sites have good hard and soft coral cover and swarms of schooling fish. Lighthouse has a "honey hole" on the point, which is home to schools of sweetlips and batfish, while Crystal Bommie and Castle Rock are excellent deep dives in which divers hang on with reef hooks and watch for the white tip sharks patrolling in the blue.

—*David Espinosa/Cody Shwaiko/ Sarah Ann Wormald*

Alor
The East's Dream Destination

Alor is a small island lying at the end of the Nusa Tenggara chain, north of West Timor. The numerous dive sites center mainly around the three islands framed by Alor and Pantar: Buaya, Ternate and Pura. The diving here, with much of the topography dominated by steep walls, ledges and caves, is world-class and its relative remoteness guarantees the type of diving that most only dream of. Alor is a popular liveaboard destination but there are a number of shore-based operators in the area now who offer dive and stay packages.

Graeme and Donovan Whitford, a father and son team, pioneered this

Access 5 minutes by speedboat from liveaboard; 1–2 hours from Kupang

Current 5–50 meters

Reef type Varies up to 5 knots

Highlights Excellent

Visibility Walls, sloping reefs, pinnacles

Coral Excellent

Fish Pertamina Pier and Kal's Dream, as different as two sites can be

magnificent group of islands in the early 1990s. Today they operate both Kupang-based DiveAlorDive and DiveKupang-

Large schools of barracuda are not uncommon in Alor when the currents are running.

Alor Dive Sites

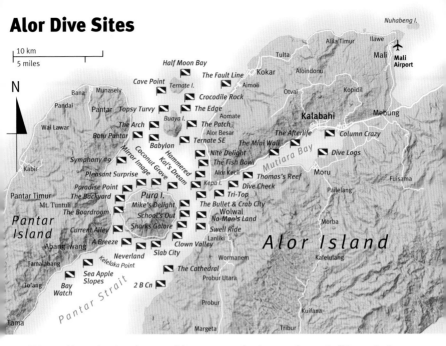

10 km
5 miles

N

Nuhabeng I.

Alila Timur — Ilawe
Tulta — Mali — Mali Airport
Half Moon Bay
The Fault Line — Kokar — Aloindonu
Cave Point — Ternate I. — Aimoli — Otvai — Kopidil
Bana — Munasely
Pandai — Crocodile Rock
Pantar — Topsy Turvy — The Edge — Aomate — Kalabahi — Mebung
Wai Lawar — Buaya I. — The Patch — Alor Besar
The Arch — Alor Besar — The Afterlife — Column Crazy
Batu Pantar — Ternate SE — The Mini Wall
Babylon — Nite Delight — Mutiara Bay — Dive Logs
Symphony #9 — The Fish Bowl
Kabir — Pleasant Surprise — Alor Kecil — Moru
Paradise Point — Kepa I. — Thomas's Reef — Fuisama
Pantar Timur — The Backyard — Pura I. — Dive Check — Pailelang
Mt. Tuntuli — Mike's Delight — Tri-Top
The Boardroom — School's Out — The Bullet & Crab City — Morba
Current Alley — Sharks Galore — Wolwal
Abang Iwang — A Breeze — No-Man's Land — Kafelulang
Neverland — Clown Valley — Swell Ride
Tamalabang — Kelelaka Point — Slab City — Lanliki — Alor Island
Sea Apple Slopes — Wormanem
To'ang — Bay Watch — 2 B Cn — The Cathedral
Probur Utara — Kuifana
Tama — Probur — Tribur
Margeta

Pantar Island

Pantar Strait

Mirror Image — Coconut Grove — Kal's Dream — Hammered

Dive and have developed many of the more than 40 sites that are dived today. This list begins, and for many divers ends, with Kal's Dream.

A DREAM COME TRUE

"I [David Espinosa] first experienced **Kal's Dream** in 1995, at the tender age of 18. At that time I was still a rank amateur with only a handful of dives under my belt. Graeme's son Donovan took me under his wing, and for the first two days we experienced superlative dives at **The Arch**, where we were buzzed by eagle rays and sharks, the **Fish Bowl**, the **Boardroom** and **Cave Point**, where the steep walls covered in a profusion of colors dizzied me. These, however, were only a prelude to the real show.

On the morning of the third day, Donovan felt I was ready for Kal's Dream, a small pinnacle that rises from the deep and sits in the middle of the strait. I can still remember that dive as if it was yesterday. The Dream is marked by a vertiginous wall on the south side and a rather gentle slope on the north. We perched ourselves on a small outcropping on the north side at 30 meters and watched the show unfold.

Numbers of grey sharks swam up from the abyssal depths and began circling our roost. One particularly frisky shark passed a few times, getting nearer with each pass. Down in the depths, bus-sized groupers slowly swam about, while schools of enormous tuna patrolled the reef top. The visibility was gin-clear, and we could see as barracuda swarmed a tip opposite our ledge.

Suddenly, a large, indistinguishable figure loomed from the dark. The ever-nearer and increasingly worrying grey shark quickly scattered, and before it disappeared back into the shadows I caught a brief glimpse of my patron saint and protector—a giant 3.5-meter hammerhead.

To this day, not one dive on the Dream has equaled that first experience, but they come close. It is without a doubt a dive to dream about...."

IN AND AROUND ALOR

Because Kal's Dream must be dived at slack tide—any other time would be insanity—operators there have looked to the many other walls and reefs in the area as alternatives.

On Pulau Pura's southwest tip lies a marine anomaly that few divers have ever been able to comprehend. **Clownfish Alley** is an unremarkable slope, but what it lacks in topography it makes up for in marine life. From 2 meters down to 30 meters, and for 1 km, every boulder and rock and pebble is covered in anemones, a remarkable sight.

Mandarin House is situated in front of the north village on Pura. It is a rather unprepossessing though healthy reef slope on which mandarinfish can be seen cavorting—during the day! If currents are minimal, divers can also gather there at dusk to witness the mating of these magnificent dragonets.

To the east of Mandarin House is one of Pura's healthiest reef walls, **The Boardroom**, a "hidden" point near the local village. The wall, where several caves and overhangs give shelter to thousands of glassfish, begins just below the waterline and drops to a sand slope at 50 plus meters. At these depths, schooling jackfish, snappers and fusiliers swim in the currents, which can gust up to 2 knots. If the current is running, divers can drift to either side of the point to finish the dive in peace. The wall is even topped by a large rock, home to nudibranchs, leaf scorpionfish and even the blue ringed octopus.

Pertamina Pier is in the harbor, only minutes away from the town of Kalabahi. This black sand slope sits at the base of the old Pertamina Pier and is home to a fantastic range of muck critters—anything from seahorses to ghost pipefish, the wonderpuss, juvenile batfish in the

This anemone in Alor is inhabited by numerous Amphiprion sandaracinos (a species of clownfish), which is not unusual in Alor where the reefs are teeming with life.

seagrass to the east and harlequin shrimp at various depths. Though the visibility is typically poor, this is still an awesome dive! At night it only gets better because stargazers, Pegasus sea moths and bizarre moray eels come out to play.

Even though the various operators don't agree on the name, **Dead Chicken Run** is an amazing site. Near the road on the north edge of the narrow bay adjacent to three large trees there is a small cliff which extends 5 meters below the waterline. At dusk, hundreds of flashlight fish pour out from a small crack in the wall to disperse throughout the reef. After the light show, divers can wander about the silty, sandy slope below the wall, which on occasion has juvenile batfish, juvenile and adult frogfish, ghost pipefish, seahorses and other invertebrates.

—*David Espinosa/Sarah Ann Wormald*

Maluku and Raja Ampat
Remote and Incredible, the Ultimate Dive Destinations

THE BANDA SEA

The islands of Maluku were the first in the archipelago to capture the imagination of European explorers, but not for their beauty, although these coconut-fringed islands with powder white beaches and constant sunshine fit most tourists' definition of paradise. The Europeans went to the Moluccas in search of one of the world's most coveted commodities—spices.

While the islands there are still sunbleached and redolent of exotic spices like the clove, this is also one of those rare spots on earth where seemingly every dive location you drop in on abounds in fantastic life. If the current political state of affairs was not so volatile, divers would flock to this region.

The **Banda Islands**, rising from a depth of over 4,000 meters in the Banda Sea, are one of Indonesia's best diving destinations. The wounds from the political and religious turmoil that racked

Access On liveaboard, 2–5 minutes; from land-based operations, 1 hr

Current Fair to excellent, 10–20 meters in the off season, 40 meters at best

Reef type Varies: weak to very strong

Highlights Excellent undamaged reefs

Visibility Vertical walls, slopes

Coral Excellent numbers and superb variety

Fish Pristine sheer walls in Banda; wrecks and untouched reefs in Raja Ampat

Ambon and Banda in 1999 have been played out and numerous liveaboards now visit the area. Serious divers will enjoy diving in Banda as there is a choice of excellent muck locations and high-voltage pelagic sites, from the shallow lagoon between Banda Neira and Gunung Api to the vertical walls of Hatta, and countless other sites at Manuk, Ai and Koon.

The Banda Islands are formed by steep volcanoes rising up from a very deep ocean bed.

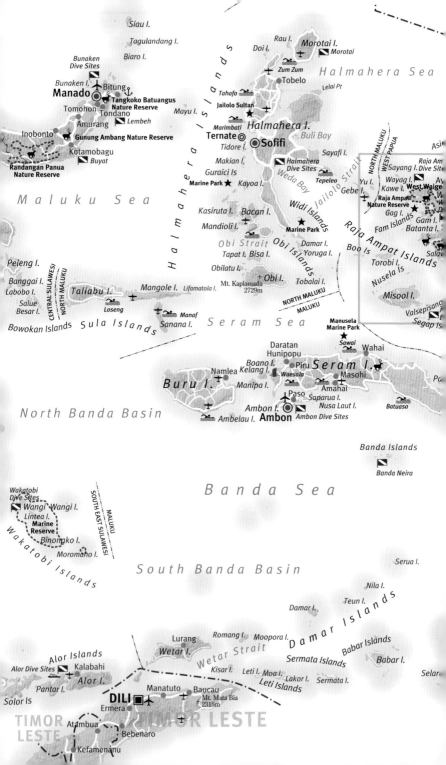

Maluku and Papua
Dive Sites

200 km
100 miles

N

RAJA AMPAT DIVE SITES MAP

Mt. Irau
2582m
Gunung
Meja
Reserve
Ambon
Tamrau Mts
Manokwari
Mt. Mebo
2940m
Numfoor I.
Ransiki
Wolnui Strait
Mt. Umsini
2970m
Rumberpon I.
Papua
Miosvaar I.
atan
Cendrawasih
Marine Reserve
Bintuni Bay
Roon I.
Berau Bay
Wondiwoi Wandamen
Mountains Reserve
I.
g Pt
Fakfak
sir Putih
Semai I.
Triton Bay
Gusawi R.
Karas I.
Tongeram Pt
Kaimana
Kumafa Mts
Aiduma I.
Nambima Pt
Adi I.
WEST PAPUA
MALUKU
Papisol Pt
la
s

Kai Islands
Kai Besar I.
Kai Kecil I.
Pasir
Panjang
Wokam I.
Maikoor I.
Kobror I.
Koba I.
Baun Reserve
ate I.
Trangan I.
Warkai I.
Larat I.
na I.
Southeast Aru
Nature & Marine
Reserve
mlaki
ne Park

Arafura Sea

The Nembrotha kubaryana species of nudibranch are found on ascidians, on which they feed, and are recognizable by the vivid orange tips of their rhinophores.

STILL GOOD AFTER ALL THESE YEARS

The Banda Sea is just one of those few places that divers only dream of adding to their logbooks. The variety and numbers of fish are both excellent, and the chances here are always good to see several big animals. The reefs have sustained damage in some areas but in others they remain pristine, with little signs of fish bombing or other man-made degradation. Currents can be tricky at times, but on a good liveaboard with a knowledgeable crew the risks should be negligible.

There is some good diving near **Banda Neira** at Keraka and Sonegat, and slightly further away at **Lontar**, and the two isles to the north—**Batu Kapal** and **Sjahrir**. But it is the islands off Banda Neira where the best diving can be found.

Hatta Island, formerly Rosengain, is great because it offers a variety of fish in excellent numbers. The sheer wall at Tanjung Besar ends in white sand at 40 meters. The surface is honeycombed with small grottoes and overhangs covered in an unusual variety of soft corals that hang from the roofs of these crevices and caves. There is an abundance of moray eels and gorgonians as well as angelfish, butterflyfish and more.

This coral bommie is typical of Raja Ampat where numerous species of soft coral, hard coral, feather stars and tunicates compete for space on the reef.

Together with Hatta, **Ai**, some 25 km to the east of Banda Neira, offers some fantastic diving. Both the north and southwest coasts are ringed with flawless coral walls, rugged and full of caves harboring plenty of fish. The southwest features a vertiginous wall that drops to more than 70 meters. Tube and barrel sponges and great quantities of soft corals of all hues can be found growing on a wide terrace on the west coast. The sheer drop-off, the number of caves and fissures and the overwhelming richness of life here compares only to the very best sites in south Komodo and a few isolated islands in the Banda Sea.

MUCK DIVING IN AMBON BAY

For serious muck divers and macro photographers, a trip to Ambon should not be missed. Ambon Bay is frequented by liveaboards but there are now also a couple of shore-based dive resorts, such as Maluku Divers, that offer diving at the numerous dive sites (almost 50) in the bay. The bay is certainly not one of Indonesia's cleanest areas, but whilst it hosts an array of debris and rubbish ranging from tin cans to occasional

household appliances it is also home to some of Indonesia's most intriguing critter life. It is no wonder that Ambon Bay is starting to rival the Lembeh Strait in the "critter capital" stakes. The list of species found here is quite staggering: blue ring octopus, rhinopias, numerous frogfish species, seahorses, pipefish, flamboyant cuttlefish, bobtail squid, scorpionfish, stonefish, an array of nudibranchs and several species of octopus, to name but a few.

For critter lovers, two weeks diving the sites here would still not be enough. For those who want a break from the "muck" there is also a deep wreck to the north of the Bay—the ***Duke of Sparta***, which is a dive not to be ignored—with a mast head that is still standing upright on the deck and towers up from 30 meters to just below the surface.

WEDA BAY, HALMAHERA

Further north in Maluku, positioned between Sulawesi and the Bird's Head Peninsula of West Papua, sits the island of Halmahera. The area around Halmahera is frequented by liveaboards, but for those who are looking to really

Raja Ampat Dive Sites

20 km
20 miles

N

mahera Sea

Ayau Island

Piai I.

Sayang Island

Wayag Island ★

Wayag Island   *Quoy I.*

Coquille I.   *Uranie I.*

Bougainville Strait

Uta Island

Yu Island
Omnial

Kawe Island

Balabalak I.   *Roibe I.*

Mey I.   *Salio*

Schun I.   *Sepatu I.*   *Go*   *Missigit*

Manuran I.

Wariai Point

Lam Lam Kabarei   *Warkori*   *Bone I.*

Warai Pt

be
nd
+ *Gebe Airport*

nera

Bururtirio Point

Ayel I.

Sarpele

Waigeo

Waigeo Island

Wairemah

**West Waigeo
Nature Reserve**

Wagailom

Waigeo Island

Poeper

Yenbekaki

Batang Pele I.

Yu I.

Minyaifun I.

*Gof
Besar I.*   *Gemin I.*

Wauyai

Manyaifibit Bay

Mumos

Rabia

Wakre

Mansikor Po   *Urbinasopon*

Mamiyai I.

Yasbekar I.

The Passage

Tsiep I.   *Walparen Bay*

Pef I.   *Gam I.*

Wurai I.   *Tapokreng*

Kabui Bay

Yenbesar   *Gaman Bay*

Saonek Kecil I.

Mioskon

Yenbekwan Po

Waim I.

Gag Island

Yeben I.

Airborek

Airborek I.

Fam Besar I.

Keruo I.

Saonek I.

Mike's Pt

Sardine Reef

Kri Island

Manta Sandy

Mansuar Island

Mansuar Corner

Dampier Strait

Klaarbeek I.

Andau Besar I.

Yar I.   *Inus I.*

Fambemuk I.   *Merpati I.*

Waai I.

Kasuari Pt

Miosyepban I.

Kommerrust I.

RAJA AMPAT NATURE RESERVE

Marandanweser

Batanta Island

Wailebet

Wensawai

Makoi Point

West Batanta

Jodlo

Sagewin Strait

Weiyaar Bay

Sorong ◎

Dum I.   *Klawasi*

Jeffman Airport ✈

Serikoberi

Matalamagi

Mabo Point

Dadi Point

Warangke

**North Salawati
Nature Reserve**

Waijaar   *Waiwo*

Flaur

Waiji I.   *Yawya I.*

re I.
Kecil I.

Jailolo I.
Eftorobi I.

Deer I.   *Hebera*

Gebe Is

Kofian Island

Walo I.

Ayuan I.
Tabek I.

Kuluai

Kapot Bogin Pt

Igiem I.

Kebu I.

Salawati Island

Kampung Samodir

Sele Strait

Waiboe

Jeflio

**Sorong
Daratan
Airport**

Yef Danga I.

Sapraan

Matugu

Salebam

Loslos I.

Sailolof

Mara   *Yefasim I.*

Papua

Fuilu I.

Lopon I.

Syeitmogan I.

Yapdio I.
Efwai I.

Weeim I.   *Mesluput I.*

Tacon I.   *Dua Is*

Deni I.

Sele Point

Seget

Kasim

Kampung Baru

Jemur I.

Kalukedi

Klasafet

Wakamoek

Segun Bay

Lawat I.   *Gewie I.*

Lie I.   *Kalies I.*   *Kabu I.*

Gam I.   *Haitlai I.*   *Ebo I.*   *Len Malaas*

Senyu I.   *Kananowat I.*   *Atkri*

Yamtu Point

Nukari Bay

Fafan I.

Nanisa I.

Solal   *Gepo*

**Misool Island
Reserve**

Folley

Seram Sea

ampale I.

Kanari I.

Waigama

Jangfubo

Tip

Kalalio

Fet Dom Point

Misool Island

Tamulol

Adua

Malolo

Mustika I.   **3 Rocks**

Igom   *Biga*

Pet Rock

Erwang

Kapocol   *Lelintah*

Yabatano I.   *Farondi Is*

Plateau

Warna Berwarna

**Razorback
Rock**   *Gemut I.*

No Contest
Andamo

The Candy Store

Andy's Ultimate

Tinanka Is   **Barracuda
Rock**

Yellit I.

Pelee I.   *Kalig I.*

Bao Rock

Daram I.

Wayilbatan I.   **Magic Mountain**

Orange Peel

Tank Rock   *Warakaraket I.*

travel into the depths of "Wild Indonesia" there is a land-based resort now operating in the Weda Bay area to the southeast of Halmahera. Although traveling here takes time, divers are rewarded by staggering coral walls, stunning atolls in the mid-ocean, some thrilling seamounts and a handful of excellent muck dives. **Weda Reef and Rainforest Resort** is positioned on the banks of the bay with a backdrop of lush rainforest. Bird watching is also offered in addition to diving, and on a non-diving day it is possible to wake up early and trek into the jungle to watch the birds of paradise in their display tree, a remarkable experience.

WEST PAPUA AND RAJA AMPAT

A wild region of glacier-topped mountains, swamps and islands covered with vast areas of rainforest, West Papua is Indonesia's easternmost province. West Papua occupies the western half of New Guinea Island, which it shares with Papua New Guinea. Few decent roads exist on the island because of the rugged terrain, and tourism is therefore limited to those boarding liveaboards or traveling to one of the few Raja Ampat Islands that offer resort-based diving.

There are still reefs within the Raja Ampat Islands, off the west coast of West Papua, that are so full of schooling fish that divers sometimes can't see each other. The diversity of Raja Ampat is also mind-blowing. Whilst West Papua is rich in timber, minerals and valuable natural resources, marine scientists believe it might also be richest in something far more precious—the Raja Ampat Islands are now thought to sit in the most species-rich sea in the world! During a three-week survey in 2002, the Conservation International research team recorded 950 fish species, 450 coral species and over 600 mollusk species. They anticipate that

Surgeonfish schools gather in the blue at a number of dive sites in the Dampier Strait.

over 1,100 fish species exist in the area. (Dr Gerald Allen, one of the lead researchers for the team, reported 374 species on a single dive on Sorido Bay Resort's House Reef, Cape Kri, in Raja Ampat, his 30-year lifetime record fish count!)

KRI AND MISOOL

The islands of Raja Ampat are mainly dived by liveaboards, but both the area around Kri Island and Misool Island are home to land-based eco resorts: Kri Eco and Sorido Bay on Kri Island and the Misool Eco Resort on Batbitim Island in the Misool area. The majority of liveaboards and Misool Eco Resort operate from mid-September to mid-June due to the south monsoon. Kri Eco Resort and Sorido Bay operate year round.

West Papua was a major battleground in World War II, and it was the vast numbers of wrecked aircraft and ships that lured pioneer Max Ammer to the area around Sorong. After vast exploration of the area, Max opened an eco-resort on Kri Island. Today he operates two resorts from the Island—**Kri Eco Resort** and the more luxurious **Sorido Bay Resort**. A tough, resourceful and personable Dutchman with family ties to the area, he manages the logistics of spare parts, bad fuel and relationships with local villagers and bureaucrats to provide superb diving in the protected area around Kri. In addition, he supports research teams, spearheads conservation efforts and uses only local Papuan people to build and staff his operation, bringing much-needed income and attention to the area.

In the shallow water around Kri Island guests can watch as small sharks, schools of fish, starfish and clumps of sargassum weed occupied by frogfish drift by. On most nights, everyone gathers at twilight on the jetty to watch the schools of fish and colorful hard corals fade in the light, to be overtaken by spectacular sunsets above the surrounding islands. By night, it is peaceful and dark. There are few lights and no man-made noises to distract the senses. Only a moving school of flashlight fish competes with the stars for attention.

Each morning guests awaken to the smell of local cooking and the sounds of exotic birds. On a non-diving day, guests can visit a nearby island to see the red bird of paradise. Small kangaroos, cus-

cus and other endemic animals are often seen in the grounds of the resorts.

And the diving is good, too. **Cape Kri**, of Dr Allen's record fish count, is the house reef for Sorido Bay Resort. Near the point, huge schools of fish parade by. Barracuda and pale or blue tail surgeonfish patrol the reef top, while below schools of trevally and fusiliers whiz past and encircle divers. Meanwhile, schools of snapper and batfish cruise slowly between the colorful soft corals and fans. Divers typically stay deep to avoid the current at the top of the reef, current that would suck the unwary into a whirlpool that leads down to 40 meters.

There are more than 50 excellent sites in the north of Raja Ampat area. **Mike's Point**, named after Max's son, is a rock island that was blown apart in the war. With the wake that strong currents create around the island, it is no wonder that the pilots thought this site was a ship! Schooling barracuda, surgeonfish, snapper and fusiliers hang in blue water or swirl in endless circles over the slope of green tubastrea coral trees, leather corals, red soft corals and sea fans. Hundreds of sweetlips gather in coral-covered crevices below the wall. When there is no current, divers look for pygmy seahorses, nudibranchs and small cowries with red mantles on the soft corals, golden sweepers and a large area covered with anemones and clownfish.

The other sites near the resort (5–20 minutes away by boat) are best dived during "prime time" when currents bring the biggest and brightest fish. **Sardine** and **Chicken Reef** (so-named because of a diver afraid to find sharks) are dives with a large quantity of fish. Bannerfish, sailfin snappers, three species of barracuda, fusiliers and snappers, bumphead parrotfish, Moorish idols, trevally, batfish, rabbitfish, golden sweepers, goatfish,

Water bungalows at Kri Eco Resort offer comfort and privacy right at the water's edge.

bream and unicornfish are common. On one dive it is not impossible to see seven species of sweetlips. "Drop me in where I came out!" is not an infrequent request. Tasseled wobbegong sharks frequent these sites along with white and black tip sharks.

For the best sites in the area, divers armed with sunscreen depart early in the morning to the islands further out. Day trips are made to **The Passage**, **Dayang** or **Melissa's Garden**, and the 45–60 minute ride to these protected areas with less current is worth the effort. Raja Ampat boasts amazing natural scenery, rainforests fringed by powdery white sand beaches, incredible rock islands and deep lagoons which divers can visit between dives or explore on specially arranged expeditions.

The **Misool Eco Resort** further to the south in the Raja Ampat Islands offers luxury accommodation and superb diving in its vast protected zone which now covers an astonishing area (twice the size of Singapore)! The area is patrolled and protected by Misool Eco Resort rangers and the effects of this are staggeringly noticeable as soon as one enters the water. Schools of glassfish crowd the walls, the soft corals are ones most divers dream of, with candy shop colors, and gorgonian fans that are meters across. Shark numbers are healthy and are continuing to increase thanks to the conservation efforts here, and grey tips, white tips, black tips, epaulette and wobbegongs are frequent visitors to the dive sites, not to mention manta rays, stingrays, bumphead parrotfish, Napoleon wrasse and tuna.

Dive sites such as **Magic Mountain**, which is home to a manta ray cleaning station, **Boo Windows** with its stunning topography, and the underwater seamount known as the **Birthday Cake** leave divers searching for more space in their logbooks. Not only is the fish life here prolific—critters abound on these reefs too—pygmy seahorses, nudibranchs, all manner of shrimps and crustaceans can be found amongst the dazzling corals.

Dive trips are typically scheduled in a similar fashion to liveaboard diving, with a morning dive followed by breakfast, another dive before lunch and then afternoon and evening dives later in the day. Two or three dive boat trips are also scheduled when visiting dive sites that are further away, and often lunch will be eaten on a paradisiacal white sand beach where rangers have camps to protect the areas nesting turtles and their eggs.

In the evenings, guests can relax in their bungalow's hammock, which hangs over the water of the bay in which juvenile black tip reef sharks swim in the gin-clear water. A well-prepared dinner is then the perfect end to the day as the sun sets over the horizon.

The Misool Eco Resort was constructed on an island that was originally home to a shark finning camp. The shark finning laborers were retrained by the resort to assist in its construction, which was built entirely from reclaimed timbers rather than from the logging of more trees. Additional labor all came from local villages. Most of those involved in the construction were later trained to become resort staff, thus bringing needed employment and income to the area.

The resort now focuses on numerous conservation projects in the area in addition to its no-take zone, and as the biomass in the area continues to increase it seems that these projects are heralding great results. With the continued efforts of Misool Eco Resort, the reefs around the Misool area only stand to get better and better.

—*David Espinosa/Deborah Fugitt/*
Sarah Ann Wormald

Indonesian Liveaboards
Diving Indonesia's Most Remote Areas

Although the wealth of dive resorts in Indonesia has taken the sport to new heights, in some areas, such as Komodo, Raja Ampat, the Banda Sea and areas further east in Indonesia, a vast amount of the diving is done by liveaboard. Liveaboards not only provide unlimited diving but can operate in areas not readily accessible from land. Divers need only to worry about the diving and can leave everyday details to the crew.

Diver safety is ensured as many operators rigidly adhere to international guidelines. There are many packages offered to fit most budgets (remember liveaboard prices include full board accommodation and diving), from 5-star luxury to more modest offerings. If you are considering a liveaboard option, book early as cabins on the more popular vessels can be fully booked over a year in advance!

There are a number of factors to consider when choosing a liveaboard. But much depends on one's personal interest in diving. The current trend in scuba diving is increasingly towards greater involvement and understanding of marine animals. This interest usually manifests itself in underwater photography, which is within the means of many divers, especially those on liveaboards.

Indonesian liveaboards cater to this market and offer a level of service unparalleled in the world. Cameras are gently lifted in and out of tenders, rinsed after use and generally pampered. The crew does everything but take the photo and set the lighting! Dive guides have even been known to lead photographers around by the arm, spotting for animals big and small, even to the point of having "addresses" on the territorial fish.

The Tambora liveaboard features a large, comfortable saloon area for guests.

Blue Marlin Komodo offer dive and stay packages with modern accommodation and fast speedboats for accessing the best dive sites.

LIVEABOARD DESTINATIONS

The two most popular areas for live-aboards in Indonesia are Raja Ampat and the Komodo National Park, with many of the high-end vessels alternating season-ally between the two. November to May tends to be the Raja Ampat season and July to September is the main Komodo season. In between these two periods, many of the liveaboards are moving from one region to the other, which means that these are amongst the best months for those wanting to explore the places that lay in between, such as East Nusa Tenggara, the Banda Sea and Maluku. The Komodo National Park is also home to many vessels that operate year round in the park, moving from the south to the north of the park seasonally. However, most of the boats that operate in the Raja Ampat area, particularly the south-ern routes, leave for July, August and September due to the south monsoon.

LIVEABOARD OPERATORS

The islands in and around Komodo are host to the largest number of liveaboards in Indonesia. But this large number doesn't mean crowded sites. In fact, the opposite exists. Reputable operators tend to be in contact with one another, sharing observations about where the big fish are and making sure that their boats aren't anchored in the same locations at the same time.

The big franchise boats were notably absent in Komodo until 2002 when Peter Hughes' *Komodo Dancer* began opera-tions. Through the Aggressor and Dancer Fleets, there are now numerous boats from which to choose, ranging from more basic boats to luxury liners.

The *Komodo Dancer*, a 30-meter wood-en *phinisi* ship built in 2001, began op-erations in March 2002. It offers 8 staterooms for up to 16 guests and space for 15 crew plus an additional 3 dive staff. All rooms are air-conditioned with private facilities. A large saloon area is situated on the main deck along with the galley and there is a spacious upper sundeck for those wanting to relax and admire the scenery.

The *Ikan Biru*, operated by **Blue Marlin Komodo**, is permanently sta-tioned in the Komodo National Park and operates on a "hop-on, hop-off" basis, whereby guests are brought to wherever the boat is located by transfer boat. They stay for their requested number of nights and are then transferred back. Sleeping arrangements on the *Ikan Biru* are underneath the stars, on the comfortable upper deck, rather than cabin-based.

Mermaid Liveaboards offer a more high-end experience and they are also a popular choice in Komodo. Although they operate two vessels, *Mermaid I* and *Mermaid II*, these are usually fully booked well in advance.

There are ships, and then there are *ships*. The *Pelagian*, operated by **Wakatobi Dive Resort**, is the undisputed queen of the liveaboard fleet in Indonesia. This classicly designed steel-hulled vessel was built as a Lloyds-classed private yacht in 1965 and has been painstakingly restored in Thailand by owner/captain Matt Hedrick.

The *Pelagian* is a world unto itself, the QEII of the liveaboard world, oozing luxury, comfort and the highest level of professionalism. The diving and on-board facilities are staggering, with quiet being

the word of the day; you can be sitting next to the outboards and not be aware they are on! The food and service are impeccable. In fact, everything is so perfect it is hard to believe you're on a dive boat and not a private yacht.

The *Pindito* is one of the longest serving liveaboards in Indonesia. Built in Borneo by Swiss owner/operator Edi Frommenwiler in 1992, it has been in continuous service ever since. Edi pioneered diving in the Banda Sea, moving to the Sorong region of West Papua when Ambon disintegrated into communal violence. The *Pindito* now operates in both Raja Ampat and Komodo as well as the numerous islands in between.

A trip on the *Pindito* is a memorable and enjoyable experience. This wooden ship looks and feels great and is as solid as can be humanly made. And with such a wealth of experience in diving and

The Pelagian liveaboard is operated by Wakatobi Resort and guarantees luxury and world-class diving.

The Seven Seas is another phinisi which has been adapted with divers in mind to maximize comfort and space.

sailing Indonesian waters, the trips are well organized, efficient and guarantee some fantastic diving.

In Raja Ampat during the season, there are now around 40 liveaboards operating in the region, which is vast so overcrowding is not an issue, and they are ranging similarly from more budget offerings to high-end luxury. Check with operators what their schedules are and what is included or not included in the price prior to booking. Some operators include beverages, for example, whilst others will levy additional charges for these.

The Arenui is one of Indonesia's most luxurious liveaboards. It promises adventure and all the creature comforts of a high-end hotel.

The *Shakti* is one of the longest serving liveaboards in Raja Ampat and offers reasonably priced trips around the region. For those looking for more upmarket and high-end trips, there are several liveaboards whose service, facilities and standards are exceptional. These include the *Amira, Arenui, Aurora, Damai, Seven Seas* and *Tambora*.

Liveaboards offer trips ranging from 7–14 night stays to expeditions of longer duration. For those wanting to link a liveaboard trip with a land-based experience, check with your operator. It is usually possible to arrange embarkation or disembarkation to link in with other travel arrangements providing the operator is aware of your plans in advance.

The majority of vessels offer nitrox for diving and some *require* guests to use it, so you may find that you need to either obtain a nitrox certification prior to your trip or else take the course once on board.

The Tambora is an Indonesian phinisi that covers many areas of Indonesia.

Equipment hire is not frequently provided, so taking your own gear or hiring gear beforehand is usually essential.

The Shakti is permanently based in Raja Ampat and has many years of experience operating in this area.

Philippines's Best Dive Sites

400 km
200 miles

Luzon

Babuyan I.
Calayan I.
Daiupiri I.
Fuga I.
Camiguin I.
Palaui I.

Abulug
Kabugao
Laoag
Tuguegarao
Vigan
Tabuk
Ilagan

Santiago
San Fernando
La Union
Hundred I.
Baguio
Cabarroguis
Alaminos
Dagupan
San Carlos
Baler
Tarlac
Cabantuan
Angeles
San Fernando
Subic
Queson City
Subic Bay
Balanga
MANILA

Nasugbu
Dasmariñas
Labo
Batangas
Lucena
Lopes
Anilao
Batangas
Puerto Galera
Verde Island
Puerto Galera
Boac
Calapan
Panamalayan

Lubang I.

Pallilo I.

Calagua I.

Naga
Pili
Virac

Cantanduanes I.

Marinduque
Burias I.
Legazpi
Sorsogon

SEE SOUTHERN LUZON DIVE SITES MAP

Philippine Sea

Philippines Trench

Luzon Sea

Apo Reef

Mindoro

Mindoro Strait

Tablas I.

SEE BORACAY DIVE SITES MAP

Ticao I.

Sibuyan I.
Masbate I.
Catarman
Samar
Catbalogan

Masbate
Borongan

Boracay

Kalibo
Roxas
Panay
Iloilo
Bacolod
Malapascua
Naval
Leyte
Tacloban

Cebu
Mactan

San Jose
Buenavista
Jordan
San Carlos

Cebu
Bohol

Moalboal
Kabankalan
Bohol
Tagbilaran

Negros
Sumilon
Surigao

Dumaguete
Siquijor
Apo Island
Mambajao
Camiguin I.

Dinagat I.
Siarg
Bucc
Granc

Tanda

Prospe

SEE VISAYAS DIVE SITES MAP

Palawan Passage

Busuanga I.
Culion I.
Coron Bay
Linapacan I.
El Nido
El Nido
Boayan I.
Dumaran I.
Taytay

Cuyo West Pass
Cuyo Is.
Cuyo East Pass

Palawan

Puerto Princesa

Cagayan I.

Jessie
Beazley
Tubbataha
Reef

SEE NORTHERN PALAWAN AND BUSUANGA DIVE SITES MAP

Dipolog
Dapitan
Oroquieta
Cagayan De Or

Sindangan
Iligan
Malaybalay

Sulu Sea

Bugsuk I.
Balabac I.
Balabac Strait
Banggi I.

Basterra

Sulu Archipelago

Zamboanga

Pagadian
Tubod
Mindanao
Nabunt

Ipil
Karomatan
Parang
Sultan
Kudarat

Gayamcam
Moro
Gulf
Cotabato City
Kabuntalan
Kidapawan

Dav
Samal I.
Davao

Shariff Aguak
Digos
Koronadal

Isabela
Basilan I.
Isulan
General
Santos

Malaysia

Sandakan

Lahad Datu
Bongao
Simunul I.

Pangutaran I.
Jolo
Tapul I.
Siasi I.
Jolo I.

Mindanao Sea

Sarangani I.
Balut I.

Diving in the Philippines
World-class Diving and a Well-developed Industry

As a diving destination, the Philippines is hard to beat. Walls, drop-offs, coral reefs, wrecks, submerged islands and lagoons abound. Divers can choose from a staggering array of locations, both easily accessible and hard to reach. Choices range from off-the-beach resort diving to dive safaris and daily boat dive trips. Among these options are a variety of liveaboard boats and other vessels which visit not only the popular and well-known sites, such as the Sulu Sea and the Visayas, but also numerous more remote locations.

Whether you're a humble scuba enthusiast with a limited budget or a wealthy aquanaut with a taste for the luxurious, the Philippines can accommodate your every whim at a price to suit your pocket.

SCUBA POTENTIAL

Since the early 1960s, when scuba diving first started to gain popularity, entrepreneurs were quick to realize the potential of a country with 7,107 islands (counted at high tide), each with its own unique coral and reef formations.

Anilao in Batangas Province, to the south of Manila, became the very first dive center in the country and probably one of the first in Asia. Since those distant days, diving has caught on in a big way. Resorts all over the country have invested in diving equipment and there are scuba diving instructors and divemasters everywhere.

In fact, the Philippines is an outstanding place to learn diving or to upgrade your certification level. Courses from open water to professional levels are widely available and can be taught in languages as varied as English, French, German, Italian, Hebrew, Swedish, Japanese or various Chinese dialects by multilingual instructors of many nationalities who have made the Philippines their home. You'll find international certification agencies such as PADI, NAUI, SSI and CMAS well established here, and there are numerous PADI course directors and SSI instructor trainers running instructor courses. Professional training is a big industry in the Philippines and

Asia Divers in Puerto Galera offers a seafront dive center and accommodation at El Galleon.

A photographer, eager for the ultimate close-up shot, peers into a marvelously colored feather star on Balicasag Island.

instructor courses are widely available in La Union, Anilao, Puerto Galera, Boracay and the Visayas, to name but a few. In fact, most areas now have professional level courses running at some point throughout the year.

Although many operators have invested in fiberglass speedboats, diving is still

A spotted hermit crab gingerly peeking out from its borrowed shell house.

largely done from native *banca* boats— motorized outrigger canoes that can vary in size from 6 to over 25 meters. As a general rule, the smaller the boat, the less stable it is likely to be. Care should be taken when stowing gear and selecting a place to sit as the balance can be critical, especially in smaller *banca*. The driest part of such a *banca* is usually right in the front, beneath the plywood covering the bow. Stow items you want to keep dry there. Let the *bancero*, or boatman, take charge of this and try not to make any sudden movements. Inform the boatman when you are about to enter the water or get back on board after a dive as he may have to provide counterweight to avoid capsizing. Another useful tip is to arrange the price for your trip before leaving and pay when you get back. There are, sadly, uncommon but verifiable stories of divers who have paid up front and then been left to fend for themselves once they are in the water.

If the *banca* has no steps to get back on board, another useful tip is to take a length of rope, tie one end to the outrigger close to where it joins with the hull and tie a stirrup, or loop, at the other end at about water level. Then, by placing a foot in the stirrup and standing up, you can avoid the embarrassment of struggling to get back in the boat, otherwise accomplished by pulling oneself up by the arms. If you are climbing back on board, do not remove your fins. Kicking as you pull yourself up also makes the process much easier.

PROTECTING THE SEAS

Spear fishing, dynamite fishing, the collection of corals and shells and other destructive practices are illegal in the Philippines, but that doesn't seem to worry the many fishermen and gatherers who make their living from the sea.

Dynamite fishing is still practiced and the damage is horrendous in some places. Sodium cyanide and other poisons are sometimes used to stun fish for collection for the aquarium and live food fish trade, a practice that burns dead patches into the coral and invertebrate cover. Then there is *muro-ami* fishing, where teams of swimmers bounce rocks tied to string with streamers attached across entire reefs to drive the fish into a net at one end. This practice strips a reef of its fish and destroys the coral at the same time, yet another factor contributing to the degradation of the Philippines' estimated 27,022 sq km of coral reef at the 10-fathom level.

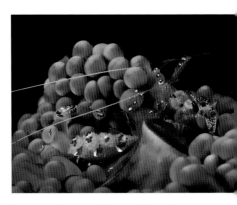

Anemone shrimp carry their eggs with them. The eggs here are clearly visible.

Although various attempts have been made to cope with the problem and many projects are now underway and showing signs of success, local politicians and influential supporters in many areas have effectively negated any serious effort to stop the devastation. The coast guard suffers from a lack of vessels and other resources, meaning that policing of marine sanctuaries and other likely targets of the *dynamiteros* is a haphazard and arbitrary affair. In a country in which millions rely on the fishing industry for their livelihood, it is ironic that the fishermen themselves, through the harmful techniques they employ, are the main culprits behind the declining fish stocks which they so vocally complain about.

The scuba diving industry in the Philippines has always been at the forefront of the struggle to protect the magnificent resources nature has bestowed on the Filipinos. In Anilao, for example,

Butterflyfish are often found in pairs, such as these two spotted at Anilao, Batangas.

The colorful reefs around remote Palawan offer numerous photo opportunities.

there is a long history of co-operation with the coast guard, and an ongoing, aggressive, pro-environment sentiment among the large scuba diving community there. In Puerto Galera, the industry has developed in harmony with the local population who can see the benefits that tourism has brought to their little corner of paradise. As with Anilao, there are some superb sites around the area because of this concern.

In the Visayas, the story is the same. On Mactan Island, there can be no doubt that the presence of so many scuba diving operations over the years has considerably slowed down the ravages of illegal fishing. Sites that are frequently visited by divers—and there are a lot of divers in the water every day around the island—are perceived as too risky by most illegal fishermen. While there are some areas bombed out beyond hope, there are also some incredible spots just waiting to be discovered and no shortage of knowledgeable guides to take them there.

Around Bohol, especially at Panglao and Balicasag islands, the locals seem to have held their marine resources in higher regard than some others because they are precious jewels in the crown of Visayan diving. Apo Island, to the south of Cebu and east of Negros, is another outstanding site not to be missed.

Obviously, the remoteness of a location can be its salvation, though some *muro-ami* vessels are quite seaworthy and can stay at sea for long periods, over six months, if necessary. The Sibuyan Sea to the northeast of Boracay and southeast of Marinduque Island, is still less visited by

These big eye snappers were pictured in the Bohol Sea.

Green turtles in the Bohol Sea allow divers to approach at close quarters.

divers. Banton Island and the wreck of the *Maestre de Campo*, two popular Sibuyan Sea sites, are now regularly accessed from Boracay and Puerto Galera, and returning divers praise them with gushing superlatives. Other even more remote sites that are often frequented by liveaboard vessels on transition runs are described as either fantastic or devastated, with few assessments of anything in between.

PROFESSIONALISM IN THE INDUSTRY

The **Philippine Commission on Sports Scuba Diving** (PCSSD) was formed in 1987 to promote the development of the sport, oversee the conservation of the country's marine resources and register and license dive establishments and professionals in the industry. This regulatory body has done a lot to improve and develop scuba diving.

Numerous dive establishments and diving professionals in the Philippines are registered with the PCSSD. Air from registered dive centers is tested twice annually and licensees are required to

conform to an ethical and environmental code. It is always a good idea to check that a dive center is registered with the PCSSD as it may say a lot about the integrity of the operation. To view a list of accredited operators, check www.dive-philippines.com.ph. The PCSSD works closely with the industry to promote the country as a diving destination and visitors are always welcome at their office in the Department of Tourism Building in Manila. The PCSSD also works closely with a recompression chamber in Cebu.

In the private sector, most of the popular dive areas have attempted to organize an association of local dive operators. The Dive Industry Trade Organization of the Philippines (DITO Philippines) was set up in 1999 to act as a focal point for interested parties such as media groups, trade show organizers and travel and industry professionals. The Haribon Foundation is another effective environmental group working with divers, as is Mario Elumba's Scubasurero project at Anilao. Scubasurero is a play on the Tagalog word for a garbage collector, a *basurero*, and that's what participating divers do: pick up plastic bags and other garbage strewn over affected reefs.

A PRICE FOR EVERY POCKET

But don't be put off by tales of dynamite and plastic bags. A visiting scuba diver is not short of superb destinations from which to choose. For most, deciding which area to choose will be based on financial considerations and the amenities on offer. From a US$500 plus a night resort with an array of facilities to a hut on the beach for backpacker rates, the choice is yours. In the US$45-75 per night range, the possibilities are almost endless. These days, most dive centers have good equipment, many offering niceties such as rental of dive computers and underwater videos, and are run by professional, competent businessmen. Many conservation-minded dive centers are also running reef monitoring projects and courses.

Porcelain crabs live in the base of anemones where they are protected by the anemone's tentacles.

Various consultants and specialized tour operators, such as Whitetip Divers and Dive Buddies, both located in Manila, can give valuable tips on most areas as well as up-to-the-minute information on weather and dive conditions around the islands, advice on travel, accommodation, amenities, night life, dining and other points of interest.

—*Heneage Mitchell/Sarah Ann Wormald*

El Galleon Resort is the perfect spot to relax after a day of diving in Puerto Galera.

La Union
Calm Waters and Pleasant Beaches

Approximately a 4–5 hour drive from Manila, La Union was one of the first beach resorts to be developed in the Philippines. The US Air Force had around 150 men stationed at Wallace Air Station until 1992, many of whom learned scuba diving in the warm, clear waters of La Union's Lingayen Gulf.

Unfortunately, indiscriminate dynamiting and other illegal fishing techniques have wreaked havoc over the years on the once prolific inner reefs. Nonetheless, there are enough interesting sites in the usually calm and gentle waters of the gulf to justify several days of lingering around to enjoy both the diving and the beaches of Bauang, Paringao and San Fernando.

Access Banca boats, 20–90 minutes

Current Good but seasonal, 20 meters on average

Reef type Usually negligible

Highlights Damaged but pretty in certain places

Visibility Rocky: crevices, caves and corals

Coral Skittish, fair variety, small numbers

Fish M10-1A World War II tanks, caves

THE TANKS

This is the most famous dive in the gulf. Resting 39 meters down on a ledge protruding from the almost vertical western wall of **Fagg Reef**, about 2 km off Poro Point, three World War II M10 tanks are now home to a variety of marine life.

Hard coral heads are the base for many soft coral growths and together they form coral bommies.

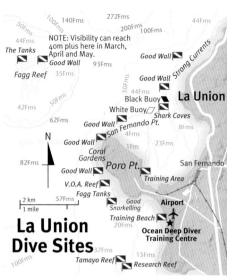

La Union
Dive Sites

272Fms
140Fms
200Fms
100Fms
44Fms
50Fms
100Fms
44Fms
NOTE: Visibility can reach 40m plus here in March, April and May.
The Tanks
Good Wall
Good Wall
Strong Currents
Fagg Reef 35Fms
93Fms
Good Wall
42Fms
50Fms
44Fms
Black Buoy **La Union**
White Buoy
Shark Caves
62Fms
Good Wall
San Fernando Pt.
8Fms
4Fms
N
Good Wall
23Fms
Coral Gardens
1Fm
San Fernando
82Fms
Poro Pt.
Good Wall
Training Area
V.O.A. Reef
Fagg Tanks
57Fms
Good Snorkelling
Airport
2 km
1 mile
Training Beach
20Fms
Ocean Deep Diver Training Centre
37Fms
15Fms
100Fms
Tamayo Reef
Research Reef

Moray eels open and close their mouths to force water through their gills to breath.

Currents can be tricky this far out but it is usually possible to come up from this deep dive and drift across the top of the reef while decompressing and still see plenty of interesting stuff. I have come across pelagic white tip and whale sharks on the wall at Fagg, as well as wrasses, dorados, the occasional Spanish

Marble rays, one of the larger species of stingray found in the Philippines, can measure up to 2 meters across.

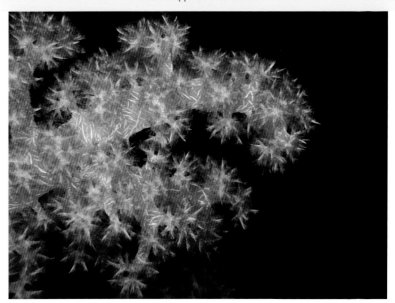

Unlike hard corals, soft corals do not have a rigid calcium carbonate skeleton.

mackerel, king barracuda and leopard rays. There used to be plenty of hawksbill turtles but sadly they are rare now.

The caves on **Research Reef** are another popular dive, with an average depth of around 15 meters. A series of easily penetrable tunnels and canyons rather than actual caves, expect to see lobsters (usually young), parrotfish and lionfish as well as almost any kind of other tropical reef fishes, though usually small and timid, at this site. It's an excellent site for a night dive.

VOICE OF AMERICA REEF

In the next cove to the north, you'll find VOA Reef, so named because of the half-million watt Voice of America transmitting station which still occupies a large section of Poro Point. From the white coral sand at 6 meters to the bottom of the wall at 22 meters, VOA is a delightful, easy dive. In common with the other local sites, there is a profusion of table, basket, staghorn, brain, star, flower and finger corals, together with a wide variety of soft corals and anemones. La Union makes up in shell life for what it lacks in fish, and following trails in the sand will usually lead to something interesting. There are eggshell, map and tiger cowries as well as green turbans, a variety of augers, cones (be careful!) and Murex. There is generally more fish life—groupers, parrotfish, squirrelfish, snappers and lionfish—at the southern, deeper end of the wall, although visibility is usually not as good here.

Visibility in the **Lingayen Gulf** is unusually good year round. In peak season (March to June), it can get to 40 meters. In the middle of the rainy season (from June to December), it rarely falls below 7 meters and is often better at many sites. The gulf is protected from all but the worst weather by the Cordillera mountain range to the east, and is well north of the usual typhoon tracks, and so enjoys mild weather all year round.

—*Heneage Mitchell/Sarah Ann Wormald*

Subic Bay
A Choice of Wrecks in a Perfect Natural Harbor

Just a few hours northwest of Manila are the coral and wreck sites of duty-free Subic Bay. During the years the US Navy held sway over the perfect natural harbor in the bay, diving and fishing were off-limits in many areas. Since their departure, 12 wreck sites have been discovered and a number of reef sites. Visibility can reach 25 meters in the bay, though it is usually between 5 and 15 meters. There is virtually no current and the water is almost always calm enough for diving.

Probably the most accessible wreck, and the most interesting one to dive on, is the battleship **USS *New York***. Built in 1891, the ship saw service in the Philippine American War, the Chinese Revolution and World War I.

Access Banca boats, 5–60 minutes

Current Usually fair, 10–25 meters

Reef type Usually none

Highlights Fair variety in places

Visibility Sand, mud bottom, some corals

Coral Good variety, prolific in places

Fish Excellent wreck diving

Decommissioned in 1931, she rode at anchor in Subic Bay for the next 10 years until she was scuttled by retreating US forces to prevent her massive 43-cm cannons from falling into Japanese hands. She lies on her port side in 27 meters of water between the Alava Pier

The large soft coral in the center of the image has retracted its polyps revealing its white stem. The soft corals to the left and right have open polyps displaying bright colors and a "bushy" appearance.

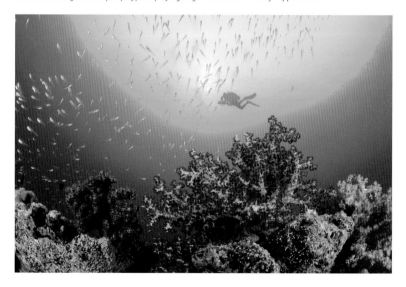

This nudibranch is from the Chromodoris family and is specifically known as the kuniei species.

and the runway at Cubi Point, and is home to a variety of marine life, including barracuda, lionfish, spotted sweetlips, groupers, lobsters and spotted rays. The cannons are still intact and the photo opportunities are outstanding.

A SUNKEN FREIGHTER

Not to be missed is the ***El Capitan***. Lying on its port side, the stern is in only 5 meters of water while the bow rests at 20 meters. A small freighter, the *El Capitan* is safely penetrable. The accommodation area is now taken up by a wide variety of tropical fishes. Look out for glass eyes, wrasses, tangs, gobies, spotted sweetlips, lobsters, crabs and clownfish. Visibility is usually between 5 and 20 meters depending on the tide.

There are several other wrecks visited regularly by local dive centers, including the ***Oryoku Maru***, an outbound passenger ship carrying over 1,600 prisoners of war when it was attacked and sunk 400 meters off Alava Pier. Despite having been flattened by US Navy demolition divers for navigational safety reasons, this is still a good dive with plenty to see, including a shoal of barracuda that are known to patrol the site overhead.

GOOD CORAL REEF DIVES

Coral reef fanatics are also well served in Subic. Apart from the ever popular sites at nearby **Grande Island**, a former R&R center for US servicemen, there are a number of other good reef dives. These

Dive sites off Nabasan Point in Triboa Bay are suitable for reef divers and offer a mix of hard branching, soft and sponge corals which provide habitat for small, colorful damsel fish.

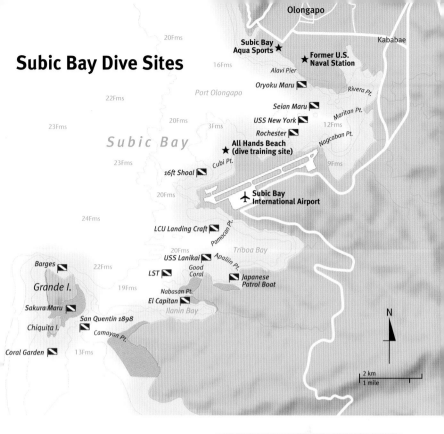

Subic Bay Dive Sites

Olongapo

Kababae

Subic Bay Aqua Sports ★

★ Former U.S. Naval Station

Alavi Pier

Rivera Pt.

Oryoku Maru

Port Olongapo

16Fms

20Fms

22Fms

Seian Maru

Maritan Pt.

USS New York

12Fms

20Fms

3Fms

Rochester

Nagcaban Pt.

23Fms

All Hands Beach
★ (dive training site)

Subic Bay

9Fms

23Fms

Cubi Pt.

16ft Shoal

20Fms

✈ Subic Bay International Airport

24Fms

LCU Landing Craft

Pamacan Pt.

Triboa Bay

20Fms

USS Lanikai

Apaliin Pt.

Barges

22Fms

LST

Good Coral

Grande I.

19Fms

Japanese Patrol Boat

Nabasan Pt.

Sakura Maru

El Capitan

Ilinan Bay

San Quentin 1898

Chiquita I.

Camayan Pt.

Coral Garden

13Fms

N

2 km
1 mile

include sites such as the coral gardens off **Nabasan Point** in Triboa Bay. Their healthier than average condition is due to the fact that they have been protected from fishing and divers for many years. Expect to find examples of various brain, table and star corals as well as a profusion of crinoids, sponges and crustaceans.

Subic is now a duty-free port and is a good place to buy diving equipment (remember to take your passport along). Complete diver training is offered by numerous dive centers from Olongapo to Barrio Barretto, a popular laid-back beach resort area a few kilometers to the north of the city of Olongapo.

—*Heneage Mitchell/Sarah Ann Wormald*

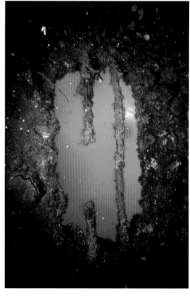

A close-up view of a pothole on the El Capitan wreck in Subic Bay.

Nasugbu and Fortune Island

Easily Accessible Diving from Manila

A few hours' drive to the south of the capital of Manila, in the province of Batangas, is the coastal town of Nasugbu. Facing onto the waters of the South China Sea, this region has long volcanic sand beaches and no shortage of good diving.

FORTUNE ISLAND

Perhaps the most famous dive sites around here are at Fortune Island, a small privately owned resort island a few miles out to sea west of the town itself. Except for the Bat Cave, the visibility here is usually good and can reach 30 meters and even more.

On one particular site, the **Blue Holes**, there are large groupers, sweetlips and parrotfish everywhere as well as angel-

Access By boat, 10–60 minutes

Current Average 20 meters depending on the site

Reef type Can be strong in places

Highlights Good variety, prolific in places

Visibility Walls, drop-offs

Coral Good variety

Fish Fortune Island, walls and caves

fish, puffers, wrasses, gobies, butterfly-fish and damselfish, to name but a few. Squid and cuttlefish are also spotted here. The corals and other reef organisms are prolific and diverse. You'll find gorgonians and barrel sponges, vast slabs of star coral with plume worms all over

The red banded wrasse (Cheilinus fasciatus) is a popular fish among divers because it often allows a close approach.

Nasugbu Dive Sites

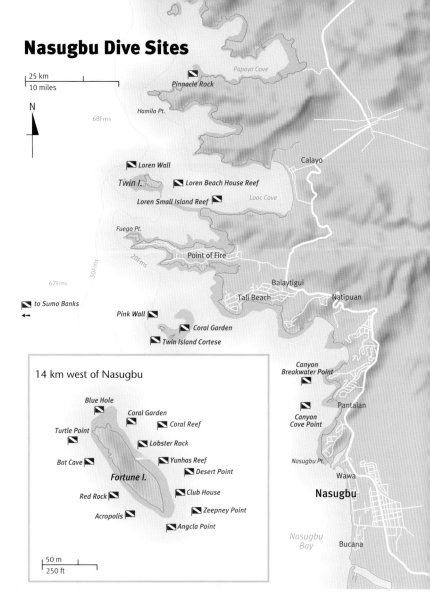

25 km
10 miles

N

Papaya Cove

Pinnacle Rock

Hamilo Pt.

68Fms

Loren Wall

Twin I.

Loren Beach House Reef

Loren Small Island Reef

Calayo

Looc Cove

Fuego Pt.

20Fms

Point of Fire

50Fms

Balaytigui

67Fms

Tali Beach

Natipuan

to Sumo Banks

Pink Wall

Coral Garden

Twin Island Cortese

Canyon
Breakwater Point

14 km west of Nasugbu

Blue Hole

Coral Garden

Coral Reef

Turtle Point

Lobster Rock

Bat Cave

Yunhas Reef

Fortune I.

Desert Point

Red Rock

Club House

Acropolis

Zeepney Point

Angcla Point

Pantalan

Canyon
Cove Point

Nasugbu Pt.

Wawa

Nasugbu

Nasugbu
Bay

Bucana

50 m
250 ft

them and anemones galore. There are three sinkholes which converge into an open cavern, and a coral overhang at 28 meters. Hawksbill turtles and shoals of leatherjackets frequent the area, plus several species of pelagics.

Also at Fortune Island are the remains of an old freighter lying in 20 meters or so of water. Not much is left now except box sections, but the wreck is very penetrable and excellent for photography. Look out for lionfish and scorpionfish that are often camouflaged against the wreck's surfaces.

The **Bat Cave** is also a popular site, another 20-meter dive, which leads to a

The lifeguard tower on the beach in Nasugbu sits in the shadows of towering palm trees.

semi-submerged cave with bats hanging around inside. Cuttlefish breed here, and there are abundant soft corals around.

SUMO BANK

Several miles further out, this is another excellent local dive. Among other features is an abundance of cauliflower-shaped corals that cover the sandy bottom. White tips and other sharks roam these waters, and a wide variety of tropical reef fish make their homes here. The corals, soft and hard, are prolific, and the area is well suited for the more experienced diver.

Closer inshore are **Twin Islands**, two large rocks jutting up out of the sea. There are several good dives here, the Pink Wall being our favorite. An almost sheer drop-off starting at 8 meters, the wall is covered by thousands of soft, pink corals. There are lots of small tropical fish and occasionally turtles frequent the area. Visibility doesn't usually exceed 20 meters but the diving is memorable.

SUNKEN BOOTY

At **Fuego Point**, almost 900 meters directly north of Twin Islands, a boulder-strewn bottom hides the remains of a galleon, the *San Diego*, sunk in 1600 by a Dutch warship and discovered in 1992, of which the anchor and chain can still be seen. The fish life is not impressive, but lots of small tropicals are swimming around. Visibility is seldom much above 15 meters but the drop-off, which goes past 30 meters, usually enjoys better visibility—between 12 and 25 meters—and is draped with colorful gorgonians and other hard and soft corals. Tuna and other pelagics cruise the waters, and there are also plenty of small tropical reef fish to enjoy.

The dive sites around Nasugbu are busy sites, due to their proximity to Manila. The PADI dive center at the popular Maya Maya Reef Resort offers daily diving around these sites.

—Heneage Mitchell/Sarah Ann Wormald

Anilao

The Birthplace of Philippine Scuba Diving

A two and a half hour drive through the lush Southern Luzon countryside from Manila, Anilao can justifiably claim to be the birthplace of scuba diving in the Philippines.

In the mid 1960s, Dr Tim Sevilla transplanted an entire coral reef onto a large rock formation a short distance off shore from his Dive 7000 resort. At the time, the conventional thinking about coral reef growth regarded transplanting a coral reef to be futile but Dr Sevilla proved them wrong, and to this day **Cathedral Rock** is a much visited site, a vibrant, colorful dive with a profusion of small reef fish, soft and hard corals and even a small underwater shrine.

This cross at Cathedral Rock was laid by President Fidel Ramos and blessed by Pope John Paul II.

Access	Banca boats, 10–60 minutes
Current	Usually fair, 10–25 meters
Reef type	Can be stiff in places
Highlights	Prolific and varied
Visibility	Walls, drop-offs
Coral	Prolific in places
Fish	Outstanding macro photography

The shrine is in the form of a cross, and was blessed by the Pope and placed at about 13 meters between two coral carpeted pinnacles in 1982 by Lt General Fidel V. Ramos, who would later become the President of the Philippines.

Anilao has remained at the forefront of the scuba industry since then, and is still an excellent place for snorkelers, novices and experienced aquanauts alike.

However, don't expect to find much beachfront along the rugged Balayan Bay coastline. You don't come to Anilao to laze around on beaches. Trips here are definitely focused on water sports and, in particular, scuba diving.

Photographers inevitably have a field day here, and professionals come in time and time again from around the world to shoot the area's diverse sites. The macro photographer will enjoy the legendary photo opportunities this dive destination affords while wide-angle enthusiasts won't be disappointed either.

Unfortunately, the pressures of an ever increasing population has put a lot of stress on the local ecosystem, typical of many premier dive destinations else-where. Being just round the corner from

Anilao Dive Sites

Balayan Bay

LUZON

Ligpo
Parang
Bau
Dalig Pt.
Dive & Trek
New Dangl
Locloc Pt.
San Andreas
Locloc
Santa Maria
Janao Bay
Mabini Bay
Galung Pt.
4 km
2 miles
344m
N

Vistamar Anilao Pier
Mato Pt.
Basura
Anilao
Mainaga
Biluga Pt.
Matu
San Jose
Pier Uno
Solo
Mabini
Outrigger
Calumpan Peninsula
Talaga
Pungo Pt.
Aquaventure
Ligaya
Cathedral Rock
Bagalangit
Masaging
Eagle Point
Bagalangit Pt.
Balabag
Batangas Bay
Beatrice Rock
Koala
Sombrero
Batok
Larry's
Garden
Arthur's Rock
Dilao Pt.
294m
Sombrero I.
Bajura
Dead Palm
San Teodoro
300m
Layag-Layag
Kirby's Reef
Balai
Red Rock
Sepoc Pt.
Caban I.
Twin Rocks
Mainit
Mainit Bubbles
Sepoc Wall
Daryl Laut
Nagiba
Mainit Point
Mapating
Caban Cove
Cazador Pt.
Tres Cuevas
Hot Springs, Good Coral ★
Merrel's Rock
Bethlehem
Maricaban Strait
391m
excellent macro-photography
Maricaban
Red Palm
Batalan Rock
Tingloy
Soft Corals
Talahib
Gamao
Mapating
Burijar Pt.
Gamao Pt.
Balahibong
Manok
Devil's Point
Masasa Pt.
Maricaban I.
Bonito I.
Nelson's
Rock
100m
Gorda Pt.
Pisa
Hot
Springs
521m
300m
Bonito
Malajibomanoc I.
Papaya Pt.
500m

a major port, Batangas City, located at the mouth of Batangas Bay, Balayan Bay has not escaped the negative effects of shipping and the constant movemen of water.

The many thousands of Filipino divers who trained and still dive regularly in Anilao have long been on the cutting edge of the social, environmental and political issues affecting all marine areas of the Philippines, from Mactan to Marinduque. Dynamite and other illegal fishing techniques, collection of corals and shells, overfishing and pollution, these are just some of the harmful influences that have put immense pressure on the environment. Action is being taken against such practices at many levels and by an increasing number of people throughout the islands.

Anilao has led the way in programs such as the Scubasurero (a play on the Tagalog word for a garbage collector) clean-up operation and has attracted wide interest from such prestigious organizations as the Haribon Foundation and the PADI Project AWARE Program. This is not to say that diving around Anilao is in any way deficient. Far from it. But it is important to recognize Anilao's importance to the development and to the future of scuba diving in the Philippines. The fact that the local diving continues to attract many thousands is testament to the continuing struggle between the ecologically aware locals and the diving community on the one hand, and the forces of industrialization and the unending demands for resources on the other.

Anilao is still, and plans on continuing to be, an extremely popular year-round destination, and there is certainly no shortage of excellent diving available here. Most of the better sites are not actually in Balayan Bay but around the islands of Sombrero and Maricaban, each located a short *banca* boat ride to the south of Anilao.

SOMBRERO ISLAND

Uninhabited, Somrero Island has a delightful beach which is often used as a picnic spot between dives. The diving is good all the way round the island but perhaps the best site is **Beatrice Rock**, just off the northern point. From depths of 6 meters down to 25 meters, there are plenty of good hard corals. Currents are often strong, which encourages pelagics to visit the site. Several species of ray can be found here, including the occasional eagle ray, as well as rainbow runners and yellowtails. Look out for another small statue placed here at a depth of around 13 meters.

At nearby **Bajura**, east of Sombrero and north of Caban Island, the reef is over 1 km long and descends from 12 meters to around 37 meters. There are lots of caves and overhangs, often providing a temporary home to sleeping sharks. The drop-offs and walls here are covered in a profusion of table, staghorn, mushroom and other hard corals as well as a wide variety of crinoids and gorgonians. The prolific fish life is impressively diverse, with plenty of parrotfish, butterflyfish, triggerfish, wrasses, lionfish, scorpionfish, moray eels, aggregations

of sweetlips, the occasional octopus, some angelfish, a few batfish, schools of surgeons and snappers, and from time to time eagle rays and white tip sharks. However, you should take care here as the currents are unpredictable and can be strong, but as this is an excellent dive experienced divers shouldn't be dissuaded by this possibility.

At **Mapating**, off the northwest shore of Maricaban, the reef has excellent soft corals and small fish in depths of only 3–12 meters. As with most sites around Anilao, the macro photography here is outstanding. The wide variety of nudibranchs are an ever popular subject. Then there is a big, long wall starting at 18 meters which drops off to over 60 meters. Another shelf at 20 meters has some good hard corals and provides temporary shelter to occasional nurse and cat sharks. Schools of snappers and surgeons often swim by when the current is running, as do some very large southern rays and white tip sharks. For those divers who are qualified to make a really deep dive, there is a huge cave here between 37 and 43 meters.

This juvenile lionfish was pictured in Anilao where macro photography is a focus for many divers.

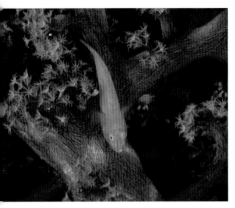

Soft coral goby Pleurosicya on Dendronephthya soft coral are not so easy to spot.

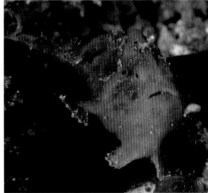

Frogfish have a lure, much like a fishing rod, attached to their head, which entices prey to come within striking distance.

PINNACLES AND POINTS

To the southeast at **Devil's Point** there is a large submerged rock between 6 and 12 meters with pleasant corals and lots of small fish. The rock formations are picturesque but, again, watch out for the current.

At **Mainit**, which means "hot" in Tagalog, there is a rocky, ridged slope with a good selection of hard and soft corals on it. At 18 meters, you'll find a submerged pinnacle and a shark cave at 6 meters. Generally, the site hosts an abundance of small reef fish. Currents can be strong, but they also produce a few pelagics when they are running so it's usually worth the effort. Afterwards, check out the hot springs on the beach.

Just off Layaglang Point on the northeastern tip of Caban Island is **Kirby's**, a pinnacle which goes down to 28 meters. There's a small wall with moray eels, lionfish and lots of colorful crinoids.

Between Culebra and Malajibomanoc (which means "chicken feather" in Tagalog) islands is **Nelson's Rock**, which tops out at 16 meters and drops down to a depth of over 30 meters. The pinnacle is carpeted most of the time by a profusion of blooming coral polyps and large gorgonians, while the water is usually a haze with lots of damselfish. You'll also see caves that often host sharks, some stingrays and a few pelagics when the current is running.

A little to the east are the **Hot Springs**, a very unusual dive site affording the opportunity to try out a neat trick. At 21 meters, hot volcanic gas bubbles out of holes in the seabed, and you can place an egg to cook on one of the holes while you swim off into a fairytale landscape of multihued pastels, bright greens and vivid yellows. Because the water is warm, the visibility here is always good. Walking fish, such as frogfish and anglerfish, are common in one spot, and sharks and rays are known to pass through. When you are ready to ascend, don't forget to collect your egg; it should be hard-boiled by the end of your dive.

It is hard to include all the favorite dive sites in and around Anilao. This choice is inevitably very subjective. Suffice to say that Anilao has plenty to offer divers of all levels.

—*Heneage Mitchell/Sarah Ann Wormald*

Verde Island
A Fabulous Wall and Good Corals

This is a favorite dive spot for regulars in the Puerto Galera and Anilao area. Situated in the aptly named Verde Island Passage between southern Batangas on the mainland of Luzon and the northeastern tip of Mindoro, Verde has one of the best wall dives north of Palawan. There are also several beaches where divers picnic between dives. Please clean up afterwards and take your rubbish home.

Access By boat, 30 minutes–3 hours

Current Usually good, 15–30 meters

Reef type Very strong in places

Highlights Prolific, colorful and good variety

Visibility Walls, drop-offs

Coral Often prolific and good variety

Fish Pristine wall, excellent corals and fish

The diver in this photo is only marginally taller than the barrel sponge in the foreground!

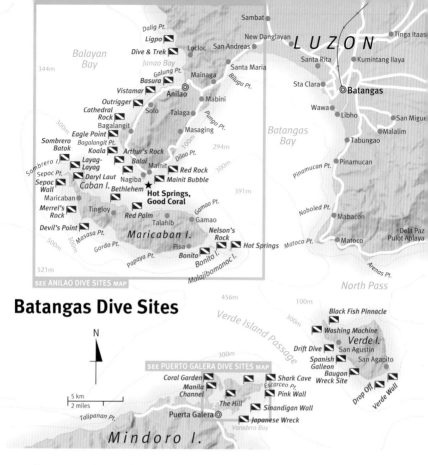

Batangas Dive Sites

Currents can be a problem here though they do create some interesting drift dives. The island's west coast has gentle drop-offs starting from the shore and sloping down to abyssal depths. There used to be the remains of the keel of a Spanish galleon sitting in a few meters just off the beach. History relates that the galleon had just left Manila bound for Spain with a cargo of silks and spices from China when it ran aground. No one was killed but the incensed crew and passengers immediately constructed a gallows and hanged the unfortunate navigator. The keel has now been raised and preserved in the National Museum. Divers who have sifted through the sand where the galleon sank have been known to come across a few ballast stones, fragments of pottery and even ancient musket balls.

Jumping into the sea anywhere off this west coast will put a diver onto the gentle slopes of the fringing reef, which is criss-crossed with gullies and ravines. The current usually provides a free ride, but nonetheless care should be taken. There are lots of soft and hard corals here but not so many reef fish around because most of these lurk in the gullies out of range of the current. It is worth investigating the various patches of sand with coral heads blooming out of them as they are home to anemones, clownfish and spotted rays as well as a variety of crustaceans.

THE VERDE ISLAND WALL

It is the Verde Island Wall that attracts most divers to the island. Easily identifiable by the rocks sticking out of the water off the southeastern tip of the island, the wall descends from the surface almost straight down to seemingly unfathomed depths. Around the corner from the drop-in point, the wall curves in a bit, which allows divers to collect themselves in calm waters before starting to explore the surroundings.

There are vast slabs of star corals draped all along the wall as well as giant gorgonians and large, cascading soft corals. Sea fans and anemones billow in the constantly moving water, and you can't help but be amazed by the impossibly diverse colors that meet the eye everywhere. The first time our party visited Verde, we encountered two large Napoleon wrasse who casually swam up and inspected us. On other dives, we have seen mantas, eagle rays, white tip and black tip sharks. Schools of jacks and tuna are not uncommon, and there are plenty of sweetlips, batfish, wrasses, emperors, surgeons, soldiers and tangs everywhere.

You must take care to control buoyancy and watch the depths on this particular dive. As the reef starts at the surface, safety stops can be made while still on the wall. Look out for schools of curious unicornfish coming in close to check out decompressing divers. Serious photographers should bring two cameras (or interchangeable lenses), one for the larger animals and one with a macro lens to capture the nudibranchs which are generally plentiful around here.

—*Heneage Mitchell/Sarah Ann Wormald*

Jackfish are a schooling fish that swim in the water column above tropical reefs.

Puerto Galera
Diving from a Popular Holiday Resort

The discovery of an ancient inter-island trading vessel laden with Chinese dragon jars and other ceramic goodies in the picturesque Batangas Channel of Puerto Galera was the precursor to the incredible growth of the scuba diving industry that thrives there today.

There are over 30 excellent dive sites within an hour of whichever of the many coves or beaches you may be staying at. Usually, there is fine snorkeling just offshore. There is no shortage of dive centers in the area competing for business, most of which offer a full range of courses, fun diving, equipment hire and other dive services.

A place of outstanding natural beauty, Puerto Galera's underwater delights are

Access	Banca and customized dive boats, 10–30 minutes
Current	Usually fair, 10–30 meters
Reef type	Very strong in places
Highlights	Prolific, colorful and good variety
Visibility	Walls and coral gardens
Coral	Often prolific, good variety
Fish	Shark caves, coral gardens

some of the most popular diving sites in the country.

Probably the most famous dive hereabouts is **Shark Cave** off Escaceo Point. Prone to treacherous currents (one local veteran has been swept away into the

Puerto Galera Dive Sites

Verde Passage twice now, fortunately surviving to tell the tale), this is not a dive for the faint-hearted or the inexperienced. The divemaster assesses the current and the divers descend to 18 meters. This is often a drift dive. You swim over a ledge to a patch of sand and there, under the ledge, you can usually spot a few white tip sharks, often with large grouper and other big fish. A little deeper and there is another, narrower cave which also accommodates sleeping sharks. This cave is popular with photographers as one can get really close to the sharks, but it is quite deep (28 meters), so bottom time is limited.

Ascending from here to around 12 meters you'll find the **Pink Wall**, so-named for the profusion of soft cauliflower corals that have created an impressive overhang. A great spot for photography and a popular night dive.

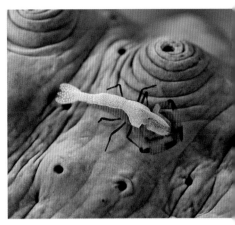

Emperor shrimps have a symbiotic relationship with sea cucumbers, where they live on the underside for protection.

THE CANYONS

The Canyons is probably the most visited dive site in Puerto Galera and is especially popular with technical divers. Usually starting at the **Hole in the Wall**, a natural hole that's large enough to pass through one at a time, divers swim along a wall and then into a series of canyons. These are encrusted with all sorts of soft and hard corals, sponges, sea fans and feather stars. The sea is alive with moray eels, lionfish, sweetlips, jacks, tuna and frequently white tip sharks. If you're lucky, you may even catch a glimpse of a passing hawksbill turtle. The dive ends at an old anchor covered with soft corals and small sea fans, often a good spot for seeing lionfish.

Sabang Point is another site worth visiting. A booming coral reef starting at 7 meters and descending to 18–20 meters, the reef is covered with feather stars, pot sponges, sea whips and sea pens. At one point there is a beautiful wall covered with different corals and home to moray eels multicolored nudibranchs and fluorescent blue triggerfish.

Puerta Galera dive sites range from calm sites for beginners to more challenging sites with currents for experienced divers. Dive courses for all levels are available across the island.

Eight kilometers to the west of the town of Puerto Galera proper, past the secluded White Beach and out from Talipanan Beach is another reef for the serious diver, with strong currents, pelagic fish and stunning corals of all kinds. This reef, being a little further away from the majority of dive sites, is visited less often but is none the worse for that. Dorado and Spanish mackerel have been spotted here as well as tuna and other pelagics. Expect to find humphead wrasse, parrotfish, sweetlips, angelfish, lionfish and the peculiar crocodilefish, which, though difficult to spot, is quite common around Puerto.

Visibility in the area can reach 35 meters but is typically 20 meters or less depending on the site and the season. As mentioned earlier, currents can be very tricky, even on some seemingly innocuous shallower dives, so always plan to go with a professional dive guide to avoid trouble. Puerto is increasingly being visited by passing liveaboard boats and is also a jump off point for regular liveaboard trips to Apo Reef, Coron Bay and the Sibuyan Sea. Trips are usually arranged at short notice.

Local dive operators own an interesting variety of vessels, from traditional *banca* to custom dive boats, yachts, catamarans, v-hulls and converted local wooden fishing boats. For snorkelers, ocean kayaks are available for rent.

An active dive store owner's association works hard to ensure visiting divers have healthy reefs to dive on. They provide mooring buoys at popular dive sites and promote environmental and infrastructure projects. A number of artificial reefs have been created since 1996 by sinking derelict vessels in the area. This professional attitude to safety and service that has developed over the years explains why so many divers just keep coming back to Puerto Galera.

—*Heneage Mitchell/Sarah Ann Wormald*

Action Divers in Puerto Galera is one of many operators that uses traditional-style outriggers to ferry divers.

Marinduque
Outstanding Dives in the Tablas Straits

A short flight or around a five-hour drive and ferry ride south of Manila finds you in Marinduque. Famous for its Moriones festival, Marinduque and environs are far more rewarding to the diver for the profusion of outstanding underwater sites.

Wreck divers, wall divers, reef divers, cavern divers and photographers are well catered for, and many experienced divers who have visited some of the outlying islands in the Tablas Straits reckon them to be superior to anything they have seen anywhere, including the Red Sea, the Great Barrier Reef and the Sulu Sea. High praise indeed.

To get to the choicest spots, it is necessary to plan full day trips and dive safaris of several days. Trips usually originate from Puerto Galera or Boracay. There are 11 main diving areas adjacent to Marinduque, from Natanco in the northwest to the Maestre de Campo Islands to the southwest and Banton Island to the southeast. Each has something special about it and has more than one dive site to recommend it.

NATANCO AND BALANACAN
Natanco is noted for its walls and drift diving. On one section we found an unbelievable coral structure, white, like a huge avalanche of snow stretching for several meters. At another wall we came upon a huge shoal of tuna at 20 meters. We also found some great gorgonians and big groupers.

Though the current will toss this anemone about, the pink clownfish is determined to keep his home safe from any menace, Balicasag Island.

Access	Liveaboard boats, 1–5-day trips
Current	Good, 10–50 meters in season
Reef type	Can be strong in places
Highlights	Outstanding variety and prolific
Visibility	Walls and drop-offs
Coral	Many species, great numbers and all sizes
Fish	Pristine diving, superb corals and fish, wrecks

At Port Balanacan, the Japanese torpedo boat is not a dive for amateurs. This small 35-meter-long casualty of World War II is sitting upright with a badly smashed bow in 36–40 meters of water. The visibility can be a problem sometimes, and averages around 10 meters. The prop is missing but there's still a multi-barrelled gun on the deck.

ELEFANTE ISLAND

Elefante Island is a privately owned island but there are a couple of good dives
around here. To the north, there is a wall
off the beach with a fairly stiff current (3
knots or more at times). The bottom of
the wall is deep; we reached 40 meters at
one point and it still kept going. Large
gorgonians adorn the face. A little further
south there's an area with more of that
incredible white coral, this time flatter
and resembling a snow-covered field.
There are a lot of colorful fish here and
photo opportunities abound.

BALTHAZAR ISLAND

At Balthazar, to the west, there is a cave
you can enter at 20 meters and exit at 28
meters. There are lots of stonefish everywhere, so be careful. The gorgonians are
particularly beautiful here, too. A little to
the south is a great night dive with prolific corals and plentiful fish life and an
army of spiny lobsters.

Further south and west again, at
Maestre De Campo, there are several
excellent dives, including the MV
Mactan, a ferry boat that went down in
1973. In good condition, she lies north
to south on a sandy slope from 25 to
55 meters. The bow is to the south.
Sweetlips, grouper, barracuda and a lot
of lionfish and clouds of small tropicals
have made this wreck their home.

At **Port Concepcion**, there are two
Japanese wrecks in the harbour. A little
scratching around in the muddy bottom
usually rewards the searcher with bottles
and other relics. The visibility is not so
good and careful finning is necessary.

There are also the remains of World
War II planes dotted around the place,

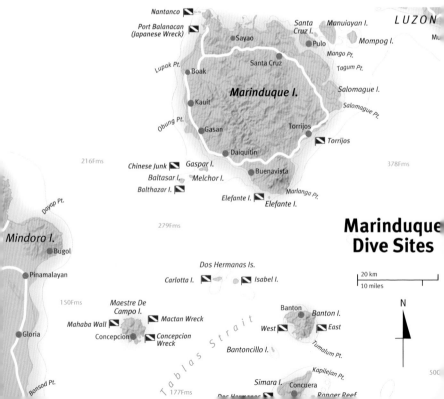

Marinduque
Dive Sites

Schools of big eye jackfish can include thousands of individual fish.

and there is also good coral diving on the west side of the island.

At **Isabella** in Dos Hermanos to the east, there is a maze of crevices and lots of corals and reef fish. The area has been visited by local hookah fishermen in the past and the fish remain skittish. A little to the west there is an excellent night dive area.

At **Torrijos**, on the east side of Marinduque, there's a shallow (15 meters) dive with cracks, fissures and canyons everywhere that is full of interesting things to explore, and a wall with large gorgonians, colorful sponges and lots of big fish. Expect to see tuna, barracuda, grouper, sweetlips, shoals of tropical reef fish of all shapes and sizes and Tridacna clams. The current is not usually too bad here.

BANTON ISLAND

Further south and east again finds the island of Banton. The inhabitants of Banton process copra though many of the younger islanders have found work abroad, apparently remitting sufficient funds to maintain their families comfortably. Perhaps that's the reason the locals don't fish the surrounding reefs as much as they do in other parts of the Philippines, and that's why the reef fish are so abundant and frisky around the island. The west side has areas of stunning coral encrustation, hard and soft corals of all kinds everywhere, with pennant butterflies, huge grouper, snapper and sweetlips darting in and out of the holes and cracks in the reef. Several species of shark and ray are sometimes seen, as are dolphins, which are very common all around the surrounding Sibuyan Sea.

The **North-West Wall** is simply awesome, one of the best wall dives you will find anywhere.

The weather can kick up on this exposed westerly side, making it a site you should plan to visit during the relatively benign months of March, April and May.

On the west coast of Banton, the story is pretty much the same, pretty white

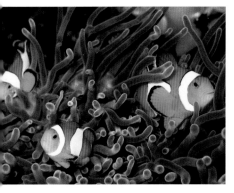

One anemone can host several clownfish, with the biggest one being the dominant female.

sand coves, some with fantastic unspoiled diving in coral gardens which reach 20 meters.

The Slab, a block of rock in a few meters of water about a third of the way south along the west shoreline, has an interesting cave that stretches into the darkness and is penetrable for several meters. Visibility often exceeds 35 meters here during season (December to June), and the profusion of pelagic and reef fish of all sizes is simply staggering.

SIBUYAN SEA

The Sibuyan Sea, which stretches south and east of here is one of the more remote areas for divers but there are numerous operators in the region. Some areas that have been visited over the last few years are reported to be heavily devastated by illegal fishing techniques. Others are spoken of in awe by the few divers lucky enough to have reached them.

One last point to make about Marinduque is that, up to now, scuba instruction is not as easily available as it is in the more touristic regions of the Philippines.

—Heneage Mitchell/Sarah Ann Wormald

Wall diving is a highlight of the Philippines but requires divers to have mastered buoyancy control.

Boracay

Stunning Beaches with First-class Dive Sites Nearby

The fabulous powdery white sand beaches of Boracay have made their name as some of the world's best. The diving industry is booming here with numerous dive centers doing good business around this small island, making it an excellent place to learn scuba. Diving courses range from discover diving to PADI master instructor.

Many dive outfits operate safaris to hard-to-reach locations, such as the Sibuyan Sea, Tablas, Romblon and Semirara Island, as well as to the west coast of Panay and the outlying reefs and islands.

Closer to Boracay there are some first-class dive sites catering to divers of all levels and some good, easily accessible snorkeling.

Friday's Rock, close to the west shore and at a depth of between 10 and 18 meters, is a favorite dive site. Here you will find a variety of soft and hard corals, butterflyfish, wrasses, tangs, damselfish, snappers and stingrays, and big scorpionfish and lionfish.

A little to the northwest of Friday's Rock there are two dive sites named **Punta Bonga 1 & 2**. One is shallower, a drop-off to 24 meters, and the other starts at 30 meters and goes down to 50 meters. On the shallow dive, the top of the reef is covered with soft corals. Triggerfish, groupers and angelfish are commonly seen. Diving on the deeper wall, you'll find large gorgonians of all colors and big stingrays. There are plenty

Access	By boat, 10 minutes–1.5 hours
Current	Usually good, 7–25 meters
Reef type	Strong in some areas
Highlights	Good variety and quite prolific
Visibility	Walls and coral gardens
Coral	Prolific in places, good variety
Fish	Easy access, awesome walls

of sizeable sweetlips and tuna about, and occasional barracuda and sharks.

CROCODILE ISLAND

Southeast of Boracay, Crocodile Island (named for its shape, not any resident reptile) is another popular site but one

Boracay Island New Wave Divers is one of many operators offering full service dive trips and courses.

Sea snakes are air breathers so they make frequent trips to the surface and back to the reef in the blue.

with current as it is right in the channel between Boracay and Panay. The bottom of the wall is around 24 meters at its deepest, the top of the reef about 10 meters. You'll find just about everything here: sweetlips, triggerfish, wrasses, butterflyfish and snappers. There are a few banded sea snakes, too—we've seen some over 2 meters long—but as they are docile by nature no one has been bitten

Large soft coral fans feature on wall dives where they have a solid substrate on which to anchor and flowing current to supply them with nutrients.

Cathedral Cave

Carabao I.

San Jose

Benihagen

178Fms

50Fms

Schooling fish, pelagics and great gorgonians

303Fms

Yapak 4   Bat Cave

Yapak 3

Guiniut Pt.   Puka Beach   Lapuz Lapuz Pt.

Yapak 2

Yapak 1

Santos Place

1 & 2 Punta Bunga

Balinghai Wall 1 & 2

Diniwid

Friday's Rock   Balabag

Friday's Reef

Virgin Drop   Lobster Rock

Camia

Coral Garden   Angol

Tribird

Angol Point

Channel Drift

Boracay I.   Ilig-iligan

Bulaboc Pt.

Laguna de Boracay

Tulobhan Reef

Malabanot

Tambisaan

Crocodile I.

Laurel I.   Lau

Potol Pt.

Caticlan

44Fms

160Fms

Channel Drift

Nasog Point   Black Rock

Walls   Nasog Pt.   Malay

Pelagics

Sharks

Buruanga   Panay I.

Big Gorgonians

Ariel's Pt.

10 km
4 miles

**Boraca
Dive Site**

The markings of the clown triggerfish are amongst the most distinct in Boracay.

by one. Look out also for the pretty blue gorgonians.

Another excellent dive close by is **Laurel Island**. Currents can get very strong here, but it is these currents that encourage the corals to open up their fantastic yellow and orange polyps to feed on microscopic elements, festooning the walls of an 8-meter-long tunnel at the tip of the island. There are also big sponges and large gorgonians.

At the northern end of Boracay is **Yapak**, a deep wall starting around 30 meters and descending beyond 60 meters depth. Currents are often tricky here and the water is usually rough, but for experienced divers and lovers of big animals this is the best Boracay has to offer. Covered with a profusion of soft corals, there are also some outstanding gorgonian fans hanging off the wall. Snappers, sweetlips, surgeons, pennants and rainbow runners are all plentiful, as are barracudas, white tip and grey reef sharks. Occasionally, a hammerhead will fin by. Manta rays have also been spotted from time to time. This is not a dive for beginners.

To the north, nearby Carabao Island has some fairly good spots. **Cathedral Cave**, a wide-mouthed cave at around 28 meters, is our favorite for its plentiful groupers and colorful soldierfish.

NEIGHBORING PANAY

To the southwest of Boracay, the west coast of Panay has some excellent sites. At **Buruanga**, off Nasog Point, **Black Rock** and **Dog Drift**, the walls and drop-offs start at around 10 meters and then go down to 40 meters. A variety of hard and soft corals are home to snappers, sweetlips and big triggerfish. Keep an eye open for large pelagics.

—*Heneage Mitchell/Sarah Ann Wormald*

Lionfish are closely related to scorpionfish and likewise have poisonous spines.

Visayas Dive Sites

The Philippines—Boracay

Palanas
Calbayog
Tagapulan I.
Cataingan
Almagro I.
Sto. Nino I.
Santa Magarita
Gandara
Samar

Masbate I.
Recodo
Naro I.
Placer
Limbuhan
Maripipi I.
Catbalongan
Motiong

Balud
intotolo I.
Esperanza
Kawayan
Culaba
Daram
Calbiga
Villareal

Visayan Sea
Naval
Biliran I.
Caibiran
Talalora
Santa Rita

SEE MALAPASCUA DIVE SITES MAP
Caruasa I.
Marias Point
Gato Island
Calubian
Biliran
Cabucgayan
Basey

Guintacan I.
Bantigue North Point
San Isidro
Leyte
Barugo
San Miguel
Taclobon

Panay I.
Buntay Pt.
Malapascua I.
Chocolate Island
Bulalaquit Pt.
Villaba
Tabango
Kananga
Carigara
Alangalang
L

Concepcion Bay
Pande Azucar I.
ago I.
Malangaban I.
Igbon I.
Bantayan I.
Daanbantayan
Villaba
Kananga
Hot Springs
Jaro
Santa Fe
Palo
Tanaua
Ma

agubanban I.
Bantayan
Medellin
Kalanggaman I.
Kalanggaman Island
Matag-ob
Palompon
Dagami

Cadiz Vijeo
San Remigio
Bago Bay
Bogo
Isabel
Merida
Ormoc
Burauen

Cadiz
Don Islands
Mangcao Pt.
Capitancillo Island
Albuera
La Paz
Dulag

Sagay
Molocaboc I.
Ponson I.
Leyte I.
Mayorga

Escalante
Molocaboc Pt.
Camotes Islands
Mac Arthur

Negros I.
Toboso
Tuburan
Pacijan I.
Poro I.
Javier
Abuyog

Calatrava
Carmen
San Francisco
Baybay
Sil

Asturias
Danao
Camotes Sea

Balamban
San Carlos
Cebu I.
Liloan
Inopacan
Canipaan

Toledo
Consolacion
Bagacay Pt.
Sogod
Bontoc
Hinuna

Vallehermoso
Mandaue
SEE MACTAN DIVE SITES MAP
Hilongos
Bato

Pinamungajan
Cebu
Mactan I.
Olango I.
Mahanay I.
Basaan I.
Peter's Mouund
San Ju

Minglanilla
Talisay
Lapu-lapu
Jaguiliao I.
Jau I.
Malitbog
Liloa

Guihulngan
Naga
Babacon I.
Talibon
Lapinig I.
Ghost Town

Thermal Spa
San Fernando
Talibon
Ubay
Pitogo
Maasin

Dumanjug
Bariii
Carcar
Bohol Sea
Padre
Burgos
Sanak Point

La Libertad
SEE MOALBOAL DIVE SITES MAP
Inabanga
Bohol I.

Ayungon
Sibonga
Pangangan I.
Carmen
Guindulman
SEE SOUTHERN LEYTE DIVE SITE

Bindoy
(Payabon)
Sharks Point
Cabilao I.
Loon

Manjuyod
Argao
Sandingan I.
Napacao Pt.
Guindulman
Bay

Dalaguete
Tagbilaran
Jagna

Tanjay
Napaling
Panglao I.
**Hot Spring
& Bathing
Resort**

Marine Sanctuary
Panglao I.
Rudy's Rock
Pamilacan
Pamilican I.

Sibulan
Sumilon I.
SEE BOHOL DIVE SITES MAP
Bohol Sea

Dumaguete
Tuapus
N

**Ancient
Church on Sea**
Tonga West
Tongo Pt.
Siquijor I.
Yungbing
Mambajao

Apo I.
Solangon
Catarman
Mahinog
Camiguin I.

Apo Island Marine Sanctuary
Sagay

SEE SUMILON DIVE SITES MAP
Talisayan
Magsaysay

Salay
Medina

40 km
20 miles
Balingasag
Gingoog
Mindana

Mactan

A Popular Resort Close to Cebu City

Looking a little unprepossessing from the air, the island of Mactan, 45 minutes from the heart of Cebu, comes alive underwater. Visited by thousands of divers every year, Mactan's east coast has several good dive sites along its walls. The Hilutangan Channel, which separates Mactan from adjacent Olango Island, is extremely deep and, as a consequence, one can hope to see several species of large animals on a lucky diving day. Although visibility can exceed 30 meters it usually averages around 18 meters, and divers should note that currents are a factor to be reckoned with.

Access Local boats, 10 minutes–1.5 hours; also liveaboards

Current Often excellent, 10–50 meters

Reef type Can be stiff in places

Highlights Good variety, pristine in places

Visibility Walls and drop-offs

Coral Good variety, good shells

Fish Fans, gorgonians and pelagics

DIVING OFF THE RESORTS

The **Tambuli Fish Feeding Station** is an excellent opportunity to get to know many smaller species of fish that abound in the warm and generally clear

Adult hawksbill turtles grow up to 1 meter in length and weigh an average of 80 kg.

waters off Mactan Island. This used to be a feeding station but only the name of the dive site has remained. Photographers will appreciate this dive, as literally hundreds of fish swarm all around in close quarters. A small light aircraft has also been sunk offshore and lays at around 22 meters. This artificial reef attracts a great number of resident reef fish.

The soft corals off **Mar y Cielo Resort** are another interesting dive, a gentle slope covered with elephant ear coral and barrel sponges.

Although a little deep, with an entrance at 26 meters, the **Marigondon Cave** is another popular dive well worth visiting. The cave stretches inward for about 45 meters and comes to end at a depth of 25 meters where there is a small grotto, home to dozens of flashlight fish. These fish have adapted to life in the dark by developing a neat patch of bioluminescence under each eye. Divers poke their heads into the narrow opening and turn off their torches to be rewarded with a wonderful light show as the fish dart around and hundreds of eyes appear to be winking back out of the dark recesses.

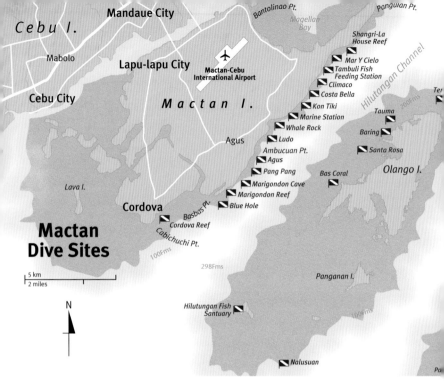

GOOD WALLS

Just to the south of the cave on **Marigondon Reef**, there is a wall starting at 12 meters and descending to around 45 meters. Its attraction is that the face is covered in a wide variety of colorful sponges, soft corals, brain corals and gorgonians, a feature that characterizes most dives off Mactan. Not to be missed here is a sizeable colony of garden eels. There is usually a fair current and thus most dives are drift dives.

To the north is **Pang Pang**, another wall dive popular for night dives. Lucky divers occasionally spot passing sharks.

The wall just off **Kon Tiki Resort** is another fine site. A short swim from the resort finds one on a gently sloping coral covered rocky seabed at 5 meters. This soon gives way to an impressive drop-off, festooned with fan corals, sea stars, feather stars and myriad crinoids. Barracuda are sometimes known to pass through.

OLANGO ISLAND

Across the Channel at Olango Island there are a couple of sites of interest, including **Santa Rosa**. Here, a white sand bottom with a profusion of soft corals leads to a steep drop-off at 15 meters. This bottoms out around 50 meters where big grouper can be seen in the small caves that are dotted about.

Also at Olango is **Baring**, just off the northwestern tip of the island. A sloping sandy bottom starting at around 15 meters with several small caves, this area is home to a number of large fish. Sharks can also be seen.

Mactan is a major jump-off point for divers wanting to visit the outstanding, remoter dive sites around the Visayas, such as Cabilao, Panglao and Apo Island. Most dive centers on the island organize dive safaris, lasting from a couple of days to a week or more aboard a variety of boats.

—*Heneage Mitchell/Sarah Ann Wormald*

Northern Cebu
A Less Crowded Alternative to the Southern Resorts

Most of the coastal dive sites visited regularly by divers in the north of Cebu tend to be close to the town of Sogod on the east coast as it is easiest to access. The exception is those divers who are heading over to Malapascua Island, home to a number of dive resorts and, more famously, thresher sharks.

Another option for exploring this area is to use some of the Mactan-based dive operators who head north regularly, usually to visit Capitancillo, Gato and Calangaman islands.

CAPITANCILLO ISLAND

Capitancillo Island has a mushroom-shaped wall on its south side with out-standing coral formations and impressive gorgonian fans. Large manta rays are occasionally seen roaming around the teeming waters of the reef, and you can also hope to see shoals of yellow fin tuna

Access Local boats, 10 minutes–1.5 hours; also liveaboards

Current Often excellent, 10–50 meters

Reef type Can be stiff in places

Highlights Good variety, pristine in places

Visibility Walls and drop-offs

Coral Good variety, good shells

Fish Fans, gorgonians and pelagics

and large groupers. The bottom is deep here—you still can't see it when you are down at 45 meters—so care should be taken at all time to monitor depths.

As a diversion after diving, you'll find an old lighthouse on top of this small rocky island. It is worth the climb for its view.

This trapezia crab was spotted hiding amongst soft corals off Malapascua.

North of Capitancillo lies **Calang-aman**, another dive site well worth visiting. Both sites are within relatively easy striking distance and visited often by Sogod-based operators and safari boats.

Quatro Island is another location frequented by northern Cebu divers, who rave about its caves and reef formations. The hard and soft corals are outstanding here, and snorkelers favor the place as there is plenty to see even in only 1–2 meters of water. There are actually four different reefs at this site, with walls descending to 150 meters, but don't even consider trying to get near the bottom of the wall. Keep in mind that although there is a recompression chamber in Cebu City, it is far away.

At **Kimod Reef**, another one of those sunken islands, you are quite likely to run into a wide variety of pelagic life, including several different species of shark as well as eagle and manta rays.

GATO ISLAND

Gato Island is another popular spot. Between November and May it's a good area for white tips and other reef sharks. You'll also find plenty of soft corals, gorgonians of all colors, sponges and hard corals. **Gato Cave**, actually a tunnel

Gato Island is a marine reserve and sea snake sanctuary. It is also home to several dive sites.

The thresher shark's long tail fin is highly distinctive, making it vulnerable to the shark fin trade.

underneath the island, is also frequented by sharks and banded sea snakes. It is not for the faint-hearted, but definitely a must for those thrillseekers with the right experience. Currents are usually a bit stronger here than at the previous locations mentioned, so expect drift diving.

MALAPASCUA ISLAND

Malapascua Island is now one of the Philippines best-known dive destinations. Malapascua has risen to fame almost entirely due to its resident thresher sharks, which divers from across the globe flock to see. These rare, shy creatures can usually be found swimming off the seamount. They cruise in a triangular pattern, swimming in circles at each corner of the route.

Divers can get quite close to these creatures but should avoid getting in the way of the sharks as this could upset their swimming patterns and may drive them away.

The threshers and manta rays are around for most of the year and it is also possible to see hammerheads here but they tend to be seasonl, between January and April. If you are a pelagic fan, then Malapascua has a lot to offer and should definitely be on your "to visit" list!

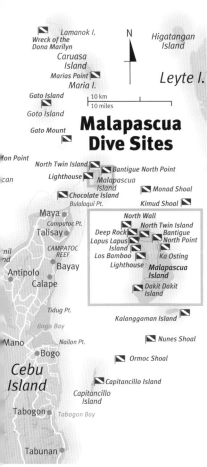

Malapascua Dive Sites

The Dona Marilyn was a passenger ferry that sank in 1988 off Malapascua.

Closer to **Sogod** there are a number of inshore sites that are worth a look. There is a series of lagoons with sheer drop-offs going down to a maximum of 40 meters, then it slopes gently to several hundred meters. All kinds of soft corals, sponges, nudibranchs and other invertebrates flourish in these waters. Chances are you will encounter dolphins and hawksbill turtles and discover shells.

—Heneage Mitchell/Sarah Ann Wormald

A rare swimming nudibranch, Malapascua.

Southern Leyte
Whale Sharks, Walls and Waterfalls

In recent years, Southern Leyte has started to flourish as a diving destination, with a number of dive resorts operating in the area. The walls, reefs and drifts promise something for everyone, but the macro life is really what makes it stand out. Topside, the topography is equally intense, with waterfalls and pristine primary forest coverage abounding.

Whale sharks are a major attraction in Southern Leyte and many whale watching tours are offered by operators.

Most of the best macro life sites are in **Sogod Bay**, also a popular whale watching area with several species of whales regularly spotted by tour boats operating from resorts along Cebu's east coast and Leyte's west coast. Southern Leyte is distinct from Cebu as it is another island and home to a different ethnic group.

Limasawa Island, a 6-km-long landmass with a fringing reef, offers walls

Nudibranch (Nembrotha) have gills positioned on their back and two rhinophores on their heads, which are their sensory organs.

Access	Boat or tricycle
Current	5–35 meters
Reef type	Sometimes strong
Highlights	Dense, prolific, untouched
Visibility	Seamounts and walls
Coral	Prolific pelagics
Fish	Whale sharks, mantas, stunning walls

and drift dives along its length. The island is known as the site of the first Christian mass held in the Far East, but it is now equally famous for its underwater attractions, especially its virginal coral gardens visited by large pelagics such as barracuda, mackerel, tuna and jacks.

Max Climax Wall is found to the north of Limasawa, just off the coast of Lungsodaan, Padre Burgos. Many crevices along the wall provide shelter for angelfish, snapper, sweetlips, grouper and Napoleon wrasse, as well as a host of smaller tropical fish. Turtles are often seen nosing around and pelagics that regularly visit include several species of shark, barracuda, tuna and eagle rays.

Tangkaan Point, to the south of Max Climax, is home to a number of dive sites on the various reefs dotted around the area, many of which have been declared marine sanctuaries. It is here that the odds of spotting a whale shark are the highest and sightings are regularly reported. Mantas are also common visitors, as are white tip and black tip sharks. Other shark species can sometimes be seen here too. The reefs are varied, from flat to rugged, some with gentle slopes,

some with steep walls. Barrel sponges are prolific in some areas, notably at the site named **Barrel Sponge Garden**, which also features large table corals as well as a good variety of hard and soft corals and sponges and tunicates. Nearby **Turtle Rock** is a likely place to spot green turtles as well as batfish, eagle rays and grouper. The corals at this site tend towards whips, gorgonians, table and brain, with plenty of soft corals and sponges filling in the gaps.

Napantaw Fish Sanctuary, also known as Rio's Wall and Toshi's Wall after pioneering divers that discovered many of the local sites, is one of the better walls in Southern Leyte. Turtles are frequent visitors, and there is a cave at 40 meters worth checking out if you can find it at the start of the dive. Don't spend too long looking for it though, as there is plenty to see higher up the wall and it's not worth risking the bends by spending too much time at depth. The currents

can be strong, which makes for prolific and healthy coral coverage, notably huge gorgonians and black coral as well as the ubiquitous soft corals liberally festooning the reef. Batfish, sweetlips and grouper are among the reef's denizens, and barracuda often pass by.

Peter's Mound is a seamount about 200 meters offshore starting at 10 meters and dropping off to well below 40 meters. Aside from the resident surgeons, fusiliers, snapper, grouper, Napoleon wrasse and other reef fish that swarm over the vibrant cora-encrusted reef, Peter's Mound is a dive worth making if only for the fact that it is a cleaning station for large pelagics who can be found finning gently against the often strong currents (the best time to see this is when the current is running) as cleaner wrasse pick off the pesky infestations of microscopic critters from their gills, teeth, fins and scales.

—Heneage Mitchell/Sarah Ann Wormald

Moalboal and Pescador
A Small but Superb Site away from the Crowds

A few hours' drive southwest of Cebu City, across the dusty mountain roads of the interior to the west coast, is Moalboal.

One of the original dive centers of the Philippines, Moalboal owes its popularity almost entirely to scuba diving. A few steps off the beach from the main resort area of Pangasama lies a reef which is home to a wide variety of marine life. The ubiquitous fan corals and gorgonians are, of course, very much in evidence, as are sponges and crinoids, nudibranchs and several different species of shells. There are sweetlips, tangs, gobies and lionfish all over the dive site. A little careful exploring will usually reveal some interesting shell life, too.

Access From the beach or by boat, 10 minutes–1 hour

Current Often excellent, 10–50 meters

Reef type Can be strong in places

Highlights Outstanding—great variety and prolific

Visibility Walls and drop-offs

Coral Good variety, prolific in places, big pelagics

Fish Pescador, Sunken Islands

The common lionfish (Pterois volitans) sometimes travels in packs, lurking around vertical formations like coral outcrops or shipwrecks.

Tongo Point, at the south end of the beach, is covered with little cracks and caves, home to soft corals and many tropical reef fish. Anemones and clownfish, nudibranchs and a host of other invertebrates make this a popular photographer's dive. Visibility can be changeable, depending on the weather. This is a great dive for novices and a popular second dive.

An underwater "island" named **Lambug** lies about a 45-minute *banca* boat ride away. Really an underwater mountain, Lambug is reached after descending through blue water for 27 meters before reaching the peak. There is often a strong current here, too, so this really is not a dive for amateurs but for those who are up to it. Lambug is an outstanding experience. Large pelagics cruise by all the time. We saw several king barracuda, a lone tuna, two manta rays and a white tip shark as well as groupers, snappers and a huge shoal of *talakitok* or jackfish, on one 25-minute dive recently.

PESCADOR ISLAND

The jewel in the crown of Moalboal's diving is tiny Pescador Island. About 2 km offshore, Pescador has been described as "a different dive every five meters". It is possible to circle the island on a shallower dive. Superb drop-offs, buttresses and impressive overhangs are the main features of this site, with a shallow reef running around the island. At 22-25 meters is a large funnel-shaped structure of about 15 meters, called **The Cathedral**. When the sunlight hits it in just the right position, the corals and sponges are dappled with beams of light, making it a beautiful sight.

Lionfish, snappers, groupers, scorpionfish and sweetlips are found at every depth, and on deeper dives white tip sharks and hammerhead sharks are not uncommon, especially between November and April. Less frequently, tiger and thresher sharks put in an appearance. The gorgonians are perhaps less profuse than one might imagine, but there is a lot of black coral around as well as sea fans, sponges of all types and nudibranchs. Divers often see Spanish dancers wriggling their way sensually around the reef.

Pescador takes on a totally different perspective after dark, and it is a favorite local night dive.

Despite its name, the melon headed whale is actually a member of the dolphin family.

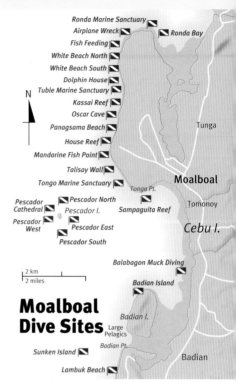

Moalboal Dive Sites

Near to Pescador Island is **Badian Island**, another spot worth visiting although the marine life is neither as prolific nor as exciting as at Pescador and Lambug. However, white tip sharks are quite common, and you may well see a banded sea snake or two, together with the inevitable anemones and sponges.

Several Moalboal dive centers arrange excursions further afield, including to Bohol, Cabilao, Apo Island and other, more remote dive sites on an ad hoc basis. Whatever you may end up doing, you can rest assured that Moalboal is sure to satisfy even the most jaded diver. It also has the advantage of excellent off the beach diving of a quality which few other dive areas in the Philippines can match.

—*Heneage Mitchell/Sarah Ann Wormald*

Bohol

Great Diving off Cabilao, Panglao and Balicasag

Bohol, in the Western Visayas, has long been regarded as home to some of the best diving in the Philippines. **Panglao Island**, connected to the mainland by a bridge, is the easiest dive area to reach and has a number of excellent sites for both divers and snorkelers.

At **Arco Point** (also known as "the Hole in the Wall"), near the exclusive Bohol Beach Club, there is a colony of sea snakes and a tunnel starting with an entrance at 8 meters, exiting at around 18 meters. Covered with a garden of soft corals, the interior has clouds of small tropical fish, including wrasse, butterfly-fish, tangs and copper sweepers.

The northwest tip of the island has a gentle drop-off leading to a bottom which becomes deeper the further south you swim. Currents can be quite strong here, so you should dive with a guide. The gorgonians are impressive, as is the mix of hard and soft corals and sponges.

Access Bancas, 10 minutes–5 hours; also live-aboards

Current 10–35 meters

Reef type Can be stiff in places

Highlights Good variety, pristine in places

Visibility Walls, drop-offs and coral gardens

Coral Good variety, good shells

Fish Fans, gorgonians and pelagics

There are other spots worth diving around Panglao Island, including the wall at **Tangnan**. Starting at around 6 meters, the wall falls away steeply to over 35 meters. Here, you will find a series of small caves that are fun to explore. Big groupers dart in and out of the holes in the corals and rocks, but it is also a good place to look out as well for wrasses, soldierfish, surgeons and the occasional barracuda, jacks and white tip sharks.

Thanks to marine preservation efforts, fish life is abundant around Balicasag Island.

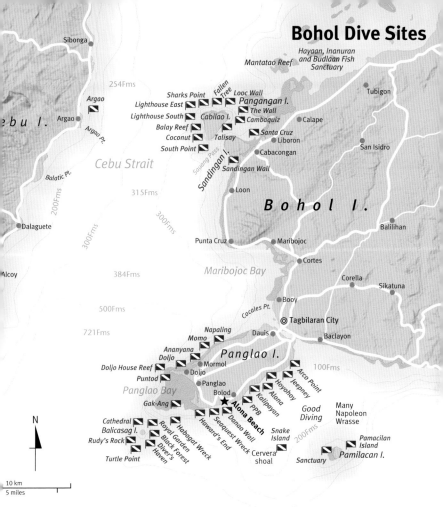

Bohol Dive Sites

Sibonga

Mantatao Reef

Hayaan, Inanuran and Budlaan Fish Sanctuary

Tubigon

254Fms

Argao

Argao

Argao Pt.

Sharks Point
Lighthouse East
Lighthouse South
Balay Reef
Coconut
South Point

Fallen Tree
Looc Wall
Pangangan I.
The Wall
Cabilao I.
Cambaquiz
Santa Cruz
Liboron
Cabacongan

Calape

San Isidro

e b u I.

Cebu Strait

200Fms

Balatic Pt.

Dalaguete

315Fms

Talisay

Sayang Pass

Sandingan I.

Sandingan Wall

Loon

B o h o l I.

Balilihan

300Fms

300Fms

Punta Cruz

Maribojoc

Cortes

Corella

Sikatuna

Alcoy

384Fms

Maribojoc Bay

500Fms

Cocales Pt.

Booy

721Fms

Tagbilaran City

Baclayon

Napaling
Momo
Ananyana
Doljo
Doljo House Reef
Puntod
Panglao Bay
Gak-Ang

Dauis

Panglao I.

Mormol
Doljo
Panglao
Bolod

Alona Beach

Arco Point

100Fms

Jeepney
Hoyohoy
Alona
Kalipayan
PPB

Good
Diving

Many
Napoleon
Wrasse

Cathedral
Balicasag I.
Rudy's Rock
Turtle Point

Royal Garden
Black Forest
Diver's
Haven

Habagat Wreck
Haward's End
Seaquest Wreck
Danao Wall

Snake
Island

Cervera
shoal

Pamacilan
Island
Pamilacan I.

Sanctuary

200Fms

N

10 km
5 miles

MARINE SANCTUARY

Diving aficionados should make sure that they take the time to venture a little further afield to **Balicasag Island**, lying to the southwest of Panglao, one of the most pristine dive sites in the world. It contains a superb marine sanctuary and has what most visitors regard as the best diving in the Visayas. Drop-offs and bottomless walls, overhangs, plentiful fans, huge table and star corals, large clumps of black coral and big fish are the main attractions of Balicasag. But that is not all that the sanctuary has to offer.

Shallower spots with a variety of hard and soft corals, sea whips, feather stars, crinoids, tunicates, anemones and sponges are a photographer's delight. On a good day, you'll encounter schools of barracuda and jacks, batfish, big parrotfish and groupers. There are plenty of lionfish about, and clouds of reef fishes.

To the east of Balicasag and southeast of Panglao lies **Pamilacan Island**. Pamilacan means "resting place of mantas" in the local dialect, and when diving you may be lucky enough to swim with one of these impressive creatures. A marine sanctuary has been set up on the northwestern side of the island, and it is here that you'll find superb gorgonians and hard corals along the walls as well as an assortment of soft corals, anemones, tunicates, sponges and sea fans.

Between Pamilacan and Balicasag is the **Cervera Shoal**. An underwater island just beneath the surface, dropping off to 20 meters, it is home to a large colony of banded sea snakes. The corals are not particularly impressive, but it is the pelagics which are the attraction here. You can expect to see several interesting species and occasional white tip sharks, as well as butterflyfish, scorpionfish, damsels and surgeons.

CABILAO ISLAND

This island is located further north, off the west coast of Bohol. Cabilao is a two and a half hour boat ride from Mactan, and it is from this island that most divers start their trip. Off the **Lighthouse** on the northwestern tip of the island there is a series of overhangs, cracks and coral gardens. Gorgonians, crinoids, sponges and soft corals can be seen adorning the walls and drop-offs, making this an exceedingly pretty dive.

But it is the hammerhead sharks for which the island is most famous. Schools of these awesome beasts congregate seasonally around the island, usually quite deep at around 40-45 meters, between December and May (April is usually the best month but it changes from year to year so check with your operator what the current predictions are). Also commonly encountered in this excellent spot are barracuda, jacks, mackerel, tuna, triggerfish, butterflyfish and humphead wrasses feeding in the strong currents.

—Heneage Mitchell/Sarah Ann Wormald

The Bohol region of the Philippines comprises more than 70 islands with white sand beaches, such as this one and also the famous Chocolate Hills.

Apo Reef

A Speck in the Midst of the South China Sea

Apo Reef in the South China Sea, off the west coast of Mindoro, is actually an underwater lagoon. Between March and June, the peak season, water visibility is usually excellent, extending to 30 meters or more at most sites. But from July to January, the sea can be turbulent, making access uncomfortable to downright unpleasant. Trips to Apo can be arranged through Pandan Island Resort (amongst others), based on the west coast of Mindoro, and from Puerto Galera, 125 km away. Most liveaboards feature Apo Reef on their itineraries. Wall diving is spectacular along many parts of the reef's perimeter and you don't need to go too deep to discover plenty of marine life.

The whale shark leads a solitary life and is only rarely seen by lucky divers when it ventures inshore.

Access Boat from Pandan Island, 1 hour; liveaboards offer various durations

Current Usually good, 15–50 meters

Reef type Can be stiff in places

Highlights Prolific and varied

Visibility Walls and coral gardens

Coral Prolific in places

Fish Outstanding macro photography

A favorite spot on the reef itself is the wreck of a small fishing boat with a bridge which divers and snorkelers love to have their photographs taken in. Lying in shallow water, the hulk used to attract snappers and groupers as well as hard and soft corals, including tables and sponges, and a variety of other tropical marine life.

DRAMATIC DROP-OFFS

The northern edge of the lagoon has spectacular walls, dropping off radically from around 5-10 meter depths. The walls are covered with gorgonians and fans due to the currents which can get quite stiff, attracting lots of pelagics as well as encouraging more impressive coral formations. Watch out for the tuna, jacks, humphead wrasses and, from time to time, mantas and hammerheads. The remains of an old steamer in shallow water on the north of the reef is also quite interesting.

To the east, **Shark Ridge** is renowned for, of course, sharks—white tips and black tips most commonly—as well as

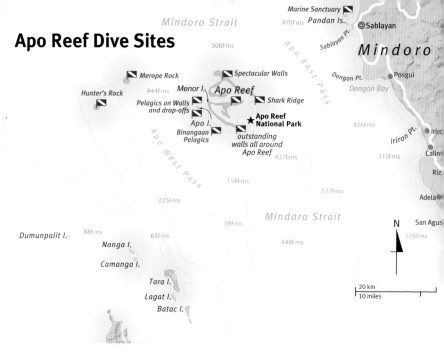

Apo Reef Dive Sites

Mindoro Strait

Marine Sanctuary
470Fms Pandan Is. ◎Sablayan

500Fms   Sablayan Pt.
Apo East Pass   *Mindoro*

Merope Rock   Spectacular Walls   Dongon Pt.   Posgui
444Fms Menor I. **Apo Reef**   *Dongon Bay*
Hunter's Rock
Pelagics on Walls   Shark Ridge
and drop-offs
Apo I.   ★ **Apo Reef**   426Fms   Iriro
Binangaan   **National Park**   Iriron Pt.
Pelagics   *outstanding*   Calin
Apo West Pass   *walls all around*   312Fms
Apo Reef 437Fms   Riz
158Fms
177Fms   Adela

225Fms   San Agus
Mindoro Strait   N   176Fms
Dumunpalit I. 88Fms   58Fms
Nanga I. 65Fms   448Fms
Camanga I.
Tara I.
Lagat I.   20 km
Batac I.   10 miles

---

manta rays. The coral is not so impressive on this sloping bottom, which gives way to sand and detritus at about 25 meters, but the animals are big and the diving can get wild!

To the southwest of Apo Reef is another excellent wall, the **Binangaan Drop-off**. Impressive gorgonians and hard and soft coral formations as well as schools of bumphead parrotfish are seen here, along with tuna and groupers, snappers, lots of interesting shells and some large pelagics.

Around Apo Island, to the west of the reef, there are also a number of superb sites to dive, mostly walls and drop-offs. Once again, mantas are not uncommon visitors all around the island, and the gorgonians are outstanding. Schools of tuna and other pelagics, turtles and groupers, snappers and wrasses, triggerfish and parrotfish seem to be everywhere. Lobsters and other crustaceans scuttle about under rocks, in crevices and fissures, while along the perimeter black

tip, white tip and hammerhead sharks, remoras and barracudas fin silently past. Currents are often strong but snorkeling can be good.

SEA SNAKES GALORE

Some 21 km west of Apo Reef, **Hunter's Rock** is an underwater island and not easy to find unless you're with a good guide.

The highlight of Hunter's Rock is that it is a popular spot for banded sea snakes. Guides often joke that to find the site you follow a sea snake down.

There can be hundreds of them on Hunter's Rock, in crevices, under coral heads and swimming about the reef. During the mating season (June through July), the sea is sometimes unnervingly carpeted with them. The reef itself is a profusion of corals and sponges alive with schools of tropicals—butterflyfish, snappers, sweetlips—and larger predatory reef fish.

—Heneage Mitchell/Sarah Ann Wormald

Sumilon
A Species-rich Marine Sanctuary

At the southeastern tip of Cebu lies Sumilon Island. While there are other sites around South Cebu visited by divers from Cebu and Bohol dive centers, Sumilon is a favorite, being the very first marine sanctuary created in the Philippines. Though it has suffered considerable damage in the past despite this status, the reefs have made an excellent recovery. Today, Sumilon enjoys better protection than before and visiting divers are asked to contribute a small sum to help preserve it once again.

The waters are outstandingly clear around the island, especially between December and May, and there are stunning drop-offs and walls to be enjoyed, with breathtaking fans and plentiful gorgonians, especially at deeper depths.

Access Day trips from Dumaguete; safaris from Cebu and Bohol

Current Usually outstanding, 15–50 meters

Reef type Can be strong

Highlights Outstanding, prolific and abundant

Visibility Walls, drop-offs

Coral Many species, prolific and large

Fish Fans, gorgonians and pelagics

All kinds of pelagics swim around Sumilon, including leopard and manta rays, yellow fin tuna and jacks. Several shark species have been noted, not only the ubiquitous white tips but also hammerheads and the occasional whale shark.

This reef octopus is flashing a white color, a sign that it is feeling threatened.

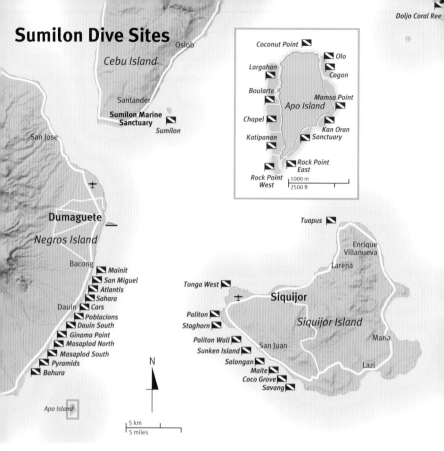

Sumilon Dive Sites

Doljo Coral Reef

Oslob

Cebu Island

Santander

Sumilon Marine Sanctuary

Sumilon

San Jose

Coconut Point

Largahan

Boularte

Apo Island

Chapel

Katipanan

Olo

Cogon

Mamsa Point

Kan Oran Sanctuary

Rock Point East

Rock Point West

1000 m
2500 ft

Dumaguete

Negros Island

Tuapus

Enrique Villanueva

Larena

Bacong

Mainit
San Miguel
Atlantis
Sahara
Dauin Cars
Poblacions
Dauin South
Ginama Point
Masaplod North
Masaplod South
Pyramids
Bahura

Tonga West

Siquijor

Siquijor Island

Maria

Paliton
Staghorn
Paliton Wall
Sunken Island
Salongan
Maite
Coco Grove
Savang

San Juan

Lazi

Apo Island

N

5 km
5 miles

APO ISLAND

To the south of Sumilon is Apo Island (not to be confused with Apo Reef in the South China Sea, off the southwest coast of Mindoro). Apo is widely regarded as one of the best dive sites in the Visayas. In fact, many dive enthusiasts claim that it is *the* best site. The marine sanctuary area on the southeast side of the island is a fairytale land of hard and soft corals, with thousands of tropical reef fish blotting out the light in every direction. Gobies, tangs, wrasses, chromis or

The colors of these hard coral formations are generated by the algae that live in symbiosis with them. Coral bleaching occurs when the algae hibernate due to the heat and the color is lost.

pullers, damselfish, surgeons, squirrel fish, butterflyfish, glass eye snappers, drums and several species of parrotfish are all there in quantity.

Pelagics are plentiful, and there is every chance of an encounter with black tip and white tip sharks as well as barracuda, tuna and game fish such as dorado and Spanish mackerel.

Apo is conical in shape, and the untouched coral reef fringes the island at 15–20 meters. All over the reef are hills of star and brain corals, magnificent barrel sponges, a variety of stinging crinoids and pillar and staghorn corals. On the walls are magnificent gorgonians and fan corals. It is an outstanding dive site!

Trips to either Apo or Sumilon Island are arranged regularly by dive operations from Mactan, Moalboal, Bohol, Dumaguete and several of the smaller resorts in southern Cebu. The best time to visit Apo Island is between December and May.

Glassfish tend to school around coral heads where they can swim up into the current stream or nestle down for shelter.

SIQUIJOR ISLAND

Between Apo and Sumilon, and a little to the east, is Siquijor Island. The inhabitants of this island are renowned (and feared) throughout the Philippines as mystics and spiritualists. Unfortunately, this did not prevent serious damage being inflicted on the reefs and shoals, and many of the great dive sites of yesteryear are history, reduced to algae covered skeletons of coral. Good recovery is evident in some areas, but not all.

There are still one or two sites worth visiting, however, including **Tonga Point** on the northwest coast. Here, a wall drops off quite rapidly from the relatively shallow fringing reef. Soft corals are plentiful here, and you'll find some reasonable gorgonians as you drift along the wall. Don't expect an abundance of fish life around this area, except at Apo Island, as overfishing has been a serious problem in the past. Divers are urged to avoid any dive outfits that encourage spear fishing.

—Heneage Mitchell/Sarah Ann Wormald

Northern Palawan
and Busuanga
Dive Sites

Ignonoc

Abra de Ilog

Maslud

Ba

Ca

Mamburao

Ulanga

Mindoro

Sta. Cruz

Barahan Salahan

SEE APO REEF DIVE SITES MAP

Sablayan

Marine Sanctuary

Tuban

Ligaya

Apo Reef

K

Calintaan

Rizal

Magt

San Jose

Mags

Calauit Island

Ilin Island

Minuit

Tara Island

Ambulong

Busuanga

Bantac Island

Island

Decalachiao

C a l a m i a n   G r o u p

Concepcion

Busuanga

Borac

Bintuan

Coron Bay

Galoc

Bonongan

Culion

Coron Island

Delian Island

Culion Island

Bulalacao Island

Linapacan Strait

P a l a w a n   P a s s a g e

Linapacan Island

Linapacan

Cabulauan Is.

Quinluban Islands

Tiniguiban

Manamoc Island

Sibaltan

Binalan

Dit Island

SEE EL NIDO DIVE SITES MAP

Iloc Island

Agutaya Island

Tapiutan Island

New Ibajay

El Nido

C u y o

El Nido

Batas Island

I s l a n d s

Guntao Islands

Oton

Casian Island

Lubid Island

Magsaysa

Bacuit Bay

Palalong

Tuluran Island

Liminangcong

Apulit Island

Cuyo Island

Pancol

Enterprise Point

Taytay

Bantulan

Maducang Island

Capnoyan Island

Imuruan Bay

Guigol

Paly Island

Calandagan Island

Calawag

SEE PORT BARTON DIVE SITES MAP

P a l a w a n

Dumaran

Island

Araceli

Peaked Point

San Vicente

Lingit

Komdong

Dumaran Bohol

Port Barton

Capayas

Saint Paul Bay

Carurai

Tumarbong

Illian

Roxas

Taradungan

Sito San
Dionisio

**Puerto Princesa
Subterranean River
National Park**

Caramay

Verde Islands

Baheli

Tinituan

Bacungan

Babuyan Tanabag

Honda Bay

Irahuan

Anepahan

SEE PUERTO PRINCESA & HONDA BAY DIVE SITES MAP

Long Point

Puerto Princesa

Apurawan

Inaguan

Aborlan

Malanao Island

Malanut Bay

Birong Plaridel

Marirong Quezon

Narra

Aboabo

Rasa Island

Panitan
Labog

*Island
Bay*

Jessie
Beazley

Pulot

*Tagalinog
Island*

Tubbataha
Reef

Brooke's Point

Tacbolubu

SEE JESSIE BEAZLEY AND TUBBATAHA DIVE SITES MAP

N

40 km

20 miles

Coron Bay

Exploring a World of Wrecks off Busuanga Island

On September 24, 1944, Admiral "Bull" Halsey, seeking a safe passage through the uncharted Calamian Islands, sent out several waves of photo reconnaissance planes. When analysts compared the pictures taken, they noticed several "islands" had changed position relative to the surrounding land. Realizing that they had discovered a camouflaged Japanese fleet, Halsey immediately ordered an air strike. Upon their return, US Navy pilots claimed 24 vessels sunk.

Today, not all 24 wrecks have been found but around a dozen are regularly dived in the protected waters of Coron Bay, lying at various depths between 15 and 40 meters.

Due to their former inaccessibility and lack of diving infrastructure, these wrecks lay undisturbed for decades. Now there are numerous operators visiting the wrecks and outstanding coral reefs of the area. Most are easily as good as the wrecks of Truk Lagoon in Micronesia but much shallower.

The diving around Coron garnered fame for its World War II shipwrecks.

Access	Banca boat, 30 minutes–2 hours; also liveaboards
Current	10–35 meters
Reef type	Moderate
Highlights	Good variety, prolific in places
Visibility	Walls, coral gardens and wrecks
Coral	Wide variety, prolific
Fish	Wrecks galore!

IRAKO AND KOGYO MARU

The southernmost wreck visited frequently by local divers here is the *Irako*. The *Irako* was a refrigeration ship, about 200 meters long displacing 9,570 tons. Now it is home to big groupers and shoals of yellow fin tuna. Lying in over 40 meters of water, the deck of this relatively intact wreck is at 28–33 meters.

To the north is the 140-meter-long freighter *Kogyo Maru*. Also known as the Tangat Wreck, she is lying upright in about 30 meters of water. Divers come onto the deck at between 18–24 meters. The cargo holds are easily penetrable, and have fish all over. Look for giant pufferfish, especially around the masts, bow and stern. Soft corals and sponges and some small hard corals have attached themselves to the remains. This is a good first wreck dive for beginners.

MAMIYA MARU

West of the *Kogyo Maru* is the *Mamiya Maru*, another freighter about 160 meters in length. Lying on its starboard side in 34 meters of water, the wreck is easily penetrable in some places. The cargo

Coron not only offers a selection of wrecks but also some picturesque reef diving.

holds still contain construction materials and anti-aircraft weapons remain on the deck. Lots of grouper have made their home on the *Mamiya Maru*, and the port side has many hard and soft corals and a variety of fish, including snappers, wrasses and lionfish.

To the northeast is a gunboat about 35 meters long on the other side of Tangat Island. Lying in only 18 meters of water, this wreck is a good snorkeling site as the bow is in only three meters.

OLYMPIC MARU

North west of the gunboat is the *Olympic Maru*, 120 meters long and lying on its starboard side in 25 meters of water. Once again, there are plenty of grouper on this wreck, and the port side, which is only 14–18 meters underwater, is covered in hard corals. Easy penetration of the cargo holds and engine room make this an interesting dive, but watch out for scorpionfish which are all over the area!

TAE MARU

Further away, to the northwest, is the *Tae Maru*, which is also known as the Concepcion Wreck, a tanker about 200 meters long lying upright in 26 meters of water. You come onto the deck at between 10 and 16 meters. The bow is completely smashed, allowing for easy penetration, and the wreck is covered in hard and soft corals and sponges. Sweetlips, grouper, lionfish, surgeons, wrasse, tang and soldierfish have made this wreck their home, and barracuda occasionally swim by overhead. The currents can be treacherous sometimes, taking an unwary diver by surprise, especially when rounding the stern or bow.

AKITISUSHIMA

Due south is the *Akitisushima*, a personal favorite, a 200-meter-long flying boat tender lying on its starboard side. The flying boat is long gone but the huge crane used to put it into the water and retrieve it is still in one piece, twisting away from the wreck into the sandy bottom at 38 meters. More or less intact, the gaping hole in the side, which caused it to sink immediately, is quite apparent.

A good boatman will put a diver onto the highest point of this unusual wreck at about 20 meters, and the average depth of a dive is usually around 28 meters or so. Shoals of barracuda, tuna and yellow fin circle the wreck, and grouper, batfish, snapper and many other species of tropical reef fish have made their home here.

Apart from the wrecks, Coron also has some outstanding coral dives, and these should definitely not be missed.

CORAL DIVING

Off the northwest coast of Busuanga lies **Dimaky Island**. Adjacent to this island are a number of excellent coral dives. On the west side of the island, a gorgeous coral garden with tame reef fish is a popular dive. A slope dropping to 17 meters is a natural home to tunicates and sponges as well as groupers and several species of parrotfish. At the far end of the wall, there's a large swathe of staghorn coral, with an abundance of barracuda, rainbow runners and goatfish. Manta rays and turtles are occasionally seen here and, more frequently, at the northern end of the island.

At **Dibuyan Island**, the reef starts around 13 meters, sloping gently to 28 meters. White tip, black tip and grey reef sharks are commonly found here, as well as surgeonfish and batfish. Manta rays, too, are occasionally seen. In the shallows, a fascinating profusion of small tropical reef fish can be found.

Busuanga is at the frontier of the struggle to preserve the natural resources of the Philippines. Among the creatures whose fates are inextricably linked with man's actions over the next few years is the harmless Dugong *dugon*,

a relative of the manatee or sea cow. Dugong are only occasionally seen by divers, but their tender flesh is a favored delicacy among native fishermen, which may lead to their eventual extinction in local waters despite the best efforts and intentions of several conservation groups operating in the area.

BARRACUDA LAKE

Coron also has one of the most unusual dive sites in the Philippines, Barracuda Lake. To get to the lake, you have to make a climb up a limestone mountain for 15–20 minutes in full gear.

The water temperature in the lake varies from between 30 and 38° C. The unique feature of this lake are the layers of fresh, brackish and salt water which are actually visible (haloclines). There is also a deep cave at the bottom of the lake, but due to its depth this should only be attempted by serious and experienced cave divers.

—*Heneage Mitchell/Sarah Ann Wormald*

Most dive centers around Coron offer buoyancy control courses to ensure safer and more comfortable dives.

El Nido

Fabulous Seascapes and Year-round Diving

A stunning collection of islands with high limestone cliffs predominates the idyllic seascapes of El Nido in northwestern Palawan. As one might expect, there is no shortage of fine diving to be enjoyed here. There are lots of pelagics, some rare and unique species, and excellent wall and drift diving. The marine life is diverse and in places very prolific.

DIVING DILUMACAD

A popular site west of El Nido town itself, situated in the southern bowl of Bacuit Bay, is on the north side of **Dilumacad Island**. This is a year-round dive site except when a strong north wind is blowing. The location features a tunnel with a cavern in the center of it, at about 15–

Access Banca boat, 10 minutes–2 hours; also liveaboards

Current 10–45 meters

Reef type Usually negligible, strong in places

Highlights Outstanding in places; soft coral covering past dynamite damage

Visibility Walls, drop-offs and coral gardens

Coral Varied, prolific; some unique species here

Fish Walls and pelagics

20 meters, and an entrance wide enough for two divers to swim abreast. Not far in, the tunnel widens out into the cavern that has a bottom of sand, and there are clouds of small fish as well as crabs

Longtail boats in El Nido are still the preferred means of water transport between islands.

El Nido Dive Sites

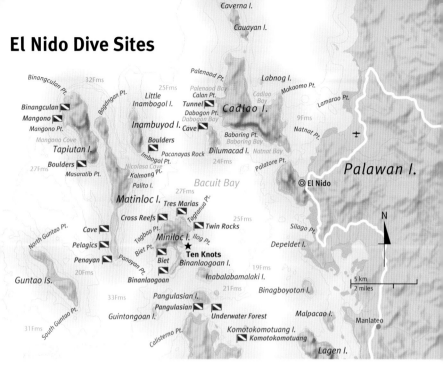

Caverna I.

Cauayan I.

Binangculan Pt. 32Fms

Palenaod Pt. Labnog I. Makaomo Pt.

25Fms Palenaod Bay
Little Calan Pt. Cadlao Bay
Binangculan Bagdngan Pt. Inambogol I. Tunnel Cadlao I. Lamarao Pt.
Mangono Dabogon Pt.
Mangono Pt. Inambuyod I. Dabogon Bay 9Fms
Cave Natnat Pt.
Baboring Pt. +
Mangono Cove Boulders Baboring Bay
Tapiutan I. Pacanayas Rock Dilumacad I. Natnat Bay
Boulders Imbogol Pt. 24Fms Palatore Pt.
Masaratib Pt. Nicolasa Cave Palawan I.
27Fms Kalmong Pt. Bacuit Bay
Palito I. © El Nido
Matinloc I. 27Fms
Tres Marias Pt. Tagtanua Pt.
Cross Reefs 25Fms
Cave Twin Rocks Silago Pt.
North Guntao Pt. Tagbao Pt. Miniloc I. Ilog Pt. Depeldet I.
Pelagics Biet Pt.
Penayan Panayan Pt. Biet Ten Knots
Binanlaogoan I.
20Fms Binanlaogoan 19Fms
Guntao Is. Inabalabamalaki I.
21Fms Binagboyoton I.
33Fms Pangulasian I. 5 km
Pangulasian 2 miles
South Guntao Pt. Guintongoan I. Underwater Forest Malpacao I. Manlateo
31Fms Calisterno Pt. Komotokomotuang I.
Komotokomotuang
Lagen I.

N

---

roaming the floor. The 10-meter-long way out is narrower, so only one diver can pass at a time. It exits at about 22 meters near lots of large rocks that frequently have big fish hanging around them. Recently, while searching for the rubber cover of his depth gauge which had fallen into a crack, my buddy collided suddenly with a very large Spanish mackerel. It was hard to tell who was the more surprised!

Further west around **Miniloc Island** there are also several worthwhile sites. South Miniloc has a dive site between 13 and 21 meters with abundant lettuce corals, sponges and a colony of blue ribbon eels. Visited by jacks and barracuda, squid, cuttlefish and angelfish also make their home here. A sheltered spot, this is one of several year-round dive sites that is worth a visit.

To the north is **Twin Rocks**, another year-round site. It is characterized by a sandy bottom at depths varying between 13 and 21 meters, and is dotted with table corals, sea whips, corals and sponges, amongst which there are small blue spotted stingrays and angelfish.

BOULDERS AND BIG FISH

Off the northwest point of Miniloc Island lies tiny **Tagbao Island**. The local boatman probably knows it as Tres Marias, in reference to the three coral reefs

Green turtles have paddle-like flippers to propel them through the water.

Irawadi 1 is one of Palawan Divers' traditional-style dive boats modified for divers.

wrinkled between the two landmasses. To the southwest is a series of vast boulders, some as large as two-story houses. Because of the relatively shallow depths, the potential for snorkeling is good here, and you'll find plentiful reef fishes and colorful corals as well as painted crayfish.

Banayan Point or **South Tip** on the larger Matinloc Island to the west is for lovers of pelagics. Most divers don't notice the richly coral-encrusted rocks as they are too busy avoiding mackerel, tuna

Female sea turtles that hatched in El Nido return there each year as adults to nest and lay their eggs on the beaches before making their way back to the open ocean.

and jacks finning by in the often stiff currents. It's best to head for the western side of the island, especially between March and June, as the east coast is generally a lot less attractive despite being accessible all year round. **Bakanayos Rock**, known locally as Picanayas, has yet more boulders on the southwest side, with a crew of white tip sharks poking in and out of the holes.

To the southwest of adjacent **Inbogal Point** (Inambuyod) there are some impressive gorgonians and green corals on a steep wall that drops down to 35 meters. Jacks, tuna and mackerel pass by, and this site is home to a unique species of angelfish, *Pomacanthus annularis*, distinguished by its additional stripe. It is only known here and at Tres Marias.

Of the many other local dives in the area, **Black Coral Forest** off the west of Entalula Island deserves a mention. On a steep drop from 35 to 40 meters, it sprouts lots of acropora and black coral.

—*Heneage Mitchell/Sarah Ann Wormald*

El Nido is a tropical paradise for snorkelers.

Puerto Princesa and Port Barton

Honda Bay, Taytay and Port Barton

Puerto Princesa is the capital city of Palawan Island in the western Philippines. Located on the island's east coast, it is a quaint, laid-back city, the base for dive sites. Adjacent Honda Bay has some quite good sites worth a visit, serviced by numerous dive centers in Puerto itself and Dos Palmas resort in Honda Bay. To the north, Taytay Bay is a good option, and in the west Port Barton has some excellent sites.

HONDA BAY

Around the resort island of Dos Palmas there are several easily accessible shallow sites. **Helen's Garden** is diveable most of the year and is a popular night dive. It is a small, rounded reef richly carpeted with hard and soft corals, including some impressive clumps of table and black corals. Juvenile black tip

Long stretches of white sand bordered by crystal clear waters and tropical palms are a stereotype of the Philippines for good reason.

Access Some beach dives, mostly by boat

Current 5–35 meters

Reef type Mostly negligible

Highlights Prolific, varied and colorful

Visibility Mostly small drop-offs, fringing reefs, seamounts

Coral Mantas (Honda Bay), pelagics (Taytay Bay), prolific reef fish (Port Barton)

Fish Baby blacktips, juvenile whale sharks, (Honda Bay)

sharks are usually spotted here as the island is a breeding ground. Sergeant majors, snapper, wrasse and trevally are among other residents you are likely to spot. **Henry's Reef** fringes Arrecife Island, another shallow dive up to 10 meters with small caves and crevices to explore. Best dived during the dry season as it is buffeted by sometimes fierce winds and waves during the rainy season, this site features lionfish, cardinals, snapper, sweetlips and a good variety of nudibranchs and is a good area for photographers. Honda Bay is also blessed with resident juvenile whale sharks and almost all operators offer whale shark trips. Mantas can sometimes be found cruising in Honda Bay; **Pandan Island** is a likely place to encounter them. The reef on the east side of the island features a steep slope to 18 meters, liberally festooned with a variety of hard and soft corals and home to blennies, triggerfish and several species of parrotfish.

Puerto Princesa and Honda Bay Dive Sites

Palawan I.

Bacungan

Tapul I.
Bush I.
Buguias I.
Parunponon I.
Henry's Reef
Fondeado I.
Verano Rocks (Twin Rocks)
East Pandan
Arrecife I.
Starfish I.
Snake I.
Fraser I.
Meara I.
Helen's Garden
Pandan I.
Cowrie I.
Honda Bay
Tagburos
Ramesamey I.
N
5 km
2 miles

TAYTAY BAY

Further north of Honda Bay, about a five-hour drive from Puerto Princesa, Taytay has some excellent sites to visit. It also offers a choice of dive centers and a variety of resorts. Some of the offshore diving is excellent, and the inshore sites are also worth a visit.

PORT BARTON

On the west coast of Palawan, about a five-hour drive from Puerto Princesa, Port Barton offers some rewarding dive experiences for those willing to make the trip across the rugged interior. The furthest of the dive sites in the area, **Shark Point**,

is a large rock you can circumnavigate in a single dive, but you'll probably want to make more than one dive here as there is a lot to see. Shark Point can experience rough seas, especially during the rainy season, so it is best to suit up in calmer water and be ready to hop off the boat on top the site to avoid seasickness and the hazards of trying to kit up in an unstable boat. Black tip and white tip sharks are quite common, the corals are impressive and there is a host of tropical fish as well as painted crays and several species of crab that call the place home. On good days, whale sharks are also occasionally spotted here.

Honda Bay is home to some good reefs, anemones and black corals. It is diveable most of the year round.

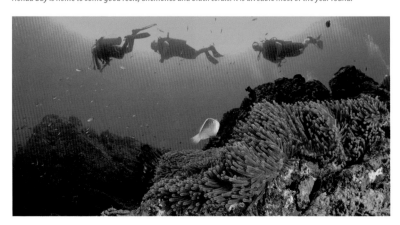

Port Barton Dive Sites

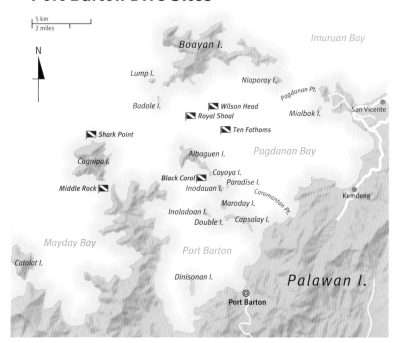

5 km
2 miles

N

Imuruan Bay

Boayan I.

Lump I.

Niaporay I.

Pogdanan Pt.

Badole I.

Wilson Head
Royal Shoal

Mialbok I.

San Vicente

Shark Point

Ten Fathoms

Cagnipa I.

Albaguen I.

Pagdanan Bay

Black Coral
Cayoya I.
Paradise I.

Middle Rock
Inodauan I.

Caramantan Pt.

Kemdeng

Inoladoan I.
Double I.

Maroday I.
Capsalay I.

Mayday Bay

Port Barton

Catalat I.

Dinisonan I.

Palawan I.

Port Barton

Royal Shoal is a seamount found at 12 meters with some of the best soft and hard corals in the area. The bottom is quite deep at 40 meters, so watch your depth and pressure gauge. Expect to see plenty of fish life, including soldierfish, a variety of angelfish, tangs, squirrelfish, gobies and sergeant majors.

Ten Fathoms is another seamount, this one starting at 18 meters, where you may get lucky and see hammerheads, leopard sharks and nurse sharks. Brain, star and pillar corals festoon the reef, grouper and snapper cruise the deeper sections, and there are plenty of smaller tropical reef fish to observe.

*—Heneage Mitchell/
Sarah Ann Wormald*

The Puerto Princesa subterranean underground river is a unique sight.

Davao

General Santos City

Davao City, home to the ubiquitous, smelly but delicious durian fruit, has several dive sites worth visiting, mostly adjacent to the Pearl Farm Resort. There are numerous dive centers in town, most based around Sta. Ana Wharf, offering everything from fun diving trips and courses to discover scuba dives for first-timers.

Access Boat or beach

Current 5–35 meters

Reef type Unpredictable, can be strong along walls

Highlights Dense, prolific

Visibility Walls and fringing reefs

Coral Prolific pelagics (General Santos), good variety of reef fish (Davao)

Fish Pelagics, gorgonians (General Santos), coral gardens (Davao)

The **Ligid Caves** are amongst the most popular sites around this area. A two-cave system with several entrances, the larger of the caves has some interesting black coral formations inside it as well as a variety of sponges and tunicates. The reef itself is liberally festooned with leather corals, and lionfish, rabbitfish and parrotfish make this their home. Look for the large gorgonian fan coral and you are near a cave entrance, which is a good site for photographers.

Pinnacle Point is another good dive for photographers, with a huge variety of fish life, including cardinalfish, big eye trevally, octopus and moray eels. Watch out for the currents here, though, as they can be tricky. The southeast side of the reef is home to schools of surgeonfish and jacks as well as a variety of angelfish. The center of the reef has some beautiful pink soft corals and plenty of hard corals. Further down on the leeward side, you'll discover clumps of black and fan corals with hundreds of little anthias darting in between them.

Sponge corals grow individually and in clumped formations like these pictured here.

Pindawon Wall is just about the best wall dive in the area, with lots of over-hangs, gorgonians, black and table corals. Grouper and snapper roam the deeper sections of the wall. At the shallower portions of the reef, expect to find sea snakes around the large cabbage corals.

Marrissa 1, 2 & 3, named after the daughter of Pearl Farm Resort's owner, are three shallow (18 meters) reefs which also provide for good snorkeling, lots of

sea stars, staghorn and elkhorn corals and an interesting topography.

General Santos, or Gen San as it popularly known, is another destination that is increasing in popularity as the word spreads. The tuna fishing capital of the Philippines, Gen San's tuna fleets ply the adjacent rich seas.

The main attraction for divers is the huge **Tinoto Wall**, running for over 10 km along the coast to the west of the city in Sarangani Bay. The wall drops off to well over 40 meters, so watch your depth here! There are over 20 sites visited by local divers on this impressive structure, all with different features. Currents can be a factor. At some points they can be fairly strong, making even a drift dive an improbable option, but an experienced dive guide can usually give a warning a few minutes before the onslaught and can get divers onto the shallow topside reef before they get washed out to sea. Huge gorgonians, sponges and a good variety of hard and soft corals festoon the wall, home to an endless variety of critters, both large and small.

Stilted resorts and accommodation over the water give guests a complete marine experience

White tip reef sharks often take refuge in small caves and under ledges.

Depending on which location you dive, you can expect to see hammerheads, black tip and white tip sharks, manta, eagle and other rays, tuna, rainbow runners, barracuda, Napoleon wrasse, grouper, snapper and patrols of sergeant-majors—an impressive list for even the most seasoned of divers. The topside of the wall is shallow, good for snorkeling, and extends in most places for about 50 meters from shore. Some of the more popular sites along the wall include Amadora's Diving Resort and Barracuda Point or Lau Tengco.

Nearer to town is **Maharlika Beach Resort**, home to a shallow reef with plenty to see, and popular as a training site and as a night dive. Turtles are quite often found here, as are Moorish idols, parrotfish, wrasses, emperors, tangs, filefish and cowfish. Squid are also known to lay their eggs among the copious staghorn corals. Look out for the resident shoal of yellowtail barracuda.
—*Heneage Mitchell/Sarah Ann Wormald*

Batfish are an easily identifiable species of reef fish because of their extended dorsal fins.

General Santos Dive Sites

© General Santos
Maharlika Beach   Alabel
Lago Cove
General Santos International Airport   Lun Pequeno
5 km
5 miles
N
Rajah
Palalisan
Sarangani Bay   Malapatan
Bailat
Tampat Pt.   Sapa Bay   Sapu
Padidu
Tampuan Pt.   Tango Pt.   Kapatan
Tampuan   Tango
(Tinoto Wall)   Canalasan   Glan Peidu
Sumbang Pt.   Cove

Sulu Sea

Diving Tubbataha, Jessie Beazley and Basterra Reefs

The Sulu Sea is bounded on the west side by the long, thin island of Palawan and on the east by the islands of Panay, Negros and Mindanao. Some of the best diving in the Philippines, and perhaps the world, is to be found at several remote locations within the Sulu Sea, the most famous of which is Tubbataha Reefs.

Despite its inaccessibility and its relatively short season—mid-March to mid-June—berths on any of the several liveaboard boats visiting the Sulu Sea are much sought after. It's best to book as early as possible to avoid disappointment. If you are looking for a shore-based option, then **Lankayan Island Resort** offers excellent macro life, four wreck dive sites and seasonal passing whale sharks from March through to May.

The Philippine Siren offers luxury liveaboard trips around the Southern Visayas and in Tubbataha.

Access	Liveaboard boats from Puerto Princesa
Current	Mostly excellent, 20–50 meters
Reef type	Variable
Highlights	Outstanding variety, pristine and prolific
Visibility	Walls and coral gardens, sand banks
Coral	Awesome variety, prolific in all sizes
Fish	Probably some of the best diving anywhere

TUBBATAHA REEFS

Tubbataha Reefs National Marine Park consists of two atolls, North and South Tubbataha, separated by 6.5 km of water with depths reaching an incredible 650 fathoms. Most liveaboards, and the one or two large pump boats that make the trip regularly in season, start out from Puerto Princesa, capital of Palawan, and take 10 hours or so to motor to the reefs. Puerto Princesa is actually located 158 km to the northwest of the reefs. Most liveaboards leave Puerto Princesa after dinner and arrive in Tubbataha early the next morning, ready for diving.

The first stop is most likely to be the southern reef, which is sometimes called **Lighthouse**, as it encloses a small islet with a solar-powered lighthouse that identifies the area. It is worth climbing up to the lighthouse for the view of the reef and the large lagoon inside it is truly spectacular from this vantage point.

Underwater, the east side of the reef is like gently rolling hills of hard and soft corals and sponges. A wide variety of squirrel fish, angelfish, grouper, parrotfish and butterflyfish hover and swim about in an underwater fiesta of colorful abandon. You may even see a crocodile-fish on the bottom between coral heads. The reef slopes down to 18–24 meters in a few spots before reaching the edge of the wall stretching north for about 12 km.

What remains of the ***Delsan*** wreck lies partly submerged near the edge of the drop-off. The vertical walls are covered with a wide variety of soft corals, tube sponges and sea fans. Moorish idols, triggerfish, surgeons and other schooling tropicals are quite common near the drop-off, while white tip and black tip sharks cruise deeper along the wall. Occasionally, barracuda, either alone or in a pair, will cruise by, and if you are really lucky manta rays may pass by close enough for a good photograph.

The west wall starts more abruptly. Winding slowly towards the northwest for almost 11 km, the drop-off has large pink, purple and burgundy colored soft corals. Red and violet sea fans reach outward, and occasionally small schools of crevale

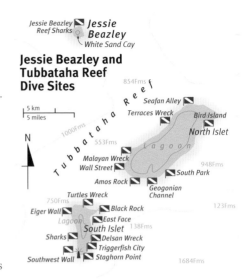

Jessie Beazley and Tubbataha Reef Dive Sites

jacks swim by. When the current is running, mackerel, tuna and shark also cruise close to the wall.

The north side of the reef, known for its turtles, has the same gently sloping

When diving with the sun overhead, shots up to the surface give an excellent depth of field and sense of drama.

The whale shark (Rhincodon typus) is the largest fish known. Although this is a small specimen, it has been known to reach 15 m.

incline leading to the actual wall, but the drop-off is not so steep in places. Hawksbill and green turtles are usually to be seen, either resting or gliding leisurely near the edge of the reef. Around the area called **Black Rock** there are likely to be currents. Unpredictable and often swift, these can catch an unwary diver and cause problems.

Amos Rock on North Tubbataha is in the south among the sandy cays. Here, you will find a gently sloping bottom covered mostly with branching hard corals interspersed with soft corals, sponges and sea squirts. Sandy patches at around 6-10 meters are home to sea pens and Cerianthid anemone. This area is ideal for night dives, when a good variety of cones, cowries and olive shells can be found by sifting through the white sand. With a little bit of patience and close observation, we invariably spotted a fine assortment of species, including several Triton shells.

On the west side of the islet, the reef winds from the southwest to the northeast. The walls are not so vertical but numerous varieties of sea whips, sea fans and soft corals abound among the hard corals. Coral fishes hover about, facing mild currents, and further off the wall are schools of surgeonfish and jacks. The wreck of a small-sized tugboat, now inhabited by plenty of small fish and an increasing number of coral colonies, sits near the wall's edge, and it offers either good snorkeling or a shallow second dive.

The north wall, near **Bird Island**, starts in 5-8 meters. Numerous fissures lead into the near vertical wall and open up into the shallows. Here, crevices and horizontal ledges cut into the drop-off where nurse sharks and, less commonly, leopard sharks may sometimes be caught resting or sleeping.

As you swim along further to the northeast, the edge drops gradually deeper. Black coral adorns the wall as well as plentiful lush soft corals and tube sponges. The sandy bottom that slowly rises to the shallows is dotted with coral heads and wide table corals. It is not unusual to find lobsters underneath these corals. Look underneath, also, for sheltering blue spotted stingrays and small sharks.

Keen-eyed divers have often found guitarfish (also called the shovel nosed shark) motionless on the sandy bottom, while we have often had good sightings of manta rays in the slightly deeper waters.

The north islet is known also as Bird Island for the thousands of terns and boobies that inhabit this pocket handkerchief of land. This is an excellent spot for birdwatching and photography, but be careful of where you step as the boobies lay their eggs in the sand.

JESSIE BEAZLEY REEF

This reef lies about 18 km northwest of North Tubbataha. It is a small, circular reef that rises up almost to the surface of the sea. The surrounding blue water plunges to depths of over 500 fathoms. Marked by the shifting sand cay and the contrasting greens of the shallows, Jessie Beazley has similar features as Tubbataha Reefs, except that it is only half a kilometer in diameter. During calm, sunny days, water visibility averages an impressive 27–37 meters although currents can be quite strong in places. The reef typically slopes to 7–12 meters before the edge of the wall

itself, which drops off to over 50 meters. The shallows here are predominantly covered with Porites and Acropora corals. Near the edge, at a depth of 16–19 meters, are cave-like crevices with a colony of lobsters (*Panulis versicolor*). Turtles can also occasionally be seen perched among coral heads. Hanging off one side of the reef is an old anchor, encrusted with a variety of colorful corals.

Anthogorgia sea fans, *dendronephthya* and *antipatharian* black corals lace the wall as you descend the steep face. The wall itself is etched with small undercuts and ledges at 21–35 meters. Massive basket sponges, some of which measure as much as 3 meters, cling to the rock face along with a diversity of tube sponges. Small white tip and black tip sharks are commonly seen, and sometimes a nurse shark can be found on the sandy ledge. On the larger end of the scale, hammerhead, mako and thresher sharks are known to occasionally cruise the clear, blue waters of the reef.

BASTERRA REEF

Also known as **Meander Reef**, Basterra Reef is rarely marked on maps and is not easily identifiable on most charts, but it lies around 77 km southwest of

The engine of the wreck of a Tristar B at Basterra Reef is encrusted with corals.

Tubbataha and 177 km southeast of Puerto Princesa. It is much smaller than the Tubbataha reefs and slightly bigger than the Jessie Beazley Reef, but what it lacks in size it more than makes up for in real fish action.

Surrounded by waters plunging to 1,000 fathoms, Basterra Reef pushes up to the surface, a massive pinnacle capped by a sandbar. A wreck, the *Oceanic II*, lies to the north. The majestic walls and corals of Basterra are bursting with myriad forms of marine life. In fact, the almost round reef is considered by many to be the best diving spot in the entire Sulu Sea.

At **Barracuda Slope** you'll find a gentle slope of white sand, with porites and acropora corals almost breaking the surface, shelves to the edge of the wall at about 16 meters. Multitudes of small, colorful fish such as anthias, swarm like confetti around large coral heads and the table corals. These become more and more dense as you approach the edge of the wall. Perciform fish swim around in the light current and a large school of red snappers is usually seen cruising around the edge of the drop-off.

The red toothed triggerfish has a distinct C-shaped tail fin.

If you are lucky, then from a distance you should be able to pick up what appears to be a silvery-grey cloud in the water. At first sighting it seems stationary, suspended in mid-water, but as you move closer you realize that the cloud is a thick school of almost motionless barracuda, which regularly inhabit this area and after whom this site has been named.

The white, sandy slope is also an excellent place for night diving. A wide variety of shells, including terebras and *Murex*, make their home here, as does a colony of garden eels, which can be spotted peering from their holes during the day. Deeper down the wall, the common black tip and white tip sharks are almost always present.

From the southwest to the west side of the reef, a thick growth of massive brown corals, piled almost on top of one another, borders the impressive vertical wall which drops off from 5 to 10 meters to unfathomable depths. Squirrelfish, big eye jacks, assorted snappers and butterflyfish join schools of Moorish idols and bannerfish. Check out the crevices, too, for lobsters are found here. Coral encrusted fishing lines stretch out almost horizontally from the wall, which is covered with a profusion of soft corals, sponges, black corals and gorgonians.

As you swim along, you may see another silvery cloud cascading from the shallow reef to the depths in the distance. Closer inspection reveals it to be thousands of jacks, often mingling with a large school of sweetlips and surgeonfish.

Moving northward along the wall, in the shallower parts of the reef, there is a series of depressions that are etched into the wall. The most prominent one resembles a crater and is home to multitudes of small tropical fish, frequently

Turtles are commonly spotted on reef tops where they have easy access to the surface for air.

including the uncommon leaffish. Deeper, you'll come across boulder-like formations of massive corals at 12-15 meters, and this is where the current may start to move in the opposite direction, attracting plenty of fish. Look out for surgeonfish amidst jacks and tuna. From here, the action really begins.

Named **Expressway** for the current's speed at this dive site, the reef hosts an abundance of fish life that includes large manta rays, grey reef sharks and even white tip sharks. Not as creviced as other areas around Basterra, the edge of the wall starts at around 3-4 meters before plunging radically to unrecorded depths, forming an awesome cliff that angles inward to create a truly impressive overhang. This is one dive which cannot fail to excite any diver, however comprehensive his diving experience! If you can tear your gaze away, common black corals and dendrophillias are scattered sparsely along the wall.

A WRECK, TOO

The scattered wreck of a large twin-hulled boat, the ***Oceanic II***, complete with well established coral growth, provides shelter to a variety of snapper, grouper and spadefish as well as smaller fish like wrasses, chromis and thou-

sands of sergeant majors. What used to be one of the engines lies in 13 meters of water close to the nesting site of some triggerfish.

Near the wreck to the north, the reef is characterized by a thick growth of a variety of hard corals. Here, you may see manta rays, mating pairs of hawksbill turtles and a few solitary barracuda. Patches of coral rubble near the edge of the wall at 18-24 meters are favorite hangouts of sharks. Barracudas, dogtooth tuna and mackerel are commonly seen off the wall that gradually curves away to the east.

Further south, the slope steepens then drops vertically from depths of 18-22 meters on the east side of the reef. Every so often, divers should watch the blue water to the east for sightings of grey reef sharks, mantas, tuna, jacks and turtles. Unicornfish and other varieties of surgeonfish are quite common in this part of Basterra. The beautiful and colorful clown triggerfish may be seen in the shallower areas, where brightly hued clams also thrive. Check out the crevices, too, for blue triggerfish and tangs.

—Louie and Chen Mencias

Green sea turtles (Chelonia mydas) can weigh up to 160 kg and are listed as endangered by the IUCN.

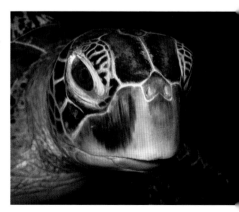

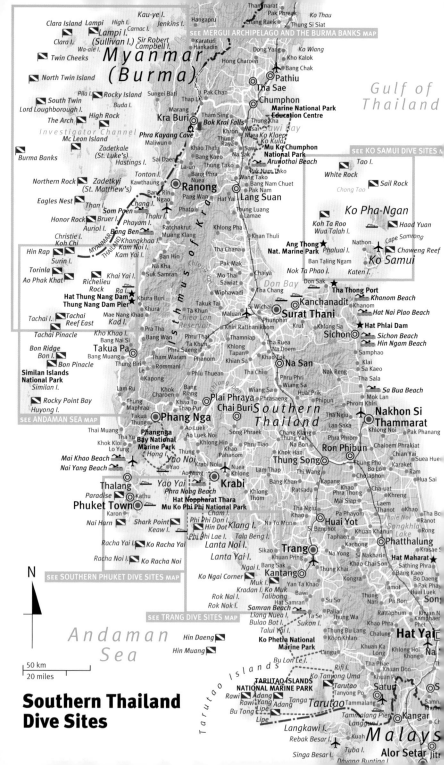

Diving in **Thailand**
A Kingdom Straddling Two Oceans

Thailand's diving industry is one of the biggest in Southeast Asia, with thousands of divers traveling here for recreational diving as well as those who want to get certified in warm, clear water. One of the reasons that the area has become so popular is not only the diving but the friendly locals who are familiar with tourists, which makes communication, organization and arranging trips far easier than in some Asian countries where tourism is still developing.

Thailand is blessed with two bountiful seas, the Gulf of Thailand in the east and the Andaman Sea—part of the eastern Indian Ocean—in the west. The riches that these oceans contain are a delight to those of us who have had the pleasure of diving here. Furthermore, the Thai kingdom is blessed with a remarkable history and culture, friendly natives who offer friendly service, beautiful national parks covering 13 percent of the country, a wide range of accommodation at every price level and some of the most delicious food in the world.

Often referred to as the "Land of a Thousand Smiles", Thailand is a joyous country to travel in. One of the first Thai phrases travelers learn is *mai pen rai*, which literally translates as "it is nothing." It also is used in the same way as "never mind" or "that's OK". However, *mai pen rai* is more than that; it is almost a philosophy that teaches one to hide problems and keep one's "public face" smiling and happy. For the visitor, this attitude creates a feeling of burdens lifted. It makes you feel satisfied, content and cheerful. While exploring the country you'll feel carefree, lighthearted and safe—you'll feel *mai pen rai*. Is it any

The beautiful island of Ko Tao offers diverse marine life on its surrounding coral reefs and the opportunity to see sharks and rays.

This whale shark, pictured near Ko Tao, has attracted some remora suckerfish which will live in symbiosis with it.

wonder so many of us expatriates have decided to stay, or does it surprise that people visit Thailand time and time again?

Thailand's territory stretches from the eastern border with Cambodia to the western border with Myanmar (Burma), and then south to Malaysia. Because of its varied topography and delightful people, Thailand offers the visiting diver diverse undersea experiences along with an unbelievable amount of topside recreation. It's the perfect place for a diving holiday. World-class diving, heavenly tropical islands and immaculate white sand beaches await the explorer. With water visibility often exceeding 30 meters, an average ocean temperature of 27° C, and uncommonly calm sea conditions, Thailand has some of the most comfortable and safe diving environments anywhere in the world.

DEVELOPMENT OF A DIVING INDUSTRY

There are a number of reasons why Thailand's diving industry has grown much faster and started sooner than in other countries in Southeast Asia. First,

tourism, in general, developed early in Thailand, with backpackers paving the way for a booming travel industry.

Second, Thailand's infrastructure has vastly improved, making it easier to communicate with the people who offer the diving—the dive centers. Third, the diving boats, diving resorts, diving operations and diving staff have improved their services and amenities so much they now cater to the most discerning diver.

Professional level diving services are the norm in Thailand. The diving industry, particularly dive instruction and training, is thriving and the standard of service and professionalism in Thailand is amongst the best in Southeast Asia. Most dive centers are affiliated with PADI, but SSI, CMAS and BSAC instruction (amongst others) is available in many places. Prices vary depending on what you are doing, where you are going and how comfortable you want to be. It is always best to contact diving centers before arriving to arrange your holiday, since at certain times of the year, especially in Phuket and other large tourist centers, dive boats are often fullly booked. If you are planning a liveaboard to the Mergui Archipelago or to the Similans, prebooking is essential.

Most diving activity is supervised by a divemaster or instructor. If you are a beginner, it is generally suggested that you find out as much about the dive site and the guide as possible before booking. Not all dive sites in Thailand are suitable for beginners. If you are concerned about your ability to dive in a certain area, let the dive operator know in advance so that they can plan appropriate sites.

Most dive centers offer both beginning and advanced or professional level courses. Courses are generally of a good standard and prices are reasonable. In most areas, there is a good choice of dive sites offering easy to medium conditions, making learning easy and safe.

Diving takes place in three general areas: Pattaya, near the capital of Thailand, Bangkok; around the southern islands of the Gulf of Thailand; and in the two triangles of diving in the Andaman Sea on the west coast of Thailand's isthmus. The pages that follow will describe these areas in detail and will give you an idea of what to expect.

Andaman Sea To the northwest of the island of Phuket lie the most famous and best-loved dive sites in Thailand, the Similan Islands, visited by many liveaboards. Approximately 180 km to the northwest of these islands stretches the vast Mergui Archipelago, a group of islands and banks covering 10,000 sq km. This archipelago is only accessible by professionally equipped liveaboard boats. About 600 km further to the northwest are the Andaman Islands. Then there is Richelieu Rock, known for its whale sharks and one of the highest densities of marine life in Southeast Asia.

South of Phuket lie a number of islands, most of which can be enjoyed in a day's diving excursion. Look out for trips to Ko Racha Yai and Noi, Shark Point and the delightful Phi Phi Islands. Further to the south are the province of Trang and the pinnacles known as Hin Daeng and Hin Muang, which can offer diving quality on par with Richelieu Rock.

Gulf of Thailand The friendly laid-back islands of Ko Samui and Ko Tao are located a moderate distance from Thailand's east coast city of Surat Thani. Originally coconut plantations, these islands have developed into a paradise for people searching for a completely relaxed lifestyle. Exotic dive site names such as Ko Wao, Hin Bai and Chumpon Pinnacle all lie within easy reach of Ko Tao and Ko Samui, and some of the diving here can be spectacular. These sites present the casual diver with a pleasant diversion from such sybaritic activities as relaxing on the beach, drinking from cool coconuts fresh off the tree or dancing to the sounds of techno music at one of the local nightclubs. Interesting diving combined with a very pleasant stay ensure an all-around great time.

East Coast Pattaya is located just a short 2-hour drive from Bangkok. A weekend escape for those living a life in the chaotic capital, Pattaya's dive sites stretch from Pattaya Bay to the areas near the border of Cambodia. Although mainly a popular place in Thailand for diving instruction, the waters around Pattaya can offer the experienced diver the opportunity to dive on shipwrecks and at the same time stay in Thailand's most comprehensive tourist resort. Further to the east, Ko Chang also has a well developed tourist infrastructure and amenities.

ENVIRONMENTAL PROTECTION

There have been a number of setbacks for Thailand's reefs in the past, which can be attributed to a variety of causes. In 2010, there was a rise in sea temperatures that resulted in some serious coral bleaching across the entire region. Some areas in Thailand are showing good signs of recovery whilst in other areas there are still dead corals, but these are mainly on the reef tops and not evident when diving deeper than 10 meters. Areas north of the Similan Islands, such as Bon, Tachai, Richelieu Rock and Mergui, have almost completely recovered from the bleaching of 2010, as have Hin Daeng and Ko Ha to the south.

Ko Phi Phi was where "The Beach", featuring Leonardo Di Caprio, was filmed.

The 2004 tsunami also damaged a number of the more popular sites in the Similan Islands and, to a certain extent, also Ko Bon. These areas have not recovered to their previous condition as they were hit harder and deeper.

Divers have long been aware of damage to coral reefs through dynamite fishing and anchoring, but dive centers began to recognize the damage done by the divers themselves many years ago. For this reason, most centers have a hands-off policy. This has resulted in Thailand having some of the most environmentally progressive dive shops in the world, operating numerous reef restoration, conservation and monitoring projects which, in some areas, have been desperately required. Divers are asked to respect the wishes of the diving community by not gathering or collecting any corals or shells, even from the beaches (removing dead shells also deprives a creature, such as a hermit crab, of a potential home). Marine items from shell shops should also be boycotted.

Environmentally, Thailand's diving fraternity continually rallies to protect their reefs but with so many divers, often beginners, entering the water every year, conservation is, and needs to be, an ongoing process. Many of Thailand's best dive sites have become protected under law. Over the past 15 years, there have been major improvements in the quality of diving in almost all regions around the country except, as of 2015, where coral bleaching took its greatest toll. While other areas in Southeast Asia and the rest of the world have suffered major degradation of their reefs, Thailand's government and its dive centers have instigated sound policies in controlling damage to the coral and fish populations. These policies have included educating people on the destruction of reefs by dynamite, mooring projects in the Similans, Ko Racha, Ko Phi Phi, Ko Samui and Ko Tao, and a strict hands-off policy for divers.

As long as this positive trend continues, diving in Thailand's waters will bring pleasure and thrills to many people, and hopefully to their children and grandchildren as well. You will find Thailand's seas, islands and culture to be full of life, full of wonder—and full of surprises.

—*John Williams/Sarah Ann Wormald*

Similan Islands
Nine Gems Offering Some of Asia's Best Diving

Ko Similan is by far the most beautiful group of dive sites in Thailand and one of the best areas for diving in the entire world. Many divers find that the most unusual aspect about the Similans is that there are two radically different types of environment neatly packaged into one destination.

The Similans, located about 100 km northwest of Phuket, are composed of nine granite islands covered in tropical jungle, washed by a clear blue tropical ocean and blessed with some of the world's finest beaches. The word Similan is a corruption of the Malay *sembilan*, which means "nine", and history has it that it was a Malay fisherman who named the group "The Nine Islands". Today, the

Access Overnight by liveaboard boat

Current Great, 18–30 meters plus

Reef type Variable, sometimes strong

Highlights Excellent condition, unbelievable variety

Visibility Boulders, coral walls

Coral Small sizes but fantastic

Fish Unusual formations, dramatic scenery, swim-throughs, large fans and beautiful beaches

Similan Island has warm, crystal clear waters and some of Thailand's best dive spots.

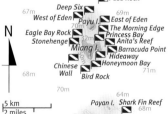

Similan Islands Dive Sites

North Point, Triple Arches, Three Trees, Christmas Point, Batfish Bend, Mooring Rock, Bangu I., Breakfast Bend, Donald Duck Bay, Snapper Alley, The Boulders 72m, Cinnamon Bay, Turtle Rock, Turtle Gulley, Fantasy Reef, Atlantis Wreck, Similan I., Beacon Reef North, Beacon Reef South, Elephant Head Rock, Beacon Point, Pusa Rock, Deep Six, 67m, West of Eden, Payu I., East of Eden 69m, Eagle Bay Rock, The Morning Edge, Stonehenge, Princess Bay, Miang I., Anita's Reef, Barracuda Point, Hideaway, Chinese Wall, Honeymoon Bay, Bird Rock, 68m, 71m, Payan I., Shark Fin Reef 64m, Payang I., Boulder City, Hobbit Land, Coral Garden, Huyong I., Surgeon Rock, Rocky Point Bay, South Rock, Rocky Point, 29m islands are identified by a Thai name and a corresponding number, for example, Ko Huyong (Island #1), located at the southern end of the chain.

The islands have national park status, and thus are fully protected under Thai law. The National Park Authority maintains their presence on two of the islands, Ko Similan (Island #8), the largest, and Ko Miang (Island #4). The islands have also come to the special attention of the Thai royal family, which, we hope, continues to protect them even further.

By drawing an imaginary line from north to south, the area divides into the two separate types of environment. The east coast, with its powdery beaches, features hard coral gardens that slope dramatically from the surface down to approximately 30–40 meters, where sand takes over as the water depth increases. On this side, the most popular activity is drift diving among healthy coral gardens and their reef inhabitants. In several sites, large bommies or coral heads rise from the bottom and are covered with soft corals, sea fans and an enormous number of critters and unusual fish. Here, the diving is easy and navigation simple, allowing each buddy pair to explore at his or her own pace.

The west coast, just a short boat ride away, can offer faster paced, more exhilarating diving as currents swirl around the huge granite boulders, some larger than the largest of houses. These smooth, rounded boulders create dramatic underwater formations, holes and overhangs or swim-throughs, where divers can enjoy just swimming with the current through the openings. The drama of looking up through the clear water at these huge rocks is satisfaction and experience enough for some divers, as there are very few places like this on earth. Growing on these boulders are some of the most colorful soft corals imaginable, in many places so thick that the rock is no longer

Soft coral trees (Dendronephthya) can grow from as small as 2.5 cm to more than 1.2 meters tall.

From November to May, when the Similan National Park is open, divers can experience diving along stunning biodiverse reefs.

visible. In the larger passages between the boulders, the fans grow to a size sometimes 3 meters across, and are often so tightly bunched together that it makes it impossible to swim through the channels. Most of the dive sites on the west coast are best seen with a dive guide since navigation can be tricky. By diving with an experienced guide, you'll almost certainly increase your enjoyment of the area.

If you enjoy watching and photographing small fish, the Similans are hard to beat for the sheer number and variety of tropicals. Large fish, however, are a different story, and the Similans are not well known for consistent big fish action. For this kind of diving, you must travel further north to Richelieu Rock or the Mergui Archipelago. However, luck brings an occasional whale shark, while large cow tail rays are fairly common. And, of course, the leopard shark makes his appearance on a regular basis. White tip and black tip sharks are also sighted once in a while, and a few times over the years we've seen pods of false killer whales.

Like diving in all areas of Southeast Asia, you should enjoy the Similans for what they are justly famous for—wild, unspoiled beaches, magnificent coral growth, prolific fish life, crystalline waters and sensational underwater rock formations. Because of the distance from the mainland, the best way to visit the Similans is on a liveaboard boat.

Thai liveaboard vessels tend to be of a decent standard, with private cabins, air-conditioning and ensuite bathroom facilities being the norm rather than the exception. There are now a huge range of boats operating around Thailand's west coast to the Similan Islands and areas further north catering to a range of budgets. The boats are safer than they were in the past, with modern navigational equipment and safety items in line with Western standards. In general, food served aboard is excellent. Moreover, Phuket has become such an international place that many Western food items are available at reasonable costs. Only wine is still shamefully expensive because of the high taxes. My advice is to bring your own supply.

Trip lengths vary from 3 to 5 days, but are often longer if the boat is including the Similans as a stop on the itinerary. One-day trips are sometimes possible but are generally not recommended.

The high season in the Similans is from October until May but diving is possible all year round. The water tends to be clearest in the summer and in the fall, but visibility is usually fairly good in the Similans, averaging 18–25 meters and at times exceeding 40 meters! There are scores of charted dive sites in the Similan chain and the following descriptions of a few of the favorites will give you an idea of the kind of diving to expect.

Zebra sharks are a species of carpet shark that are nocturnal and spend most of the day resting on the sea floor.

Christmas Point, Island #9, Ko Bangru

One of the most dramatic dives in the Similans, this dive begins with a series of large arches at a depth of about 24

Crinoids, such as these, are also commonly known as bushy feather stars. They attach to larger corals and often contain crinoid shrimps and squat lobsters.

meters. The soft coral growth and sea fans are as large as they are anywhere, and the fish action is fast. We often encounter small schools of blue fin trevally feeding on schools of small fry. End your dive near the island for the best swim-throughs in the Similans and keep your eyes open for surprisingly large jacks that hide in these passageways.

Beacon Reef (south), Island #8, Ko Similan

One of my favorite dives in the past, probably because this is where I saw my first whale shark, this reef features a steep drop-off with striking diversity of hard corals from a depth of 35 meters almost all the way to the surface. This dive could easily have had the largest variety of healthy hard corals in the Similans, probably exceeding 300 species. There were plenty of nudibranchs around the coral heads as well as rare, nervous firefish (*Nemateleotris magnifica*), one of the most beautiful fish in the tropical sea. One of the ugliest residents of this reef are the big eyes (*Priacanthus hamrur*) that slowly cruise the reef flats. These fish have an amazing ability to change from a deep red color to a contrasting vivid silver. It almost appears as if they are changing their

Lionfish are closely related to scorpionfish and have 18 venomous spines. Treatment for stings includes removing spines, cleaning and hot water.

Coral reef groupers are a retiring species and are often found resting in shady crevices in the reef or in caves and recesses.

color to fit their mood. Much of this site has deteriorated but diving on the west coast is still viable and worthwhile.

Elephant Head, Island #8, Ko Similan

This dive site, named after an unusually shaped rock that juts out of the water just south of Ko Similan, remains the most famous dive in the group. The three rocks that form Elephant Head also create a natural amphitheater that feels like diving in a huge aquarium. Yellow goatfish and snappers always hang around at the deepest level of the bowl as well as several species of lionfish, coral trout and the occasional hawksbill or Ridley's turtle. The swim-throughs at deeper depths are dazzling and worth the dive experience alone. The soft corals at this dive site are also amazing.

West of Eden, Island #7, Ko Payu

This has become the choice site for divers now that East of Eden is still recovering from the 2010 bleaching. West of Eden can be a deep or shallow dive, but generally don't go too deep as the current can shift and take you in the wrong direction. Follow the divemaster on this dive. The dive site features large granite boulders with soft coral growth, and as you move shallower,

you'll find swim-throughs. Look for turtles, rays and barracuda.

Anita's Reef, Island #5, Ko Miang

Going by various names over the years, Anita's Reef or Point has become one of the favorite sites. It's still in great shape after the bleaching and is recovering faster than most of the other east coast dive sites. Depending on the current, you may start north or south of the small island to the east of Island #4. Starting from the south, you descend over a beautiful shocking white sand patch looking up to the coral ridges or bommies that reach up towards the surface. You'll find garden eels in the sand here. It's a beautiful dive to drift along and just watch the scenery in very clear water, or follow your divemaster to look for frogfish, ghost pipefish and anemone fish.

One last important comment about the Similan Islands—they are unique for another reason. Mooring projects and other environmentally protective measures have been introduced over the past and in place for years, and happily the diving has actually improved. One thing is for sure, the Similan Islands will give all that you ask for and more.

—John Williams

Ko Tachai and Richelieu Rock
Plus the Sites at Ko Bon and Ko Surin

North of the Similans lie the islands of Ko Bon and Ko Tachai, the Surin Islands and Richelieu Rock. All of these areas, with the exception of Surin, offer world-class diving that differs from the Similan Islands. You should try to make this part of your itinerary when you visit the south of Thailand.

Ko Bon This island is located about 20 km north of Similan Island #9 and features one of the few vertical walls in Thailand. The dive site is on the south-western point and consists of a 33 meter wall facing a small cove and a step-down ridge that carries on to depths of over 45 meters. Leopard sharks are sometimes seen on the ridge and on the sandy flats below the wall. Although the soft corals

Access Liveaboard boat

Current Good, 15–30 meters

Reef type Variable, sometimes strong

Highlights Excellent

Visibility Walls, ridges, pinnacles, boulders

Coral Fantastic

Fish Whale sharks, guitar sharks, soft corals in a rainbow of colors, schooling pelagics

are not as high profile as they are in the Similans, the colors of the corals are radically different and include shades of turquoise, yellow and blue besides the more common pinks and purples. Ko Bon is one of the best places in the Andaman Sea to see manta rays. They are common and it's

A close encounter with a zebra shark is one of the main attractions of diving in the Andaman Sea.

Andaman Sea

Bruer I.

Phayam I.

Christie I.

50 km
20 miles

Koh Chi

Kam Nui I.

Hin Rap
Surin Nua I.
Kam Yai I.
Ao Mai Ngam
Turtle Ledge Reef
Torinla
Ao Chong
Khat
Surin Tai I.
Richelieu Rock
Ao Phak Khat

N

Ra I. ◎

One of the best
places in the
world to dive with
white sharks in
clear water

Ban Ko Ko

Khat I.

Tachai I.
Tachai
Reef East

Pra Tha

Tachai
Pinacle

Bang Wan

Bon I.
Bon Ridge

Takua Pa◎

North
Point

Bon Pinacle

Bang Sak

SEE SIMILAN ISLANDS DIVE SITES MAP

Bangu I.

Similan I.
Beacon Point

Thailand

Miang I.
Similan
Islands

Ban Jam Ru

Payang I.
Shark Fin Reef
Ban Thap Lamu
Plai Hang

Huyong I.
Rocky Point Bay

Ko Tachai Twenty-five km north of Ko Bon, this isle has an offshore underwater ridge that runs perpendicular to the island. This is considered to be one of the finest dives in the kingdom and is famous as a place to see not only the more common species of corals, fans and schooling tropical fish but also larger animals such as rays, leopard sharks, nurse sharks and hawksbill turtles. Whale sharks make an appearance on a semi-regular basis. Ko Tachai also boasts a breathtaking sandy beach on its north-eastern shore. It consistently has manta rays throughout the season.

Surin Island Although visited by several dive operators from Phuket, these islands are more famous for their beautiful coves, bays and dense jungle than for their diving. Spending a few idyllic days on a sail boat or other yacht here is the stuff dreams are made of, yet the serious diver will be bored easily after a few

not at all unusual to see them both along the ridge, at the pinnacle and in the bay.

Colorful soft corals such as these pink Dendronephthya are perfect for wide-angle and macro shots as they host candy crabs and often aeolid cowries.

The common reef cuttlefish (Sepia sp.) has the remarkable ability to change color by flexing its iridiophores, cells in the skin that bend and reflect light.

dives because of the generally poor visibility and lack of fish. This area is also accessible directly from Ban Ko Ko on the mainland and takes around 4 hours.

Richelieu Rock Surin's ace is a small, submerged rock about 18 km east of Surin. Richelieu Rock—just exposed at the lowest of tides—rates as one of the best dive sites in the world due to the unbelievable diversity and concentration of marine life. It was also one of the best places in the world to swim with whale sharks, the largest shark in existence. In recent years, the sharks have become rarer. We still see them on a regular basis but not in the numbers we used to. Hopefully, whatever caused their decline in numbers will change and we will again see these gentle giants as before. Nonetheless, the dive site is still incredible and gets better each year as less fishing is done than previously.

Besides the appearance of the whale shark, Richelieu Rock offers lush soft corals, large schools of pelagic fish and countless small organisms clinging to the rock. Octopuses are frequently seen here. Recently, we had a chance to observe cuttlefish in their courtship behavior on almost every dive. The ritual can be likened to a dance as their tentacles wave wildly in all directions and they go through rapid color changes which appear to be like a quick change of costume between dance acts. Richelieu is good also for shell spotters. Murex, cowries and cones are all relatively common. Try and dive here either very early or much later in the afternoon, if the tides permit, as this site can become very busy with divers throughout the day.

These days, most of the vessels that offer four-day or longer itineraries to the Similan Islands visit these dive sites as well. In addition, most of the boats that visit the Mergui Archipelago include two or more of these dive sites in their program. Boats depart from Phuket, Ko Phi Phi and Khao Lak, north of Phuket.

—*John Williams/Sarah Ann Wormald*

Mergui Archipelago
A Huge Unpopulated Group of Islands and Reefs

In the early 1990s, several dive operators out of Phuket, looking for new diving frontiers in the Andaman Sea, began exploring a series of underwater mountains 145 km northwest of the Similan Islands that came to be known as the **Burma Banks**. In a very short time, the banks became recognized as one of the best places for divers to observe sharks close up and personal, something lacking in Thailand. As it turns out, this was just the beginning. Even though these banks lie in international waters, by the middle of the decade the Myanmar (Burmese) authorities became aware and uneasy about the activity off their coastline and asked the dive boats to seek official permission from the government to dive there. After three years of negotiations, in 1997 consent was finally given to not only

Access At least five days by liveaboard boat

Current Variable from 5–50 meters

Reef type Strong in many areas depending on tides

Highlights Varies from excellent to poor

Visibility Sloping mountains, walls, canyons, caves, pinnacles

Coral Several species of shark, ghost pipefish, seahorses, frogfish

Fish One of the last pristine areas in the world

The Similan Islands don't just attract divers. Snorkelers, cruise trippers and naturists also visit the island in the season. Purchasing a permit in advance is recommended.

Mergui Archipelago and the Burma Banks

50 km
20 miles

N

visit the now famous Burma Banks but also the islands in Myanmar's inshore waters. This opened up a whole new range of diving possibilities in the Andaman Sea, and operators soon began promoting these new destinations offering multi-day trips. Some boats visit both Thailand and Mergui on the same itinerary, while others confine the journey to Myanmar alone. The main obstacle the area has to conventional diving is the distances between dive sites. A typical seven-day circuit including Thailand and Mergui can cover over 1,000 km. Obviously, day trips are not practical for exploring the area.

LUSH, UNEXPLORED AREA

Historically, the archipelago had been an important area for trade between Eastern and Western civilizations, particularly in

This giant potato cod (Epinephelus tukula) is resting in a field of coral rubble.

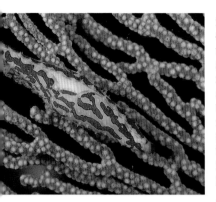

Allied cowries, prized by shell collectors, are difficult to find because they adapt very well to their surroundings, usually sea fans and soft corals.

the 18th century. After World War II, with the major political changes that took place in Burma and the rest of Southeast Asia, the archipelago fell into obscurity, resulting in over 50 years of very little human activity. With over 800 islands, some of them the size of Singapore or Phuket, and most of them completely uninhabited, the area is a dreamland for divers, yachties, naturalists and other pleasure seekers.

A user fee is charged by the Myanmar authorities to enter and dive the Mergui Archipelago. The permits are usually organized by your liveaboard operator, but check if the price is included in your cruise price or if it is an additional fee payable when you arrive. Divers planning to visit the Mergui Archipelago should also check what current visa restrictions apply, if any, prior to making a confirmed booking.

The Burma Banks are no longer the prime reason to visit the area as there are so many better dive sites. Although sharks and rays are seen on a regular basis both at the Burma Banks and at the islands lying further inshore, environmental problems, including long-line

fishing and trawling, have had an effect on this type of wildlife. Much has been written about the area being a place to see sharks and other large fish but the main reason for visiting, honestly, is to see the incredible variety of smaller fish and reef invertebrates, many of which are not found in Thai waters. This, and the sheer immensity of the area, are reasons to go. If catching sight of large animals is the only reason for visiting the archipelago, divers will be disappointed.

DIVERSE DIVING ENVIRONMENTS

There are four types of diving environments in the Mergui Archipelago: shallow inshore fringing island reefs where visibility is often poor but the diversity of marine life is unsurpassed; offshore fringing reefs where the visibility is considerably better and the coral is much healthier; pinnacles and small rocky islands that rise from the depths of the ocean and attract larger marine life, such as sharks and rays; and banks that rise up from depths of over 300 meters and attract different types of marine life altogether. All in all, the Mergui Archipelago contains some of the most diverse and interesting marine ecosystems in the world.

Far inshore, the islands are lush, with vegetation and primary jungle, and contain some of the last jungle cats, elephants and other large mammals to be found in Southeast Asia. For those who are interested in more than diving, jungle walks and river trips can and should be considered as part of your trip. Birdwatchers and other observers of terrestrial life will be thrilled.

Further offshore, the islands are drier and lay in deep enough water to afford good visibility. Here, the corals, sea fans, and fish life are similar to that found in Thailand but with much more diversity of species. This makes the diving better and more exciting than in the waters to the east or to the south.

FACE TO FACE WITH SHARKS

At least nine species of shark have been reported in Burma, including bull, tiger, hammerhead, grey reef, nurse, mako and spinner. At the Burma Banks, white tip, tawny nurse and silver tip sharks are the ones to look out for.

Some of the more interesting dive sites in the archipelago are described below, taking a general south to north route. Keep in mind that these are just a few of the sites that you would visit on a live-aboard cruise as there are scores of dive sites here, and like everywhere some are better than others.

WESTERN ROCKY ISLAND

This limestone island features beautiful underwater terrain, including a tunnel— on good days it is occupied by tawny

nurse sharks—which traverses the island about 20 meters down. The island is more like a series of pinnacles rather than one big rock and the soft limestone makes for crevices offering shelter for a wide variety of sea creatures. Some of the marine life that it is possible to see here includes mantas, gray reef and spinner sharks and eagle rays in the open water next to the island, while leopard sharks and spotted rays can be found lying on the bottom. On and around the rocks, spiny lobsters, cowrie shells, feather stars, anemones and an assortment of crabs abound. Reef fish include blue ringed angelfish, moray eels, snappers, frogfish and ghost pipefish.

BURMA BANKS

Not officially part of the Mergui Archipelago as there are no islands here, the Burma Banks, located about 130 km west of Kawthaung, are a series of seamounts that rise up from over 300 meters to just

The yellow snapper is just one species of schooling tropical fish common to the Andaman Sea. They typically school close to the reef.

below the surface. Depths average 15–22 meters on the flat areas on top, dropping off slowly on the edges. Some banks have a more dramatic drop-off than others, but nowhere will you find a vertical wall. Guided drift dives are the norm, usually starting on the edge of the bank in 35 meters of water where divers stare out in the blue looking for sharks.

If the sharks don't happen to be around, the dogtooth tuna, Spanish mackerel and jackfish that patrol the reef edges will delight you. You never know what you're going to see out here. Most boats don't visit the Banks any longer as there is much better diving to be found inshore. Once the archipelago opened, there was very little reason to travel so far offshore where there is no anchorage.

THREE ISLETS (SHARK CAVE ISLAND)
One of the most extraordinary dive sites, these three rocks that rise out of the sea from depths of 40 meters or more harbor some of the best marine life in the archipelago. Huge schools of fusilier and silversides surround you upon entering the water. The sandy base of the islands reveals unusual anemones and starfish, while the walls are covered with orange cup corals, whip corals and green tubastrea coral. It is one of the better areas to try and see harlequin shrimps and harlequin ghost pipefish.

If you're looking for drama, there is a canyon that leads to a tunnel connecting the northern and southern part of the main, middle island. There is tremendous sponge growth around the cave entrance and nurse sharks are still seen here on occasion. Spotted rays are more common but divers visit this dive site for critters. It's one of the best critter dives in the Andaman Sea.

These three islands are treated as three different dive sites and are dived separately. Boats usually spend one or more days at this site because it is one of the best in Mergui.

NORTH TWIN PLATEAU
Located just northwest of North Twin, this large plateau starts at around 6 meters and carries on down to between 24 and 30 meters. It's quite a large dive site, and it's best to start in the deeper areas and find an interesting vein to explore as you move toward the surface. Lots of large sea fans make this look similar to many

This small rock, typical of the sites in Mergui, is covered in a profusion of life—yellow tubastrea corals, a golden sea fan and a lone urchin, swarmed by hundreds of fusilier fish.

of the west coast dives in the Similan Islands. Barracuda and rainbow runners cruise the outer edges of the reef, and sandbar sharks have also been sighted here.

BLACK ROCK

Probably the most spectacular site with the most potential for big stuff in the archipelago, Black Rock is a rocky island about 100 meters long, located about 80 km north of North Twin Island. Here is the closest you'll come to having a true wall dive, with depths of over 60 meters and a dramatic drop-off in most areas. Although visibility can change dramatically here due to strong currents at certain times of the month, there is plenty to see and many dives are possible on this one site. The currents can also make this an advanced dive, with up and down

currents, not to mention the sideways ones, causing all kinds of fun and games for divers. Be careful of your depths and try and stay close to the rock itself to duck out of the currents.

Some of the fish you will see here include black spotted pufferfish, spotted hawkfish, scorpionfish and blue ringed angelfish. If you are a moray eel fan, then this is your dive site. Many unusual and rarely seen morays are residents here, including extra large common green, zebra, fimbriated and white eyed morays. Octopus and cuttlefish can also be seen at the site.

Moving north, we find dive sites that are not dived as often as the southern sites because of the distances involved. For that reason, they tend to be quieter with fewer divers in the water and for that reason alone they are worth noting.

The tawny nurse shark (Nebrius ferrugineus) inhabits shallow reefs and is commonly seen in this area.

The crown of thorns sea star (Acanthaster planci) feeds on live corals.

TOWER ROCK

Located off Northeast Little Torres Island, this island rises dramatically out of the sea and plunges over 60 meters to the bottom. Schools of mobula rays are frequent. It's also a good place to spot sharks, but the remarkable landscape and the chance of seeing a wide variety of smaller species is the more reliable interest.

WEST CANISTER

Located almost 130 km north of Black Rock, the island looks almost exactly like Ko Bon in Thailand, just flipped 180° C. The best site is a pinnacle located almost in the middle of the small bay, and is almost connected to a ridge that runs from the westernmost point of the island. On dives we've done there, the top of the rock acts as a cleaning station for manta rays. It's a huge granite rock starting about 15 meters and continuing to over 40 meters. From there, you'll find a hard coral reef sloping down to over 60 meters. Large sea fans swathe the granite boulders, with purple, pink and orange soft corals covering most of the rock. Barracudas, fusiliers, jacks, Spanish mackerel and rainbow runners cruise over the top of the reef. Painted crayfish hide in the overhangs.

The Mergui Archipelago has something for everyone, and although the dive sites here can often lean toward the advanced, even intermediate divers will love the place as long as the dive sites and dive times are picked carefully. As always, consult with the divemaster before diving to make sure you aren't getting more than you bargained for. Conditions change constantly due to fluctuating tides, and your dive professional is the best source of current information.

—*John Williams*

Shark Point
Shark Point, Anemone Reef and the King Cruiser Weck

By far the best and most popular dive sites by day trip from Phuket or Phi Phi, these two pinnacles and the wreck dive are located approximately 25 km east of Chalong Bay in Phuket. Given marine sanctuary status in 1992, these three dive sites are the only day trips in Thailand that offer truly world-class quality diving, albeit with limited visibility. The rock pinnacles explode with life and the wreck attracts thousands of fish. The sheer density of marine life makes diving here a wonderful, sensual experience.

Shark Point, or Hin Musang as it is called in Thai, rises out of the water from surrounding depths of only about 18–20 meters. Considering the small extent of

Access	Full-day trips through dive centers
Current	Variable, 2–25 meters
Reef type	Variable, often strong
Highlights	Unequalled
Visibility	Coral gardens, rock
Coral	Quantities and varieties excellent
Fish	Leopard sharks, large moray eels, unbelievable amounts of marine life, great soft corals and fans

the rock above the water, the actual size of the reef underwater is a big surprise to most divers. Beginning from the relatively steep main rock pinnacle, the reef

Zebra sharks rest through the day and feed at night when they hunt for molluscs, small fish and occasionally sea snakes.

flattens out to the south until it rises toward the surface again about 500 meters away. This second rock does not break the surface, and, depending on the current, is an excellent place to begin the dive.

Like many places in Thailand, Shark Point's most colorful feature is the profusion of purple and pink soft corals that cling to the rocks. The strong currents sweeping over the pinnacle provide food aplenty for hundreds of different species of hard corals and Indo-Pacific tropical fish.

The name of the site comes from the common leopard (zebra) shark (*Stegastoma varium*), a docile creature that hangs out in the sand surrounding the pinnacle. These completely approachable, trusting sharks grow to lengths of a little over 2 meters, and most divers think that they are one of the "cutest" sharks in the ocean. Divers not accustomed to seeing sharks are genuinely surprised at how big and approachable they are. Unfortunately, many times these sharks are taken advantage of and handled unnecessarily. Handling by divers can injure the animal and expose it to infection. Touching an animal in no way benefits it and—more often than not—seriously harms it. Dive guides that handle marine life in this way should be reported to the dive center's management.

ANEMONE REEF

Hin Jom (Submerged Rock or Anemone Reef) lies just underwater, about 600 meters to the north of Hin Musang. No part of the pinnacle is exposed, and underwater the rock drops off more dramatically to a depth of between 20 and 27 meters until reaching a bottom of sand and oyster shells. Although not as colorful as Shark Point, the fish life here is excellent, and our friends, the leopard sharks, are often seen free swimming at the top of the rock in 6 meters of water.

KING CRUISER WRECK

This 85-meter-long car ferry was sunk in May 1997 after hitting Anemone Reef. The wreck rests at the bottom in about 30 meters of water and houses schools of jacks, queenfish and reef species, such as cardinalfish, snappers, lionfish and scorpionfish. Most of the hull is covered with acorn barnacles, one reason to wear gloves. Although the wreck is disintegrating, it still rises to within 12 meters of the surface, making it an easy multilevel dive.

Located just south of Ao Phang-nga and all of its freshwater rivers, visibility averages about 10 meters, often less. Although such conditions are not exactly perfect, the amount of marine life more than makes up for the poor visibility. On days when the water becomes gin-clear, diving here feels like taking a breath of fresh air. The only downsides of these sites are the visibility and the occasional strong currents, making both locations unsuitable for beginners.

—*John Williams/Sarah Ann Wormald*

The "magnificent anemone" is easily identifiable by its bright violet underside, which is only visible when it closes up, most commonly at night.

Phuket's West Coast and the Racha Islands

Diving from Phuket's West Coast and Islands to the South

Though most serious divers will immediately book a longer liveaboard boat to the Similans and beyond when contemplating a Thai diving holiday, Phuket does offer some fine day trips and shorter overnight cruises to its west coast and offshore islands. One- and two-tank, half- and full-day diving excursions are available through most of the dive centers in both Patong and Kata as well as from hotels in the Bang Tao area near the airport and Kamala Beach north of Patong.

Phuket's west coast offers casual diving, usually from a local longtail boat. Although not the easiest of boats to dive from, they do have the advantage of being able to pull right up to the beach and are relatively inexpensive to hire.

The giant potato cod can reach up to 3 meters and weigh up to 110 kg.

Access	Half-day and full-day trips arranged by dive centers
Current	Average to poor, west coast. At Racha, 10–30 meters
Reef type	Variable, can be strong
Highlights	Good
Visibility	Coral gardens, rocky points, boulders
Coral	Good
Fish	Unusual fish life, easy to get to areas, good fun, fast dives at Racha. Beautiful topside scenery

Some of the dive areas off the west coast include Patong Bay, Freedom Beach, Paradise Beach, Bang Tao, Kata Beach and Ko Pu. All of these spots are popular training areas and actually do offer some pleasant and easy diving, although Phuket's offshore areas are much better. One of the more promising areas is right off the beach in **Kata** where the coral reef parallels the bay's northern rocky point. Averaging a depth of only 5–6 meters, the amount of marine life surprises even the most seasoned divers. I've seen all sorts of unusual fish here, including a ghost pipefish, dragon wrasses, a crocodilefish and sea robins. I've also had a lionfish swim up to a diving class and peer into each student's individual mask as if looking for an explanation. Whilst the diving is not world class, you should expect the unexpected when diving Phuket's west coast.

Phuket Island
Kathu
Patong
Paradise
Medidien Reef
Freedom Bay
Patong Bay
Na Kha
Phuket
Karon Noi
House Reef
Karon
Karon Beach
Ko Pu
Pu I.
Kata Yai
Kata Beach
Kata Bay
Kata Noi
Kata Noi House Reef
Chalong
Bay
Phuket Bay
Makham Bay
Taphao Yai I.
Tang Khon
Bay
Lon I.
Nai Harn
Rawai
Nai Harn
Rawai Bay
Aeo I.
Promthep Cape
Kaew Yai I.
Hey I.
Coral Island
Kaew Noi I.
Maphrao I.
Mali I.
Khai Nui I.
Khai Nok I.
Pak Khlong
Khai Nai I.
Marine Sanctuary
Lo Po Lai Ok
Laem Hua Lan
Hua Lan Cape
Ko Doc Mai
Doc mai I.
Mai Thon I.
Anemone Reef
King Cruiser Wreck
SHARK POINT
Keaw I.

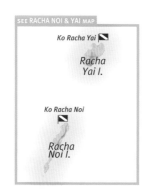

SEE RACHA NOI & YAI MAP

Ko Racha Yai
Racha Yai I.

Ko Racha Noi
Racha Noi I.

N

10 km
5 miles

Southern Phuket Dive Sites

To the south of Phuket lie the twin islands of Ko Racha Yai (Big Racha) and Ko Racha Noi (Small Racha), which offer significantly better diving than Phuket's western beaches. Almost all diving operators offer one-day trips to both of the islands, sometimes on the same day. There are a number of dive shops on Ko Racha Yai as well as several resorts catering for a range of budgets.

KO RACHA YAI

Racha Yai's best diving is off its east coast, which makes it especially attractive during Phuket's off season in the summer. Although visibility varies, it can be as good as 25 meters or more. A typical dive is a gentle drift along a sloping rocky face sprinkled with hard coral forests of many, many varieties. Especi-

ally prominent are staghorn corals of blue and tan. Often there are large schools of false barracudas hovering over the reef, while on the reef itself are octopus and cuttlefish, in addition to the more common tropical species. Divers of all levels of experience and snorkelers can visit Racha Yai without concern over dive hazards as the diving is easy and gentle. Water depths range from 3 to 30 meters.

KO RACHA NOI

This spot is popular for the more experienced diver as depths are generally greater and the currents frequently stronger than at its sister island to the north. The northern tip features a large pinnacle where spotting larger marine life is possible, while the southern point

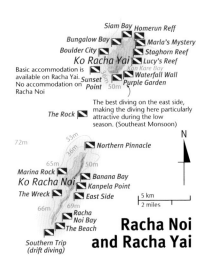

Siam Bay *Homerun Reff*
Bungalow Bay — *Marla's Mystery*
Boulder City — *Staghorn Reef*
Ko Racha Yai — *Lucy's Reef*
Basic accommodation is — *Kon Kare Bay*
available on Racha Yai. Sunset — *Waterfall Wall*
No accommodation on Point 50m *Purple Garden*
Racha Noi

The best diving on the east side, making the diving here particularly attractive during the low season. (Southeast Monsoon)

The Rock

N

72m 55m
36m *Northern Pinnacle*
65m 50m
Marina Rock
Ko Racha Noi — *Banana Bay*
The Wreck — *Kanpela Point*
East Side
66m 69m 5 km / 2 miles
Racha Noi Bay
The Beach
Southern Trip (drift diving)

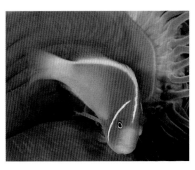

This pink clownfish is seeking protection in the underside of the poisonous anemone.

Racha Noi and Racha Yai

is a nice drift dive with the added bonus of having a beautiful little beach to visit during your surface interval. For some reason, Racha Noi is one of the better places for divers to see manta rays throughout the year. The diving here is definitely more challenging than at Racha Yai but the rewards can also be much greater.

As in most places around the country, accommodation has improved significantly here since tourism first began and although there probably will never be accommodation on Racha Noi, Racha Yai has a range of options for places to stay. There are also ferries that run regularly between Phuket and Racha Yai.

—*John Williams/Sarah Ann Wormald*

Phuket is an international magnet for beach lovers and beginner divers. It was one of the first islands to boast international five-star hotels but now many consider it too touristic and the diving only average.

Phi Phi Islands
Beaches, Bommies and Birds' Nests

Over the past several years, Ko Phi Phi (pronounced "pee pee") has grown from a peaceful little Muslim fishing village to one of the busiest international tourist destinations in the country. It now boasts a hoard of dive centers, several expensive international hotels and a variety of cheaper bungalows and guest houses. Literally thousands of people visit Ko Phi Phi daily, but after the last boat leaves, around mid-afternoon, the island regains some of its original peaceful allure.

Located about 45 km east of Phuket, the Phi Phi Island group—actually part of Krabi province—is composed of the islands Ko Phi Phi Don, Ko Phi Phi Lae (meaning "Phi Phi of the Sea"), Ko Yung (Mosquito Island) and Ko Mai Pai (Bamboo Island).

Access Day trips and overnighters from Phi Phi and Phuket

Current Variable, 3–30 meters

Reef type Variable, often strong, good drift diving

Highlights Colorful soft corals, healthy hard corals

Visibility Coral gardens, limestone rock, walls

Coral Excellent quantities and varieties

Fish Leopard sharks, dramatic landscape above and below, caves, vertical walls, diveable year round

Although the scuba diving is generally not considered to be at the world-class level, depending on your definition, Ko

Striped eel catfish (Plotosus lieatus) are characterized by four pairs of barbels around the mouth. Juveniles are found in schools such as these.

Maya Bay on Phi Phi Lae was made famous by the movie "The Beach".

Phi Phi offers the keen diver a wide range of diving possibilities and occasionally some absolutely fantastic diving. It is a delightful place to spend a few days relaxing on its exquisite beaches, exploring its numerous coves and bays, climbing its steep vertical peaks, investigating the huge caves that hide the edible nests of swifts and, last but not least, enjoying some colorful and enticing scuba diving.

DRAMATIC SCENERY

What sets Ko Phi Phi apart from other dive destinations in Thailand are two features. The first are the amazing limestone cliffs that rise dramatically out of the sea and then plunge equally spectacularly straight down underwater. The second is the remarkable variety of dive sites that are concentrated in such a small area.

Nature has created the limestone rock formations and islands which form Ko Phi Phi and which have become known the world over as one of the most stunning settings in Southeast Asia. These cliffs soar over 500 meters in some areas, and beautiful green trees and bushes grow on the tops and sides of the cliffs. Swimming in a protected little cove at the base of one of these steep cliffs conjures up visions of an unearthly paradise and, no matter how popular Ko Phi Phi becomes, the stunning scenery will always create that special feeling that no one has ever been here before you.

Underwater, these towers shape a rugged, interesting environment for scuba divers, and over time the elements have created long caves, dramatic overhangs and swim-throughs in this soft rock. Some caves penetrate the rock as

Peacock mantis shrimp have the most complex eyes of all the animal kingdom.

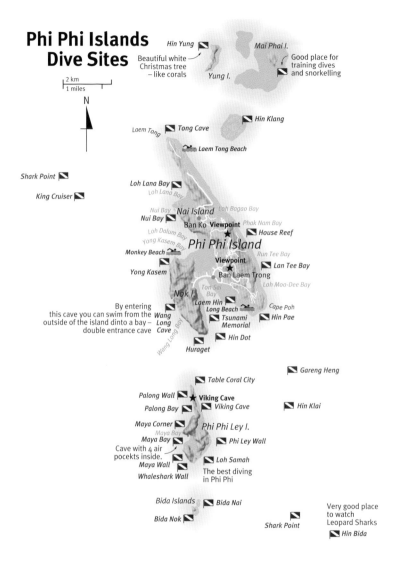

Phi Phi Islands Dive Sites

2 km
1 miles

N

Hin Yung

Beautiful white Christmas tree – like corals

Mai Phai I.

Good place for training dives and snorkelling

Yung I.

Hin Klang

Laem Tong — Tong Cave

Laem Tong Beach

Shark Point

King Cruiser

Loh Lana Bay
Loh Lana Bay

Nui Bay — *Nai Island* — *Loh Bagao Bay*
Nui Bay — Ban Ko — **Viewpoint** — *Phak Nam Bay*
★ House Reef
Loh Dalum Bay — **Phi Phi Island**
Yong Kasem Bay
Monkey Beach — **Viewpoint** — *Run Tee Bay*
★ — Lan Tee Bay
Yong Kasem — Ban Laem Trong — *Loh Moo-Dee Bay*
Nok I. — *Ton Sai Bay*
Laem Hin
By entering this cave you can swim from the outside of the island dinto a bay – double entrance cave — *Wang Long Cave* — Long Beach — *Cape Poh*
Tsunami Memorial — Hin Pae
Wang Long Bay — Hin Dot
Huraget

Gareng Heng

Table Coral City

Palong Wall — ★ **Viking Cave**
Palong Bay — Viking Cave — Hin Klai

Maya Corner — *Phi Phi Ley I.*
Maya Bay
Maya Bay — Phi Ley Wall
Cave with 4 air pocekts inside. — Loh Samah
Maya Wall — The best diving in Phi Phi
Whaleshark Wall

Bida Islands — Bida Nai
Very good place to watch Leopard Sharks
Bida Nok
Shark Point — Hin Bida

much as 100 meters or more and provide the ingredients for exciting dives—if they are well planned and carried out under the supervision of a professional dive operator. Indeed, in other dive areas the scenery is often incidental to the flora and fauna, but here you'll find that the underwater landscape, itself, is impressive.

Other types of environments include vertical walls that plunge from the surface to over 25 meters. On these walls grow a profusion of soft corals, large orange-colored fans, black coral and long, stringy sea whips. Several types of unusual coral trees grow in the waters surrounding Ko Phi Phi, including a

Two different species of eel, a dark spotted moray and a white eyed moray, inhabiting the same hole.

distinctive white coral bush that looks like a frocked Christmas tree, covered with ornament-like growth in the form of oysters and colorful crinoids.

In many places, the islands are fringed with hard coral gardens, home to a wide array of tropical creatures. Most of the coral is healthy, although in the more popular shallow areas damage has occurred due to bleaching and unscrupulous boat operators dropping anchor. But in most areas coral growth and fish life and plentiful and most, but not all, of the same fish species that live in the Similans can be found around Ko Phi Phi.

KO BIDA NOK

One of the most popular dive sites in the group is located at the southern tip of this tiny island. The dive normally begins in a shallow bay on the eastern side of the islet. Upon descending to about 10 meters, you'll find vast healthy growths of staghorn and star corals and incredible numbers of anemones and anemonefish. In fact, this is one of the best places in Thailand to observe the aggressive little anemonefish *Amphiprion ephippium*, which is otherwise rare in Thailand. Watch carefully as they will make a

harmless attempt to bite the unwary diver. Because of their aggressiveness, these fish are easier to photograph than their more common cousins, the clown anemonefish (*Amphiprion ocellaris*), since they are constantly trying to bite your camera.

Continuing south on your dive, you'll reach a vertical wall that is exhilarating to sail over, and continue your descent head first. You'll come to sand at about 22 meters, but there is a gorgeous little bommie off the wall, ending at almost 27 meters, that is often covered with thousands of glassfish, large sea fans and pink and purple soft corals.

This pair of clownfish were left without a home after the host anemone folded up into a tight purple ball.

Ko Phi Phi is a popular destination for snorkelers.

Swimming west along the wall, the terrain becomes less vertical and schools of blue striped snapper seek safety in numbers along the rocky bottom. You'll meet the usual pairs of butterflyfish and plenty of small tropicals in the shallower depths. Octopuses are repeatedly found here if you look carefully in the numerous nooks and crannies, and large green moray eels are almost surely spotted.

Towards the end of the dive, you'll find a small cavern in the rock that makes a sharp right turn just past the entrance. This cavern is a great place to spend a few minutes of your safety stop since the light filtering through holes close to the surface creates lovely patterns on the sandy bottom.

Just be sure that you leave the shallow cavern with at least 50 bar in your tank to avoid a messy out-of-air situation, and that you stay near the entrance.

GETTING ABOUT

The most common type of transportation available in the Phi Phi Islands remains the simple wooden longtail boat. Powered by gasoline, they have a propellor at the end of a long pole that they submerge in water. For hire practically everywhere, these water taxis will take you—for a modest fee—to secluded beaches, the birds' nest caves and any other scenic areas around the islands.

Many dive operators also use these boats for diving trips, and they are quite comfortable to dive from if you listen carefully to the pre-dive briefing. If nothing else, it is a cultural experience to spend the day watching your friendly Thai captain (who usually does not speak much English, nor does he normally know how to swim) ply the waters of Ko Phi Phi, wielding his longtail boat.

—*John Williams/Sarah Ann Wormald*

Trang
Hin Daeng and Hin Muang, Two Jewels of the South

Located just south of the town of Krabi is Trang, which is not as commercially developed as some of the other sites around the country such as Phuket and Phi Phi, which makes it more difficult to get to, but some of Trang's diving spots are decidedly world-class. When conditions are right, the pinnacles of Hin Daeng and Hin Muang triumph over anything in the Similan Islands.

There are four principal places for diving in this area, located south of Ko Phi Phi. These are Ko Ha Yai, Ko Rok, Hin Daeng and several islands inshore from Ko Rok and just south of Ko Lanta.

KO HA

This is a small group of islands almost directly west of Ko Lanta. These tiny islands, separated by channels over 50 meters deep, jut straight out of the

Access Day trips from Ko Lanta, but only by liveaboard to the best dive sites

Current Variable, often strong

Reef type Coral gardens, pinnacles and walls

Highlights Deep drop-offs, lush marine life, stunning islands

Visibility Inshore, 5–10 meters. Offshore, 20–40 meters

Coral Healthy and colorful

Fish Prolific big and small fish, sharks and rays

Andaman Sea. However, unlike Ko Phi Phi, the water here is quite clear and visibility frequently exceeds 25 meters. The diving highlight is a series of caves, or caverns, on the largest of the islands, **Ko Ha Yai**. The caverns are safe to enter,

Dive vessels in parts of Thailand can cater for large numbers of divers and include onboard bathrooms, kit-up areas, sundecks and even spaces for eating.

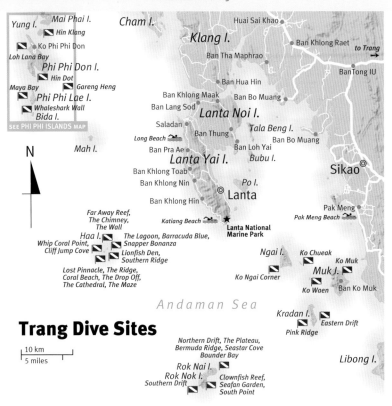

Yung I.
Mai Phai I.
Cham I.
Huai Sai Khao
Hin Klang
Klang I.
Ban Khlong Raet
to Trang
Ko Phi Phi Don
Loh Lana Bay
Ban Tha Maphrao
Phi Phi Don I.
BanTong IU
Hin Dot
Ban Hua Hin
Maya Bay
Gareng Heng
Ban Khlong Maak
Ban Bo Muang
Phi Phi Lae I.
Ban Lang Sod
Whaleshark Wall
Lanta Noi I.
Bida I.
Saladan
Tala Beng I.
SEE PHI PHI ISLANDS MAP
Long Beach
Ban Thung
Ban Bo Muang
N
Mah I.
Ban Pra Ae
Ban Loh Yai
Lanta Yai I.
Bubu I.
Ban Khlong Toab
Ban Khlong Nin
Po I.
Sikao
Lanta
Ban Khlong Hin
Pak Meng
Far Away Reef,
The Chimney,
Pak Meng Beach
The Wall
Katiang Beach
Lanta National
Marine Park
Haa I.
The Lagoon, Barracuda Blue,
Whip Coral Point,
Snapper Bonanza
Cliff Jump Cove
Lionfish Den,
Ngai I.
Ko Chueak
Southern Ridge
Ko Muk
Muk I.
Lost Pinnacle, The Ridge,
Coral Beach, The Drop Off,
Ko Ngai Corner
The Cathedral, The Maze
Ko Waen
Ban Ko Muk

A n d a m a n   S e a

Trang Dive Sites

Kradan I.
Eastern Drift
Pink Ridge

10 km
5 miles
Northern Drift, The Plateau,
Bermuda Ridge, Seastar Cove
Bounder Bay
Libong I.
Rok Nai I.
Rok Nok I.
Clownfish Reef,
Southern Drift
Seafan Garden,
South Point

even without a light, as the entrances are large and there is only one way in and one way out. The best part of entering these caverns is that you can surface inside the island to view stalactites hanging down from the ceiling over 30 meters above the surface. The quality of light filtering through the water from the entrance is truly magical.

Moving inshore to the south of Ko Lanta, the water clarity begins to deteriorate and the diving is quite shallow. There is one interesting place to explore here called the **Emerald Cave**, where at high tide divers can swim through a large cavern underwater to surface in a perfect little lagoon complete with its own white sand beach and splendid tropical jungle. Once inside, you are

surrounded by tall cliffs, and the only way out is through the cavern. An experienced dive guide is essential in the cave for safe exploration.

KO ROK

About 25 km south of Ko Ha are two sister islands separated by a narrow channel about 15 meters deep. These islands, **Ko Rok Nok** and **Ko Rok Nai** ("Outside and Inside") have some of the prettiest beaches in Thailand and are completely devoid of inhabitants. The islands are protected by the National Parks of Thailand so there are no privately owned businesses on them but there is a government-operated campsite where tourists can pitch a tent for a night amid nature! The islands are named after a small furry mammal called *rok* in Thai, and this animal, along with monitor lizards, can be observed onshore with just a little patience and a bit of luck.

The diving here is relatively shallow, with the best corals and fish life living above 18 meters. The bottom is composed of mostly hard corals, with small areas of soft corals at deeper depths. Black tip sharks patrol the reef shallows and hawksbill turtles are sighted regularly. But the main reason for stopping in Ko Rok is that it is the perfect jumping off point for trips out to Hin Daeng, and these twin islands make an ideal "harbor" in all kinds of weather conditions.

The sole reason that diving has become popular in Trang are two pinnacles that lie approximately 25 km southwest of Ko Rok. Hin Daeng (Red Rock) and Hin Muang (Purple Rock) offer everything a diver could want, from dramatic walls and big fish action to lush tropical underwater gardens.

HIN DAENG

This pinnacle is easily found since it protrudes about 3 meters above the surface. Although not very impressive topside, underwater the rock is huge. The

This juvenile lionfish was spotted sheltering in the branches of a pink soft coral tree.

southern side descends—straight down—to over 60 meters, forming the most radical vertical drop in Thailand's seas. The wall is dotted with light growths of soft corals and a few sea fans, but is otherwise devoid of life. On the eastern side, where the slope is more gentle, two long ridges descend into the blueness and if the currents are favorable, it is possible to swim along these ridges down to 40 meters or more. Here, the soft coral becomes more lush and tall, and huge schools of jacks sweep past the ridge, surrounding the diver with a shimmering wall of silver.

Ascending to the shallows we see needlefish, or long toms, skip along the surface. Barracudas stalk their prey through the clear water. Swimming between the three large rocks that form the surface view of Hin Daeng, large schools of fusiliers dart to and fro as if they were afraid of the water surging through the channels.

HIN MUANG

Located just a few hundred meters from Hin Daeng, this pinnacle lies completely submerged. What surprised us the first time we explored the rock was the incredible amount of marine life that clung to the rock. It is as if the rock were located in another ocean and not just a short distance away from the relatively barren Hin Daeng. The name derives from the thick purple growth of soft corals that are everywhere. The rock itself is approximately 200 meters long and less than 20 meters wide and is shaped like an immense loaf of bread with steep, vertical sides and a rounded top. The walls are decorated with large sea fans in varying hues of red, white and orange. Clouds of glassfish, or silver sides, school around the fans and rocky outcroppings. Carpets of anemones cover the more shallow sections of the pinnacle.

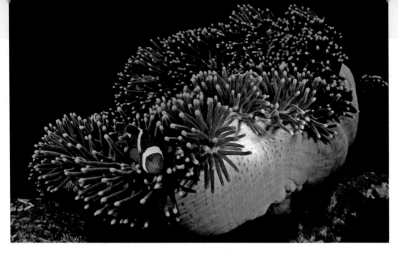

The largest clown fish in an anemone is the dominant female. When she dies, the largest male will change sex and take her place.

One July, the water was so transparent and the sea so smooth that I could see clearly, above me, the splash of someone throwing the dregs of their coffee overboard—with puffy white tropical clouds as a backdrop—from a depth of over 45 meters.

The whale shark is one animal that we see repeatedly around these pinnacles; we sighted these creatures on almost 70 percent of our trips. We even gave a name to one small 5-meter animal, since he was often present. Oscar didn't seem to mind divers at all and would swim right up to us—an impressive sight to behold. Oscar especially seemed to like to make dramatic entrances with beginning divers around, and seemed to know that this was an unnerving experience for most of them. There's nothing like a whale shark with a sense of humor!

On many occasions we have swum with grey reef sharks in the deep blue waters off Hin Daeng and Hin Muang. This is the only place in Thailand where I have seen numerous gray reef sharks together at one time. Grey reef sharks are full-bodied sharks, powerful and sleek, and they are often confused with black tips because of their similar markings. However, unlike their cousins, these sharks are true pelagic animals, and swimming with them is a stirring, emotional experience. On one occasion, I managed to hover within 2 meters of a group of these sharks who ignored me in favor of a large school of jacks. Apparently, they were more mouth-watering than I was.

—*John Williams/Sarah Ann Wormald*

The spotted pink lobster, also known as the Debelius reef lobster (Enoplometopus debelius), grows up to 10 cm and is a special find around Thailand.

Ko Samui

Diver Training Courses and Idyllic Beaches

Ko Samui's allure to tourists really began on a large scale from the early 1990s with the arrival of the traveler who came seeking a unique tropical paradise. Chasing idyllic places where locals were friendly and life was simple and cheap, they found Samui.

Today, surprisingly little has changed from those early days as the charm of Ko Samui as well as the unhurried lifestyle have remained largely intact. About the only noticeable changes today are the addition of an airport and the building of numerous top-class international resort hotels in a low-rise, relatively environmentally pleasing way.

Considering that most dive sites are situated at least two hours by boat from Ko Samui, and considering that the water

Access   Full-day trips through dive centers; some shore diving

Current   Variable, 2–15 meters

Reef type   Variable, often strong

Highlights   Fair, soft and hard

Visibility   Coral gardens, rocks

Coral   Excellent variety and color

Fish   Black coral, bull sharks, occasional whale sharks

clarity is not something the island is noted for, scuba diving is surprisingly popular on the island. Remarkably, Ko Samui has developed into one of the main diver training centers in all of Southeast Asia. Most instruction is

The Ang Thong National Marine Park is an archipelago comprising 42 islands in the Gulf of Thailand.

completed in the shallow water directly off the coast at Chaweng Beach, Coral Cove or one of the other secluded little bays and beaches that make the island so lovely. Many diving centers will offer a couple of days on Ko Tao to finish up a diving course, but the waters around Samui are adequate for training.

For the advanced diver, Ko Samui has two main dive areas, each with an approximate six-month opposite season. Hin Bai, or **Sail Rock,** located north of Samui and Phangan, is best from March until September. During the rest of the year, the **Ang Thong Marine National**

This striking red gorgonian coral was pictured at Ko Samui. Gorgonians attract small juvenile fish that seek protection in their branches.

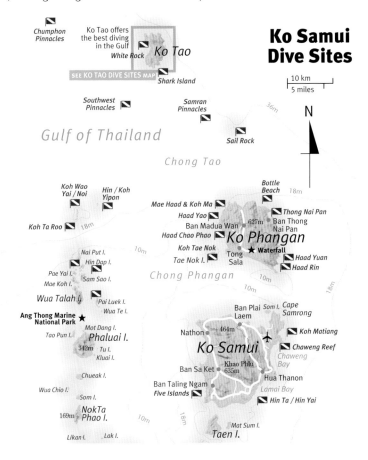

Ko Samui Dive Sites

Chumphon Pinnacles

Ko Tao offers the best diving in the Gulf

White Rock

Ko Tao

SEE KO TAO DIVE SITES MAP

Shark Island

10 km
5 miles

N

Southwest Pinnacles

Samran Pinnacles

36m

Gulf of Thailand

Sail Rock

Chong Tao

Koh Wao Yai / Noi

Hin / Koh Yipon

Bottle Beach   *18m*

Mae Haad & Koh Ma

Haad Yao

Thong Nai Pan

Koh Ta Roo   *18m*

Ban Madua Wan   *627m*   Ban Thong Nai Pan

Haad Chao Phao   *Ko Phangan*

Nai Put I.

Koh Tae Nok

10m

Hin Dap I.

Tae Nok I.   Tong Sala

★ Waterfall

Haad Yuan

Pae Yai I.

Sam Sao I.

Haad Rin

Mae Koh I.

Chong Phangan

10m

Wua Talah I.

Pai Luek I.

18m

Ang Thong Marine National Park ★

Wua Te I.

Ban Plai Laem   Som I.   Cape Samrong

Mot Dang I.

Nathon   *464m*

Koh Matiang

Tao Pun I.

Phaluai I.

Tu I.

342m

Kluai I.

Ko Samui

✈

Chaweng Reef

Chaweng Bay

Khao Phlu   *635m*

Chueak I.

Ban Sa Ket

Hua Thanon

Wua Chio I.

Som I.

Ban Taling Ngam   *Five Islands*

Lamai Bay

Hin Ta / Hin Yai

169m   *NokTa Phao I.*

10m

Likan I.   Lak I.

Mat Sum I.

18m

Taen I.

Park to the northwest is the choice spot. Both dive areas are interesting, and although most divers wouldn't take a dedicated dive holiday to Ko Samui, most divers will enjoy at least a few dives at both of these areas.

Hin Bai is the preferred day trip from Ko Samui since it offers the most exciting diving. The likelihood of seeing larger animals such as sharks is better here than in other areas. Similar in shape to the islands around Ko Phi Phi, Sail Rock juts out of the water and slopes beneath the surface, sometimes vertically, to just over 30 meters. You begin by exploring one of the deeper pinnacles away from the rock, which are covered in beautiful green trees of *Tubastraea micrantha*, and the bright yellow polyps of encrusting species of Dendrophylliid coral. Black coral trees with either lime green or reddish-brown polyps also grow out of the crevices.

Longfin batfish (Plata teira) are from the spadefish family and are characterized by their long lower yellow fins.

UP A CHIMNEY

Towards the end of the dive, you'll be shown an underwater chimney located on the northwest side, the most impressive attribute of the dive. Two divers can enter at a depth of 19 meters where the cavern continues in for about 2 meters before bending toward the surface. At 12 meters you'll spot a hole that opens up laterally. Look out for camouflaged scorpionfish! Although a tight squeeze, it is possible to swim back into open water from here. Continuing up, the chimney opens at about 5 meters of water depth, and you'll exit the hole to find yourself surrounded by a magnificent carpet of anemones, often full of pink anemonefish.

People tell stories of shark sightings around Hin Bai. Although I haven't seen sharks myself, reliable sources report that they may well be bull sharks, if not large grey reef sharks, an uncommon shark in Thai waters, that have been spotted feeding from time to time at the surface. Along with the possibility of sighting a whale shark, this surely makes Hin Bai worth repeat diving.

The Ang Thong Marine National Park is a beautiful archipelago of over 40 islets, and operators offer trips to this area from December until March. While the visibility here is often poor, the snorkeling and shallow diving as well as the striking topside scenery make an enjoyable outing. **Ko Wao** and **Hin Yipoon** (meaning "Japanese Rock") are the most popular areas for scuba diving and are noted for shallow caves and colorful soft corals.

Because of its laid-back charm, Samui combines many attractive factors with diving, making it a good place to sport dive, learn to dive or further your dive education.

—John Williams/Sarah Ann Wormald

Ko Tao

A Laid-back Island with Good Diving

The sleepy little islands of Ko Tao (Turtle Island) and **Ko Nang Yuan**, located approximately 65 km north of Ko Samui in the Gulf of Thailand, are booming with dive centers offering dive courses and dive trips. There are backpacker-style bungalows, upmarket resorts and a plethora of well-run dive centers offering a range of scuba, free diving and snorkeling services.

An idyllic tropical paradise, Ko Tao seems to attract many divers looking for lengthy stays in Thailand, and many backpackers who travel to the island end up spending months there. Some of the reasons for this are the relaxed pace of living, inexpensive accommodation, camaraderie between divers and dive centers and, of course, interesting and

Access Full-day and half-day trips through dive centers

Current Variable, 3–40 meters

Reef type Variable, often strong

Highlights Good to average

Visibility Coral gardens, boulders, pinnacles

Coral Good schools of pelagic fish, nice tropicals

Fish Whale sharks, good soft corals. Expect the unexpected

relatively inexpensive scuba diving. All these combine to bring back visitors time and time again.

One of the best things about diving around these two small islands is the fact that the dive sites, unlike Phuket's and

Ko Tao, part of the Chumphon Archipelago, is the smallest of the famous island trio of Ko Samui, Ko Pha-Ngan and Ko Tao.

Chumphon
Pinnacle
The best dive
in the gulf.
Sometimes
whale sharks
are seen here.

Cape Namtok

Mango Bay

Green Rock

Nang Yuan
Pinnacle

Mamuang
Bay

Cape Grachom Fai

Cape Grachom Fai

Lighthouse

Ko Nang Yuan

119m

Japanese
Garden

Lighthouse Bay

Bouyancy World

Kluay Theuan Bay

No Name Pinnacle

Twin Rocks

★ Nanyuan Terrace

Mountain Viewpoint

White Rock

379m

210m

Hin Wong Pinnacle

Pee Wee Rock

★
Whale Skeleton

H.T.M.S. Sattakut Wreck

Mahaena Bay

Hin Wong Beach
Hin Wong Bay

Sairee Reef

Sairee

Sairee Bay

310m

King Rama V Boulder ★

Ko Tao

Mao Bay

Junkyard Reef

Laem Thian
Pinnacle

Ship Wreck

Mae Haad Bay

Two Views

Cape Thian

Pottery Pinnacles &
Three Rocks

Jansom Bay

Mae Haad

Khao Mae Haad
313m

Tanote Bay

Tanote Bay

N

Dive Tuk Tuk

Padi Diving
Centres

★
Golden View

★
Tanote View

Lang Khaay Bay

Lang Khaay Bay

Sai Tong Beach

Sangjan

Ao Leuk Point

Sai Nuan Beach

Leuk Bay

Cape Je Ta Gang

Chalok Baan Kao

Hin Ngam Bay

2 km
1 miles

June Juea Beach

Viewpoint

New Heaven

Hin Ngam Bay

**Ko Tao
Dive Sites**

Cape Gul Juea

John Suwan
Rock

Thian Og
Bay

Shark Island

Shark Island

Taa Toh Rock

Taa Cha Bay

Cape Taa Ton

Budha Rock

Biorock
Artificial Reef

Samui's, are only minutes away. Including Ko Nang Yuan, which is only a short hop from Ko Tao, there are more than enough dives sites and site diversity to keep even seasoned divers entertained. Sites range from deep water pinnacles to shallow coral gardens to rocky points complete with swim-throughs such as are found in the Similan Islands. Although water clarity can sometimes be limited, frequently the water becomes as transparent as the Andaman Sea, with visibility over 30 meters.

IN SEARCH OF THE BIG ONES

One day a couple of years ago, I was visiting Ko Tao with a friend from the US. The day was perfect, the sea glassy and smooth and the water crystalline, so we decided to take a dive or two. There had been much talk of whale sharks over beers

the night before, since I had seen quite a few on the Phuket side that year. Everyone had high hopes of today being the day that the big boys would be out to play. Well, the boys were out and then some.

As we pulled up to **Chumphon Pinnacle**, someone shouted "whale shark!" and, sure enough, there she was next to the boat. While everyone jumped in with snorkeling gear, I hurriedly slapped on my tank so that I could follow her more easily. As the snorkelers crowded around her, she slowly moved off and only a videographer and I were able to follow. We spent the next 20 minutes swimming easily along with the shark before she swam off.

But that wasn't all. As I swam back to the boat to meet up with my buddy, a 4-meter-long swordfish swam lazily below me almost the whole way back. He was a light tan color and had a nose on him that extended over a meter in length.

Then, upon reaching my buddy and finally going to the dive site proper, we descended through a spiraling school of large jacks numbering well over 1,000 individuals. We felt we were lost in some monstrous whirlpool of fish, and we were so mesmerized we completely lost sight of the rock—again.

It was another long swim back to the boat with no air remaining. But it wasn't over. Some type of huge animal, surely over 12 meters, was swimming around the rock with a black back and a tiny black fin. We knew it couldn't be another whale shark with those markings, but only when we jumped in the water did we find out that two fin-back whales were frolicking with our group. Divers swam with these whales for over an hour. This was definitely a dive of a lifetime—even though we never found the dive site.

It is a longish trip to Ko Tao, but as it offers the best diving in the Gulf of

Schooling barracuda at Sail Rock.

Thailand, combined with the pleasantries of a sybaritic shore life, it is well worth a visit. You may not see whale sharks or swordfish sailfish on every dive, but you'll certainly be more than charmed by the local inhabitants of the reefs.

—*John Williams/Sarah Ann Wormald*

Ko Tao became famous for diving because of its whale shark encounters. This one has a school of remoras.

Pattaya and Ko Chang

Fun Resort with Some Interesting Diving Options

Pattaya, Thailand's first resort built for foreign tourists, became infamous as an R&R destination for American soldiers during the Vietnam War. The first dive shop opened for business during this time and, as a result, many servicemen and their visiting families became some of the first foreigners to scuba dive recreationally in Thailand. Today, huge high-rise hotels follow the curve of the bay and Pattaya, while still popular with international visitors, has become more attractive as a weekend getaway for residents of Bangkok.

Although this city by the sea is far more densely populated than other tourist areas in Thailand, its remains popular because it is bustling and energetic. Even though it has received considerable negative press, it has a certain character that people return for. Pattaya is definitely an

Access	Full-day trips through dive centers; liveaboards
Current	Variable, 2–25 meters
Reef type	Variable, often strong, especially on wrecks
Highlights	Good in some places
Visibility	Coral gardens, rock, boulders
Coral	Not bad, some unusual animals
Fish	Wreck diving

active resort and diving enthusiasts will find plenty of different dive sites and courses to keep them busy.

Since Thailand's recreational diving industry was born in Pattaya, dive centers there have set valuable examples to other more recently opened diving businesses in other parts of Southeast Asia. Their main activities are teaching introductory courses and open water certification courses to new divers. In addition, they specialize in advanced training programs for divers, offering scheduling that is especially suited to residents working in Bangkok, both foreign and Thai. All dive centers in Pattaya conduct one-day diving trips and some also operate liveaboard vessels, offering longer trips to Ko Chang near the Thai–Cambodian border.

One problem that frustrated dive operators in the past was the lack of a clear environmental policy. Combined with rapid population growth as tourism developed, this caused many dive sites to deteriorate. To side step this, many operators were forced to go further afield.

Myriads of small reef fish in shallow water, such as these sergeant majors, have made Thailand a famous snorkeling destination.

Nong Pla Lai
Takhian Tia
8Fms   8Fms   4Fms
Ko Luarn   Na Klua
Luarn I.   Khram Wreck   Ko Sak Kood Wreck   Pong   Khao Mai
Phai I.   17Fms   Sak I. Pattaya Beach   Nong Prue   Kaeo
Ko Phai   Khrok I.   **Pattaya**
Klung Badan I.   *Larn I.*   Ko Khrock   Phana Nikhom
Ko Klung Badan   Pethra Wreck   Jomtien
Man Wichai I.   8Fms
12Fms   Pottery Wreck 4Fms
Ko Man Wichai   *Jomtien Beach*
Huai Yai
14Fms
North Rock   9Fms
Hin Khao I.
Ko Rin   5Fms   Na Chom Thian
Hin Ton Mai I. South Rock
Klet Kaeo I.   Bang Sare   Samnak Thon
12Fms   Ko Khram Noi   Klet Kaeo
Khram Noi I.   Map Ta Phut
Khet   Phlu Ta Luang
36Fms   Udomsakdi
Khram Yai I.   Ban Chang
N   I-ra I. Sattahip   U-Taphao
Petchburi Bremen Wreck   Nen I.   Airport
Submarine Rock   Tao Mo I. Phra I.
Mu I.   Samae San
I-lao I.
Yo I.
25Fms   Charakhe I.
35Fms   Kham I. Raet I.
10 km   Shark Fin Rock   39Fms
5 miles   *Samae San I.*
Changkluea I.
Pattaya Dive Sites   Hardeep Wreck
Chuang I.   Ko Chan
32Fms   Ko Chuang   Chan I.

Fortunately, the National Marine Park is now better protected and many dive operators are actively involved in environmental and conservation projects to improve and protect the reef and its marine inhabitants.

Visitors to the area will soon discover that some of the best wreck diving in Thailand is found here. Although there are several wrecks around, the three best sites in the area are the *Hardeep*, the *Bremen* and the Vertical Wreck, now renamed Pak 1 or the Horizontal Wreck.

The **Hardeep** is considered to be one of the best wreck dives around Pattaya, and stores offer one-day and two-day trips to the site. Located between Ko Samaesan and Ko Chuang, the *Hardeep* is a 42-meter-long freighter that sank in 1942 and now rests on her side in 21–27 meters of water. As with all wrecks, one of the main reasons people dive on it is because of certain eerie emotions they experience when the ship first becomes visible through the gloom. This aside, the best reason for diving on sunken ships is that they are a magnet for incredible amounts of marine life.

Today, the wreck is still and tranquil, except for the masses of tropical fish that have made this disaster their home. It is also home to colonies of fan corals and large barrel sponges. Although visibility is not dependably clear here—averaging about the same as in the rest of the Gulf of Thailand—the prolific marine life and the possibility of a safe penetration (experienced divers only) into the wreck makes the dive one of the most inviting in the whole area.

The second popular wreck is the **Bremen**, located near the village of Sattahip, south of both Pattaya and Jomtien. Although the profile of this 100-meter steel ship is weakening each year due to gradual deterioration, the wreck attracts large schools of yellow tail snappers and barracudas during slack tide. An excellent deep dive for an advanced course, the wreck rests at a depth of about 25 meters and visibility ranges from around 7 to 10 meters.

The **Vertical Wreck** was, no doubt, the most famous wreck dive in Thailand. This freighter, when she sank in 1996, was still full of gas and the stainless steel tanks, located on the bow, still held gas which made the bow buoyant. Thus, when the ship sank, the stern sunk to 60 meters and the bow remained just below the surface. This is why it was called the Vertical Wreck. However, in 2003 the Thai Government sank the wreck completely as it had begun to refloat and was considered a danger to shipping. The wreck (renamed the Horizontal Wreck or Pak 1) now lays upright on the bottom in around 42 meters of water and is much closer to mainland Thailand, approximately 48 km offshore.

Despite being resunk and relocated, the wreck is still an excellent dive, especially on days when the visibility is good. The cabin and bridge area, in particular, are worth spending some time exploring. Penetration is easy in the bridge area but other parts of the ship are more tricky and penetration should always only be undertaken by divers with the right training.

Due to the depth of the wreck, Pattaya dive shops offer technical diving, including Tri-mix and deep air courses. This makes Pattaya one of the few areas in Thailand that can offer such courses and have the diving to back them up.

For those divers interested in more than shipwrecks, coral diving in Pattaya can be satisfying as well. Often dive centers will offer a coral dive during their trip to the *Hardeep*, as Ko Chuang and Ko Samaesan have healthy coral down to as deep as 30 meters. Although larger animals such as sharks and rays are occasionally seen, the big attractions here are the abundance of corals, both soft and hard, and beautiful colorful anemones.

The island of **Ko Rin** probably offers Pattaya's best diving. The underwater profile is more interesting here compared with other places, and water clarity can be excellent, sometimes exceeding 25 meters. Rocky canyons form swim-throughs, which are not only wonderful for divers but create currents to wash around the rocks, causing great environmental conditions for the vast array of marine life that lives here. Although the day can be long due to the distances involved in getting to different sites in the area, those looking for clearer water will find the longer traveling times more than worthwhile.

SOUTH TO KO CHANG

Ko Chang is actually Thailand's second largest island, but despite this the tourism industry here was very late to catch on. However, despite a late start, since the early 2000s it has developed at an alarming rate and now boasts a range of accommodationfrom budget bungalows and rooms to international-style resorts, numerous dive centers, bars and all of the other ancillary services that you would expect from a popular tourist destination. It is still not on a level with Phuket and it has still retained some of its original charm despite its exponential growth. The island is also home to long, beautiful, powder white sand beaches, lush vegetation, waterfalls and a range of terrestrial wildlife and birds. This actually makes Ko Chang an ideal destination for those who want to mix diving with some topside adventure and lively nightlife.

Some people claim that the diving in Ko Chang is at least as good as in the Similan Islands. However, the area suffers from very inconsistent visibility and the dive sites lie very far apart. So, instead of making a comparison between the Similans and Ko Chang, a more reasonable comparison would be with Ko Tao. The best time to visit Ko Chang is from November to May, which are the driest months and the visibility is therefore a little more consistent, although diving is available all year round.

Ko Chang, like Ko Tao, has become a massive center for diver training and there are courses available for all levels, from discovery to instructor and also technical diving. There is decent wreck diving in the area, the **HTMS *Chang*** is good for wreckdiving courses and is a good dive in itself.

As with the island of Ko Samui to the south, Pattaya is probably not the place for a dedicated diving holiday. But for those divers looking for an active sporting life, or a busy nightlife as well as diving, Pattaya or Ko Chang could be the answer. For the student of scuba, both areas offer many opportunities for all levels. For a weekend away, Pattaya has the potential to keep even the most active diver happy. For a longer, more relaxing stay with an island vibe, Ko Chang ticks all the right boxes.

—*John Williams/Sarah Ann Wormald*

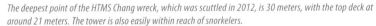

The deepest point of the HTMS Chang wreck, which was scuttled in 2012, is 30 meters, with the top deck at around 21 meters. The tower is also easily within reach of snorkelers.

Malaysia Practicalities
Malaysia Telephone Country Code: 60

Malaysia has radically developed its tourist infrastructure in the past few decades and continues to do so. Now travelers have a wide choice of accommodation and travel options almost everywhere in the country. The capital, Kuala Lumpur, boasts shops as sophisticated as those in Hong Kong or Singapore, yet, happily, at grass-roots level, kampung or village life remains much the same as ever. The Malaysians are a hospitable people, whether Malay, Chinese, Indian or mixed race in origin. The diving can be very good, particularly off the island of Sipadan. *Note*: Malaysia can be dialed directly from Singapore.

Air travel

Kuala Lumpur International Airport is 60 km from Kuala Lumpur and is the air travel hub of the country. Apart from the national carrier, **Malaysian Airlines**, numerous airlines (major and smaller) serve the city from all continents. In total, Malaysia has over 100 airports ranging from international terminals to small airstrips. Other destinations of interest to divers in Malaysia that have international airports include Langkawi, Penang and Kota Kinabalu. Shuttle services exist between Kuala Lumpur and neighboring Singapore while frequent flights link Peninsular Malaysia with the East Malaysian states of Kuching and Kota Kinabalu.

Staying in contact

Cell phones By far the easiest way to stay in touch from Malaysia is to buy a local pre-paid SIM card on arrival. They are relatively inexpensive to buy and usually include a small amount of credit to get you started. The best coverage throughout Malaysia is through **Maxis** or **Celcom**. **Digi** is also a popular choice. If you are traveling to a more remote area, ask your operator beforehand which network provider is best in their area. Credit is known locally as "recharge" or "reload" and there is a range of packages available depending on what you require. "Recharge" is sold at almost all small streetside shops as well as in larger supermarkets and stores. Look out for network provider signs. The main network providers also have stores at the airport but queues can be longer there. It is possible to purchase credit that can be used for phone calls or for Internet data. *Note*: When you purchase a local SIM card, your handset needs to be unlocked and the SIM has to be registered. This process is done through the main SIM menu on your device, and the best way to deal with this is when you purchase the SIM ask the seller to register it too if not done automatically). It only takes them a few minutes and they do not charge for it; they are doing it many times a day!

Internet Most cafés, bars, restaurants and resorts in tourist areas have free Wi-fi hotspots and you simply need to make a purchase (just a drink will suffice) and ask for the password. The strength of Internet reception in Malaysia is variable. In major towns and tourist hotspots it tends to be better than in more remote areas. Checking emails and browsing is not generally a problem but uploading or downloading large files from remote areas can be an issue. If you need Internet access whilst you are away, check with your operator beforehand what the situation is, particularly if you are making a liveaboard trip. If you buy a local SIM card (see above), you can make use of data packages for Internet through your cell phone, which you can then use directly to go online or "tether" as a mobile hotspot if you prefer to use your computer.

Land travel

Travel within Malaysia is equally convenient. Shared taxi services exist between many large towns and the country has a good railway system. Air-conditioned express buses also operate regularly on inter-city and inter-state routes.

Sea travel

Ferry services link the country's many islands with the mainland. Along the east coast, ferries operate on a regular basis to the most popular islands of Tioman, Perhentian and Redang and there is no short supply of ferries running between Kuala Perlis or Kuala Kedah and Langkawi. There are also high-speed catamaran services between Penang and Langkawi.

Visas

All travelers must be in possession of a passport valid for at least six months from the date of departure from Malaysia. Citizens of most Commonwealth and EU countries are granted a visa-free entry for 14 days. Extensions can be made for a period up to three months at immi-gration offices providing an onward ticket is shown and any other current requirements are met. If you are unsure about your eligibility to enter Malaysia, check on the Malaysian Foreign Office website for up-to-date information.

Health

This rarely presents a problem in Malaysia. A tropical country, it does have mosquitoes but malaria is rare. The most common complaints are usually too much sun and upset stomachs. Both can be remedied by taking preventive measure or paying a visit to a pharmacy or clinic, found all over the country. In emergencies, there are government-run and private specialists in all the major towns with doctors who speak English. Generally, the water throughout the country is safe, though opting for boiled or bottled water is a wise precaution.

Money exchange

Banks and money-changers will convert foreign currency to the Malaysian dollar, or ringgit Malaysia (RM), as it is known, in all the major cities. Credit cards are widely accepted but you should expect to pay a small percentage fee. Carry plenty of small change and notes as these are invaluable for taxis and buses.

When exchanging currencie, travelers should check for regular updates as to current exchange rates.

Weather

Divers in Malaysia will enjoy tropical weather year round. During the northeast monsoon (November to late March), the eastcoast is mostly wet and the west coast,dry. With the westerlies between April and October, it is the east coast that is dry and the west that is rainy. The same is largely true of Sabah. Temperatures at sea level rarely fall below 22° C and infrequently rise above 32° C.

Accommodation and food

There is no shortage of luxury hotels in Malaysia's capital and resort destinations. However, there is also a wealth of less expensive accommodation, simple guest houses and backpacker style rooms throughout the country. When staying in resorts and hotels or when booking dive and stay packages, be sure to check with your operator prior to booking as to what is and what is not included in the package price. Some will include full board or breakfast, transfers, diving, equipment hire, etc., whereas others may bill for these separately.

Malaysian cuisine is spicy and delicious, combining pungent spices with local vegetables, fish and fowl. Throughout the country hawker stalls serve fast food, Malaysian style, for less than a few dollars. Malay, Chinese and Indian cuisine are all widely available, while international dishes can be found in restaurants in the more popular resort areas and major towns and cities.

What to bring

Divers should bring only the essentials if they want to avoid excess baggage fees on domestic flights. Weight restrictions apply on some of the services offered by small domestic airplanes. Check your booking confirmation carefully for how much baggage you are allowed and how much you can pay for in addition. All resorts and dive operations will rent the basic equipment, but a suit is a recommended extra. A long 3 mm will generally be fine and offer adequate skin and thermal protection. Bring sufficient batteries, sun cream, a small first aid kit and spares for your dive gear if you are diving off the islands. If you are planning to bring your own gear, think about what you really need and what you can hire/borrow from your operator.

Dive emergencies

The best advice for divers is always to dive conservatively. If an emergency arises, there are naval decompression chambers at Tanjong Gelang on the east coast (near Kuantan) and Lumut on the west coast of Peninsular Malaysia.

Kuala Lumpur City code: 03

Dive operators

There are a number of dive operators based in Kuala Lumpur. The following are recommended:

Borneo Divers and Sea Sports (KL) Known for its excellent PADI 5 star IDC facility and diving operation in Sabah, this company runs tours to Sipadan and the islands in Tunku Abdul Rahman Marine Park. See the section on Sipadan below for full details. The head office is based in Kuala Lumpur and is a fully licensed travel reservation agency for bookings to its Sabah-based diving and beyond. Head Office, 9th Floor, Menara Jubili, 53 Jalan Gaya, 88000 Kota Kinabalu, Sabah. Tel: +6088 222226; information@BorneoDivers.info.

Planet Scuba This PADI 5 star IDC is located at No. 2A Jalan Telawi 5, Bangsar Baru, 59100 Kuala Lumpur. Tel: +603 228 72822; www.planetscuba.com.my; info@planetscuba.com.my.

Scuba Dynamics PADI 5 star dive center offering dive trips, PADI dive courses and equipment sales. Lot 32-2, 2nd Floor, Jalan 27/70A, Desa Sri Hartamas, 50480 Kuala Lumpur. Tel: +603 2300 1489; contact@scuba-dynamics.com.my.

Sipadan, Mabul and Kapalai

Sipadan Island is located in Sabah, East Malaysia, off the coast of northeast Borneo. Access is either via Singapore, Johor Bahru or Kuala Lumpur to Kota Kinabalu, the capital of Sabah, then by a domestic service to Tawau, which is approximately one hour by car from Semporna from where boat services to Mabul, Kapalai and Sipadan depart.

Diving around Sipadan Island is strictly regulated through a permit system operated through the **Sabah National Parks Parks Office** (www.sabahparks.org.my). Permits were introduced in 2005 to limit the number of divers visiting the area daily and the permits are highly sought after, sold to operators and often sell out six months in advance. Booking beforehand is highly recommended. When booking a one-week trip, you should expect only 1–2 days of the diving to be around Sipadan Island. If you arrive without a booking it may be possible to wait around for 2–3 days until one becomes available but this is not guaranteed and, in peak season, highly unlikely. Also since 2005 there are no resorts on Sipadan Island itself. Divers need to stay on either Mabul or Kapalai islands, which is where the main dive operators and resorts are based. There are some cheaper alternatives in nearby Semporna for those traveling on a budget.

Diving in the Sipadan Park area is restricted to the hours of 6am–4pm with no night diving allowed at all. Usually operators coming to the park will make 3–4 dives during these hours to ensure value for money for the permits. When booking diving packages, check how many days diving at Sipadan are included and how many dives on each day. The days you are not diving around Sipadan itself will probably be spent diving around Mabul or Kapalai, both of which offer some nice dive sites and a range of critters and marine life.

When to visit

July through September are busiest and theoretically the best months to dive off Sipadan, with the northeast monsoon. Late November through January are the worst, with decreased visibility, colder air and waters, but a greater possibility of seeing larger pelagics and different shark species. The best visibility tends to be from April to June.

Diving

Sipadan is not always the easiest place to dive and currents can be strong. Most operators require an advanced level certification and usually will not take you to Sipadan for your first day of diving. This gives them chance to access your ability first, especially for less experienced divers

What to bring

UW flashlight, insect repellent and a wet suit of at least 3 mm thickness.

Dive operators and resorts

The following operators purchase permits in advance and are recommended, but be sure when booking to check how many Sipadan dives are included in your package:

Borneo Divers Operates dive trips to Sipadan as well as Tunku Abdul Rahman

National Park. Tel: +6088 222226; www.borneodivers.net; information@borneodivers.info or reservations@borneodivers.info.

Scuba Junkie Operates both a 5 Star PADI Dive center and dive lodge located in Semporna and a PADI IDC Center on Mabul Island. If you are based in Semporna, their speedboat takes approximately 1 hour to reach Sipadan Island for a 3 dive trip, including lunch. If you are based in Mabul, they offer a 4 dive trip to Sipadan Island (20 minutes boat travel time), which includes breakfast and lunch. Scuba Junkie also offer a range of PADI courses and diving around the neighboring islands. Dive and stay packages can be arranged along with transfers from Semporna to Mabul. www.scuba-junkie.com.

Sipadan Scuba Offers a 3 dive trip to Sipadan Island from their dive base at the Hotel Sipadan Inn in Semporna. Departure is around 8.30am and returns at around 5pm, lunch included. www.sipadanscuba.com.

Sipadan-Kapalai Dive Resort An upmarket stilted water village resort located just a few minutes by boat from Sipadan. Dive and stay packages are available and dives are around Sipadan, Mabul and Kapalai. Transfers to and from Semporna are also available. www.sipadan-kapalai.com.

Liveaboards in Sipadan

Liveaboard possibilities can be checked out through the marinas at Tanjung Aru (Kota Kinabalu) and Port Klang (Kuala Lumpur). For liveaboards in the Sipadan area, booking in advance is required and make sure that you check when booking how many days you will be able to dive around Sipadan Island. For Sipadan fanatics, the MV *Celebes Explorer* is the only Malaysian liveaboard operating in the area and the only vessel that will allow you to dive Sipadan *every* day of the week except Sundays. The boat is not maintained as well as it could be and you shouldn't expect any luxuries (at all) but it will get you the most days diving on Sipadan.

Kota Kinabalu City code: 088

Kota Kinabalu can be reached by regular daily flights from Kuala Lumpur with Air Asia, Malaysian Airlines and Firefly. Local buses run from the city center to the beach at Tanjung Aru and to other suburban locations. Taxis are available at ranks in the center and are metered.

Accommodation and food

Hotel rooms vary from expensive to simple, with everything in between. Kota Kinabalu excels in its seafood and has a wealth of temperate climate vegetables from the highlands. You can pay anything from US$5 for a simple meal in an open-air market to US$100 for a lavish dinner in a fancy hotel restaurant.

Dive operators for Tunku Abdul Rahman Park

Borneo Divers Operates trips to Tunku Abdul Rahman National Park as well as Sipadan. Tel: +6088 222226; www.borneodivers.net; information@borneodivers.info or reservations@borneodivers.info.

Scuba Junkie 623 Wisma Sabah, Kota Kinabalu 88000, Sabah. Organizes dive courses and dive trips around Kota Kinabalu and the islands around the Tunku Abdul Rahman National Park as well as Sipadan. Tel: +608 8255 816; www.scubajunkiekk.com; scubajunkiekk@gmail.com.

Layang-Layang

Layang-Layang Atoll is a one hour flight north of Kota Kinabalu and is home to only one resort and a Malaysian Naval Base with landing strip. The naval base is used purely for training and surveillance purposes. If you are hoping to see hammerheads then Layang Layang should be on your list.

Layang-Layang Island Resort The only commercial operation on this remote oceanic atoll, Layang-Layang Island Resort was renovated in 2013 and now this upmarket resort boasts 86 guest rooms, a 150 seat restaurant, bar, swimming pool and massage center. Full board dive and stay packages are offered and booking in advance is required. Tel: +603 2170 2185; www.avillionlayanglayang.com; res@avillionlayanglayang.com.

Pulau Payar City code: 04

Pulau Payar is accessible from the island of Langkawi (around 45 minutes by boat), a popular tourist destination island off the west coast of Peninsular Malaysia.

Getting there

By Air: There are direct flights to Langkawi with Air Asia and Malaysian Airlines from Kuala Lumpur. The airport is situated in Padang Matsirat, which is located 20 minutes away.

By Sea: Ferry options are widely available from Kuala Kedah, Kuala Perlis and Padang.

Accommodation and food

Langkawi's hotels and beach resorts offer a wide range of accommodation, from 5 star deluxe class to moderately low-priced hotels and chalets at budget prices more suitable for backpackers. There is something for every traveler here.

Seafood is a specialty in Langkawi and there are plenty of small restaurants in Kuah. Breakfast or lunch may cost as little as RM10 per person and dinner around RM30.

Dive operators

East Marine Offers daily dives and snorkel trips to Pulau Payar as well as PADI, BSAC and SSI courses. East Marine Holidays Sdn Bhd, Royal Langkawi Yacht Club, Jalan Dato Syed Omar, 07000 Kuah, Langkawi, Kedah. Tel: +604 966 3966; www.eastmarine.com.my; info@eastmarine.com.my.

Langkawi Coral Eco Offers fun dives and both PADI and SSI courses around Langkawi. Contact: Langkawi Saga Travel & Tours Sdn Bhd, 16 Jalan Tanjung Bungah, Georgetown, 11200 Penang. Tel: +604 899 8822; www.langkawicoral.com; sales@langkawicoral.com.

Terengganu

This state's coastline offers a score of delightful offshore islands and the best snorkeling and diving in Peninsular Malaysia.

Getting there

Kuala Terengganu airport (Sultan Mahmud) has a few daily flights from Kuala Lumpur and from there it is around a 2-3 hour drive to Kuala Besut, which is the main entry point to the Perhentian Islands. However, transit through Kota Bharu in Kelantan offers better conections to Kuala Besut by both train and air. If you are planning to stay on Redang Island, then Marang is the main ferry point. The two islands of Perhentian lie at the furthest extremity of Terengganu, some 23 km offshore, and are accessible by ferry from Kuala Besut. All of the coastal villages and towns are linked by bus or taxi from the state capital, Kuala Terengganu, and with Kuantan, further south in the state of Pahang.

If visiting a resort, the hotel boat will usually pick you up at the relevant port. If you want to dive or snorkel on an individual basis, you have to negotiate a fare with one of the boats that ply the route. If you are going to try this option, it helps to team up with other travelers as you will generally get a better overall per person price for a larger group.

Dive operators and resorts

The companies and dive operators listed under Kuala Lumpur offer inclusive-cost dive trips to these islands. Most of the better hotels along the coast also have operational headquarters and booking offices in Kuala Lumpur.

Universal Diver Located next to Tuna Bay Island Resort on Perhentian Besar. PADI 5 star dive center. Offers diving around Perhentian as well as trips to Redang and Lang Tengah and a range of PADI dive courses. Contact: Oceanaut Marine Bhd, 120 Jalan Besar, Kuala Besut, 22300, Terengganu. Tel: +609 691 1621; www.universaldiver.net; info@universaldiver.net.

Turtle Bay Divers With dive shops on both Perhentian Besar (Longbeach) and Perhentian Kecil (Mama's Place Chalet). Offers PADI dive courses, fun diving around Perhentian and trips to Redang. Tel: +601 9333 6647; www.turtlebaydivers.com; diveturtlebay@gmail.com or turtlebay93@gmail.com.

Bubbles Dive Resort Located in Tanjung Tukas, south of Perhentian Besar. PADI dive center offering courses and fun diving plus dive and stay packages. The resort is also involved in numerous conservation projects. Tel: +601 2983 8038; www.bubblesdc.com; reservation@bubblesdc.com.

Redang Pelangi Resort Offers accommodation and diving through Dive Redang dive center. Dive packages and dive courses are available. Tel: +609 624 2158; www.diveredang.com; reservation@redangpelangi.com.

Tioman and Aur

Tioman offers visitors plenty in the way of recreation, beaches and tourist facilities. There are international-standard hotels, an 18-hole golf course and scores of other smaller, bungalow-style guest houses and hotels. Pulau Aur has recently boomed in tourism and the diving is just as good as that around the better known Tioman Island.

Getting there

Access to Tioman and Aur is from Mersing jetty on the southern east coast of the peninsula. The easiest way to reach Mersing from Singapore is by Transnasional buses which travel direct (www.transnasional.com). The journey takes around 3 hours depending on traffic. Be sure to allow enough time so you do not miss the last ferry from Mersing. **Blue Water Ferries** are the main operator and the journey to Tioman takes around 2 hours depending on sea conditions (www.tiomanferry.com). Aur can be accessed also by ferry direct from Mersing (around 4.5 hours) or via Tioman. Many operators will arrange transfers for you from Singapore. Check when you are booking what your agent or operator is able to offer.

Dive operators

Tioman Dive Center Operates from two bases, one at Panuba Inn and one in Tekek at the Swiss Cottage Resort. Offers fun diving, full range of PADI courses, reef monitoring, conservation and educational projects. Tel:

+609 4191 228; www.tioman-dive-centre.com; enquiries@tioman-dive-centre.com.

Eco Divers PADI 5 star dive center offering a range of courses and fun diving. Conservation-minded dive center. Tel: + 601 3602 2640; www.

eco-divers.net; mail@eco-divers.net.

DiveAsia PADI dive centre on Tioman Island offering courses and fun diving. Tel: +609 419 5017; www.diveasia.com.my; diveasiatioman@yahoo.com.

Indonesia Practicalities
Indonesia Telephone Country Code: 62

Indonesia is an archipelago of some 17,000 plus islands. Levels of tourism vary widely across the region, but visitors can travel and lodge in reasonable comfort throughout the country. Bali, the best-known Indonesian destination, offers resort facilities of the highest standard. As one travels progressively east across the archipelago, infrastructure and amenities become more rudimentary but there are numerous dive resorts located in most corners of the country that provide Western-standard levels of comfort and facilities.

Air travel

Major European, Asian, Middle Eastern and Pacific airlines serve the capital, Jakarta, and Denpasar (Bali) daily. The airports in Manado, Makassar and Lombok also receive international flights. For access to other airports located in Indonesia, domestic flights are required.

The national airline, **Garuda**, and its sister internal carrier, **Merpati**, serve islands large and small and are reasonably efficient in handling bookings from abroad. Both Garuda and Merpati accept online bookings, as do

Lion Air, Trans Nusa, Sri Wijaya, Xpress and a number of other smaller carriers. Some online bookings require an Indonesian credit card so an agent may be required to process purchase. Many dive operators will also handle domestic flight bookings for guests.

Garuda Indonesia www.garuda-indonesia.com
Sriwijaya Air www.sriwijayaair.co.id
Lion Air www.lionair.co.id
Merpati www.merpati.co.id
Transnusa www.transnusa.co.id
Xpress Air www.xpressair.co.id

Staying in contact

Cell phones By far the easiest way to stay in touch from Indonesia is to buy a local SIM card on arrival. They are usually around a couple of dollars and this includes a small amount of credit to get you started. The best coverage throughout Indonesia is through **Telkomsel** (also known as Simpati). **XL** is also reasonable but not quite as good. Credit is known locally as "pulsa" and can be purchased in the form of a card that you scratch off a panel and input a code to your phone or it can be done electronically through the seller's cell phone. Pulsa is usually purchased in Rp 25,000/50,000/100,000 vouchers and sellers add around Rp2,000–5,000 to the total (their commission). Pulsa is sold at almost all small *warung* and streetside shops as well as in larger supermarkets and stores. Once you have credit on your phone, you can make calls that will be taken directly from your credit or you can buy a data package (which can include Internet) through the menu on your phone. *Note*: When you purchase a local SIM card, it needs to be registered. This process is done through the main SIM menu on your device but the instructions are in Indonesian. The best way to deal with this is when you purchase the SIM, ask the seller to register it too (some will do this automatically. It is not a strange request and only takes them a few minutes and they do not charge for it.

Internet Most cafés, bars, restaurants and resorts in tourist areas have free Wi-fi hotspots and you simply need to make a purchase (just a drink will suffice) and ask for the password. In more remote areas, such as Raja Ampat, Internet is available and in some places it is free whilst in others the operators sell packages. Very few areas in Indonesia have no Internet coverage, but as it is usually provided through cell phone networks if you are in an area with no cell reception it is unlikely that you will have Internet reception. The strength of Internet reception is also variable. In major towns and tourist hotspots, it tends to be better than in more remote areas. Checking emails and browsing is not generally a problem but uploading or downloading large files from remote areas can be an issue. If you need Internet access whilst you are away, check with your operator beforehand what the situation is, particularly if you are making a liveaboard trip. If you buy a local SIM card (see above), you can purchase data packages for Internet through your cell phone that you can then use directly to go online or "tether" as a mobile hotspot if you prefer to use your computer.

Land travel

Taxis are commonly used in all Indonesian cities but are an expensive way to travel long distances. As most land travel is difficult to arrange and book in advance, the majority of operators based in areas that require long land journeys provide pickups and transfers either included in the package price or for a surcharge.

Sea travel

Given the cheap price of domestic flights, travel by sea is not usually necessary and is considerably more time consuming and less reliable than traveling by air. The national passenger line, **Pelni**, calls at scores of ports, large and small. Only the adventurous—or masochistic—would want to travel in any berth other than in first class. Ships are often sold out, if not overbooked, long in advance of sailings. Schedules are erratic and it is not possible to plan sea trips from abroad. Many ports have no wharves and transfer is by small boat. Do not attempt this unless you are in peak condition. The Pelni website has schedules and contact information for most areas: www.pelni.co.id

Visas

A 30 day tourist visa can be purchased on arrival in Indonesia for US$35. Sixty day tourist visas are also available but must be purchased prior to arrival in the country through a branch of the Indonesian Embassy. Tourist Visas may be extended through immigration offices within Indonesia. Passports must be valid for at least six months upon arrival. There are hefty fines for overstaying your visa. Check current visa regulations prior to departure as they change regularly!

Health

Tetanus should be up to date, and many recommend gamma globulin against some forms of hepatitis. Malaria is endemic in many areas of East Indonesia as well as rural Java. Always consult your doctor prior to travel for up-to-date information. The best protection is caution. Search out clean food and water and avoid exposure to mosquitoes. After sundown wear trousers and long-sleeved shirts. Mosquito coils are available everywhere, and much better are room and body sprays from stores and supermarkets in larger towns and cities. Major pharmaceutical companies manufacture and distribute in Indonesia, but have your prescriptions refilled before departure.

Dive emergencies

Jakarta and Bali have the best health care providers in Indonesia and both areas offer a range of international hospitals and clinics. Other major cities, such as Manado and Makassar, also have international hospitals but in more rural areas local clinics are the norm where facilities, equipment and medical supplies can be limited and the training of the staff questionable. In the event of serious illness or injury, you should leave immediately for Singapore, Bali or Jakarta if help is not immediately available. A private medevac could be financially ruinous (US$25,000 and up), so if your health plan does not cover your trip, travel insurance is essential. A policy should include medevac to the nearest recompression chamber and a 24 hour worldwide hotline. **Divers Alert Network (DAN)** and **SOS International** provide good secondary

coverage. The non-profit DAN researches dive safety, provides medical advice to injured divers, keeps an updated list of operational hyperbaric chambers and offers affordable insurance. Annual membership prices vary according to the level of cover you opt for, but fully comprehensive cover that includes medivac is strongly recommended.

DAN Southeast Asia-Pacific, located in Australia, has regional responsibility for Australia and New Zealand, Papua New Guinea, Fiji, Indonesia, Malaysia, Vietnam, Singapore, Cambodia, Myanmar, Philippines, Vanuatu, India, Solomon Islands, Brunei, Thailand, Hong Kong, Korea, China and Taiwan. 24-hour emergency hotline number: +61-8-8212-9242; danasiapacific.org; info@danap.org.

Weather

Indonesia's wet and dry seasons depend on the monsoons. Dry southeast winds blow dry from May to September, while the northwest monsoon brings rain from November to March. This delineation has become increasingly erratic with El Nino and perhaps global warming. Wet season diving is often disappointing in areas where visibility is affected. Check weather conditions at all times.

What to bring

Snorkel, mask and fins, and light and alkaline batteries are good basics to have. Rental equipment quality and maintenance varies, as does availability. Check with your chosen operator beforehand what is and is not available for hire. A Swiss army style knife and/or a basic tool kit may come in handy.

Money exchange

The Indonesian rupiah (Rp) has fluctuated wildly over the last few years. Banks and currency exchanges in major cities will change major currencies but the US dollar is always the best bet. Bali's small money-changers offer good rates but are well known for trickery and sleight of hand. US notes must be clean, unmarked and not torn or they may be refused or changed at a lower rate. Euros are also easy to change in tourist areas. Traveler's checks are rarely accepted and so are really not worth the trouble. The best bet is to bring your ATM card from home. All major networks, such as Visa, Mastercard, Cirrus, Maestro, etc. are online. Stock up on rupiah at ATMs and keep some US cash for the more remote areas. This is much safer than bringing all your funds for the trip. VISA and MC are widely accepted, Amex less so. Credit card payments usually incur a fee of around 3 percent.

EAST KALIMANTAN
Derawan and Sangalaki

Traveling to Derawan and Sangalaki is not easy, but for guaranteed mantas and big fish almost anyone should make the effort. Operators will assist with transfers and domestic flight bookings but be aware that baggage allowances can be quite limited, so excess fees may apply.

There are a limited number of operators that offer dive and stay packages for diving the sites of Kakaban, Sangalaki, Derawan and Maratua.

Derawan Dive Resort This resort is operated by Sulawesi-based Tasik Divers and offers dive and stay packages on Derawan Island. Advance booking is required. Tel/24h: +62 431 824445 or (manager) 0821 89262599; www.derawandivelodge.com; info@derawandivelodge.com.

Sangalaki Dive Resort Based on Sangalaki Island, dive and stay packages are available. Contact is through their website: www.sangalakiresort.net.

NORTH SULAWESI
Manado

Manado, the entry point to diving North Sulawesi, is a large city and well connected by air to the rest of Indonesia. The Dr Sam Ratulangi airport is 7 km outside of town and taxi cabs are readily available. If you reserve ahead with one of the dive operators, they will meet you at the airport.

In the past, just getting to Manado was a

long and expensive proposition but this has now changed. There are direct flights from/to Singapore. Manado receives domestic flights from Makassar and Jakarta on a daily basis.

Accommodation

There is now a multitude of hotels available to travelers, ranging from luxurious 4-star properties at US$300+ a day to small, simple *losmen* at US$15 a day. However, if you come to Manado to dive seriously, or even as a serious snorkeler, there is no reason to stay anywhere except at one of the many dive resorts.

Formed in 1998, the **North Sulawesi Watersports Association** (www.divenorthsulawesi.com) now serves as the primary forum for marine tourism operators in the area. Besides promoting North Sulawesi as a world-class marine eco-tourism destination, the NSWA serves to allow members to voice their concerns and actively prevent environmental degradation in Bunaken National Park, the Lembeh Straits and other reef areas of North Sulawesi through cooperation with NGOs and government agencies in solving common environmental problems.

At the core of NSWA's efforts to protect North Sulawesi's rich but threatened marine resources is an innovative program of "3Es"—Employment, Education and Enforcement.

The NSWA strongly believes that an important way to relieve the pressure on North Sulawesi's reefs is to provide alternative employment to villagers who otherwise depend on extracting reef resources. The NSWA's programs to achieve this goal include a commitment from all members to recruit staff from local villages within the park. Additionally, the NSWA has instituted a village handicrafts program to produce a variety of reef-friendly handicrafts for sale to tourists, including embroidered marine life handkerchiefs, coconut shell carvings of marine animals and miniature replicas of traditional dugout canoes. Numerous villagers in Bunaken are also now employed in patrol and entrance fee systems.

Educational programs by NSWA include production of reef-friendly tourism information brochures, a television video on the problems of marine trash disposal, beach clean-ups and book donations to schools, with the centerpiece of their educational efforts a scholarship program designed to provide young adults from villages within Bunaken National Park and the Lembeh Strait with educational marine-related opportunities in local universities. The NSWA also sponsors younger children from poor families to attend primary school.

Regarding enforcement, NSWA's active participation in the development of an entrance fee system for Bunaken National Park has insured sustainable financing for an effective patrol system to curb illegal and destructive practices, such as blast and cyanide fishing techniques. The association also instituted a ban on all anchoring within Bunaken National Park and has brought in internal regulations to prevent degradation of dive sites by tourism activities. In some areas, the NWSA has funded mooring buoys.

Finances generated through the marine park entrance fee system are used to fund numerous worthwhile projects within the park.

Dive operators

Bunaken and Siladen

Siladen Resort and Spa An upmarket eco resort on Siladen island with private bungalows and swimming pool, dive and stay packages, courses, nitrox, equipment hire available. Up to 3 dives per day plus night dive. Home of the Siladen Island Turtle Sanctuary. Tel: +62 (0) 431 856 820; www.siladen.com; info@siladen.com.

Two Fish Divers Reputable Bunaken-based dive resort, courses up to instructor level, dive and stay packages with a range of bungalows. Has resorts also in Lembeh and Nusa Lembongan, multi-location packages available. Tel: +62 (0) 813 5687 0384; www.twofishdivers.com; info@twofishdivers.com.

Living Colours Diving Resort Upmarket Bunaken dive resort. Tel: +62 (0) 812 430 6063; www.livingcoloursdiving.com; info@livingcoloursdiving.com.

The Village Bunaken Pleasant all inclusive dive resort and spa located on Bunaken Island. Tel: +62 8134 0757 268; www.bunakenvillage.com; info@bunakenvillage.com.

Tasik Ria Resort Manado Diving resort option based on mainland Manado. Tel: +62 (0) 431 824 445; www.tasikria.com; info@tasikria.com.

Lembeh Strait

Divers Lodge Lembeh Eight eco bungalows catering for up to 14 people with fan cooling and hot water, all with views over the strait. Good value dive and stay packages include 3 meals per day, 2–3 boat dives per day plus night dive options, unlimited dive times, tailored schedules also possible. Nitrox available. Two destination trips available with Weda Reef and Rainforest Resort, Halmahera. www.diverslodgelembeh.com; info@diverslodgelembeh.com.

Kungkungan Bay Resort Upmarket resort with all inclusive bungalows situated in a private bay. Nitrox, equipment hire, courses and swimming pool. Web: www.divekbr.com.

Lembeh Resort Upmarket dive resort and spa overlooking the Lembeh Strait. Renowned for being a center for world-class photographers with extensive camera facilities, the only operator in Lembeh with both an onsite, full-time dedicated Photo Pro and a Marine Biologist, camera and housing repairs available in resort. Lembeh's leading operator with excellent dive guides, small groups, first class service and a dedicated team of professionals. Resort offers a swimming pool, poolside bar, a la carte and buffet restaurant, spa, luxurious surroundings and a touch of class throughout. Highly recommended. Tel: +62 438 550 3139; www.lembehresort.com; info@lembehresort.com.

It is worth noting that the following operators have resorts on both Bunaken and Lembeh: **Two Fish Divers** www.twofishdivers.com; **Bastiano's** www.bastianos.com; **Froggies Divers** www.divefroggies.com; **Murex Dive**, the original operators in the area with a wealth of experience, www.murexdive.com.

Bangka Island

Murex Dive Resorts Murex operates resorts in Manado and Bangka and also works with Lembeh Resort in the Lembeh Straits, enabling them to offer 3 destination trips with logistics taken care of. **Murex Manado** offers excellent diving around the Manado coastline and in the Bunaken Marine Park. The resort offers a range of rooms in a tropical garden setting on the seafront. **Murex Bangka** boasts stunning diving around Bangka Island and the northern tip of the Sulawesi coastline. Accommodation in Bangka is in beachfront bungalows looking out onto a white sand beach. Both resorts are family friendly with top-class guides, excellent service and years of experience in the area. Tel: +62 (0) 431 838774; www.murexdive.com; reservations@murexdive.com.

Togean Islands

There are now a handful of operators in the Togean Islands, most of which will assist with the logistics of traveling there.

Black Marlin Dive Resort Beautifully located on Kadidiri Bay, dive and stay packages, range of accommodation, restaurant and bar, massage center, dive center, equipment hire, daily dive trips, PADI and SSI courses, pickup/drop off service by boat from Wakai, experienced guides and small groups. Tel: +62 (0) 856 5720 2004; www.blackmarlindiving.com.

Walea Diving Resort and Spa Upmarket resort on Walea Bahi Island. Offers pickups and transfers from Luwuk Airport. Tel: +62 (0) 411 402 101; www.waleadiveresort.com.

SOUTH AND SOUTHEAST SULAWESI

Selayar

With stunning reefs and incredible wall dives, beautiful beaches and varied marine life, the central and southern regions of Sulawesi are a diver's dream.

Selayar Dive Resort Diving and full board accommodation packages, boutique eco beach resort with 8 bungalows, all with hot water and ocean views, AC available, restaurant and dive center, maximum of 15 minutes to dive sites. The area around the resort is a protected no-take zone and offers the best dive sites around Selayar Island. Closed May–October due to sea conditions. www.selayar-dive-resort.com or www.selayar-dive-resort.de; info@selayar-dive-resort.com.

Mangga Lodge German dive resort in Bira offering full board dive and stay packages. Diving is around Bira and neighboring islands. Web: www.mangga-lodge.com.

Wakatobi and Tomia

Now home to a number of dive operations, diving in the Wakatobi Marine Park is becoming more accessible and offers a stunning diversity of marine life and world-class dive sites.

Wakatobi Dive Resort Luxury eco-dive resort based on Onemobaa Island offering a range of individual bungalows, full-board dive and stay packages, up to 3 boat dives per day plus night dives and unlimited house reef dives. Nitrox, equipment hire, courses and private guide options available. Air transfers from Bali using the resort's private plane and airstrip on neighboring Tomia Island. Also operates the Pelagian Liveaboard. Tel: +62 (0) 361 759 669; www.wakatobi.com; office@wakatobi.com.

Tomia Scuba Dive Dive center on Tomia Island, offers diving only or full-board dive and stay packages using local guest houses with choice of fan or AC rooms. Daily dive trips, night dives and equipment hire available. Web: www.tomiascubadive.com.

Wangi Wangi

Wakatobi Patuno Resort Dive resort on Wangi Wangi with a range of bungalows. Full board dive and stay packages with 2–3 dive day options, free airport transfers from Wangi

Wangi. Equipment hire and courses available. Tel: +62 (0) 811 4002221; www.wakatobipatunoresort.com; info@wakatobipatunoresort.com.

JAVA

Jakarta is the center of Indonesia's government and commerce as well as being the hub for diving West Java and Pulau Seribu. There are several dive operators in the city to choose from. While these diving centers primarily provide scuba diving instruction, they also organize regularly scheduled weekend trips.

Jakarta and Pulau Seribu

Jakarta dive centers/trip organizers
Divemasters Jalan Bangka Raya No. 39A pela Mampang Jakarta 12720. Tel: +62 (0) 21 7199045; www.divemasters.co.id.

Bubbles Dive Center Jl. Guru Mughni No. 18, Jakarta. Tel: +62 (0) 21 52922233; www.bubblesdivecenter.com.

Kristal Klear Dive Hotel Kristal, Jl. Tarogong Raya, Cilandak Barat, Jakarta Selatan 12430. Tel: +62 (0) 21 75818025. www.kristalkleardive.com.

Pulau Seribu resorts
Alam Kotok All inclusive resort on Kotok Island. Tel: +62 (0) 21 5356958; www.alamkotok.co.id.

Sepa Island Beach Resort All inclusive resort. Tel: (agent) +62 (0) 21 68274005; www.sepaisland.com.

BALI

To make someone jealous, tell them you're going to Bali. The word itself will conjure up an intoxicating vision of a tropical paradise.

The waters off Bali are very rich, and while the diving is not as immediately impressive as that in Eastern Indonesia, it is very good, and gets more interesting the more you dive. Bali's combination of beautiful surroundings, convenient diving, tourist services and interesting culture is hard to beat.

Getting there
Flights to Bali arrive at the Ngurah Rai International Airport (airport code: DPS). Despite often being referred to as "Denpasar", it is actually on the isthmus connecting the Bukit Badung peninsula to Bali, much nearer to Kuta Beach than to Bali's capital city. Numerous daily domestic and international flights connect to Ngurah Rai. Most international airlines flying into Ngurah Rai have offices in Bali. Check with your flight operator for their Bali office contact details prior to departure from your home country if they are not included on your travel itinerary.

Getting around
Airport taxis One-way fares from Ngurah Rai Airport to the tourist centers are fixed. You pay a cashier inside and receive a coupon, which you surrender to your driver. (There will be touts and freelancers offering their services but these are never a better deal. It is faster and cheaper to go to the official airport taxi counter at the exit to the terminal.) If you are using taxis for getting around, it is wise to agree with the driver that he will operate the meter rather than trying to haggle a fare.

Minibuses Many major hotels have minibuses and cars for hire with a driver or an English-speaking driver/guide. Rates vary according to the distance you wish to travel, number of passengers and type of vehicle. Check with your hotel what is on offer. Some hotels also offer free shuttle services to the major malls and shopping areas.

Bemos Public minibuses in Bali (usually small green buses) are called *bemos*. They drive circular routes and passengers simply flag them down and hop on and hop off. This is the way the Balinese travel and is the cheapest way to get around the island. Fares are very cheap, particularly if you can speak a little Indonesian. Rp5,000 is an acceptable amount for a short distance. If traveling a longer route, expect to pay up to Rp10,000. Be careful that the drivers do not "misunderstand" and ask for a taxi rate as this will be considerably more expensive and will not guarantee a private ride.

For a diving visitor to Bali, *bemos* are most useful for short day trips around the area or to hop locally around town. Get one of your diving guides or someone at the hotel to explain the ins and outs of the local routes.

Vehicle rental It is best to leave the driving in Bali to someone who knows how to negotiate the roads and traffic. The roads are narrow, twisting and full of hazards—unmarked construction sites, chickens, dogs, children, scooters and motorcycles as wide as cars due to huge baskets of produce, and tough, unflinching truck drivers, to name just a few. You can rent a small (150cc) motorcycle for up to US$10 per day. You will not be asked to show your license by the vendor but an international license is required by law and the police issue fines to tourists driving without the correct documentation. A motorcycle helmet is also required and strongly recommended.

Renting a car runs to US$20 per day for little Suzuki jeeps, more for larger, more comfortable Toyota Kijangs. Rent through an agency or from numerous local rental companies. Ask at your hotel or comb the streets where there's an agent on nearly every block. Be sure your rental includes insurance for loss and damage. The same regulations regarding driving licenses apply to motorcycles (see above)

Diving and photography equipment

It is possible to buy both diving equipment and photography equipment in Bali and Jakarta. Outside of these areas usually requires an operator to ship it and it takes too long. Equipment reatilers include:

Divemasters Indonesia Aqualung supplier with retail outlets in both Bali and Jakarta. Also stock Apeks, Trident, Suunto, Underwater Kinetics, Sea and Sea, Intova, Light and Motion, Ikelite, Bauer compressors and Luxfer cylinders. Aqualung service and repairs also carried out. Web: www.divemasters.co.id. Email: enquiries sales@divemasters.co.id.

Bali Branch: Jalan Ngurah By Pass Rai No. 314, Sanur, Denpasar 80228. Tel: +62 (0) 361 283138; Fax: +62 (0) 21285736.
Jakarta Branch: Jalan Bangka Raya No. 39A Pela Mampang 12720. Tel: +62 (0) 217199045; Fax: +62 (0) 217198974.

Dive Sport Bali ScubaPro supplier based in Sanur, Bali. Also stock Uwatec, BARE, Sub Gear and GoPro. Repairs and mainainance services available. Staff are helpful and the service is excellent. Jalan By Pass Ngurah Rai No. 25 B. Tel: +62 (0) 361283463; www.divesportbali.com; info@divesportbali.com.

Ocean King Mares dive equipment supplier based in Sanur, Bali. Jalan By Pass Ngurah Rai No. 19. Next to Lotte Marte traffic lights. Tel: +62 (0) 361710990; www.okdiveshop.com; sales@okdiveshop.com.

Dive operators

Bali is home to literally hundreds of dive operators and, in general, the standards are above average. However, the range of services available in Bali can vary from excellent to frightening. It is worth sticking to a reputable operator who provides decent equipment hire, experienced guides and professional services and facilities.

Most operators on the island are based around the south, particularly around Sanur where most of the major dive schools have set up their bases. Some of these maintain branches, with tanks and compressors, in the northwest or on the east coast, and there are local operators clustered around the most popular dive areas, such as Tulamben, Padang Bai, Pemuteran and on Nusa Lembongan.

Bali is not very big, and you could dive any site on a day trip starting from a hotel anywhere in the south. We don't recommend this, however, as you probably will spend half of your vacation cooped up in the back of a van or minibus as your driver fights his way through an unending stream of local traffic.

If this is your first trip to Bali for diving, you should plan to stay at Tulamben for at least a couple of days. This is the most popular purely diving area, and from here you can run across to Menjangan on a day trip without too much trouble (it is a pleasant drive along the relatively empty north coast road; there is nothing pleasant about the drive from the south) or, going the other way, run down to Padang Bai to dive the east coast. A few days based on Nusa Lembongan also allows you to explore the dive sites around Lembongan and its neighbouring island, Nusa Penida, a must if you are hoping to see manta rays or the oceanic sunfish.

If you are a serious diver, and you have the time, a "dive safari" is highly recommended. This involves staying a few days at Pemuteran, diving Menjangan, then a few days at Tulamben, diving that area, then a few days at Candidasa or Padang Bai, diving the east coast, and finally a few days staying on Nusa Lembongan to catch the drift dives around Nusa Penida. Operators in the south also offer day trips by boat to Penida but the operators based on Lembongan arrive at the sites earlier. Most operators in Lembongan will also assist you with logistics. This will give you a taste of the island's different diving areas and also its different towns and environments with the minimum amount of driving.

Any of the bigger dive operators will book you a package that includes any combination of the sites. Booking in advance is recommended, especially for diving during the peak season from July to October.

Courses

Like everywhere else in the world, and for the same business and marketing reasons, most of the operators in Bali are or have become PADI affiliated (some SSI, but on a smaller scale), with the larger operators offering 5 star services and everything from discovery dives to instructor level training. Dive courses are competitively priced, averaging US$350-500 for an open water certification.

Bali is not a bad place to learn to dive, and Tulamben and the east coast probably offer the easiest conditions for this. If you decide to do this, we recommend that you make your decision on who to take a course from based on the knowledge, attitude and experience of the person who will be teaching you.

Prices

The cost of diving in Bali is pretty standard among operators, and is almost always priced in dollars. A basic day's package, including two full tanks, weights, transportation and a guide, runs US$40-60 for shore dives (e.g. Pemuteran, Tulamben), US$65-90 for a dive that requires a boat ride (e.g. Menjangan, Tepekong, Penida if diving from Lembongan), and US$100-150 for a dive that requires a long boat ride (e.g. the far side of Nusa Penida from Sanur, Gili Selang).

NORTHWEST BALI

This is the furthest area from the airport and the resorts of the south. Although most of Bali's operators offer Menjangan packages, unless you want to spend half of your day on the road, you are better off staying at one of the resorts in the area. Those in Pemuteran offer the most variety with the majority of upmarket operators and resorts being positioned directly on the beachfront. Cheaper accommodation and homestays are available back from the main road.

Werner Lau Dive centers based at both Pondok Sari and Matahari Beach Resort and Spa. Both centers offer nitrox, equipment hire, courses, fun diving within the Menjangan Park and Pemuteran and dive and stay packages. Staying outside of the two resorts in local accommodation is also an option. Local hotel pickups provided. www.wernerlau.com; bali@wernerlau.com.

Bali Diving Academy Based on Pemuteran Beach. Daily fun diving, courses, equipment hire and dive and stay packages at either Taman Sari or Amertha Villas. Tel: +62 (0) 361 270252; www.subali.com; info@scubali.com.

Mimpi Resort Menjangan Large resort offering dive and stay packages; also with a resort in Tulamben. Tel: +62 (0) 362 94497; www.mimpi.com; info@mimpi.com.

Tulamben and Amed

Many divers travel to Tulamben as part of a day trip package booked through one of the larger operators based in Sanur. The car journey can be long, around 3 hours or longer if there is traffic. From 9am onwards, as day trippers start to arrive at the dive sites, the diving can become very crowded, particularly on the wreck.

Operators in Tulamben are able to start diving earlier when the sites are still quiet. Most offer tanks, weights and equipment rental, along with guides. Tulamben offers a range of accommodation to suit all budgets and there are some excellent dive resorts now offering high-end dive and stay packages.

Villa Markisa An upmarket dive resort based on the outskirts of Tulamben providing quiet, relaxing surroundings and high-end accommodation with swimming pool, spa facilities and restaurant. Dive center offers Nitrox, equipment hire, experienced guides and two purpose-built speedboats. The resort offers excellent access to dive sites, including the *Liberty* wreck. The house reef here is "Seraya Secrets", which is located directly in front of the resort. Dive and stay packages and pickup and drop off services available. Tel: +62 (0) 8123873108; www.villa-markisa.com; info@villa-markisa.com.

Tauch Terminal Tulamben Dive Resort Well situated on the beach directly in front of the Coral Garden Dive Site. Offers daily fun diving and dive courses in Tulamben and day trip boat safaris to Amed, Padang Bai, Nusa Penida and Menjangan. Two swimming pools, accommodation (dive and stay packages available), restaurant, bar, spa, equipment hire

and nitrox available. Pickup and drop off service. Professional operation, based in a beautiful resort, small groups and experienced guides. Tel: +62 (0) 361 774504; www.tulamben.com.

Tulamben Wreck Divers www.tulambenwreckdivers.com Tel: +62 (0) 363 23400. PADI Dive center with a range of accommodation and swimming pool. PADI courses and daily fun diving at Tulamben sites and day trips to further afield around Bali.

Mimpi Resort Tulamben Large resort offering dive and stay packages also with a resort in Menjangan. Tel: +(62) 363 21642; www.mimpi.com; tulamben@mimpi.com or info@mimpi.com.

Padang Bai and Candidasa

It is not too inconvenient to dive the east coast sites from the south, nor is it difficult to dive them from Tulamben (the drive is more pleasant). But if you are serious about this area, it is best to stay in either Candidasa or Padang Bai. These sites are very dependent on conditions. It's nice to be able to look out at the actual water you are going to be diving in the mornings and evenings, to get a feel for what you are up against.

Padang Bai is a quiet and somewhat odd little town. The local Balinese community seems very tight and still curious about the ways of foreigners, as if this isn't a tourist town at all. Yet this is the terminus of the Bali–Lombok ferry and a constant stream of backpacking tourists pass through.

Candidasa itself is quiet and less crowded than Kuta and Sanur to the south, but it is a veritable New York City compared to Tulamben. It has numerous hotels, resorts and homestays and plenty of restaurants.

Bali Scuba Organized and professional operator based in Sanur offering 2–3 dive trips including hotel pickups and drop offs, transfers to Padang Bai, lunch and diving. Tel: +62 (0) 361288610; www.baliscuba.com; letsdive@baliscuba.com.

Geko Dive Established operator based in Padang Bai. Tel: +62 (0) 36341516; www.gekodivebali.com; info@gekodivebali.com.

Aquamarine Diving Bali Sanur-based operator offering hotel pickups and drop offs, 2–3 dives around Padang Bai including lunch. Tel: +62 (0) 361 4738020; www.aquamarine-diving.com; info@aquamarinediving.com.

Nusa Penida and Lembongan

Operators based in the south of Bali (Sanur) offer 2–3 dive trips to Nusa Penida, but by far the best way to explore these sites is by staying on Nusa Lembongan, Penida's smaller neighboring island. Nusa Lembongan is home to around 20 dive centers that offer 2 dive trips each day to the sites around Penida, Lembongan and Ceningan. Due to their proximity to the sites, the Lembongan boats tend to arrive earlier and the local guides have extensive experience, a major plus when diving in areas with current. Lembongan has a range of hotels from 5 star luxury with fine dining to a myriad of local homestays. Lembongan is often compared to Bali 20 years ago before major tourism took hold. If nothing else, the views over the seaweed farms in the Bay to Mount Agung at sunset are stunning.

World Diving Lembongan Reputable dive center offering daily fun diving trips and PADI courses from beginner to assistant instructor. Operates the only large *jukung* (comfortable and spacious,traditional outrigger boat) on the island plus smaller speedboats, equipment hire. Professional service, experienced guides, small dive groups and safety conscious. Tel: +62 (0) 8123900686; www.world-diving.com; info@world-diving.com.

Blue Corner Dive A 5 star PADI IDC facility located to the north of Jungutbatu offering a full range of PADI dive courses (including professional levels) and fun diving, equipment hire, bar and accommodation attached. Friday nights at the Blue Corner Bar are popular amongst divers. www.world-diving.com; info@bluecornerdive.com.

Other reputable dive operators based on Nusa Lembongan include:

Big Fish Diving Based at Secret Garden Bungalows and also offering courses, fun diving, accommodation packages and yoga at the Yoga Shack; www.bigfishdiving.com.

Two Fish Divers Also offer courses, fun diving and accommodation packages at Villa Jepun. www.twofishdivers.com.

Lembongan Dive Center Locally owned operation offering PADI courses and fun diving. www.lembongandivecenter.com.

Bali Diving Acadamy Based at No. 7 Bungalows offering PADI courses and fun diving, dive centers also located around mainland Bali. Multiple destination trips are available. www.scubali.com.

THE SOUTH

Most of Bali's tourist services and dive operators are clustered in the south, mainly around Sanur, Kuta and Seminyak. We would use a south-based operator only for diving at Nusa Penida if you do not have time to take a trip to Nusa Lembongan, or for a single day on the east coast. Because of travel time, for diving the northwest or for serious diving in Tulamben or the east coast, it is better to stay in those areas.

Kuta

Kuta has grown up around the beach to become the tourist center of Bali. It now extends north up to Legian and bustles with activity, its streets and tiny alleyways lined with shops, restaurants, bars, nightclubs and homestays. Kuta is now a popular destination for younger backpackers, nightclub goers and sun seekers. If you are expecting a quiet Balinese town, then you will be disappointed. Kuta is where the action is!

AquaMarine Diving Reputable and experienced operator offering courses, fun diving and hotel pickups and drop offs. Jalan Petitenget 2A, Kuta, Bali. Tel: +62 (0) 3614738 020 or outside of office hours (emergency) +62 (0) 85339465151; www.aquamarinediving.com; info@aquamarinediving.com.

Sanur

Sanur was Bali's first resort town and is, in a sense, the gray eminence of the tourist triangle. Compared to Kuta, it is quiet and dignified (or just dull, depending on your point of view and, inescapably, your age) and compares to Nusa Dua as old wealth does to new. The town is very quiet at night and the beach here, protected by the reef flat, is very calm. People who intend to spend a long time on Bali often stay in Sanur.

Bali Scuba Friendly, organized, experienced and professional 5 star PADI Career Development Center, full range of courses from introductory dives to instructor levels, purpose-built dive training pool, daily fun diving trips to all areas of Bali and Penida, hotel pickups and drop offs, all vehicles with AC, equipment hire, nitrox, retail store. Tailor-made safaris also an option. Jl Danau Poso 46, Sanur. Tel: +62 (0) 361 288610; www.baliscuba.com; letsdive@baliscuba.com.

Other reputable operators in the Sanur area that offer excellent services include:

Crystal Divers www.crystal-divers.com
Blue Season Bali www.baliocean.com
Atlantis www.atlantis-bali-diving.com
Bali Diving Academy www.scubali.com (with operations in Tulamben, Pemuteran, Lembongan and Sanur)
D-Scuba Club www.d-scubaclub.com

Professional training in Sanur

Sanur is now at the forefront of professional training in Southeast Asia with instructor courses being held every month.

Bali Scuba is Indonesia's PADI award winning Career Development Center. Facilities include multi-media, air-conditioned classrooms, 4-meter-deep training pool, 3 course directors on staff, equipment rental, dive shop and store,

high-powered speedboats for easy access to dive sites, professional and friendly crew. Bali Scuba also offer a pass guarantee on instructor courses and good value for money. A range of free workshops are included in their pricing. For professional courses: www.bali-idc.com; letsdive@baliscuba.com.

Tanjung Benoa

Nusa Dua offers luxury, and isolation from touts, peddlers, stray dogs, cold water showers and other indignities. It's also quite antiseptic, preferred by the international jet set. The lodgings here are not cheap.

Bali Hai Diving Adventures Specialist operator for Lembongan Island and Nusa Penida offering packages for day trips and longer stays. Courses also available. Tel: +62 (0) 361720331; Fax +62 (0) 361720334; www.balihaicruises.com; sales@balihaicruises.com.

Recommended operator for multiple destinations

If you want flexibility, a taste of everything and are staying in South Bali, then **Bali Scuba** is an excellent choice. Based in Sanur, they offer day trips to Padang Bai, Tulamben, Nusa Penida and Lembongan, Amed, Seraya and the northern dive sites. They are a professional set up and provide hotel pickup and drop off and all logistics are dealt with for you. Equipment hire is available as is a full range of PADI Courses. Excellent guides, instructors and facilities. PADI award winning 5 star dive center. www.baliscuba.com; letsdive@bali-scuba.com.

EAST OF BALI

The season for the best diving conditions varies for many of the sites east of Bali. Like the sites in north Komodo, the best months to dive Moyo, Sangeang, Satonda and Maumere are from March through December. Sumba, in the south, is best from December through April.

Moyo Island

Amanwana Resort Once the preferred choice of Princess Diana, this opulent tent resort spoils guests with outstanding location, service, diving and dining. Tel: +62 (0) 371 22233; Fax: +62 (0) 371)22288; www.amanresorts.com; amanwana@amanresorts.com.

Liveaboards (Komodo/Raja Ampat)

Seven Seas A 45-meter Indonesian sailing schooner with 8 state cabins for 16 guests. www.thesevenseas.net; info@thesevenseas.net.

Amira A 52-meter Indonesian style *phinisi* with 8 double cabins and 2 single cabins. www.amira-indinesia.com.

Arenui A 43-meter luxury liveaboard with 8 cabins catering for 16 guests. www.thearenui.com; info@thearenui.com.

Aurora A 40-meter *phinisi* style liveaboard covering a number of destinations; www.auroraliveaboard.com; info@auroraliveaboard.com.

Ikan Biru Excellent budget liveaboard option which is great for those with limited schedules, stationed in Komodo National Park operating on a hop on, hop off basis. Up to 8 recreational divers or 6 technical divers, sleeping arrangements on the upper deck. www.ikanbiru.com; info@bluemarlinkomodo.com.

Pindito Reputable liveaboard with 8 cabins which comfortably accommodate up to 16 guests. Pindito has over 20 years cruising experience in Indonesian waters and offers both Raja Ampat and Komodo routes plus others. Tel: +41 (0) 448700207; www.pinditio.com; info@pindito.com.

Tambora Purpose-built mid-range liveaboard with 8 suites catering for 16 guests. Nitrox and gear rental available. www.tamboradive.com; info@tamboradive.com.

Shakti A more budget option for Raja Ampat. www.shakti-raja-ampat.com.

Komodo

Komodo is a popular area for liveaboard operators although there are numerous shore-based operators in the harbor town of Labuanbajo on Flores. These operations are increasingly using more powerful speedboats that enables them to visit sites further into the park in single day trips, offering usually 2–3 dives.

Blue Marlin Komodo Facilities include speedboat-operated 3-dive trips, PADI courses with designated student boat, accommodation, purpose-built dive training pool, equipment hire, restaurant, bar, dive and stay packages (also operate Ikan Biru Liveaboard). Boats are equipped with GPS and VHF radios. Jalan Soekarno-Hatta. Tel: +62 (0) 81237757892; www.bluemarlinkomodo.com; info@bluemarlinkomodo.com.

Wicked Diving Day trips, liveaboard and dive training. Jalan Soekarno-Hatta. Tel: +62 (0) 81337182258; www.wickeddiving.com/komodo.

Dive Komodo Day trips, liveaboard and dive training. Jalan Soekarno-Hatta. Tel +62 (0) 385 41862; www.divekomodo.com.

The Komodo National Park encompasses the three main islands of Komodo, Rinca and Padar plus 26 smaller islands and was founded in 1980 to protect the world's largest species of lizard, the Komodo dragon. In 1991, it was declared a World Heritage Site by UNESCO and conservation efforts have been extended to cover all aspects of marine and terrestrial life. The park is protected from all types of destructive fishing practices, including dynamite fishing, cyanide and long-line fishing.

Dive operators in the Komodo area have a number of initiatives underway to help monitor, protect and conserve the natural environment, including reef monitoring, manta ray databases, mooring buoy projects and educational programs for local people. Divers who are visiting the area are urged to choose an operator who follows marine conservation-aware dive practices and who is involved in marine protection initiatives.

Alor

To dive Alor, guests must first fly to Kupang, the capital of West Timor. Since there are no international flights to Kupang getting to Alor requires a little planning. There are flights from Bali, but these typically have stopovers in towns like Maumere, Bima or Labuanbajo along the way. The travel time may be long and arduous but is well worth the effort.

For Kupang's only operator, DiveAlorDive (also trading as Dive Kupang Dive), guests must overnight in one of the hotels in Kupang before catching a morning flight to Kalabahi, Alor's provincial capital. Once there, you will lodge in basic but clean and comfortable *losmen* style rooms and depart early each morning for a 2/3/4 dive trip on a comfortable vessel with lunch and refreshments served after each dive. DiveAlorDive is managed by Donovan Whitford. (It was Donovan and his father Graeme who pioneered diving in the Alor archipelago and Donovan still guides all dives booked through DivaAlorDive.)

If divers are staying at one of the shore-based operations in the Alor archipelago, they are met from the airport in Alor (usually after an overnight stopover in Kupang), transferred to the harbor by car and then transferred to their resort by boat.

Liveaboard embarkation and disembarkation varies from operator to operator.

Dive Alor Dive Operated by Donovan Whitford since 1990. Tailor-made packages, including a range of accommodation in Kalabahi (small local hotels or guest houses only—do not expect anything more than basic in Kalabahi), up to 4 boat dives per day, equipment hire, domestic flight booking service, pickup service in Kupang, PADI courses available in English and Indonesian. Kupang and Alor combo packages available. Tel: +62 (0) 8123960107; www.divealordive.com; info@divealordive.com.

Alor Divers More upmarket French-managed dive eco-resort on Pantar Island offering full board dive and stay packages. www.alor-divers.com; info@alor-divers.com.

La Petite Kepa Budget accommodation and diving situated on Kepa Island. www.la-petite-kepa.com; la_petite_kepa@hotmail.com.

Banda Sea and Malukus

Much of the Banda Sea and the Maluku area remain solely liveaboard territory. However, there are shore-based operations in Ambon Bay which offer phenomenal muck diving and also in Weda Bay (Halmahera) for wall diving.

Banda has two dive seasons, one in April, the other in October. The months before and after are usually quite good. Visibility in the off-season is restricted to 15-25 meters, but during the peak months can reach upwards of 40-50 meters.

Maluku Divers Centrally positioned on the west side of Ambon Bay, which is renowned for the best muck diving sites in the area. Diving packages available, up to 4 dives per day plus night dives, nitrox, equipment hire, camera room, camera processing desks and lights in all rooms, full board accommodation, tailored packages available. Airport pickups and drop-offs included. Tel: +62 (0) 9113365307; www.divingmaluku.com; info@divingmaluku.com.

Weda Reef and Rainforest Resort Weda Resort offers diving, birding and eco tours. The resort features 6 cabins overlooking the bay. Full board dive and stay packages are available. The resort operates two speedboats equipped with GPS and oxygen. The resort has been constructed with minimal impact to the environment. Tel: +62 (0) 8124433754 or +62 (0) 81340044758; www.wedaresort.com; info@wedaresort.com.

West Papua

Papua Diving Resorts Owned and operated by Max Ammer who pioneered diving in Raja Ampat. Papua Diving operates two resorts on Kri Island, both of which offer a range of dive packages, full board accommodation, PADI courses, nitrox and equipment hire. Papua diving is committed to conservation projects in the area through the work of the RARCC

(Raja Ampat Research and Conservation Center) and donates 10 percent of their profits to conservation and community initiatives. Across both resorts, Papua Diving employs almost 100 local Papuan staff who they have trained and continue to support. www.papua-diving.com; info@papua-diving.com.

Kri Eco Resort Offers dive and stay packages in rustic water bungalows with fans and choice of shared or private bathroom. Dive packages include up to 4 boat dives per day.

Sorido Bay This is a truly remarkable resort which offers the remoteness of Raja Ampat combined with the all of the comforts of home. High-end dive and stay packages with luxury cottages and upmarket service. Packages include up to 4 boat dives per day.

Misool Eco Resort Luxury resort situated on Batbitim Island, full board dive and stay packages with stunning water bungalows over an exquisite aquamarine lagoon boasting a population of juvenile black tip sharks. Dive center, conservation center, daily fun diving; 4 dives per day and night dives, nitrox available, equipment hire and PADI courses available on request in advance, spa, speedboat transfers from Sorong. www.misoolecoresort.com; info@misoolecoresort.com.

Liveaboards in West Papua

If you are opting for a liveaboard experience in West Papua, there are a number of considerations that you should take into account when selecting your operator, including:

Price

Make sure you are completely clear on what is and is not included in the price prior to booking. Operators vary in what they charge additionally for.

Food

Most ships, particularly high end, cater a mix of European and Asian menus. The more expensive packages include imported meats and condiments. In some packages soft drinks and alcohol are included but in others these are billed separately. If you have any allergies or dietary requirements, let your operator know when booking. Most requirements/requests will not be an issue if operators know in advance.

Tenders

Tenders may be fiberglass, aluminum or inflatable, but all are powered by outboard motors. For the environmentally minded, four-stroke engines are the least polluting outboard by far. Entry from the mother boat to the tender is usually by gangway. Getting in the tender after diving is most important. Is there a ladder or must you pull yourself up?

Air

Does the boat use airbanks or compressors? Airbanks allow tanks to be filled quickly and quietly, otherwise the compressors are working non-stop. Are the compressors regularly maintained? Is nitrox available?

Dive guides

Are the dive guides Western or Indonesian? Are all the guides internationally certified? Do the guides cater to photographers? Do the guides give thorough briefings before each dive?

Camera facilities

Are there camera tables? Are there dedicated rinse tanks for camera equipment? Are there plenty of sockets for chargers in the cabins? Is there an on-board TV for playback of video?

Comfort zone

Is there hot water? Are there on-deck showers? Are towels provided? Is there a water-maker on board? Is there adequate refrigeration? Does the crew speak English? Are the bathrooms private or shared? AC in the cabin?

Safety zone

Does the ship have life rafts and life preservers? Does the ship have radar, sonar and GPS? Does the ship have a satellite phone? Are safety sausages, dive computers and diver alert horns available? Do tenders have walkie talkies? Are there fire extinguishers readily accessible? Is there a ship's emergency briefing?

Communication
Does the ship have a satellite phone? Is there an email capability? Is there an on-board computer with maps and descriptions of dive sites? How can people contact you in case of an emergency? Can the ship access real-time weather reports?

Conservation
How does the ship handle its garbage? Do the guides routinely handle marine animals? Does the ship use moorings when available? Is the crew environmentally aware? Does the operator support local conservation groups?

The Philippines Practicalities
Philippines Telephone Country Code: 63

The Philippines is an island nation—it has 7,107 islands at the latest count. Travel and trade between the islands has been a predominant feature of life in the country for centuries. Tourism is a major dollar earner and there is no shortage of domestic destinations. The traveler these days also has a wide range of transportation options, from jet planes and air-conditioned coasters to simple inter-island ferries, fast super cats and colorful, crowded jeepneys. A welter of development throughout the islands is continuing to produce world-class hotels and resorts, both luxury and budget in concept, in some of the most unique and intriguing corners of the country. Eco-tourism is gaining ground as well, and divers arrive in droves to discover what must be one of the best organized industries in Asia, given the tyranny of distance and poor communications which still plague some parts of the country.

In Manila and many provincial capitals, such as Cebu and Davao, giant shopping malls are becoming part of the everyday scene. The Philippines, despite its often stormy political and economic fluctuations, continues to grow at a pace which amazes even some Filipinos themselves, but the outgoing, friendly character of the people is more or less intact.

Money

The currency in the Philippines is the Philippine peso (Php). The prices listed below have been converted into US dollars at a rate of 45 Philippine peso to 1 USD.

Air travel

The county's leading gateway, **Ninoy Aquino International Airport (NAIA)** in Pasay City, Manila, has been subject to much criticism in the local press for its lack of infrastructure. In fact, if travelers follow a few simple rules, they will survive NAIA easily. After exiting the airport, one can avail of the coupon taxi system, which, although costing more than a regular taxi, is a fixed price paid in full before departure which negates the need for any "bargaining" with the driver. If you are being met by a hotel or travel agent's representative, look for the person carrying a sign identifying themselves after exiting customs. NAIA has a comprehensive English website which also contains travel advice, terminal information and FAQs.

You can also opt for a DOT approved metered taxi. Although technically monitored by the DOT, in our experience there may sometimes be an attempt to negotiate what is supposed to be a metered taxi fare. Stick to your guns and request the meter be used.

Mactan International Airport on Mactan island, Cebu, is now a bustling airport handling numerous domestic airlines and it is also served by airlines flying direct from Japan, Singapore, Malaysia, Korea and elsewhere. Taxis in Cebu and Manila are *always* supposed to use their meters. Ignore any protestations to the contrary.

Both airports have tourist information centers, currency exchange facilities and duty free shops as well as car rental agencies and hotel hospitality desks.

There is a departure tax to pay when leaving. Check the airport website to check for the current rate or check with your dive operator. They will usually be able to tell you. International flights require you to check in at least two hours before departure as exit queues can be long. For domestic flights, you should arrive at least one hour in advance.

Do reconfirm your onward flight within 72 hours of departure unless your airline specifies otherwise and allow for the often heavy traffic, especially in Metro Manila and when it is raining.

Domestic airlines

Several domestic airlines serve the provinces. Prices are very reasonable, and the coverage is quite extensive. Divers (and other sport equipment carrying people) can pay an additional US$25 to Philippine Airlines for sports equipment. This will automatically increase your baggage allowance by 15 kg. To take advantage of this option, stating so when booking your ticket is best. Domestic flights require check-in one hour before departure. Unclaimed seats are often given away to standby passengers 35 minutes before take-off.

Domestic airports around the country are mostly quite efficient, though take-off and landings can sometimes be a bit hairy. Departure taxes are payable for domestic flights but note that regional airport charges vary. Manila airport has four terminals. Check which one your flight is leaving from in advance so you can let your taxi/driver know where to drop you.

Domestic airline destinations

Although domestic routes are subject to change, the following list of domestic airlines and the destinations they fly is accurate as of going to press.

Philippine Airlines Destinations: Manila, Cebu, Cagayan de Oro, Kalibo (Boracay), Puerto Princesa, General Santos. Reservations: www.philippineairlines.com or (632) 855-8888 (24 hours).

AirAsia and ZestAir Destinations: Manila (NAIA), Cebu, Davao, Kalibo/Boracay, Puerto Princesa, Tacloban, Tagbilaran. Reservations: www.airasia.com or (632) 742 2742 (7am–10pm daily).

Cebu Pacific Air Destinations: Manila, Clark, Iloilo, Cebu, Davao, Laoag, Taguegarao, Cauayan, Naga, Virac, Legaspi, San Jose,

Busuanga, Caticlan, Kalibo, Roxas, Tacloban, Bacolod, Puerto Princesa, Siargao, Surigao, Tagbilaran, Dumaguete, Butuan, Dagupan, Cagayan de Oro, Ozamis, Pagadian, Cotabato, Zamboanga, General Santos, Tawi-Tawi. Reservations: www.cebupacificair.com or Manila (632) 7020 888 and Cebu (6332) 230 8888.

Tigerair Philippines Destinations: Luzon, Clark, Manila, Puerto Princesa, Bacolod, Cebu, Iloilo, Kalibo/Boracay, Tacloban, Davao, General Santos, Cagayan de Oro, Butuan. Reservations: www.tigerair.com or (632) 798 4499 (5am–10pm daily).

Sky Jet Airlines Destinations: Manila, Coron, Batanes, Baler, Boracay. Reservations: www.skyjetair.com or (02) 863 133.

Staying in contact

Cell phones By far the easiest way to stay in touch from the Philippines is to buy a local SIM card on arrival. They sell them at most international airports even before you clear customs.

They are usually around a couple of dollars and this includes a small amount of credit to get you started. There are two main providers, **Smart** and **Globe**. There's little difference between the two in terms of cost, but if you are traveling away from major cities you might find one has much better reception that the other. It pays to wait until you arrive at your destination and then ask the locals which SIM they use.

Credit can be purchased in the form of a card which you scratch off a panel and input a code to your phone or it can be done electronically through the seller's cell phone. Credit (known as "Load") is usually purchased in Php50/100/500 vouchers and sellers add around 2–5 peso to the total (their commission). "Load" is sold at almost all small booths and streetside shops as well as in larger supermarkets and stores. Once you have credit on your phone, you can make calls which will be taken directly from your credit or you can buy a data package (which can include Internet) through the menu on your phone. *Note*: When you purchase a local SIM card, it needs to be registered. This process is done through the main SIM menu on your device but the instructions are in Filipino. The best way to deal with this is when you purchase the SIM ask the seller to register it too (some will do this automatically). It is not a strange request and only takes them a few minutes and they do not charge for it. They are doing it many times a day!

Internet Most cafés, bars, restaurants and resorts in tourist areas have free Wi-fi hotspots and you simply need to make a purchase (just a drink will suffice) and ask for the password. In more remote areas, such as Malapascua, Internet is available and in some places it is free whilst in others the operators sell packages. Very few areas in Philippines have no Internet coverage but as it is usually provided through cell phone networks. If you are in an area with no cell reception, it is unlikely that you will have Internet reception. If you need Internet access whilst you are away, check with your operator beforehand what the situation is, particularly if you are making a liveaboard trip. If you buy a local SIM card (see above), you can purchase data packages for Internet through your cell phone which you can then use directly to go online or "tether" as a mobile hotspot if you prefer to use your computer.

Land travel

Filipinos love to travel and there is always a way to get somewhere. A wide variety of buses, from luxury air-conditioned liners to diesel spewing behemoths serve anywhere that can be reached by road. Jeepneys and motorized tricycles go where the buses can't, which can make for exciting, if uncomfortable, excursions. Carry all your valuables with you, preferably in a belt bag, as bag slashings are not uncommon on some routes, especially on regular buses plying the Batangas to Manila route.

Sea travel

Many visitors who have the time might prefer the option of sailing between the islands. While luxury yachts can be chartered by the affluent few, several shipping lines, such as **WG&A**, **Negros Navigation** and **Sulpicio Lines** have excellent services connecting

Manila and Cebu, with dozens of ports around the country. Accommodation ranges from deck space to first-class suites, and there are quite passable restaurants and discos aboard some of the vessels.

Inter-Island travel around the Visayas is often on fast **Super Cat Ferrys**.

At some point, it will almost certainly be necessary for you to board a *banca* boat, the ubiquitous motorized outrigger canoe. Sit where the boatman tells you and be prepared to get splashed now and again. The driest part of the boat on a smaller *banca* is usually under the bow, so stow anything that has to be kept dry there. Taking a roll down dry bag is recommended for anything valuable (or electronic) that must stay dry.

Visas

Most foreign nationals with valid passports and an onward ticket are given a 21 day visa on arrival, depending on the visitor's country of origin. For longer trips, visa extensions up to one year can be arranged in the country at regional Bureau of Immigration offices or through a local travel agent, but if you plan to stay longer, you should apply for a 59 day Temporary Visitor's Visa at any Philippine Embassy or Consulate.

Health

The Philippines has some excellent medical facilities,and others which are not so excellent. Dentistry is cheap and often of extremely high standards, and there are several good medical centers in Manila.

Most sicknesses occur through over indulging in the many delicacies of the islands. Overexposure to the sun is another common cause of discomfort, especially for fair-skinned divers soaking up a few rays between dives. Proper precautions should be taken to avoid sunburn as the local remedy of applying vinegar or other, more pungent, liquids on affected parts is best avoided.

Tap water is often heavily chlorinated in cities and mostly not to be consumed before prolonged boiling outside of them, especially by those with delicate stomachs. Bottled mineral water is the safest option and is widely available, but watch out for the ice in the soft drinks and washed salads.

Weather

There are two seasons in the Philippines: the dry season (from March to May) and the rainy season (from June to February). Tropical depressions, storms and typhoons affect parts of the country from June to October, especially in the so-called "Typhoon Belt" from Southern Luzon to the Visayas.

Between storms, the weather is often quite balmy for long periods. December through February are the coolest months. Average temperature is 22° C, humidity is 77 percent.

Money exchange

Visitors can bring in any amount of currency, but you should declare any amount over US$3,000 or equivalent in cash to avoid any complications when exiting. The export of more than 1,000 pesos is disallowed, but note that it is necessary to produce official Central Bank Receipts issued by authorised currency exchange dealers to change your excess pesos back to another currency before leaving.

The easiest way to access funds in the Philippines is through ATMs drawing directly from your home bank (debit) account. Alternative banking, such as arranging transfers can be awkward in the Philippines. In an emergency, it is usually safer to use the Standard Chartered or the Hongkong Bank to have funds telegraphically transferred (TT'd) from outside the country. Most international credit cards are honored after verification. Most urban centers now have ATMs that will give a cash advance in local currency with a credit card. It is advisable to check first before booking into a resort or paying for services as some merchants cannot verify cards quickly. Traveler's checks are now almost completely outdated in the Philippines and not worth bothering with when ATMs are relatively easy to find.

Photography

There are few places which restrict the taking of photos,and there are always plenty of interesting subjects to shoot. In many areas, the locals, especially children, love to have their pictures taken and to view them on your camera screen.

Extras for digital cameras and their housings are not readily available outside of major population centers and many spares for cameras and strobes, especially O-rings, seals, gaskets, etc., are almost non-existent, so be sure to pack plenty of spares.

Communications

In recent years, the Philippines have undergone a communications revolution and even when you are diving in some of the most remote areas you will find that you still have a decent phone signal and in many resorts Wi-fi is available throughout the resort. The cheapest way to maintain communications with home is to purchase a local SIM card upon arrival. It is best to check with your operator first which service provider has the best reception in their area.

All telephone numbers listed in this section are listed with the local area code. If you are dialing from a landline with the same area code, drop the part in brackets. To dial any telephone, cellular or otherwise, from outside the country, drop the zero and add the international access code and country code (63). Thus, a Manila number 123 4567 becomes (02) 123 4567 when dialed from outside Manila and (63-2) 123 4567 when dialed from outside the country.

Note: To the absolute annoyance and frustration of subscribers, telephone numbers tend to change periodically as the country's booming telecommunication providers upgrade their systems.

Technical diving

Technical diving is widely available throughout the Philippines, IANTD, TDI, PADI, SSI and ANDI being the most popular certification agencies. Most areas frequented by divers have several interesting sites for "techies", such as caves and wrecks as well as deep drop-offs and walls. Needless to say, getting the proper instruction for any intended dive is vital, and there is no shortage of highly qualified technical instructors available at most destinations.

In 2001, John Bennett set the world record for the deepest mixed gas dive (308 meters) in Puerto Galera. Although this record has since been broken by divers in the Red Sea, the level of support he got from other local techies is a testament to the popularity and professionalism of technical divers in the Philippines.

Manila City code: 02

Manila Bay is not recommended as a dive spot. However, Manila is a good place to start planning your diving vacation as it is home to several retail stores worth a visit as well. The **Philippine Commission on Sports SCUBA Diving (PCSSD)** (www.divephilippines.com) is also headquartered in Manila. The PCSSD is the regulatory body of the local scuba industry. Registered dive operators are bound by a code of ethics and safety. The PCSSD operates two recompression chambers, one in Manila and one in Cebu. There is a hyperbaric chamber hotline which deals with both chambers: +63 928 242 6237. Whenever possible, check to see if the dive center you plan to dive with is registered as it can say a lot about the operator's integrity.

There are a number of other recompression chambers in the Philippines but divers should always check with their insurer prior to attending. It may be that your insurance company only approves certain facilities and most insurance policies require divers to contact them prior to seeking treatment.

The Philippine Diver (www.diver.com.ph/diver/) has been around for almost 20 years in magazine form and is now an unbiased and complete online resource for divers visiting the Philippines. The printed magazine is distributed to leading dive centers throughout the country (for free) and it provides news, dive site information, operator contact details and numerous articles. Tel: (+632) 713-8882, for more details.

Most liveaboard vessels and many resorts around the islands have offices in Manila and there are several dive tour specialists around town as well.

Aquaventure Whitetip Dive Supply (www.aquaventurewhitetip.com) One of the country's leading wholesale and retail suppliers of dive gear and related products, the company was formed when Whitetip Divers and Aquaventure Philippines merged in 2002. Branches are located in Cebu, Manila, Mactan, Puerto Galera and Boracay. Sells products from the following manufacturers: Apeks, Aqualung, Bauer (compressors), Luxfer and Catalina (tanks), Dive Rite, PADI, Suunto, Deep Sea, Intova, Nuvair, Tovatec, Catic, Coltri (compressors) and more.

Scuba World Inc (www.scubaworld.com.ph) Scuba World started out in 1988 and now operates in Makati City, Cebu, San Juan and Mactan. Scuba World Inc. operates a network of dive shops and supplies dive equipment, equipment servicing, diving courses and travel packages. They also have strong conservation and environmental policies. If you are looking to buy gear, they are stockists of the following manufacturers: Hollis, Mares, Aqualung, Suunto, Oceanic, Pelican, Underwater Kenetics, TUSA and others. For purchasing enquiries Email: sales@scubaworld.com.ph. The Makati City Branch can be contacted by telephone on (632) 8953 551; San Juan (632) 726 0115; BF Homes Branch (632) 809 4268; Boracay Branch (63-36) 288 3310; Cebu City (032) 254 9554; Mactan Branch (63-32) 495 1382.

Asia Divers (www.asiadivers.com) Another large equipment supplier in the Philippines with stores located in Puerto Galera (point@asiadivers.com), Manila (manila@asiadivers.com), Cebu (cebu@asiadivers.com), Boracay (boracay@asiadivers.com) and Alona (alona@asiadivers.com). Stores stock products from the following manufacturers: Cressi, Waterproof, Body Glove, L&W Compressors, Underwater Kinetics, PADI, Surface Marker, Divers Unlimited Internations (DUI), Apeks, Halcyon, and A.P. Valves, plus others.

Other dive centers around Manila you should check in with include:

Nautilus Dive & Sport Center Makati City. Specialists in equipment rental and sales.

Stockists of Apeks, Aqualung, Aquatec, Scubapro, Halcyon, OMS, Henderson, Unidive, Apollo, ORCA, Mares, Suunto, Uwatec, Pelicon, Poseidon, Bare, Ikelite plus others. Tel: (632) 403 9786 or (632) 664 2953; www.nautilus-dive.net; nautilusphilippines@gmail.com.

Ocean Zone Explorers 54 Timog Avenue, Quezon City, Philippines 1103. PADI and UTD Dive courses, equipment sale, rental and servicing. Dive trips to the following areas are offered; Anilao, Subic Bay, Puerto Galera, Bohol and Cebu. Tel: +63 2709 9001; www.oceanzoneexplorers.com; oceanzoneexplorers@instructor.net.

Cocktail Divers Large organization offering all inclusive diving services from day trips to holiday packages, including transfers, diving and accommodation. This organization operates in multiple regions across the Philippines so they are a good operator if you are looking to dive in more than one destination. Tel (Europe) +49 (0) 89 6429 9226 and (Philippines) +63 (0) 917 812 6625. www.cocktaildivers.com; info@cocktaidivers.com.

La Union City code: 072

Getting there

La Union is accessible by road from Manila. It takes around 6–7 hours depending on the time of day and the traffic. If you prefer not to rent a car, with or without a driver, there are several bus companies running regular air-conditioned buses daily to La Union from Manila. **Partas Transportation Company** terminal is a short taxi ride from the airport (816 Aurora Boulevard, Cubao, Quezon City) and they have buses running 24/7 from Quezon to Laoag. If you ask to be dropped off at Urbiztondo in San Juan, this is directly in front of the beach resorts. Bus fares should be less than US$10. Partas Transportation Company Tel: (+63) 2727 8278 or (+63) 2724 9820.

Autobus Transport Systems also operate buses from Manila to San Fernando from which San Juan is a short jeep ride away.

(Autobus Transport Systems: Dimasalang Street Cnr. Laong Laan Street, Sampaloc, Manila. Tel: (+63) 2735 8098). Buses are not in short supply and the transit is easy to arrange once you are in Manila. Other bus operators include Dominion Transit, Farinas Transit Company, Genesis Bus Lines, Rabbit Business Lines, RCJ Transit and Maria De Leon Transit.

Ocean Deep Dive Centre Ocean Deep offers all levels of training from beginner to professional as well as diving trips, equipment sales, rentals and hotel and travel reservations can also be made at Ocean Deep. Located in San Fernando, La Union. Tel: +63 (072) 700 0493. www.oceandeep.biz; twaukshun@yahoo.com.

Cocktail Divers See page 244 for services and contact details.

In La Union, jellyfish particles are quite common in the warmer upper layers of water at some times of the year, so full coverage, such as a lycra suit, is recommended. 14 Mile Reef and further north can be arranged. Diving is mainly done off *banca* boats, which can sometimes get a little hairy. A few miles to the north of San Fernando is a good surfing beach with cheap cottages at San Juan.

There are several smaller resorts next to each other along the coast here, all with reasonable rooms and good restaurants.

Sunset Bay Beach Resort This a reasonable option with a range of facilities and rooms starting from US$50 US per night. Canaooy, San Fernando, La Union, Philippines 2500. Tel: +63 (0) 726 075 907; www.sunsetbayphilippines.com; admin@sunsetbayphilippines.com.

Subic Bay City code: 047

Getting there

Just a 2-3 hour car drive from Manila, Subic is visited by hordes of duty free day trippers from Manila, eager to spend their duty free allowance at the stores inside the Free Port Zone, formerly a US Navy Base. If traveling by bus, **Victory Liners** is the easiest way to get there. They run several air-conditioned trips daily to and from

Olongapo, departing hourly from Manila from 4am. They have terminals in Pasay City, Caloocan, Sampaloc and Cubao. **Saulog Transit** is another popular bus company covering the route to Olongapo. They are based at Dr Lopez Jaena Street, Cavite City, Saulog. They operate hourly departures from 2am to 2pm. Tickets are under US$10.00 for both companies. From Olongapo City bus terminal, Subic Bay is just a quick jeepney ride and it is easy to organize.

For those who do not want to use buses, then taxis are available to Subic from Ninoy Aquino (Manila) Airport. Car hire is also easy to arrange (with or without a driver), although these options are more expensive than the bus companies.

A wide variety of accommodation is available locally, from 5 star hotels to small nipa huts and bungalows at prices to suit all pockets. The beaches bordering the bay are popular as weekend getaways for Manila-based families, and there is a variety of nightlife and dining options available.

Blue Rock Beach Resort is a popular place to stay along the beachfront in Baloy Long Beach, with rooms starting from around US$50 per night. All rooms have AC, hot water and minibar and there is a pool, bar, restaurant, dive center and a range of other water sports and activities on offer. Baloy Long Beach, Olongapo City, Bo. Barretto, Philippines. Tel: +63 (0) 917 805 0201 or Mobile +63 (0) 47 252 9978; www.bluerocksubic.com; bluerocksubic@yahoo.com.

There are several other places to park yourself, ranging from cheap backpacker rates with basic amenities to more upmarket places with a range of facilities.

El Coral Reef Dive Centre Offers a range of dive courses plus guided fun diving trips. Tel: +63 929 585 8244; www.elcoralreefdivecenter.ph; email enquiries are through the contact form on their website.

Arizona Dive Shop PADI dive center offering courses and guided fun dives. 47 National Highway Barrio Barretto, Olongapo City, Zambales, Philippines 2200. Tel: +47 222

0962; Mobile: +63 939 924 0946. www.arizo-
nadivesubic.com; arizonadiveshop@gmail.com.

Nasugbu

Getting there
Southwest of Manila, after a 2-hour drive that
takes you over the mountain at Tagaytay with
its breathtaking views of Taal volcano poking
out of Taal Lake, is Nasugbu in western
Batangas. There are several decent places to stay
along the coast here, at nearby Matabungkay
Beach, for example, along with some cheaper
options in the same area.

If you are traveling under your own steam,
then there is a regular bus service to Nasugbu,
but a hire car is a better bet. If you are arranging your trip through an agent or operator, ask
if transfers are included or if they can be
arranged.

There are several beach resorts along the
coast from Nasugbu to Matabungkay and
further south with varying degrees of value
and amenities available. These are worth
checking out. There are also many small resorts, bungalows and cottages for rent along
the coast from Balayan to Nasugbu for those
traveling by their own transport.

Jo and Johnny's Beach and Dive Inn This
is by far the best option for any serious divers
exploring the area. Jo and Johnny's small
resort offers 2 suites, 3 cabanas and 2 rooms.
The focus here is on diving and they have a
wealth of experience in the area. Tel: +63 (0)
2 807 3416; www.tali-beach.com; booking.
office@tali-beach.com.

Canyon Cove Hotel and Spa Resort style
accommodation with swimming pool and a
range of rooms with views over the water. Far
East Road, Piloto Wawa, Nasugbu. Tel: +63 (0)
2 908 1111; www.canyoncove.com.ph; email
contact is through the enquiry form on their
website.

Chateau Royale Sports and Country Club
This resort offers a mix of accommodation
from rustic log cabins through to international
hotel style Skylight Premier Rooms. A range of
facilities and activities are available. Tel: +63
(0) 2 7428 016–17; wwwchateauroyalebatangas.
com;chateauroyalefrontoffice@yahoo.com.

Anilao

Getting there
Most dive operators in Anilao can provide their
guests with some form of transfer if they need
it. Adventure lovers without their own car can
take a bus to Batangas and then a 30 minute
or so jeepney ride over some quite bumpy
roads to Anilao. Once there, one can negotiate
a *banca* boat at the town pier or take a chance
on getting another jeepney along the road that
winds along the brows of the lush, tropical
hills overlooking the sparkling Balayan Bay.
With Anilao being one of the more popular
tourist destinations, traveling to the area is
actually remarkably straight forward.

Anilao is all about diving. Since 1967, when
Thelma Zuniga of the Aqua Tropical Resort first
built two little nipa huts on the rugged coastline to accommodate visiting divers, Anilao has
blossomed and grown. In Anilao, the diving is
still excellent and most of the better established resorts serve great buffets at meal-
times. Time for beach hopping, in reality more
like rock hopping, is limited for most visitors.
Listed are only a few of the many resorts along
the rugged Balayan coastline offering SCUBA
diving packages.

Acacia Resort and Dive Centre Upmarket
resort and dive center with standard rooms
starting from US$145 per night. Full service
dive center offering guided dives, PADI and
GUE courses, camera assistance and tech
facilities. Resort facilities include swimming
pool, bar, restaurant, Wi-fi and cable TV.
Airport pickups from Manila are also available.
Brgy Ligaya, 4202 Mabini Batangas. www.
acaciadive.com; info@acaciadive.com.

Aiyanar Beach and Dive Resort Upmarket
resort, rooms with AC, swimming pool, club-
house, reatuarant, bar, games room and Wi-fi.
Full service dive center offering courses, dive

packages, guided fun dives, equipment hire, photography services. Sitio Looc, Barangay Bagalangit, Mabini, Batangas. Tel: +63 917 594 0056; www.aiyanar.com; info@aiyanar.com.

Aqua Reef Club Rooms with AC and hot water, bar, swimming pool and massage service. Dive Centre offers SDI, PADI and TDI dive courses, technical diving, equipment hire and guided fun diving trips. Barangay Bagalangit, Mabini. Tel: +63 2584 1328. Email: booking@ aquareefclub.com.

Dive & Trek Resort This is a diver friendly resort that offers reasonable package prices. Accomodation varies from superior, standard and tent style rooms. San Pablo, Bauan, Batangas. Tel: +63 9209 064123; www.diveandtrek.com; sales@diveandtrek.com.

Balai Resort Resort and dive center offering diving packages and buffet meals. Tel: (+632) 240 2927; www.balai-resort.com; balairesort@ yahoo.com.

Puerto Galera

Getting there
Regular air-conditioned BLTB and JAM Transit buses leave from Cubao Bus terminal in Manila (Quezon City) to Batangas Pier, where numerous ferries leave for Puerto Galera daily. Allow at least 3 hours for the bus trip. Most resorts and dive centers in Puerto Galera can arrange painless transfers at any time of the day or night with short notice (depending on the the water conditions in the Verde Island Passage).

The **Sikat Bus and Ferry** service leaves promptly at 8.30am every morning from the Citystate Tower Hotel on Mabini Street, Ermita. The price is around US$35 for the bus and ferry together and you reach Sabang around 1pm in the afternoon.

Ferry prices are fixed but watch out for ticketers trying to charge higher rates. On arrival in Puerto Galera, there is no shortage of people offering you transport to wherever you wish to go.

There are numerous budget rooms on the many beaches within 5 km of the picturesque port of Puerto Galera.

From busy Sabang Beach in the east to the beautiful White Beach to the west, nipa huts and cottages, with or without catering facilities, can be rented for a range of rates to suit all budgets. There are also several self contained dive resorts, such as Capt'n Greggs on Sabang Beach and PADI 5 star CDC dive resorts such as Atlantis Hotel on Sabang. Dive centers employ multilingual instructors and divemasters who are readily available to teach any number of courses and specialties, including technical diving and rebreather courses.

Many of the dive centers carry a range of equipment for sale as well as having gear for rental during your stay, so bringing your own is not essential. Ask at any dive center for the latest information on dive safaris to the Sibuyan Sea, Apo Reef, Coron and other remote sites originating in Puerto Galera. Technical diving is very popular in Puerto, and many dive centers offer courses with SSI, PADI, CMAS and others. Nitrox and technical diving courses and complete technical diving equipment, including rebreathers, are widely available.

Sabang Beach
Among the many choices available, **Capt'n Greggs** (Tel: +63 43 287 3070) was the first dive center to open on Sabang Beach and remains a popular choice. **Atlantis Dive Resort** (Tel: +63 (0) 43 287 3066; www.atlantishotel.com; reservations@atlantishotel.com), is a PADI 5 star Career Development Centre offering a full range of courses, including professional levels, technical diving and rebreather courses. Atlantis hotel has 40 guest rooms ranging in rates and facilities. **Sea Rider Dive Center** (www.seariderdivecenter.com; mark@seariderdivecenter.com) offers both PADI and SSI courses and fun diving. Sabang Beach has numerous other dive centers, and divers are well advised to look around and find the center that they feel most comfortable with and which has the correct facilities to suit their requirements. Sabang Beach also has a lively nightlife scene.

Other dive centers on this beach include **South Sea Divers** (Tel: +63 (43) 287 3052; www.southseadivers.com; dive@southseadivers.com), **Cocktail Divers** (Tel: 089/64299 226; www.cocktaildivers.de—German site and info@cocktailreisen.eu) and **Mermaid Resort** (Tel: +63 (43) 287 3301; www.mermaidresort.com; info@mermaidresort.com.)

Small La Laguna Beach
El Galleon Beach Resort Hotel and Asia Divers Dive Resort A PADI 5 star CDC facility offering a full range of PADI courses, both recreational and professional. There is a range of rooms available in the resort starting from US$60 per night. Fun diving is around US$43 per dive, including equipment hire, $35 if you are using your own gear. Open water courses are approximately US$525 and the advanced open water course is just under US$400. Tel: +63 43 287 3205; www.asiadivers.com; admin@asiadivers.com.

Action Divers Offers dive and stay packages with rooms they source from local hotels ranging from luxury resorts to local homestays to suit your budget requirements. Action Divers offers dive courses and guided fun dives as well as a range of other activities such as kayaking, trekking, golf, sailing, windsurfing and vibrant nightlife activities. Tel: +63 43 287 3320; www.actiondivers.com; info@actiondivers.com.

Cocktail Divers (see listing for Sabang) is another dive franchise offering diving and courses.

Big La Laguna Beach
La Laguna Beach Club and Dive Center
Offers 45 guest rooms ranging in price according to facilties and a full service dive center offering both PADI courses and guided fun dives. Tel: +63 9177 9403 23; www.llbc.com.ph; lalaguna@llbc.com.ph.

Scandi Divers Offers a full service dive center and range of rooms. Airport pickups

from Manila are possible on request. Fun diving and PADI courses available in a range of languages. The resort features a sky bar, restaurant, swimming pool, rooms with either ocean or pool views and it is just a 10 minute walk from the buzzing nightlife of Sabang. Tel: +63 43 287 3551; Mobile: +63 915 456 6411; www.scandidivers.com; info@scandidivers.com.

White Beach
White Beach is perfect for those looking for somewhere a little less hectic than Sabang. It offers more relaxing, quieter surroundings and resorts.

Marco Vincent Dive Resort Offers 38 guest rooms, swimming pool, restaurant, massage service and full service PADI 5 star dive center. Courses and guided fun dives are available as are dive safari trips to Apo Reef. www.marcovincent.com; mvresort@marcovincent.com.

Pacific Divers PADI courses and guided fun dives. Tel: (+63) 920 613 5140/(+63) 947 602 7298; www.philippines-diving.com; pacificdivers@yahoo.com.

Verde Divers Offers a full range of PADI courses and guided fun diving trips. Open water and advanced open water courses are just under US$400 with the advanced course being slightly less. Fun diving with your own gear is approximately US$35 and with rental equipment around $40. Tel: +63 906 352 9489; www.verdedivers.com; info@verdedivers.com/inquire@verdedivers.com.

Boracay City code: 036

Getting there
Boracay Island can be accessed from either Kalibo or Caticlan domestic airports, both of which are situated on the mainland of Panay.

If you are flying into Caticlan, the best option is to take a motorized tricycle to Caticlan Jetty, which is around a 5 minute ride away. Ferries from Caticlan Jetty to Boracay take only 10 minutes when the sea is calm. However, from July to October the port is often closed due to the monsoon season and services are diverted to Tabon Port, which is around a 20 minute journey from Caticlan.

If you are coming to Boracay from Kalibo, there is a 90 minute air-conditioned bus ride to Caticlan through the scenic country side of the Aklan Province. At the time of writing airlines flying into Kalibo Airport include Zest Airways, Philippine Airlines and Cebu Pacific. Airlines with flights to Caticlan include Seair and Cebu Pacific.

Along the famous white beach of Boracay there are a number of accommodation options to suit all budgets. Many resorts maintain offices in Manila, too, making booking a snap. There are usually plenty of options available to travelers preferring not to reserve in advance, though in peak season, from January to May, especially around Easter, it is advisable to book ahead, if possible.

Boracay is home to a large number of full service dive centers and dive resorts. Most dive centers are also working in partnership with a range of accommodation providers, which enables them to put together a package to suit your budget. A wide range of restaurants and bars and several great nightspots complete the picture.

Many of the resorts listed here sell packages, including round trip airfares and transfers. It is worth calling first to compare prices and amenities. With comfortable rooms and suites, most with A/C, fridges in the rooms and televisions, many of the up-scale resorts are still good value for money. Check for significant seasonal and walk-in discounts. For the less wealthy but comfort-minded, there are numerous mid-range options available and budget rooms are not difficult to find. In short, every taste and pocket is catered for on Boracay!

Dive centers on Boracay are very competitively priced and can be booked directly or through agents in Manila. All have multilingual PADI instruction. Dives are priced around US$30 if you are using your own gear and just under $40 if you need to hire equipment. A PADI Open Water Course that takes 4 days is in the region of US$450–475 and the PADI Advanced Course around US$350. It is

worth shopping around a little for prices and to see what is included from various dive centers. Ultimately, though, you should choose an operator who you feel comfortable with, who has good facilities and decent equipment.

Divegurus Has some of the longest serving members of the local diving community and offers a range of courses and fun diving options for certified divers. Tel: +63 36 288 5486; www.divegurus.com; info@divegurus.com.

Victory Divers Diving packages are available as are a full range of PADI courses. For diving enquiries Tel: +63 36 288 3209 and for accommodation enquiries at **Victory Divers Beach Resort** +63 36 288 6056; www.victorydivers.com; info@victorydivers.com.

New Wave Divers Offers a full range of courses and fun diving trips and can assist with accommodation at a number of different resorts and homestays depending on your budget and requirements. Tel: +63 36 288 5265; www.boracaydiver.com; info@boracay-diver.com.

Calypso Diving Resort Located at White Beach, Boracay, this is a PADI 5 star IDC center offering a complete range of recreational and professional courses together with good facilities and equipment hire as well as fun diving. It is based in the **Calypso Beach Resort**, which offers rooms from around US$100 per night in low season (June to October) and from US$127 in high season (November to May). Rates are based on two people and breakfasts are included. Special rates apply for Christmas and New Year. Tel: +63 (0) 36 288 3206; www.calypso-boracay.com; email through the contact form on the website. Calypso Diving also offers accommodation at **Pinjalo Resort**, Calypso Beach Resort's sister hotel. Pinjalo Resort offers a range of rooms and is just a few minutes walk away from Calypso. Tel: +63 (0) 36 288 2038; www.pinjalo.com; reservations@pinjalo.com.

Scuba World Dive equipment supplier with a branch in Boracay, stockists of Hollis, Tusa,

Mares, Aqualung, Pelican, Underwater Kinetics, Suunto, Oceanic and others. Tel: +63 (0) 36 288 3310; www.scubaworld.com.ph; boracay@scubaworld.com.ph.

Marinduque

Not much goes on around this sleepy little island except for the annual Moriones Festival where the local people dress in costumes and masks depicting biblical roman soldiers. The event occurs during holy week and is really quite tame, but the diving around Marinduque is well worth the effort.

There are a number of small resorts dotted around the island. Take a jeepney or bus along the western coastal road and pick one that seems to suit you. There are no full service dive centers, but there are a few operators with scuba gear for rent who are willing to arrange full day dive trips if they are around. Check at any resort or hotel for more information, but be prepared for disappointment as the operators are unreliable and frequently not around. Most divers visit Marinduque's offshore islands to the west and south by liveaboard dive safaris originating from Puerto Galera and Boracay.

Mactan and Cebu City code: 032

Getting there

Minutes from where Cebu's first tourist, Magellan, met his untimely end while interfering in a squabble between local chieftains, Mactan's busy airport spills out planeloads of international travelers, many of them package tourists from Japan, to enjoy the resorts of Mactan and historic Cebu's cosmopolitan beat. Cebu is a hub city, a major shipping center and the jump-off point for the rest of the Visayas.

Mactan Island is separated from Cebu City on the main island of Cebu by the Mactan Straits. A single bridge spans the gap, connecting the two.

Diving and water sports have been at the forefront of the development of tourism, a top dollar earner for the region. Cebu has several retail outlets serving the booming SCUBA market, including the following:

Aquaventure Whitetip Dive Suppliers They have stores in Manila, Cebu City, Mactan Island and Puerto Galera and stock a full range of dive equipment and brands, including Apex, Aqualung, Bauer Compressors, Dive Rite, Suunto and many more. The Mactan store is located at Bagumbayan 2, Maribago Lapu-Lapu City, Mactan Island. Tel: +63 (0)32 492 0122; www.aquaventurewhitetip.com; mactan@ aquaventurewhitetip.com,

Most resorts around Mactan have diving services on the premises. If not, you are never too far away from a dive center. They are literally everywhere and offer a range of courses, including technical diving and free diving. Most dive shops arrange 1–5 day dive safaris to nearby Cabilao Island as well as to other exotic Visayan dive spots.

Scotty's Dive Center At the top of the range, Scotty's offers SSI courses as well as tech and free diving courses and fun diving trips. Located at **Shangria-La's Mactan Resort and Spa**, Punta Engano Road, Lapu-Lapu City, Mactan Island. Tel: +63 (0)32 231 0288; www. shangri-la.com; mac@shangri-la.com. Scotty's Dive Center has its own website: www.dive-scotty.com. Heading more towards the beach, you will find more down-to-earth prices and people with years of experience diving around Mactan and the Visayas.

7 seas Another decent option is this PADI 5 star dive center. www.7seas-cebu.com; dive@7seas-cebu.com. 7 Seas is located at **Plantation Bay Resort and Spa**, Marigondon Beach, Mactan Island. Tel: +63(0) 32 495 2216; www.plantationbay.com.

Kon Tiki Divers Genuinely run by divers for divers, this is a PADI 5 star dive center for the more serious diver, located in the **Kon Tiki Beach Resort** on Mactan Island. It offers the full range of PADI courses, including technical diving and fun diving. Fun dives are both from the shore and by boat and trips further afield are also offered (Cabilao, Bohol, Apo Island and Negros safaris). Dive prices are approximately US$25 for shore dives and $30 for boat dives.

Equipment hire is under $10 for a full set, PADI open water courses $400 and advanced open water $340. Rooms at Kon Tiki Beach Resort are priced at US$30–50 per night for a double room (2 people), not including breakfast. Tel: +63 (0)32 495 2471; www.kontikidivers.com; info@kontikidivers.com,

Whilst not really close to Cebu City, mention should be made of the **Argao Beach** area a few hours south of the city on the east coast (approximately 90 km). Rooms tend to be more expensive but there is some excellent diving quite close by that is otherwise hard to reach. For reasonable accommodation, try the family run **Woodruffs Beach Resort** located on the southern edge of Argao directly on the beach. The resort has air-conditioned rooms, swimming pool, restaurant and beautiful views over the water. Tel: +63 (0) 32 367 7388; www.woodruffs-beachresort.com; info@woodruffs-beachresort.com.

Moalboal

On the western side of Cebu Island, Moalboal was one of the original SCUBA diving centers in the Philippines. Most of the SCUBA operations here offer a full range of PADI recreational courses and many also offer instructor level training, technical diving and free diving as well as fun diving, equipment hire and dive safaris. Most operators employ Western guides and instructors who are multilingual. Courses are available in numerous languages. The larger operators in Moalboal can put together a dive and accommodation package for you to suit your budget if you book in advance.

The majority of operators in Moalboal offer airport pickups and it is recommended that you take advantage of this, even if there is a small surcharge. It is also possible to travel by taxi but you will need to agree a price with the driver beforehand and this can be tricky. Other alternatives include bus travel, but if you are traveling with gear the journey can be uncomfortable. Upon arrival at Moalboal, grab a tricycle and head off to Panagsama Beach. Accommodation here ranges from basic backpacker to more upmarket resorts. There is something for every budget. The food is also very affordable hereabouts, with several surprisingly good options.

Dolphin House Moalboal Spa and Diving This environmentally conscientious operator offers diving packages, high-end accommodation and excellent dining. Dive courses are available as are learning experiences at their dive college alongside marine biologists. In Moalboal they are located on White Beach, Saavedra, and also have another facility in Mactan. Both outlets are highly recommended. Tel: +63 32 358 5419; www.philippines-cebu.com; email contact is through the enquiry form on their website.

Visaya Divers Corp Based in the **Quo Vadis Dive Resort** at Panagsama Beach, Moalboal, the dive center is a PADI 5 star dive operation and offers diving from US$25 a dive if you have your own gear, $33 without, and teaches PADI open water courses for $335, advanced for $290. Tel: +63 (0) 32 474 3088. The resort offers a range of rooms, bungalows and suites to cater for varying budgets. It has a swimming pool and pool bar, Wi-fi and restaurant. Airport pickups are also available. Tel: +63 (0) 32 474 3068; www.quovadisresort.com,; reservation@quovadisresort.com.

Savedra This PADI 5 star IDC center at Moalboal is a professionally run diving outfit with complete nitrox fills and technical diving facilities. Savedra organizes accommodation through a range of local resorts to suit your requirements (and budget) and will organize a complete package, including domestic flights, airport pickups and transfers, accommodation and diving. They also offer dive safaris and island hopping trips around Cebu, Bohol and Negros. Dive rates are as follows (approximate): Single shore dive US$25, single boat dive $30, 5 boat dive package $140, 10 boat dive package $260, 20 boat dive package $495. Full set of equipment hire $7 per dive, PADI open water course US$400 and PADI advanced open water course $330. Tel: +63 (0) 32 474 3132 or +63 (0) 32 474 3488; www.savedra.com; info@savedra.com.

SeaQuest Dive Center This PADI 5 star facility offers courses, fun diving, nitrox fills, equipment hire and direct beach access to their house reef. The dive center is located next to the **Sumisid Resort**, which offers comfortable and friendly accommodation on the beach front. Sea Quest also has partnership operations in Bohol and Malapascua. Head office Tel: +63 (0) 32 232 6010 or 418 1550; www.seaquestdive center.net; info@seaquestdivecenter.ph.

Blue Abyss Dive Shop This is an IDC center offering both courses and fun diving. It operates two boat dives and house reef diving daily. Fun diving and accommodation packages are available as are courses and accommodation packages. Tel: +63 (0) 32 474 3036; www.blue abyssdiving.com; info@blueabyssdiving.com. **Blue Abyss Resort** offers basic but comfortable rooms whereas **Marcosas Cottages Resort** provides more upmarket facilities, including swimming pool, cable TV, etc.

A walk along Panagsama Beach will introduce you to most of the dive operators doing business. Ask for rates and facilities before committing. Remember, not all dive operators are created equal.

Northern Cebu

Not as well developed as the south, there are only a few places catering to scuba divers in the north.

As dive operators tend to come and go in remoter locations, it is best to ask for local advice with regards to dive operations doing business before planning a journey up north unless planning to stay at **Alegre Beach Resort** at Calumboyan, Sogod, north of Cebu City, an excellent private resort featuring 3 private beach coves and 21 cabanas. Tel: +63 32 254 9800; www.alegrebeachresort.com; reserve@algrebeachresort.com.

Malapascua Island

Getting there

Malapascua Island is one of the most raved about dive sites now because of the spectacu-

lar thresher sharks that inhabit its waters. Most operators based on Malapascua will offer a pickup service (surcharge applies) from either the airport or your hotel in Cebu. If you are making your own way to the island from Cebu, then you need to travel either by taxi (2.5 hours) or bus (4.5 hours) from Cebu to Maya. From Maya the boats leave to Malapascua Island and the trip is around 30 minutes. Private and public boats are available, with the public boat costing less than US$5 and a private boat ranging in price from $25 to $40. There are no ATMs on Malapascua Island and only a limited number of operators will accept credit cards. Marine park fees are payable in Malapascua and are currently Php150 per day (approximately US$3.40). An additional fee is payable if you visit Monad Shoal, currently Php50 per dive (US$1.20). Amongst the most established operations are the following:

Thresher Shark Divers This is a PADI 5 star IDC and TecRec center that offers recreational and professional level courses, technical diving and fun diving trips and safaris. They will arrange all inclusive packages—pickups, transfers, accommodation and diving according to your requirements. They do not have rooms but use local resorts to meet your budget and tastes as requested. They also stock Aqualung, Scubapro, Apeks, Waterproof, Cressi and Suunto equipment for sale as well as selling off old rental gear. Dive prices vary according to the number of dives you are making. A single boat dive is US$35, 2+ boat dives $33 per dive, 5+ boat dives $31 per dive and 10+ boat dives $29 per dive. Prices do not include equipment hire (tanks, weights and guide only). Tel: +63 917 795 9433 or +63 32 406 6414; www.malapascua-diving.com; dive@thresherdivers.com.

SeaQuest Dive Center A PADI 5 star dive center located next to the lobby of **Legend Resort** on Bounty Beach, SeaQuest offers a range of PADI recreational courses, fun diving trips and equipment hire and nitrox is also available. Packages can be booked with accommodation at Legend Resort which has 20 air-conditioned rooms, Wi-fi, swimming pool, "resto-bar", or at other local resorts. Tel: +63 (0) 32 232 6010 or 418 1550; www.seaquestdive-center.net; info@seaquestdivecenter.ph, Seaquest also have dive centers in both Bohol and Moalboal making multi-destination trips also a possibility.

Evolution Diving This PADI 5 star dive resort and TDI Instructor Training Facility offers PADI courses and technical diving and rebreathers, fun diving and equipment hire. Accomodation is offered at **Evolution Resort**, which has 16 rooms available. Prices per dive are on a sliding scale: 1–4 dives are US$36 per dive, 5–9 dives $33 per dive and 10+ dives are $32 per dive. Fuel surcharges apply to certain destinations as do minimum passenger numbers. The PADI open water course is US$400 and advanced $332. Equipment hire is available at US$8.50 per dive or $15 per day. www.evolution diving.com.ph; info@evolutiondiving.com.ph

Southern Leyte

Southern Leyte has stunning natural attractions above and below the water. Waterfalls and walls, caves and whale sharks now attract a large number of visitors, and as such facilities have developed, including places to stay, dive operators and tourist amenities.

Getting there

There are a number of options for getting to Southern Leyte. If you are coming from Cebu, take the fast ferry from Cebu direct to Leyte. Most operators will pick you up from harbors in Leyte (some apply a surcharge for the service but it makes the journey a lot easier). If you are flying into Tacloban Airport, operators will also pick you up from there on the same basis. If you are flying into Manila airport, numerous domestic flights are available daily to Tacloban Airport.

Peter's Dive Resort Located at Lungsodaan, Padre Burgos, this is one of the original operators in the area and offers a range of accommodation choices from dormitory style rooms with shared bathrooms through to standard rooms, condos and a complete house. Divers are given a discounted rate on accommodation.

Pickups can be provided from either Tacloban Airport or your arrival port in Leyte. Fun diving is priced at US$29 per dive and gear hire $17 for a full set. PADI courses are also available (open water US$440/advanced open water $330). Whale shark watching tours are available, which include the boat ride out to the whale shark area, one snorkeling session with the whale sharks, one additional dive (not with the whale sharks as diving with whale sharks is strictly prohibited in Southern Leyte), lunch, tank, weights and guide and conservation fee for US$83, which is about the average rate for this type of trip for this area. There is a requirement for a minimum of 6 divers for the trip (also standard for the area) as the boat ride takes 1.5–2 hours. Tel: +63 (0) 917 791 0993 or +63 (0) 915 437 7560; www.whaleofadive.com; email contact is through the form on their website.

Southern Leyte Divers This operator offers both accommodation and diving. Standard rooms with AC are around US$33 and bungalows are priced from around $42 (prices not including breakfast). Fun diving and PADI courses are available as are whale shark watching tours, which include the standard snorkeling session with the whale sharks, one additional non-whale shark dive, lunch, etc. for US$98. Tel: +63 (0) 921 663 1592; www.leyte-divers.com; info@leyte-divers.com.

Sogod Bay Scuba Resort This resort caters for a maximum of 22 guests with room rates ranging from US$25 to $50 per night. PADI courses, fun diving, equipment hire and whale shark watching tours are all available at reasonable prices. Reservations Tel: +63 (0) 916 376 0064, Resort Information Tel: +63 (0) 915 520 7274; www.sogodbayscubaresort.com; info@sogodbayscubaresort.com.

Bohol City code: 038

Bohol Island has a diverse choice of accommodation and dive services available. Most of these originate on Panglao Island, across the causeway south of the provincial capital, Tagbilaran City.

Getting there

Bohol can be reached by regular domestic flights to Tagbilaran City from Manila or Cebu, or by comfortable fast ferry boat services from Manila, Cebu and from throughout the Visayas–Mindanao region. Once there, most divers head for Alona Beach on Panglao Island, where the scuba diving business is flourishing. Most operators will provide transfers from either Tagbilaran Airport (some for free) or from Cebu International Airport (surcharges usually apply). It is recommended to take advantage of operator arranged transfers as they are the most reliable and hassle free.

There are many dive operators in the area offering a range of services. If you haven't made an advance booking, then you should shop around but rates tend not to vary too much from operator to operator. Some will include additional extras though, so it is worth asking what you are getting for your money.

Cebu Sea Explorers They have dive centers at Alona Beach, Bohol and also in Cabilao, Dauin, Malapascua and other popular destinations. The **Alona Beach Center** offers daily fun diving, dive courses and dive safaris. As Cebu Sea Explorers are located in a number of locations, island hopping dive packages are available as is technical diving and rebreathers. Sea Explorers will put together packages for you that cover accommodation to suit your budget and also transfers. Diving prices are on a sliding scale according to the number of dives you make. The following prices are without gear rental (tanks, weights, guide and boat included): 1 single dive US$38.8, 12 dive package $36.80 per dive, more than 16 dives $33.40 per dive, gear hire is $12.20 per dive or $16.70 per day for a full set. This is a long serving operator that pioneered island hopping dive packages. They have an excellent reputation for efficiency, service and experience. Their website has sample itineraries for those planning multi-destination trips. Head office in Cebu City. Tel: +63 (0) 32 234 0248; www.sea-explorers.com; cebu@sea-explorers.com.

Philippine Fun Divers Inc. A PADI 5 star center located at Alona Beach, Panglao, it offers PADI courses, daily fun diving around Bohol as well as trips to Cabilao and safaris to Apo Reef. They will also assist you with accommodation bookings through local resorts. Prices for diving are as follows: US$29 per dive (boat or shore dive with your own gear), gear hire $7.70 per dive, PADI open water course $300 and PADI advanced open water $225, which is a lower rate than many such courses. Tel: +63 (0) 38 502 4083; www.boholfundivers.com; info@boholfundivers.com.

SeaQuest Dive Center With operations also in Malapascua and a number of other locations, this is a popular operator. The head office is located in Cebu City and the Bohol operation is at Alona Beach, Panglao, at the **Oasis Resort**. Courses, fun diving, nitrox and equipment hire are available. Tel: +63 (0) 32 232 6010 or +63 (0) 32 418 1550; www.seaquestdivecenter.net; info@seaquestdivecenter.ph.

Sierra Madre Divers Located at Alona Beach, Panglao, this PADI 5 star IDC resort offers PADI courses (open water US$420 and advanced open water $329), fun diving ($29 with rental gear and $25 with your own) and dive packages. The dive center is complete with sundeck, classrooms and hammock area. Sierra Madre assists guests with accommodation bookings at a range of local resorts/homestays to meet your budget and they can also arrange transfers. Tel: +63 38 502 9789; www.dive-bohol.com; info@dive-bohol.com.

Atlantis Dive Center This operator is also located at Alona Beach, Panglao, and is based at the **Kalipayan Beach Resort**, which offers 18 rooms with a swimming pool, pool bar, restaurant and seaside terrace. This is one of the longest running operations on the island and is owned by Kurt Biebelmann. It offers both fun diving and courses. A range of rooms are available, the prices varying according to the season and room type. www.atlantisdive-center.com; email contact is through the enquiry form on their website.

Another option is to stay on nearby **Cabilao Island**, particularly if you are looking for a less developed area:

Polaris Beach and Dive Resort This offers a range of accommodation from "tree house bungalows" with cold water and fans through to air-conditioned rooms with hot water for around US$70 per night (not including breakfast). Single dives are US$35, a 6 dive package $195 and a 12 dive package $369. Gear hire is around $7.50 per dive or $14 per day. PADI diving courses are also available but should be requested in advance. The resort has a swimming pool, restaurant and bar. Tel: +63 (0) 918 903 7187 or +63 (0) 918 925 2473; www.polaris-dive.com; info.ph@polaris-dive.com.

Coron

Coron has garnered fame for its wreck diving, and as such now offers a range of accommodation from backpacker style rooms to international standard upmarket hotels. The area is also a popular liveaboard destination. A number of nearby islands offer dive resorts of varying levels of comfort and price.

Getting there

Coron is serviced by its own airport, Coron/Busuanga Airport, which can be reached by domestic flights from either Cebu or Manila International Airports. Upon arrival in Coron, many operators offer an airport pickup service and transfers, particularly the resorts that are based on nearby islands.

Dugong Dive Center Located at **Club Paradise**, Busuanga (www.clubparadisepalawan.com), the Dugong Dive Center is one of the longer established operators and offers both diver training and daily fun diving trips. There is a wreck dive 30 minutes from the resort, a house reef and they offer trips to 10 of Coron Bay's shipwrecks as well as trips to Apo Reef, Barracuda Lake and the Tara Islands, and full day excursions to a dugong feeding ground for dugong watching. Tel: +63 (0) 920 951 9100 or +63 (0) 917 866 9877; www.dugongdivecenter.com; info@dugongdivecenter.com.

Sangat Island Dive Resort Located on Sangat Island right in the middle of the best wreck diving in the Philippines, the resort has its own house wreck a few meters off the white sand beach. The resort offers hillside accommodation with stunning views. Its full service dive center offers both dive training and daily fun diving trips, 11 wreck dives, plus a selection of reef dives. Tel: (general enquiries) +63 (0) 916 400 8801 or (Resort office) +63 (0) 908 896 1716; www.sangat.com.ph; email enquiries through the inquiry form on the website.

D'Divers at D'Pearl Bay Busuanga Formerly known as Discovery Divers Coron, D'Divers is the exclusive dive service provider for **Busuanga Bay Lodge** (www.busuangabaylodge.com), **Puerto Del Sol Resort and Dive Center** (www.puertodelsolresort.com) and **AlFaro Palawan Resort** (www.alfaropalawan.com). D'Divers offers both dive trips for certified divers as well as recreational and technical diver training from beginner to instructor level courses with SDI and TDI. The dive center is ideally situated close to the wrecks of Coron Bay. A range of reef dives is also available. D'Divers has a wealth of experience when it comes to the wrecks in Coron Bay. Single dives are around US$35 with your own gear, 10 or more dives are around $31 per dive and full equipment hire is around $8. Tel: +63 (0) 917 975 9109 or +63 (0) 977 201 2223; www.ddivers.com; reservation@ddivers.com or ddivers.office@gmail.com.

Neptune Dive Center This PADI dive center is located on National Highway in Coron and offers daily diving trips as well as PADI courses and island hopping tours. Accommodation packages are available through local resorts and guest houses to suit your budget and requirements. Neptune dives the wrecks of Coron Bay as well as Barracuda Lake and also offers a number of reef dives. Tel: +63 (0) 921 760 7492; www.neptunedivecenter.com; info@neptunedivecenter.com.

Chindonan Dive Resort Located a little more remotely on Chindonan Island, the resort offers relaxing and quiet surroundings in its hillside cottages. Daily dive trips and PADI courses are available as well as a choice of cottage styles (high and low season rates apply and room rates include airport pickups, boat transfers, breakfasts and dinner buffets). Single wreck or reef dives are around US$40, House reef dives $33, PADI open water course US$480 and PADI advanced open water $355. Rates include equipment hire and environmental fee. Tel: +63 (0) 929 312 1594; www. chindonan-diveresort.com; chindonan@gmail.com.

El Nido

Getting there

El Nido is serviced by Lio Airport which receives domestic flights direct from Cebu. The flight takes around 1 hour and the airport is situated around 4 km from mid-town El Nido. This is by far the easiest way to access the town and many operators/hotels will pick you up from the airport. Jumping in a taxi is also an easy option.

The alternative is to fly to Puerto Princesa Airport in Central Palawan. From there El Nido is around 220 km by highway. This is best traversed by coach and takes around 5–6 hours. Public buses also ply this route but they are far less comfortable, less reliable and the travel time is around 6–8 hours.

The town itself is not big. You can walk from end to end with ease.

Miniloc Island Resort and **Lagen Island** Operated by El Nido Resorts, both are situated in El Nido bay and both have outstanding natural views and first class facilities. You should reserve first as both resorts are not especially welcoming to transient visitors. Miniloc Island Resort has 50 rooms and a marine sports center, which includes a PADI dive center offering fun diving trips, courses and equipment hire. Tel: +63 (2) 902 5985; www.elnidoresorts.com; holiday@elnidoresorts.com.

There are now numerous dive centers in El Nido and amongst the most popular operators are:

Submariner Diving Center A PADI 5 star and Tec Rec resort offering PADI recreational and technical diving courses, fun diving trips, equipment hire and liveaboard safari trips to Coron. Tel: +63 905 484 1764; www.submariner-diving.com; info@submariner-diving.com.

Deep Blue Dive Seafari Offering PADI recreational course and fun diving trips. Tel: +63 917 803 0543; www.deepblueseafari.com; deepblueseafari@gmail.com.

Palawan Divers PADI 5 star dive center offering PADI courses, fun diving trips, gear hire and fully serviced dive center with classrooms. Tel: +63 9 399 581 076; www.palawan-divers.org; hello@palawan-divers.org.

General Santos City

Diving around Mindanao Island and its surrounding areas is excellent and the local facilities are good and reasonably priced.

Getting there

Regular flights by PAL serve General Santos City in Mindano. There are ample choices for accommodation and entertainment. Gen San, as it is more popularly known, has one of the best walls to be found anywhere in the country.

The only major operation in the area is **Cambridge Dive Center**, formerly known as Tuna City Scuba Center, owned and run by Englishman Chris Dearne, a PADI Instructor. Contact is best by telephone: +63 (0) 83 301 613.

Davao

Getting there

Davao is served by regular domestic flights daily. A thriving city, home to the smelly durian fruit and orchid farms, Davao enjoys a balmy tropical climate year round. There are some good dive sites and several choices for discriminating divers to choose from.

Davao Scuba Dive Center Based on Monteverde Street, near Sta Ana Wharf, Davao Scuba Dive Center offers fun diving trips for certified divers and diver training. Tel: +63 082 226 2588; www.davaoscubadive.net; davaodive@gmail.com. A contact form is also available on their website.

Carabao Dive Center Offers PADI, SDI and Naui courses as well as guided fun diving trips and equipment hire and boat rental. Tel: +63 82 300 1092 or 302 6255; www.divedavao.com.

Camiguin

Camiguin Island, just south of Bohol, is a delightful tropical paradise with plenty to see and do topside as well as some outstanding diving under the waves. There is a good choice of resorts and dive centers on the island, too.

Getting there

The easiest way to access Camiguin Island is by domestic flight from Cebu International airport (Cebu Pacific have regular domestic services). Alternatively, it is possible to take an overnight ferry from Cebu or from Jagna, Bohol (the best operator from Bohol is Ocean Fast Ferries Corp.—www.oceanjet.net).

Johnny's Dive "N" Fun A PADI dive resort with dive centers located at **Caves Dive Resort** and **Paras Beach Resort**, offering fun diving trips and PADI courses. Single (local) boat dives are around US$25 and a 10 dive package (5 days of diving) is around $225, PADI open water course $310 and advanced open water $290. Course prices do not include the cost of PADI materials. Tel: +63 88 387 9588; www.johnnysdive.com; info@johnnysdive.com.

Liveaboards in the Philippines

Liveaboard diving in the Philippines is an experience which, once tasted, is usually repeated. A full range of vessels and destinations awaits divers with a yearning to discover some of the best diving in Southeast Asia.

The Sulu Sea dive sites, such as Tubbataha, Jessie Beazley and Basterra, are accessible for 3-4 months of the year (March to June) and only by liveaboard. Book early to insure a slot. Other locations frequently visited by liveaboards include El Nido, Coron, Bohol and the Visayas, Apo Reef and the Sibuyan Sea. Some operators also dive the Spratley Islands.

At the bottom end, large *banca*, or pump boats, and sailing yachts carry 6-8 people in relative comfort. Some have air-conditioning,

but most don't, though sleeping on the deck under a blanket of stars is quite okay for many people. Camps are often made on deserted islands (make sure you tidy up properly before leaving, please), and schedules are very much open. These budget liveaboard trips can be arranged through most dive shops in Puerto Galera and Boracay, and through travel agents in Manila.

For the more sophisticated diver, there is no shortage of superb, customized liveaboard dive vessels offering the absolute maximum in comfort and service. Fine dining, luxurious appointments and professional expertise are very much the order of the day on these boats. Every year, groups of divers return from around the world to take advantage of the excellent value offered by Philippine liveaboards.

Manila and Cebu are the main centers for liveaboard bookings. Embarkation points depend on where the vessel is working. For more upmarket liveaboard vessels, booking in advance is absolutely essential and through the vessel's website or agent.

Some recommended liveaboard vessels currently operating in the Philippines include:

S/Y *Philippines Siren* At the more luxurious end of the market and part of the well-known Siren Fleet, the *Philippines Siren* covers Cebu, Dauin, Tubbataha, Apo Reef, Malapascua and Donsol. The 8 cabins accommodate up to 16 guests onboard this traditional Indonesian-built gaft-rigged *phinisi* vessel. Booking in advance is essential and for some trips there are 12 month plus waiting lists. It is worth watching their website for special offers. Tel (Reservations): +66 (0) 76 367 444; www.sirenfleet.com; info@sirenfleet.com.

Atlantis Azores An upmarket vessel with 7 deluxe stateroom cabins and 1 suite, covering Malapascua, Tubbataha, Dumaguete and the Visayas. Tel: +63 (0) 43 287 3066; www.atlantishotel.com; reservation@atlantishotel.com.

Expedition Fleet The largest privately owned liveaboard fleet in the Philippines, operating **MY *Borneo Exporer*, MY *Stella Maris*, MV *Eco Explorer*, MV *Oceanic Explorer*** and

MV *Crystal Explorer*. The fleet covers Tubbataha, Apo Reef and Coron. Tel: +63 (0) 2 577 4305; www.expeditionfleet.com; expeditionfleet1539@gmail.com or stellamaris1539@yahoo.com.ph.

Thailand Practicalities
Thailand Telephone Country Code: 66

You'll find Thailand an easy country to travel in as the tourism industry here is well developed and well organized. The people of Thailand are extremely friendly and polite, and crime is relatively rare. English is widely spoken in tourist areas, but keep your requests—and language and grammar—simple. Above all, avoid becoming frustrated and losing your temper as this will lead to doors of communication rapidly closing. The attitude of *jai yen*, or "keep your cool," will go a long way toward making your time here more pleasant and enjoyable. Unless noted, prices are in US$.

Cultural considerations

Thais are very proud of their heritage—and rightly so. The country has never been colonized but was briefly occupied by the Japanese during World War II, and Thais are happy with their freedom and their way of life. Show respect and consideration and you will receive it in return.

Customs and habits in Thailand are often quite different from those of other countries and can be difficult for travelers to understand. Respect these customs and beliefs, even if they may not immediately make sense to you, and you'll find your time in Thailand more enjoyable, fulfilling and, I dare say, educational.

Always remove your shoes before entering a Thai house or a temple, even if your hosts insist it is not necessary. Removing your shoes before boarding a dive boat will also show that you know what's going on.

The head of a Thai is considered the highest point, literally and spiritually, while the feet are considered the lowest. Therefore, you should never touch a Thai on the head, even children, and make an effort not to point to or touch objects or people with your feet.

The *wai* (putting your hands together with flat palms in a prayerlike position) is a traditional and beautiful form of greeting in Thailand. Rules for who greets who with a *wai* are complicated, even for Thais, but it is generally not appropriate to pay this form of respect to children, waiters, housekeepers or those younger than yourself or of a lower social station. It is appropriate, however, to *wai* persons older than you in many situations, especially those who have been extra kind to you. For example, if you are invited into a Thai home, it is very polite to *wai* your hosts upon entering and leaving. It is rare that a tourist is ever obligated to perform a *wai*, as you are a guest in this country. However, just like a handshake in Western countries, it is an important part of Thai culture and a little bit of understanding goes a long way.

The Thai royal family is highly respected and loved, and it is in extremely poor taste to make denigrating remarks about them, even in jest. Never desecrate an image of the King or Queen of Thailand, which you will often find hanging proudly in many shops and places of business. Even stepping on a rolling coin, which bears the image of the King, is considered rude and should be avoided.

Air travel

Don Muang Airport in Bangkok is one of the busiest airports in the world, and hundreds of flights arrive daily from virtually every major country. **Thai Airways International** is the national airline and it is consistently named one of the best airlines in the world. Singapore, whose national airline is also a world champion in passenger service, is also a great place to make your entry to Southeast Asia as Changi

Airport offers multiple connecting flights to Bangkok and Phuket every day.

Air travel within Thailand is convenient and relatively inexpensive. The Phuket Airport receives numerous flights a day (the number varies between the high and low seasons) from Bangkok year round. Phuket's ever-expanding airport receives international flights as well, from Hong Kong, Japan, Taiwan, Singapore, Malaysia and Europe. Flights are available to and from Ko Samui and Pattaya on **Bangkok Airways**.

The Thai Airways office telephone number in Bangkok is (66-2) 288 7000 and in Phuket, (66-076) 360 444 or 360 400; www.thaiairways.com.

Staying in contact

Cell phones By far the easiest way to stay in touch from Thailand is to buy a local SIM card on arrival. In most airports, SIM cards are free and you buy more minutes at any convenience store. Often the lines are long at airports so if you're in a hurry, wait until you get to your hotel and go buy a SIM card for about 50 Thai baht down the road. Hotels always know where the closest store is. You'll have to show your passport to buy a SIM. Both data and voice are available and very affordable. The three main service providers are **TrueMove**, **AIS** and **DTAC**. All are good for voice, but True offers 4G data, the only company in Thailand to roll out proper 4G. It's very fast. All types of SIM cards are available, from micro-SIM to standard sizes. Credit is known locally as "top" and can be purchased in the form of a card which you scratch off a panel and input a code to your phone. The staff will input the code for you if you ask nicely. You can do this at almost any convenience store or at service centers throughout the country. Service centers are located mainly in shopping malls. There are online services, usually in English as well, but it's easier just to go and talk to a human being. Top ups can be of any value, usually 200 Thai baht will last you a few days. Once you have credit on your phone you can make calls which will be taken directly from your credit, and if you signed up for data, you'll be able to use the Internet from your phone or tablet. Usually the HotSpot or tethering tool will work in Thailand with all providers. To call overseas, all providers have a discount code you input before the country code as you dial. This saves you up to 80 percent on overseas calls. Ask your provider for the codes for their system. 006 or 0060 is the one used by True, for example, so if you were calling the UK, you would dial 00644, then the number without the proceeding "0" If you were to call the US, you would dial 00061, then the area code and number. If you use the usual "+" for overseas numbers, you will be charged the full rate.

Internet Most cafés, bars, restaurants and resorts in tourist areas have free Wi-fi hotspots and you simply need to make a purchase (just a drink will suffice) and ask for the password. Very few areas in Thailand have no Internet coverage. Most of the networks these days are high speed and you may find it better than back home. If you need Internet access whilst you are away, check with your operator beforehand what the situation is, particularly if you are making a liveaboard trip. Internet is not yet available on liveaboards except for emergencies by satellite telephone or data systems and, of course, are very expensive. The Similan Islands is the one exception. It has limited cell service on two of the islands. The Internet can be tethered to your computer when you have a signal there. But the service is still slow at the islands (GPRS) and should not be counted on for getting work done.

Land travel

Ground transportation in Thailand is very well organized and both the trains and buses are relatively comfortable and efficient. Travel by train is probably the most comfortable and least expensive, but since the trains are often full they must be booked in advance. The state government runs the rail system, and booking trains can be less convenient than privately run buses.

Buses are common and go everywhere. Buses run in three different classes: *tamada* (normal), *ae* (air-conditioned), and VIP (the best). The most comfortable are the double-decker VIP buses and their usage is common on most major routes. Be sure to bring warm clothes, however, as Thai air-conditioned buses are notorious for their extremely low temperatures!

Rot too (mini-vans) are widely available as a means of transport between tourist destinations, but the majority of drivers are extremely unprofessional and drive as if they were in a car race. Caution and a strong stomach are advised when traveling this way. You may also need to barter the rate.

Motorbike and car rental is available in most tourist areas where there are roads. If you can, buy insurance. Be careful at all times when driving due to the dual hazards of tourists not paying attention and reckless Thai drivers. Motorcycles are a fun and cheap way to get around provided you are experienced on two wheels. Thailand is not a good place to learn. A license is usually not required, but rental agencies will take your passport as a deposit against damage. Always wear a helmet.

Local taxis and buses are widely available, and prices vary from place to place. One thing you'll notice quickly: Thais rarely walk. Thus, transportation is readily available anyplace you find people.

Sea travel

Ferries travel to Ko Phi Phi, Ko Samui, Ko Tao, etc. on a daily basis. Any travel agent can book them. Obviously, some boats are more comfortable and safer than others and prices vary accordingly. Be wary of overloading on cheaper boats.

Visas

All travelers must have a passport valid for at least six months. For stays shorter than 30 days, visas are not required for Southeast Asian citizens and for most Europeans and North Americans. Visas are required for stays longer than 30 days, although some nationalities are exempt and given 90 days upon arrival. Check with the Thai embassy in your own country before departure, since entry rules do change often. Altogether, the visa process is simple, convenient and inexpensive.

Health

Thailand is a tropical country and there are certain health issues travelers should be aware of. Check with your health department before leaving. Malaria and other mosquito-born diseases are only a problem in remote areas, like the jungles of northern Thailand, islands near the Cambodian border and Ko Tao north of Ko Samui. It can be a problem in Myanmar if you spend any time on shore. If traveling to the Mergui Archipelago, see your doctor for the latest recommendations on what medication to take. We suggest you bring along a good supply of mosquito repellent, suncream and a hat as well as long pants and long sleeves for around sunrise and sunset.

Bottled water is widely available and you are well advised to drink only this type. Tap water is rarely, if ever, clean enough for Western stomachs. All water served in hotels, guest houses, restaurants and dive boats is bottled, usually coming from large 20 liter containers to help control the plastic waste problem. If in doubt, ask.

Health care, including dental work in Thailand is widely available and inexpensive. Most first aid supplies are easily purchased virtually everywhere. Any prescription medicines you need, of course, should be brought from home.

Dive emergencies

While there is a reasonable network of recompression chambers in Thailand, air evacuation remains unreliable, more so in some areas than in others. Therefore, transport time can be very lengthy, depending on your location. Even in the Similan Islands, which is relatively close to the chamber in Phuket, evacuation may take 6 hours or more. More distant areas will take even longer. Considering the lengthy transport times, it goes without saying that you should dive conservatively. Do everything you can to avoid a dive accident!

CHAMBER CONTACT INFORMATION

Pattaya
Sattahip Naval Base, located 45 minutes south of Pattaya, have urgent care available 24 hours and a recompression chamber.

Bangkok
Department of Underwater & Aviation

Medicine, Phra Pinklao Naval Hospital, Taksin Road, Thonburi, Bangkok, open 24 hours.

Phuket
Hyperbaric Services Thailand, SSS Recompression Network Phuket, 44/1 Moo 5, Chalermprakiat Ror 9 Road, Vichit, Muang, Phuket 83000. Office: Tel: (66) 76209 347, 24 hour diving emergencies: (66) 81081 9000; Phuket@sssnetwork.com.
Badalveda Diving Medicine Center, Bangkok Phuket Hospital, Tel: 076 254 425

Krabi
Krabi Evacuation Center, SSS Recompression Network, Krabi, 376/3 Moo 2, Aonang, Krabi 81000. Tel: (66) 7563 8376. 24 hour diving emergencies: (66) 81081 9222; krabi@sssnetwork.com.

Khao Lak
Khao Lak Evacuation Center, SSS Recompression Network, Khao Lak. 24 hour diving emergencies: Tel: (66) 81081 9444; khaolak@sssnetwork.com.

Samui
Samui, SSS Recompression Network. Tel: +66 (0) 77 427 427; 24 hour diving emergencies: (66) 81081 9555
Bangkok Hospital Samui: Tel: +66 (0) 7742 9500; www.samuihospital.com; info@samui-hospital.com.

Note: Keep in mind that Hyperbaric Services Thailand can charge over US$1,000 per hour for treatment (and many hours may be required), so insurance must be purchased before traveling. Government-operated chambers charge much less but are only in the Bangkok area. Dive insurance is very reasonable through DAN (insurance is available worldwide) and well worth it in case of a problem, real or perceived. See more about DAN below.

Weather
Thailand has three seasons—cool, hot and rainy. The best time to visit the west coast is between October and May, while the best time to visit the east coast is February to August.

The summer months of July and August are usually very pleasant, although it tends to rain in the evenings. September is not the best time on the islands as it tends to be rainy and the seas are generally too rough for swimming or diving.

Most of the good dive sites are on islands far enough offshore to be unaffected by runoff, and rain makes no difference to the water clarity. Visibility in the Similans, for example, is actually greatest during the summer months despite the evening rains.

Clothing

Although shorts and T-shirts are appropriate for dive boats and beaches, Thais tend to dress more formally and are actually offended by revealing clothing, especially when worn by women. Be aware of your surroundings and avoid giving offense. Topless and nude sunbathing are officially against the law although they are widespread, especially in backpacker hangouts. Thai people are very forgiving but this does not mean these practices are accepted. If you are on a beach with a majority of Thais, please wear a bathing suit.

What to bring

Try to pack as lightly as possible as the climate is very agreeable except near the northern borders in December and January. Warm clothing is available for rent there if you are planning a trek.

The diving industry is very competitive in Thailand, and equipment, usually in very good shape, is available for rent no matter where you dive. Spares are readily available in Phuket, Samui and Ko Tao as there are a number of dive suppliers/stores and most large operators also sell some new, smaller items. It is always best though to bring things like extra mask and fin straps and o-rings in case of breakages. Most centers rent wet suits.

A 3 mm wet suit (even a shorty or surfing style) or a Lycra suit is adequate for diving all year round. Keep in mind, however, that Lycra offers little or no thermal protection, and these suits are not adequate if you plan to dive three or more times per day. A full-length neoprene suit is probably best for serious diving.

Power in Thailand is 220 VAC. Although some of the more expensive dive boats offer 110VAC, you should bring a proper adapter if you have 110V equipment. *Note*: Inexpensive "shaver" type adapters will not work for such devices as laptop computers and rechargers for underwater flashes. Bring the proper type. Most places stock batteries.

Many dive shops are increasingly concentrating on the retail dive gear business. Prices vary, and if you are considering buying equipment while in Thailand, it's a good idea to have an idea of what it would cost at home first. In general, however, prices are competitive and many items will be far cheaper than they would be at home. The selection of gear available to purchase is quite surprising and most major brands are available.

Photography

Most dive centers have compact cameras with housings available for rental. If you are planning to rent a camera, it is a good idea to travel with a USB stick or SD card with a decent memory capacity for taking your images home. Some shops also rent larger camera setups for those taking photography courses or wanting to try something more sophisticated. When taking pictures, always be respectful of the marine life. The dive operator should pack the camera into the housing for you. Once that is done, do not open the housing yourself, hand it back to the operator for opening.

Communications

In Thailand it is always necessary to dial the city/province code before the number, even if you are in the same province! The easiest and cheapest way to maintain communications when in Thailand is to buy a local SIM card for your own phone and then use top up (credit) vouchers that are widely available for purchase. Vouchers are available in various amounts and calls are cheap.

If you call from overseas, do not dial the "0" after the country code (66). So, to call Bangkok from overseas you would dial +662+ the number. From inside Thailand, 02+ the number.

Internet access

Accessing email or the web in Thailand is relatively cheap and very painless, especially as it can now be accessed through your mobile phone. Most credit vouchers you buy for a Thai SIM card also allow Internet browsing and email. There are also hundreds of Internet cafés in all tourist areas, and most other areas as well. Larger coffee shops such as Starbucks also have free Wi-fi for customers as do most restaurants and bars. Just ask for the login and password.

Money exchange

Thai currency is the Thai baht (THB), but many operators will accept payments in US dollars and Euros. ATMs are widely available in towns, cities and tourist areas and allow you to take out money from your home account in baht. Charges vary according to the bank and ATM operator but are usually relatively low if using a debit card. Credit card withdrawals often cost more.

Changing money is easy except in extremely remote areas where you probably don't need much money anyway. Credit cards are widely accepted and dive centers normally do not add a service charge although many hotels and other shops will.

Accommodation

Thailand has some of the best hotels in the world and service is often of the highest standard. Thailand is a country with many levels of economy, and the choice of what class you want to fit into is definitely yours. Divers generally select one of the many inexpensive and comfortable guest houses or bungalows, although fancy hotels and upmarket dive resorts are certainly available.

On the islands, room rates range from under US$20-35 (at the time of writing) for a basic bungalow with cold water and a fan. US$50-100 will give you an enormous range to choose from with hot water, air-conditioning and a comfortable room. If you want to hang out in luxury with the heavy players, figure $275 a night or more. If you are interested in the more expensive hotels, booking in advance through an agent can save you 50 percent or more. It

pays to book in advance, except in the low season on some of the smaller islands when bargaining becomes acceptable and there can be some good deals made. In the high season, prices tend to be less negotiable.

Food

Thai cuisine is famous the world over for its remarkable variety and often blistering flavor. Experiment as often as you can. Southern Thailand—where the diving happens—is famous for its fresh seafood. Food is usually very inexpensive, but like everywhere in the world, you can pay more for atmosphere.

Rice is the staple and is served with almost every dish that is ordered here. Many different varieties of rice are available depending on what kind of food you're ordering. Curries are absolutely fantastic in Thailand and vary in degree of spiciness from mild and sweet to fiery.

Quite often the best food available is right off the side of the street. Thais are extremely creative in business and it is common to see Thai families set up a portable restaurant on a street corner. Some will have a more permanent *kwait diaw* (noodle) shop on the sidewalk. This type of food is often fresher that what you will find in the more expensive restaurants because the food stalls have no refrigerators and operators must buy their ingredients fresh every day. Don't be afraid to experiment even if it means trying the fried silkworms (astonishingly tasty with a cold Singha beer).

For those with more traditional tastes, in all the tourist areas most international cuisines are available, including American steak, Italian pasta, German schnitzel and Swedish meatballs. McDonalds, if you must, is also available countrywide as is KFC, Pizza Hut and Swensen's, among others.

Thailand is famous for its fruits, and even if you've traveled widely in the tropics you will see fruits here that you have never encountered before. The best season for unusual fruit is March to September. Thais have very creative ways to prepare fruit dishes. A favorite and delicious springtime dish is *kao neaow matmuang*, a concoction of fresh mango slices on a bed of rice marinated in coconut milk overnight. You should also try the durian, an ugly and horrible smelling fruit that many Asians insist is the best fruit in the universe. See for yourself.

Liveaboard boats in Thailand offer some of the finest food anywhere, and often people come back time and time again not only for the diving but for the incredible meals that are served onboard.

Dive operators

Professional diving services are the norm in Thailand. The industry is huge and the standard of service and professionalism is unequaled in Southeast Asia. Most dive centers are affiliated with PADI, but SSI and NAUI instruction are available in many places. Prices vary depending on what you are doing, where you are going and how comfortable you want to be.

It is always best to contact diving centers to arrange your holiday before arriving since at certain times of the year, especially in Phuket, dive boats are frequently full. If you are planning to join a liveaboard to the Andaman Islands, Burma Banks or Similan Islands, booking ahead is essential.

Most diving activities are supervised by a diving guide, either Thai or *falang* (Western foreigner, pronounced "fah-lahng" in Thai) who speak a variety of languages. If you are a beginner, it is generally suggested that you find out as much about the dive site and the guide as possible before booking. Not all dive sites in Thailand are suitable for beginners, and like anywhere, not all guides are as competent as others. It pays to look around.

On the longer journeys, which attract more experienced divers, more freedom is usually given to the individual diver, although most dive outfits discourage recreational dives past 40 meters. Technical diving centers are also common in Thailand, so deeper diving is sometimes possible. The problem is finding water deeper than 40 meters in Thailand.

All the listed dive centers offer beginning dive courses and some offer advanced and professional level instruction. All courses are generally of high quality and the prices are reasonable. Class sizes in Thailand vary from center to center. The ratio of students per pro-

fessional are usually quite good but this can be only one instructor backed up by 2 divemasters and a class of 8. Opt for smaller classes with a maximum of 4 students to each instructor. In Ko Tao, in particular, classes can be larger than ideal.

Liveaboards

Keep in mind that liveaboard dive boats, no matter how large, do not have a lot of space for luggage storage. Most dive operators recommend soft-sided luggage on the boat but will allow you to store extra bags at the dive center. Since liveaboard diving is casual, only a few T-shirts, shorts and possibly a sweatshirt for the evenings are necessary. Generally, the less you bring with you, the more comfortable you will be.

Divers Alert Network (DAN)

This US non-profit researches dive safety, provides medical advice to injured divers, keeps an updated list of operational hyperbaric chambers and offers affordable insurance. Annual membership prices vary according to the level of cover you opt for but fully comprehensive cover, which includes medivac, is strongly recommended.

DAN Southeast Asia-Pacific, located in Australia, has regional responsibility for Australia and New Zealand, Papua New Guinea, Fiji, Indonesia, Malaysia, Vietnam, Singapore, Cambodia, Myanmar, Philippines, Vanuatu, India, Solomon Islands, Brunei, Thailand, Hong Kong, Korea, China and Taiwan. 24 hour emergency hotline number: +61-8-8212-9242; www.danasiapacific.org; info@danap.org

Environmental considerations

Divers and dive operators in Thailand are, for the most part, very aware of the value of Thailand's unique natural environment and, more importantly, going to efforts to preserve it. Divers have long been aware of damage to coral reefs through dynamite fishing and anchoring, but only recently have dive centers starting thinking about the damage that can be done by divers themselves. Thailand now has some of the most environmentally progressive dive shops in the world, which has helped keep our reefs healthy and beautiful.

When diving here, please try to respect the wishes of the diving community by not gathering or collecting any corals or shells, even from the beaches. Of course, never buy marine items from shell shops as this will only encourage the proprietors to order more stock.

Please do not spear fish. Although some argue that spearfishing is not damaging because it is selective, it tends to frighten fish and make them unapproachable. Also, since spearfishing is selective, the pressure is felt only on larger animals and only on certain species. This can upset the ecological balance of the reef.

On land, you'll find that like in most countries, Thailand has its share of plastic garbage. Although this is a worldwide problem, make an effort to do your part. Take your own bag or backpack to the store and buy a canteen or reusable plastic container to hold drinking water during trips to the beach (your hotel will be more than happy to fill this up for you, especially if you explain why you are doing it this way). Think about where this plastic will end up. Don't take an out of sight, out of mind attitude, because you just may see that bottle washed up on your favorite beach the next day.

Finally, most islands in Thailand have a year round fresh water shortage. Please do not waste water. You may see green tropical foliage surrounding you but there is very little water in the ground. Shorten your showers, turn off the water while shaving and generally be conscious of water use.

National park fees

As of this writing, the Thai government has imposed fees to enter any national parks in Thailand, and there are often user fees charged as well. The charge varies from park to park, with some being as little as 100 THB but others, for example the Similans, being 500 THB plus a "user fee". There are two rates for national parks, rates for foreigners (tourists) and a much lower rate for local people. Likewise, children and adults usually pay different rates.

With tourism in Thailand being at an all time high and with an increasing number of marine parks, the Thai government is generating a large income through park fees. All we can do is hope that the money is used wisely and that a portion of it goes towards protecting the environment.

Bangkok City code: 02

Getting there

Many connecting flights are available out of Don Muang Airport. Check with your travel agent for schedules and destinations. Reservations are recommended almost all year around.

Getting around

Book your taxi at one of the offices inside the airport. Ignore touts. If you take a taxi from one of the official taxi stands in front of the arrivals terminals, the taxis run on a meter with a 50 baht airport surcharge. Ask for the meter rather than trying to negotiate a price; usually you will lose! There is also an airport bus which will drop you off at many locations in Bangkok and which runs regularly. For those who want to save this fare, walk to the public bus stop and take a bus into town for almost nothing. Be warned, however, that this takes a long time. Free transport is available from the domestic terminal to the international and vice versa. Do not be fooled into paying for this short journey. There is a walkway between the terminals which takes about 10 minutes.

Metered taxis are available throughout Bangkok and are extremely comfortable (air-conditioned) and convenient. Depending on the time of day and the traffic, it should cost around 200 baht to get you back to the airport from downtown and take around 30–60 minutes. Make sure the meter is on before you start your journey, and if no meter is available, discuss the price before you begin your journey. Bargaining is possible in many instances, but keep smiling!

The tollway or freeway system can save a lot of time but there is a small toll fee. If you are in a hurry, or traffic is bad, ask the driver to use the "tollway" (same word in Thai) and give him the amount he asks for. This is never included in the fare unless you book transportation from an agency or hotel, but it's wise to check.

Phuket City code: 076

Some 890 km south of the capital, Phuket is accessible by land, sea and air. Frequent daily buses ply the route from Bangkok. The journey by bus takes 14 hours and buses depart from the **Southern Bus Terminal**, Boromratch-chonnani Road in Bangkok and arrive in Phuket Town at the bus station in town. From there you can take a taxi, tuk tuk or bus to any of the beaches around the island. For information about buses from Bangkok to Phuket, contact the Southern Bus Terminal on (02) 435 1200 or 434 7192.

Trains also connect Bangkok with Surat Thani (3.5 hours by car northeast of Phuket) and Hat Yai (7 hours by car southeast of Phuket) in the south of Thailand. From these points, travelers can catch an inter-provincial bus to Phuket.

Numerous daily flights connect Bangkok's **Don Muang Domestic Airport** with Phuket. Tickets can cost from around US$60 depending on what deals are available and how far in advance you are booking. In addition, Phuket's modern international airport welcomes flights from a wide range of international destinations, including daily flights from Singapore.

Accommodation and food

Phuket has probably the widest range of accommodation anywhere in Thailand, from exclusive lodging at the Aman Puri Resort for more than US$1,000 per day to multiple local guest houses for often less than US$20 per day and everything in between. The most popular (and crowded) beach is **Patong**, the center for entertainment, shopping and night life. To the south you'll find **Kata-Karon**, which is quieter and classier and the home of Club Med. An integrated resort near the airport (**Bang Tao Beach**) offers first-class international hotels and many amenities for travelers. These include the Sheraton, Laguna Beach Resort and the Dusit Laguna, all of which will spoil you to your heart's content.

Food is wonderful, diverse and readily available from noodle shops on street corners, local seafood restaurants right on the ocean and international style continental restaurants that will make you feel as if you've never left home.

And yes, we finally have a McDonald's and a Starbucks for those of you who insist, right on Patong Beach.

For obvious reasons, Phuket is most famous for its seafood. However, it is not just the availability of seafood that makes it popular. Phuket's locals have many exciting, special recipes and preparation techniques that motivate even Thais from Bangkok to make that special trip to Phuket. Keep in the mind that the more seafood you eat, the less fish there are to see in the ocean, although many products are farmed. Divers please note.

Dive operators

Most of Phuket's diving centers offer one-day trips to the Racha Islands, Shark Point, *King Cruiser* wreck and Ko Phi Phi. In addition, most of the dive centers listed here can provide liveaboard diving to the Similan Islands and beyond, as well as Burma. Some of these centers can arrange charters to the Andaman Islands as well.

All of the dive centers here offer excellent diving instruction and most of them offer courses all the way up to the instructor level. Specialty courses are available, especially on the better liveaboard dive boats, some of which have onboard professional photographers.

Phuket is Thailand's center for liveaboard diving and several of the operators offer boats that cater to a very select group of divers. These boats feature modern navigational systems, international radio communications and safety features, and the stability to travel the open oceans. They also offer first-class service, crew, accommodation and meals.

Prices in Phuket for a two-dive day trip do not vary so much but what is included depends on the operator. Ideally, you should choose a day trip package which includes hotel pick-up, lunch, tanks and weights and a qualified divemaster. Gear rental is widely available but, as always, you should check out the condition of the equipment prior to diving with it. Boats certainly vary in quality, so it's best to check with individual dive centers for their particular package and vessel.

Liveaboard prices vary dramatically and the services, destinations and quality of the boat vary dramatically as well. Trips to the Similans on a basic style boat are the cheapest whilst trips to the Mergui Archipelago, Burma Banks or Andaman Islands on a very comfortable boat will be far more costly. There are many mid-range priced boats now in Phuket that are well worth the price due the higher level of comfort. The more comfortable you want to be, the safer you want to be and the further you want to gg, the more you pay.

The following operators, listed in alphabetical order, are recommended:

Aussie Divers A PADI 5 star dive facility located in Patong offering PADI courses, daily fun diving, dive trips and liveaboards. Tel: +66 076 688 113; www.aussiedivers.com.

Dive Asia Located on Karon Beach, this is Phuket's first PADI 5 star CDC center. It offers recreational and professional level training, daily fun diving and dive trips. Tel (24 hours): +66 (0) 8189 48588; www.diveasia.com; reservations@diveasia.com.

Kon-Tiki Diving & Snorkeling Center Located at 84 Taina Rd, T. Karon A Muang, Phuket, this center offers day trips, liveaboards courses and IDCs, also with Dive centers in Ko Lanta, Krabi and Khao Lak. Tel: +66 (0) 76 330 674; www.kontiki-thailand.com; info@kontiki-phuket.com.

Scuba Cat Diving A PADI 5 star CDC center in Patong offering recreational and professional PADI courses, fun diving around Phuket and the Similans (liveaboard) as well as day trips to other areas. Tel: +66 (0) 7629 3120; www.scubacat.com; info@scubacat.com.

Sea Bees Diving This is one of the largest operators in Phuket with branches at Amari Coral Beach Resort, JW Marriot Mai Khao, Outrigger Laguna Beach Resort and also in Nai Harn. Sea Bees also has dive centers in Phi Phi and Khao Lak. Tel (main Phuket office): +66 (0) 76 381 765; www.sea-bees.com; info@sea-bees.com.

Sea Fun Divers PADI 5 star dive centers located at two different resorts—Le Meridien Phuket Beach Resort in Karon Noi (+66 0 76 34 480) and Kata Thani Phuket Beach Resort in Kata Noi (+66 0 76 330 124). The company offers dive courses, day trips, liveaboards and both centers have good house reefs. www.seafundivers.com; info@seafundivers.com.

Siam Dive n' Sail This outfit offers a large range of liveaboard trips and dive safaris on a number of vessels. www.siamdivers.com; dive@siamdivers.com or siamdivensail@gmail.com

Sunrise Divers Situated on Karon Beach, this PADI 5 Star dive center offers diving around Phuket, the Similans and Phi Phi Islands. It also offers a full range of courses, day trips, overnight trips and liveaboards. Tel: +66 (0) 8 4626 4646; www.sunrise-divers.com; info@sunrise-divers.com.

Thailand Divers A PADI dive center based in Patong Beach offering PADI courses, fun diving, tours and liveaboards to the Similans. Tel: +66 (0) 87 275 3238; www.thailand-divers.com; info@thailand-divers.com.

Burma: Mergui Archipelago and Burma Banks

Your dive operator will explain the ways and what fors of a trip to the Mergui Archipelago, but at the time of writing this is the situation.

Some liveaboard trips will depart from and return to Phuket and spend at least two days diving in Thailand on the way up and back. Other trips will depart from Kawthaung (Victoria Point) in Myanmar (Burma).

The Burmese immigration officials require that you bring your passport, a photocopy of the front page of it and your Thai immigration stamp page, four passport sized photos and pay a fee, currently around US$200 depending on the length of your stay. Marine park fees are also payable as follows: Similan and Surin fees are approximately US$6 per day plus a $15 entry fee per park. Burma marine park fees are also payable and you should check these with your operator. These fees, not included by the operator in their cruise prices because they are subject to change, are usually paid by you in cash to the liveaboard staff who will then organize payment for you. For more details, please contact your dive operator as procedures can vary.

When selecting a liveaboard operator, check what is included in the price. Some operators include local wine and beer, others soft drinks only. Make sure you are clear on the price of marine park fees and how to pay them. Ask if nitrox is charged additionally or included. Recommended liveaboards operating these routes are as follows:

Thailand Aggressor A 35 meter, steel hulled yacht making 7 and 10 night Burma trips. The vessel carries a maximum of 16 guests and all cabins are ensuite. The *Thailand Aggressor* departs from Tap Lamu Pier, Khao Lak, in the evening. An airport pickup service is provided from Phuket Airport.

MV *Deep Andaman Queen* This makes 8 night trips covering the Similans and Mergui Archipelago. This 28 meter monohulled motor yacht caters for 19 guests in a mix of master, VIP and budget cabins. Trips depart and return to Khao Lak and pickups are included from Phuket Airport.

SY *Diva Andaman* This stylish 35 meter wooden hulled sailing yacht caters for 16 guests and offers trips to the Similans, which depart from Chalong in the evening, and also to Burma, which depart from Ranong in the afternoons.

Phi Phi Islands City code: 075

Some dive operators have mobile phones as business numbers (01 or 09).

Regular ferries and hydrofoil services link Phi Phi with Phuket (Rassada Pier). If you are coming from Phuket Airport by bus, it is advisable to buy a combination transfer ticket that includes bus and ferry. Alternatively, taxis from Phuket are relatively inexpensive. Various ferry companies leave for Phi Phi

at different times. Recommended is the **Andaman Wave Master** as it is most comfortable. This leaves at 8.30am and 1.30pm.

Accommodation and food

Places to stay vary widely in Ko Phi Phi, though prices are generally higher than in Phuket. On the northern shore of Phi Phi there are numerous first class restaurants, a feel of exclusivity, and freshwater swimming pools. These run from over US$100–250 plus per night.

As many Western foreigners have settled on the island, the food available varies from traditional Thai and seafood restaurants to hamburger joints with black and white checked floors and excellent bakeries. No sign of McDonald's yet; the nearest is in Krabi if you are desperate! Authentic Italian pizza and pasta are readily available, as are steaks and seafood. You name it, they have it and for a range of budgets too.

Dive operators

Some diving centers in Ko Phi Phi now have larger boats to take you to the local sites and to areas further away, such as Trang and even the Similan Islands. Boat quality is getting better all the time.

Most of the diving shops are connected with the PADI training organization and there are instructor level courses being carried out in dive centers across the island. NAUI and SSI instruction are available on the island as well. Although the majority of the dive centres are professionally run and prices do not differ much between them, as a beginner, a student, or as a serious diver who wants good information about marine life, it pays to check around before committing to a course or diving trip. Bear in mind that you generally get what you pay for and the quality of instruction and guide service may well be more important to you than the price. It is also worth checking what is included in the price, for example, lunch, pickups, gear hire, course materials, etc.

The following operators, listed in alphabetical order, are recommended:

Ao Nang Divers Integrated with the **Krabi Sea View Hotel**, this PADI 5 star dive center has a multilingual website, daily dive trips and dive courses. Contact is through the form on their website: www.aonang-divers.com.

Barakuda Dive Center Located in the center of Tonsai village, Barakuda Dive Center offers both PADI and SSI courses and focuses on keeping student and fun diving groups small. Open water courses are usually a maximum of 2 students to 1 instructor. For certified divers, daily dive trips and safaris are offered. Tel: +66 (0) 75 601 006; www.phiphibarakuda.com; info@phiphibarakuda.com

Kon-Tiki Diving & Snorkeling Center Located at 161/1 Moo 2, Tambon Ao Nang, Amphur Muang, Krabi, it offers day trips, liveaboards, courses and IDCs. It also has dive centers in Ko Lanta, Phuket and Khao Lak. Tel: +66 (0) 75 637 826; www.kontiki-thailand. com; info@kontiki-krabi.com.

Moskito Diving Center Situated at 111 Moo 7, Phi Phi Island, Ao Nang, Muang, Krabi, it offers a full range of PADI courses, including IDCs, daily fun diving and dive trips. Tel: +66 (0) 95 570 8051; www.moskitodiving.com; moskitodiving@gmail.com.

Sunrise Divers Operating out of 269/24 Patak Road, Karon Beach, Phuket, it offers diving trips to Phuket and liveaboards. Tel: +66 (0) 8 4626 4646; www.sunrise-divers. com; info@sunrise-divers.com.

Phi Phi Scuba Diving Center One of the largest operators in Phi Phi, and located in Ton Sai Bay, this center offers guided fun diving, dive trips and safaris and both PADI and SSI dive courses. Tel: +66 (0) 75 601 148; www. ppscuba.com; ppscuba@gmail.com.

Sea Bees Diving A large operator with centers in Khao Lak and Phuket, it is based at the **Holiday Inn Resort**. It offers courses, fun diving, day trips and safaris. Tel: +66 (0) 93 649 1725; www.sea-bees.com; phi-phi@sea-bees.com.

Ko Samui City code: 077

Visitors to Ko Samui have a choice of ways of reaching the island. If you are flying into Chumphon, there is a high-speed ferry to Ko Samui which stops at Ko Tao along the way.

If you are flying into Surat Thani, you need to head to Donsak Pier where the boats for Ko Samui depart from. It is best to buy a bus and ferry combo package from the airport. The bus ride is around 60 minutes to the pier and the ferry journey a further 90 minutes or so. Alternatively, travelers may fly from Bangkok or Phuket to Ko Samui with **Bangkok Airways**. There are a number of flights daily. **Thai Airways** also flies from Bangkok to Ko Samui. Seasonally, direct flights to Ko Samui from both Kuala Lumpur and Singapore are available.

Accommodation and food

Samui, like Phuket, has an incredible range of accommodation available. There are still many places with huts right on the beach for sometimes around US$20 in low season. And there is incredibly expensive, luxurious accommodation as well. You can probably still spend more money in Phuket if that's your style but the difference is not much. One very delightful thing about much of the accommodation in Samui is that the hotels have tried to maintain the traditional Thai architectural style, with huge slanting roofs and lots of wood. Even the airport is built in this way and it makes a charming first impression when you arrive.

As in all tourist centers in Thailand, food is available to suit any palate. Samui has great little beachside restaurants that normally show videos in the evenings, and many little funky places run by both foreigners and Thais that serve everything from great pasta to Muslim vegetarian food to pizza. Some of the late night food carts—restaurants on motorcycles—that hang about outside the discos after midnight offer great barbecued chicken, spring rolls and deep fried everything. This is just the thing to eat after a few too many Singha beers.

Dive operators

All of Ko Samui's dive centers offer high quality diving courses and are well organized and reliable. Your diving trips are always supervised by a professional divemaster or instructor.

Travel time to the different destinations, such as Sail Rock and the marine park, is 2–3 hours. Prices do not tend to vary significantly between the operators but it is worth shopping around for deals and packages, especially if you are planning a few days or more of diving. The average 2 dive day trip includes transportation, tanks and weights and a divemaster. Prices are sometimes reduced during the low tourist season between August and January. Most operators now also arrange diving trips to Ko Tao as well as nearby Ko Phangngan. The majority of operators are affiliated with PADI but SSI courses are also available. There are a number of larger operators on Ko Samui offering instructor level training. The following operators, listed in alphabetical order, are recommended:

Discovery Dive Center A PDI 5 star dive center offering PADI courses and daily dive trips. Tel: +66 77 310 764; www.discoverydivers.com; info@discoverydivers.com.

Samui Easy Divers A PADI 5 star IDC facility offering recreational and professional level PADI courses, tours, daily dive trips and hotel pickups and drop offs. Tel: +66 (0) 77 448 129; www.easydivers-thailand.com; info@easydivers-thailand.com.

Searobin Dive Center A PADI dive center offering PADI courses and daily fun diving from its Choeng Mon shop, which is affiliated with **Choeng Mon Beach Hotel**. Searobin's sister company, **Ko Samui Boat Charter**, offers private charters on board the luxury yacht *Blue Dragon*. Tel: 66 (0) 84 868 4842; www.divesearobin.com; info@divesearobin.com.

The Dive Academy Samui One of Samui's largest operators, this PADI 5 star IDC center offers a full range of PADI courses, small diver to professional ratios (4 : 1 max), and some good early booking discounts through their website. PADI open water course is priced at 17,000 THB, advanced open water 14,000 THB, trips to Sail Rock 4,800 THB and to Ko Tao 5,000 THB. Tel: +66 9 2464 3264; www.thediveacademysamui.com; info@thediveacademysamui.com.

Ko Tao City code: 077

Ko Tao is easily accessible from Ko Samui or Ko Phangngan by daily ferry, weather permitting. The ticket price varies according to the style of boat and crossing time, with private charters obviously being the most expensive option. A speedboat service also operates daily between Ko Tao and Chumpon.

Accommodation and food

Ko Tao has a mix of accommodation, from basic bungalows to much more upmarket offerings. Resorts have 24 hour electricity, air-conditioning and hot water but some bungalows in more remote places may still operate their own generator that runs during set hours only.

The dining scene on Ko Tao has drastically improved in recent years and there is a range of cuisines available. If you are looking for cheap Thai food, there is a lot on offer and it is basic but very good. If fine dining is more to your taste, there are several decent restaurants serving both Thai and international cuisine. As in most of Thailand, when it comes to food there is always something good on offer and new places are constantly opening up.

Dive operators

Ko Tao now has a number of PADI 5 star IDC dive centers and all shops offer high quality instruction. Many of the dive boats on the island operate with GPS navigation systems, which enable the guides to find hidden underwater pinnacles—normally the best sites—consistently and quickly.

Due to a rapid increase in the number of dive operators on the island, prices for fun diving and for dive courses are very competitive. Look out for packages that include diving and accommodation or courses and accommodation combos. Most operators also operate a sliding scale when it comes to fun diving, so the more dives you make, the cheaper they become.

The following operators, listed in alphabetical order, are recommended:

Ban's Diving Resort This PADI 5 star CDC resort offers a full range of recreational and professional courses, daily dive trips, 2 swimming pools, full service dive center and beachfront restaurant. Accommodation is also available with a discounted rate for divers. Tel: +66 (0) 7745 6466; www.bansdivingresort. com; info@bansdivingresort.com.

Big Blue Diving Ko Tao Based in Surat Thani, Big Blue offers SSI, BSAC and TDI courses, full day trips and technical and wreck diving. el: +66 (0) 77 456 050; www.bigblue-diving.com; info@bigbluediving.com.

Easy Divers A PADI 5 star IDC center operating out of two resorts—**Easy Divers Resort** and **Beach Club Resort**. This is a large operator offering fun diving, dive trips and courses. It is worth looking on their website for packages including accommodation and promos. Tel: +66 (0) 7745 6010; www.kohtaoeasydivers. com; Email contact is through their enquiry form on the website.

Scuba Junction Located in Sairee, Beach Scuba Junction offers both PADI and SSI courses, daily fun diving, dive packages and help with accommodation booking. Groups here are a maximum of 4 students to 1 instructor. Tel: +66 (0) 77 456 164; www.scuba-junction. com; Email contact is through their website.

Planet Scuba Dive Center Located at Seatran Pier, Mae Hadd, Planet Scuba also has operations in Ko Samui and Bangkok. Daily fun diving, dive trips and SSI courses are available. Tel: +66 77 456 110; www.planetscuba.net; tao@planetscuba.net.

Pattaya City code: 038

Pattaya is situated 147 km southeast of Bangkok. Air-conditioned buses link Pattaya with both Don Muang International Airport and the center of Bangkok. Buses depart from **Bangkok's Eastern Bus Terminal** every half hour and take an average of just under 2 hours to make the journey. Pattaya is well connected via Highway 7, so if you are planning to drive yourself, the route is relatively straight forward. if you prefer not to travel by bus, it is possible to hire a car and driver or take a taxi.

Accommodation and food

Pattaya was the first tourist resort built in Thailand and it's got everything, including high-end luxury resorts and villas. For those on a budget, there are also many, many small guest houses, often run by foreigners, which are sometimes available for less than US$25 per night. Since Pattaya is so big, there are always hotel rooms available and it pays to check with travel agents to find the best deals.

Although just a few years back Pattaya had acquired a poor reputation, the government has done a good job cleaning up the town and it's again a very nice place to visit.

Like Phuket, Samui, and Bangkok, Pattaya has every kind of food available. Like Bangkok, Pattaya is a 24-hour city, and street vendors sell everything from fresh tropical fruit to Chinese noodles and Indian curries to fried silkworms. Eating off the carts on the streets, like everywhere in Thailand, is where you'll find the most varieties of food prepared in the most local way. You'll also find great seafood and steak houses in Pattaya, along with wonderful Japanese restaurants.

And yes, there are McDonald's, Pizza Hut, Kentucky Fried Chicken, Dunkin' Donuts and all the rest of the chains. Why people eat this stuff when they are in the country with the best food in all the world, I'll never know, but if you've got that homesick feeling, in Pattaya you may indulge.

Dive operators

This small city was the first place in Thailand to develop a diving industry, so most of the operators are well-established. The centers listed below all offer quality diving instruction. Most of their business comes from Bangkok, so the weekends in Pattaya can be quite crowded and it pays to book ahead. Some of the shops offer special weekend dives or liveaboard trips which get the working diver back at work early Monday morning.

Because many of the clients of the Pattaya operators are regular divers coming in from Bangkok who own their own tanks and weights, boat prices are generally less than in other places, but equipment rental is more. If you need equipment, it's about the same, but if you have all of your own equipment, diving in Pattaya can be quite inexpensive.

Many of Pattaya's dive operators also offer diving trips to Ko Chang. Ask around to see what different trips are available.

The following operators, listed in alphabetical order, are recommended:

Aquanauts Dive Center A PADI 5 star IDC center offering a full range of professional and recreational courses as well as daily fun diving and dive trips for certified divers. Tel: +66 (0) 38 361 724; www.aquanautsdive.com; info@aquanautsdive.com.

Mermaid's Dive Center This experienced operator is a PADI 5 star CDC facility offering a full range of professional and recreational courses, daily fun diving, dive trips and safaris. Hotel pickups and lunches are included in their day trips. The main dive center is situated in Jomtien and they also have retail and training facilities at the Centara Grand Mirage Resort, North Pattaya and in Bangkok. Tel: +66 3830 3333; www.mermaidsdivecenter.com. Email contact is through the enquiry form on their website.

Pattaya Dive Centre This PADI 5 star IDC center offers fun diving, courses up to and including instructor level and technical deep diver training. Tel: +6638422 133; www.divecentrepattaya.com; info@divecentrepattaya.com.

Real Divers A British run PADI 5 star IDC center located in Jomtien, Real Divers offers professional and recreational courses, daily dive trips and a full service dive center. Tel: +66 (0) 38 232 476; www.real-divers.com; realdiverspattayathailand@gmail.com.

Seafari Dive Center This offers PADI and SSI courses, fun diving and dive trips. www.seafari.co.th; diving@seafari.co.th.

Andaman Islands

Dive operators

There are a few dive centers in the Andaman Islands themselves, but this is still a developing area for the diving industry. On Havelock Island is **Andaman Bubbles Dive Center** that offers PADI and SSI courses and fun diving trips. Andaman Bubbles is located next to the **Wild Orchid Resort**, which offers simple but clean air-conditioned and non-air-conditioned accommodation with bathrooms and 24 hour running hot water. If you are diving with Andaman Bubbles, they will also help to arrange an accommodation booking at Wild Orchid. Contact details for Andaman Bubbles: Tel: +91 3192 282 140; www.andamanbubbles.com; andamanbubbles@gmail.com. For Wild Orchid Resort: www.wildorchidandaman.com.

Another option is **Island Vinnies**, which offers diving and accommodation in tented cabanas and huts. Standard huts have shared bathrooms, upgraded huts and cabanas have their own. Dive courses and fun diving trips are available. Tel: +91 3192 214 247; www.islandvinnie.com; info@islandvinnie.com.

Prices are relatively the same as those in Thailand for both diving and instruction.

Liveaboards

There are a number of Thai-based liveaboard operators diving the Andamans, some departing from Port Blair, others from Phuket.

If you are embarking on a liveaboard trip from the Indian side of the Andamans, then you will most likely depart from Port Blair. Your liveaboard operator will help to arrange overnight accommodation. Check what options are available and recommended as new places are continuing to open up. There are several options for eating out and some of the local food is wonderful but you should not expect to find western fast food outlets here!

Recommended liveaboards include:

Siam Dive N' Sail This company, which has years of experience in liveaboard diving around Thailand, runs both the **MY *Infiniti Liveaboard*** and the **MV *Panunee Liveaboard***. Their website contains a lot of useful information about available charters and cruises. www.siamdivers.com; dive@siam-divers.com.

MY *Infiniti Liveaboard* This 37 meter vessel has 2 cabins on the upper deck, 4 on the main deck and 2 on the lower deck. All cabins are equipped with air-conditioning, hot water, ensuite bathrooms and storage space. The *Infiniti* cruises around the Andaman and Lakshadweep Islands. The operator can be contacted directly: Tel: +91 98202 34027; www.infinitiliveaboard.com; divetrips@InfinitiLiveAboard.com.

FURTHER READING

In addition to a good guide to dive sites, a diver is probably most interested in a fish identification book to help make sense of the more than 2,500 species swimming around the reefs of Southeast Asia.

Complete Combinations

Two excellent books, which together provide comprehensive coverage of marine life in Southeast Asia are *Reef Fish Identification: Tropical Pacific*, 2nd edn, by Gerald Allen, Roger Steene, Paul Humann and Ned Deloach (New World Publications, 2005), and *Reef Creature Identification Tropical Pacific*, 2nd edn, by Paul Humann and Ned Deloach (New World Publications, 2010). The first contains over 2,500 underwater photographs of more than 2,000 species of fish (including juveniles and various color phases). The second has excellent coverage of 1,600 shrimps, lobsters, crabs, cephalopods, nudibranchs, flat worms and everything in between. Both books are amongst the most up to date on the market and include many of the relatively new species undocumented in other publications.

Reef Fishes

Reef Fishes of the World by Ewald Lieske and Robert F. Myers (Periplus Editions, 1994) is a comprehensive guide to over 2,000 species with 2,500 color illustrations. It enables divers and snorkelers to identify the inhabitants of coral reefs wherever they are in the world.

Tropical Reef-Fishes of the Western Pacific: Indonesia and Adjacent Waters by Rudie H. Kuiter (P.T. Gramedia, 1994), a leading authority on Pacific reef fishes, is the first extensive guide to the reef fishes of Indonesia. A compact book at a manageable 300 pages, it includes 1,300 excellent color photographs illustrating 1,027 species, including males, females and juveniles where color or morphological differences exist. The book covers more than 50 families of reef fishes, just about every species you are likely to see around Indonesia's reefs to a depth of about 30 meters.

Micronesian Reef Fishes

Micronesian Reef Fishes: A Practical Guide to the Identification of the Inshore Marine Fishes of the Tropical Central and Western Pacific, 2nd edn, by Robert F. Myers (1989), also belongs in the library of every diver in Indonesia. While Myers has not sought to write a book about Indonesian species, there is a great deal of overlap in the fauna of the two regions of the Pacific and well over 90 percent of the species discussed can be found in Indonesia. Myers' book is a model of accuracy and detail, with clear color photos of more than 1,000 species, complete meristics and a concise 50–100 word description of the habitat and behavior of each species.

Other Works of Interest

The grandfather of all Indonesian fish guides is Bleeker's *Atlas Ichthyologique* (1877). It is still very accurate although not even close to being portable or even available.

Another very valuable book is Gerald R. Allen's *Damselfishes of the World* (Mergus, 1991). This fine book describes and illustrates some 321 damselfish, all that are currently known, including 16 new species. Full meristics and the range and habitat descriptions of all the species are included.

The most available series of books on Indo-Pacific reef life in the United States are those put out by Tropical Fish Hobbyist publications in New Jersey. Unfortunately, these books are problematic due to their editing, misidentified photos and poor organization.

Most reputable dive operators will have a supply of fish identification books in their dive shops or offices. Those most preferred by professional operators are the *Reef Fish* and *Reef Creature Identification* books for the tropical pacific put out by New World Publications.

Fishes

Allen, Gerald R., *Butterfly and Angelfishes of the World*, New York: Wiley Interscience, 1979.

_____, *Damselfishes of the World*. Hong Kong: Mergus, 1991.

Allen, Gerald R. and Roger C. Steene, *Reef Fishes of the Indian Ocean*, Neptune, NJ: T.F.H. Publications, 1988.

Bleeker, Pieter, *Atlas Ichthyologique des Indes Orientales Neerlandaises*, 9 vols, Amsterdam, 1877.

Burgess, Warren E., *Atlas of Marine Aquarium Fishes*, Neptune, NJ: T.F.H. Publications, 1988.

Burgess, Warren E. and Herbert R. Axelrod, *Fishes of the Great Barrier Reef*, Neptune, NJ: T.F.H. Publications. 1975.

_____, *Fishes of Melanesia*, Neptune, NJ: T.F.H. Publications, 1975.

Carcasson, R. H., *A Guide to Coral Reef Fishes of the Indian and West Pacific Regions*, London: Collins, 1977.

Myers, Robert F., *Micronesian Reef Fishes: A Practical Guide to the Identification of the Inshore Marine Fishes of the Tropical Central and Western Pacific*, 2nd edn, Guam: Coral Graphics, 1991.

Nelson, J. S., *Fishes of the World*, New York: John Wiley & Sons, 1984.

Piesch, Ted and D. B. Grobecker, *Frogfishes of the World*, Stanford, CA: Stanford University Press, 1987.

Randall, John E., Gerald R. Allen and Roger Steene, *Fishes of the Great Barrier Reef and the Coral Sea*, Bathhurst, Australia: University of Hawaii Press, 1990.

Sawada, T., *Fishes in Indonesia*, Japan International Cooperation Agency, 1980.

Schuster W. H. and R. R. Djajadiredja, *Local Common Names for Indonesian Fishes*, Bandung, Java: N. V. Penerbit W. Van Hoeve, 1952.

Weber, M. and de Beaufort, L. F., *The Fishes of the Indo-Australian Archipelago*, 11 vols, Leiden, E. J. Brill, 1913-62.

Invertebrates

Debelius, Helmut, *Armoured Nights of the Sea*, Kernan Verlag, 1984.

Ditlev, Hans A., *A Field-Guide to the Reef-Building Corals of the Indo-Pacific*, Klampenborg: Scandinavian Science Press, 1980.

Randall, Richard H. and Robert F. Myers, *Guide to the Coastal Resources of Guam*, Vol. 2, *The Corals*, Guam: University of Guam Press, 1983.

Usher, G. F., "Coral Reef Invertebrates in Indonesia," IUNC/WWF Report, 1984.

Walls, Jerry G. (ed.), *Encyclopedia of Marine Invertebrates*, Neptune, NJ: T.F.H. Publications, 1982.

Wells, Sue, et al. (eds.), *The IUNC Invertebrate Red Data Book*, Gland, Switzerland: International Union for Conservation of Nature and Natural Resources, 1983.

Wood, Elizabeth M., *Corals of the World*, Neptune, NJ: T.F.H. Publications, 1983.

Ecology

George, G., *Marine Life*, Sydney: Rigby Ltd, 1976.

Goreau, Thomas F., Nora I. Goreau and Thomas J. Goreau, "Corals and Coral Reefs," *Scientific American*, Vol. 241, 1979.

Henry, L. E. *Coral Reefs of Malaysia*, Kuala Lumpur: Longman, 1980.

Randall, Richard H. and L. G. Eldredge, *A Marine Survey of The Shoalwater Habitats of Ambon, Pulau Pombo, Pulau Kasa and Pulau Babi*, Guam: University of Guam Marine Laboratory, 1983.

Salm, R. V. and M. Halim, *Marine Conservation Data Atlas*, IUNV/WWF Project 3108, 1984.

Soegiarto, A. and N. Polunin, "The Marine Environment of Indonesia," Report Prepared for the Government of the Republic of Indonesia under the sponsorship of the IUNC and WWF, 1982.

Umbrgrove, J. H. F., "Coral Reefs of the East Indies," *Bulletin of the Geological Society of America*, Vol. 58, 1947.

Wallace, Alfred Russel, *The Malay Archipelago*, reprint, Singapore: Oxford University Press, 1986.

Wells, Sue, et al., *Coral Reefs of the World*, 3 vols, Gland, Switzerland: United Nations Environmental Program, 1988.

Whitten, Tony, Muslimin Mustafa and Greg S. Henderson, *The Ecology of the Indonesian Seas* (Parts One and Two), Singapore: Periplus Editions, 1997.

Wyrtri, K., "Physical Oceanography of the Southeast Asian Waters, Naga Report Vol. 2," La Jolla, CA: University of California, Scripps Institute of Oceanography, 1961.

CONTRIBUTORS

Gerald R. Allen is an American-born Australian ichthyologist who has written over 30 books and 400 scientific articles. He was curator of the Western Australian Museum in Perth from 1974 to 1997 and now works for Conservation International.

Charles Anderson is a British-born marine biologist who has lived and studied marine life in the Maldives since 1983. He now organizes wildlife (whale and dolphin) watching holidays in the Indian Ocean with his wife Susan.

Michael Aw is a Singapore-born marine wildlife and conservation photographer and author based in Sydney. He has won more than 65 international photographic awards.

Gary Bell is one of Australia and the world's most distinguished underwater and wildlife photographers and the founder of Oceanwide Images Stock Photo Library. He has won a string of international awards and contributed images to major nature publications.

Ashley Boyd is an Australian underwater photographer based in Thailand. He has co-authored a number of publications, including *Diving in Thailand* (2004). He teaches underwater photography courses.

Clay Bryce a marine biologist who works with the Western Australian Museum, has studied and photographed marine life for 40 years. He has a special interest in nudibranchs.

David Espinosa has worked for some 30 years in the dive industry. He is currently Editor-in-Chief of *Sport Diver*, the official publication of the PADI Diving Society.

Lynn Funkhouser is an internationally published photographer, author, lecturer and environmental activist and a strong promoter of Philippine dive travel.

Jack Jackson is an award-winning British underwater photographer who has written 20 bestsellers, mostly on underwater subjects. He managed a dive operation in the Red Sea for more than 12 years.

Ingo Jezierski is a Singapore-based travel photographer. He contributed to the photo-editing of this book.

Burt Jones and **Maurine Shimlock** are a Texas-based underwater photographic team who have worked extensively in Indonesia, Malaysia and the Philippines. They run the photo agency Secret Sea Visions.

Heneage Mitchell is a British writer, editor and entrepreneur and the publisher of Asia's first English language scuba diving magazines, *The Philippine Diver*, *Thai Diver* and *ScubGlobe Asia Pacific*.

Kal Muller is a photographer and writer who for the last four decades has specialized in exploring, photographing and writing about Indonesia. Dubbed 'the dean of Indonesian travel writers', he is the author of at least a dozen books, including the Periplus guides to the eastern Indonesian provinces.

Fiona Nichols is a freelance editor, writer, and photographer who was based in Southeast Asia for a decade, regularly diving these waters. Her published works include travel guides, photo features for travel magazines and contributions to several guidebooks.

Mike Severns is a Hawaii-based photographer. For the last 30 years he has run Mike Severns Diving, which specializes in taking out small groups of certified scuba divers for educational, personalized diving in Maui. He is the co-author, with biologist Pauline Fiene-Severns, of the acclaimed *Sulawesi Seas: Indonesia's Magnificent Underwater Realm* (1994).

Michael Stachels is an editor and writer, formerly based in Singapore.

Roger Steene is an Australia-based pioneering underwater photographer. His 13th publication on marine environments, the 3-volume *Colours of the Reef* (2014), contains nearly 7,000 of his finest photographs taken during his 50-year career.

Shaun Tierney is a Londoner who has spent years traveling the planet and capturing images of the underwater world. He and his wife Beth are the authors of *Diving the World*, (2nd edn, 2010) and regularly contribute to several international dive magazines.

Takamasa Tonozuka The late Tokyo-born Takamasa Tonozuka was a long-time Bali resident, underwater photographer and dive operator. He is credited with giving the great muck diving site in Gilimanuk Bay–Secret Bay–its name.

Scott Tuason is an underwater photographer who lives and works in the Philippines. He has co-authored two books, *Philippines Coral Reefs in Water Color* and *Anilao*, and is a founding member of the environmental group Concerned Divers for the Philippines.

John Williams is a California-born writer and PADI dive instructor who spent four years diving in the Caribbean and the Pacific before settling on Phuket in 1987. He runs Siam Dive n' Sail on Kata Beach, which offers a broad range of liveaboard diving.

Sarah Ann Wormald is a Yorkshire-born British writer and dive instructor based in Indonesia. She has been diving for two decades and has spent the last eight years exploring the Indonesian Archipelago. She is the author of the Tuttle Publishing's *Diving in Indonesia* (2015) and continues to guide divers around Indonesia's many islands.

Robert Yin is a Shanghai-born, California-based photographer who has spent 50 years filming Pacific reef fauna. His work has appeared in numerous books and dive magazines, and he is the author of *Beneath Philippine Seas* (1997).

Other Authors The publisher would like to acknowledge the following who also contributed articles to the book:

Bob Bowdey, South African PADI master instructor and co-author of *Diving and Snorkeling Guide to Vanuatu* (1995); **Danny Lim**, Malaysian writer, journalist and photographer; **Bruce Moore**, owner of Black Sand Dive Retreat in the Lembeh Strait, North Sulawesi; **David Pickell**, California-based writer, editor, cartographer and diver and co-author of *Diving Bali* (2010); **Annabel Thomas**, founder and owner-operator of AquaMarine Diving-Bali; **Cody Shwaiko**, writer and long-term expatriate resident in Bali; **Deborah Fugitt**, underwater photographer and writer and organizer of Cityseahorse liveaboard charter trips to Raja Ampat; **Louie and Chen Mencias**, staunch advocates of environmental education and preservation in the Philippines.

Additional Acknowledgements The authors and editors would like to thank the following for their invaluable assistance:

Ron Holland and **Graham** and **Donna Taylor** of Sangalaki Dive Lodge; **Dr Hanny** and **Inneka Batuna** of Manado Murex Resort; **Anton Saksono** of Pulau Putri Resort; **Michael Lee**, recreation manager of Berjaya Beach Resort; and **Henrik Nimb**, PADI course director and director of Master Divers, Singapore.

INDEX

PHOTO CREDITS

All photographs in this book have been provided by Sarah Ann Wormald except for those on the pages listed below:

Front cover, main photo © Kjersti Joergensen/Dreamstime.com; **Front cover, top far left**; **47 bottom** © Fenkie Sumolang/Dreamstime.com; **Front cover, top 2nd left** © Periplus Editions (HK) Pte Ltd, photo by Scott Tuason; **Front cover, top 2nd right** © The Arenui; **Front cover, top far right**; **54 bottom** © Periplus Editions (HK) Pte Ltd, photo by Scott Tuason; **Back cover, top far left**; **18** © Avillion Layang Layang; **Back cover, top 2nd left**; **7 bottom** © Simon Gurney/Dreamstime.com; **Back cover, top 2nd right** © Auroro; **Back cover, top far right; 2/3 top middle**; **129** bottom © Periplus Editions (HK) Pte Ltd, photo by Scott Tuason; Back cover, inset © Periplus Editions (HK) Pte Ltd, photo by Robert Yin; **1** © Periplus Editions (HK) Pte Ltd, photo by Ashley Boyd; **2 top left** © Avillio Layang Layang; **2 top right** © Orlandin/Dreamstime.com; **3 top left** © Periplus Editions (HK) Pte Ltd, photo by Scott Tuason; **3 top right** © Periplus Editions (HK) Pte Ltd, photo by Robert Yin; **4** © Fenkie Sumolang/Dreamstime.com; **5 bottom** © John Becker; **6 top** © Richard Carey/Dreamstime.com; **6 bottom** © Periplus Editions (HK) Pte Ltd, photo by Gary Bell; **7 bottom** © Simon Gurney/Dreamstime.com; **8 top** © Christopher Russell/Dreamstime.com; **9 top** © Periplus Editions (HK) Pte Ltd, photo by Lynn Funkhouser; **10 top** © Matthew Oldfield; **11 bottom** © Periplus Editions (HK) Pte Ltd, photo by Gary Bell; **13 top** © Soren Egeberg/Dreamstime.com; **14 top** © Chee Jin Neoh/Dreamstime.com; **15 bottom** © LKWID; **16** © Periplus Editions (HK) Pte Ltd, photo by Jones/Shimlock; **17 top** © Periplus Editions (HK) Pte Ltd, photo by Jack Jackson; **18** © Avillion

Layang Layang; **19 top** © Periplus Editions (HK) Pte Ltd, photo by Jones/Shimlock; **20 bottom** © Sarah Ann Wormald; **21 bottom** © Aminor Azmi Abdul Latip/Dreamstime.com; **22 top** © Simpadan Scuba; **22 bottom** © Soren Egeberg/Dreamstime.com; **23 top** © Rodrigolab/Dreamstime.com; **24 top** © Asnidamarwani/Dreamstime.com; **26 top** © Avillion Layang Layang; **26 bottom** © Avillion Layang Layang; **28 bottom** © Periplus Editions (HK) Pte Ltd, photo by Jones/Shimlock; **30 top** © R.M. Nunes/Shutterstock.com; **31 bottom** © Seanlean/Dreamstime.com; **32 top** © Bokgallery/Dreamstime.com; **32 bottom** © Armrule/Dreamstime.com; **33 bottom** © Selins/Shutterstock.com; **34 bottom** © Tioman Dive Centre; **35 bottom** © Eugene Sim Junying/Dreamstime.com; **36 bottom** © Periplus Editions (HK) Pte Ltd, photo by R.C. Anderson; **37 bottom** © John Becker; **38** © Kelvintt/Dreamstime.com; **39 top** © Sarah Ann Wormald; **39 bottom** © Weiqing Xia/Dreamstime.com; **41 bottom** © Periplus Editions (HK) Pte Ltd, photo by Jones/Shimlock; **42** © Dirk-jan Mattaar/Dreamstime.com; **43 top** © Kevin Lam/Dreamstime.com; **44 top** © Rafał Cichawa/Dreamstime.com; **45 bottom** © Howard Chew/Dreamstime.com; **46 bottom** © Rafał Cichawa/Dreamstime.com; **45 top** © Howard Chew/Dreamstime.com; **46 bottom** © Rafał Cichawa/Dreamstime.com; **48 top** © Andamanse/Dreamstime.com; **48 bottom** © Andamanse/Dreamstime.com; **49 bottom** © Stubblefieldphoto/Dreamstime.com; **51 top** © Dirk-jan Mattaar/Dreamstime.com; **51 bottom** © Periplus Editions (HK) Pte Ltd, photo by Scott Tuason; **52 bottom** © Stubblefieldphoto/Dreamstime.com; **53** top © Periplus Editions (HK) Pte Ltd, photo by Scott Tuason; **54 top** © Fiona Ayerst/Dreamstime.com; **55 top left** © Andamanse/Dreamstime.com; **55 top right** © Sophietraen/Dreamstime.com; 56 top © Daexto/Dreamstime.com; **57 bottom** © Daexto/Dreamstime.com; 60 bottom © Dirk-jan Mattaar/Dreamstime.com; **61 bottom** © Jeremy Brown/Dreamstime.com; **62 top** © Jeremy Brown/Dreamstime.com; **62 bottom** © Jeremy Brown/Dreamstime.com; **63 bottom** © Dirk-jan Mattaar/Dreamstime.com; **65 top left** © Jiří Hruška/Dreamstime.com; **65 top right** © Andamanse/Dreamstime.com; 65 bottom © Pavel Aleynikov/Dreamstime.com; **66 bottom** © Tatsianat/Dreamstime.com; **67 top left** © Greg Duncan/Dreamstime.com; **67 top right** © Petr Zamecnik/Dreamstime.com; **68 bottom** © Jeremy Brown/Dreamstime.com; **69 top** © Teguh Tirtaputra/Dreamstime.com; **70 bottom** © Nvelichko/Dreamstime.com; **72 top** © Rich Carey/Bigstock.com; **73 bottom left** © Jeremy Brown/Dreamstime.com; **73 bottom right** © Jeremy Brown/Shutterstock.com; **74 top** © Jeremy Brown/Dreamstime.com; **75 bottom** © Periplus Editions (HK) Pte Ltd, photo by Scott Tuason; **76 bottom** © fenkieandreas/Shutterstock.com; 77 top © Parnupong Norasethkamol/Dreamstime.com; **77 bottom** © Nicolas Voisin/Dreamstime.com; **79 bottom** © Rostislav Ageev/Shutterstock.com; **80 bottom** © Nick Everett/Dreamstime.com; **83 top** © Parnupong Norasethkamol/Dreamstime.com; **84 top** © Marcel Toung/Shutterstock.com; **84 bottom** © Nick Everett/Dreamstime.com; **85 top** © Ethan Daniels/Shutterstock.com; **85 bottom** © Pniesen/Dreamstime.com; **86 bottom** © John Becker; **88 top** © Periplus Editions (HK) Pte Ltd, photo by Scott Tuason; **89 bottom** © J.Croese/Shutterstock.com; **91 top** © Fenkie Sumolang/Dreamstime.com; **92 top** © Fenkie Sumolang/

Dreamstime.com; **94 top** © Periplus Editions (HK) Pte Ltd, photo by Deborah Fugitt; **95 bottom** © Kri Eco Resort; **97 bottom** © Ricky Rusli Kurniawan; **98 top** © Blue Marlin Komodo; **99 bottom** © Didi Lotze; **100 top** © Matthew Oldfield; **100 bottom** © Arenui; **101 top** © Patrick Beijk; **101 bottom** © Shakti Liveaboard; **103 bottom** © Asia Divers; **104 top** © Periplus Editions (HK) Pte Ltd, photo by Scott Tuason; **104 bottom** © Beth Watson and Asia Divers; **105 top** © Beth Watson and Asia Divers; **105 bottom** © Kkg1/Dreamstime.com; **107 top** © Palawan Divers; **107 bottom** © Orlandin/Dreamstime.com; **108 top** © Orlandin/Dreamstime.com; **109 top** © John Becker; **109 bottom** © Asia Divers; **110 bottom** © Chris Von Damm/Siren Fleet; 111 top © Sarah Ann Wormald; **111 bottom** © Chris Von Damm/Siren Fleet; **112 top** © Sarah Ann Wormald; **113 bottom** © Rich Carey/Shutterstock.com; **114 top** © Sarah Ann Wormald; **114 bottom** © Rich Carey/Shutterstock.com; **115 bottom** © Periplus Editions (HK) Ltd, photo by Jack Jackson; **116 bottom** © Periplus Editions (HK) Ltd, photo by Robert Yin; **118 top** © donsimon/Bigstock.com; **119 bottom** © Periplus Editions (HK) Pte Ltd, photo by Jack Jackson; **121 bottom** © SARAWUT KUNDEJ/Shutterstock.com; **122 top left** © Periplus Editions (HK) Pte Ltd, photo by Gary Bell; **122 top right** © Kkg1/Dreamstime.com; **123 bottom** © Howard Chew/Thinkstock.com; **125 bottom** © Dudarev Mikhail/Bigstock.com; **127 top and bottom** © Atlantis Dive Resort; **128 bottom** © Action Divers; **131 top** © John Becker; **132 top and bottom** © John Becker; **133 bottom** © Boracay Island New Wave Divers; **134 bottom** © Rich Carey/Bigstock.com; **135 top** © Boracay Island New Wave Divers; **135 bottom** © Dezay/Bigstock.com; **137 bottom** © Rich Carey/Bigstock.com; **139 bottom** © John Nightingale, Thresher Shark Divers; **140 top** © Uwe Jacobs, Thresher Shark Divers;

140 bottom © John Nightingale, Thresher Shark Divers; **141 top** © John Nightingale, Thresher Shark Divers; **141 bottom** © nicolasvoisin44/Shutterstock.com; **142 bottom** © Periplus Editions (HK) Pte Ltd, photo by Scott Tuason; **144 bottom** © Periplus Editions (HK) Pte Ltd, photo by Fiona Nichols; **145 bottom** © Dolphin House Resort; **146 bottom** © Yves Sautter/Dreamstime.com; **148 bottom** © Periplus Editions (HK) Pte Ltd, photo by Mike Severns; **149 bottom** © Periplus Editions (HK) Pte Ltd, photo by Scott Tuason; **151 bottom** © Rich Carey/Bigstock.com; 152 bottom © Mikhail Dudarev/Dreamstime.com; **153 bottom** © Rich Carey/Bigstock.com; **155 bottom** © Periplus Editions (HK) Pte Ltd, photo by Jack Jackson; **156 top** © Periplus Editions (HK) Pte Ltd, photo by Ashley Boyd; **157 bottom** © littlesam/Shuttestock.com; **158 bottom** © Mirko Vitali/Dreamstime.com; **159 bottom** © Palawan Divers; **160 top** © Palawan Divers; **160 bottom** © Plotnikov/Dreamstime.com; **161** © Softlightaa/Dreamstime.com; **162 bottom** © Hemera/Thinkstock.com; **163 bottom** © Rich Carey/Bigstock.com; **164 bottom** © Wassiliy/Thinkstock.com; **166 top** © John Becker; **166 bottom** © Periplus Editions (HK) Pte Ltd, photo by Scott Tuason; **167 top and bottom** © Sarah Ann Wormald; 168 bottom Siren Fleet © Philippine Siren; **169 bottom** © seachic51/Thinkstock.com; **170 top** © Periplus Editions (HK) Pte Ltd, photo by Ashley Boyd; **171 bottom** © Periplus Editions (HK) Pte Ltd, photo by Jack Jackson; **172 bottom** © John Becker; **173 top** © John Becker; **173 bottom** © Sarah Ann Wormald; **175 bottom** © Johnnyjoker/Dreamstime.com; **176 top** © Soren Egeberg/Dreamstime.com; **178 top** © Cartu13/Dreamstime.com; **179 bottom** © Kampee Patisena/Dreamstime.com; **180 bottom** © Periplus Editions (HK) Pte Ltd, photo by Scott Tuason; 181 top © Piboon Srimak/Dreamstime.com; **182 top** © Olga Khoroshunova/Dreamstime.com;

182 bottom © Soren Egeberg/Dreamstime.com; **183 top left** © Szczap/Dreamstime.com; **183 top right** © Vaulot/Dreamstime.com; **184 bottom** © Michal Maly/Dreamstime.com; **185 bottom** © Kampee Patisena/Dreamstime.com; **186 top** © Periplus Editions (HK) Pte Ltd, photo by Scott Tuason; **187 bottom** © Worldwidestock/Dreamstime.com; **188 bottom** © Periplus Editions (HK) Pte Ltd, photo by Scott Tuason; **189 top** © Periplus Editions (HK) Pte Ltd, photo by Scott Tuason; **190 bottom** © Piboon Srimak/Dreamstime.com; **191 bottom** © Periplus Editions (HK) Pte Ltd, photo by Scott Tuason; **192 bottom** © Periplus Editions (HK) Pte Ltd, photo by Scott Tuason; **193 top** © Kampee Patisena/Dreamstime.com; **194 bottom** © Periplus Editions (HK) Pte Ltd, photo by Scott Tuason; **195 bottom** © August1967/Dreamstime.com; **196 bottom** © Periplus Editions (HK) Pte Ltd, photo by Scott Tuason; **198 top** © Periplus Editions (HK) Pte Ltd, photo by Scott Tuason; **198 bottom** © Sarah Ann Wormald; **199 bottom** © Vichaya Kiatying-angsulee/Dreamstime.com; **200 top** © Periplus Editions (HK) Pte Ltd, photo by Ingo Jezierski; **200 bottom** © Kjersti Joergensen/Dreamstime.com; **202 top** © Periplus Editions (HK) Pte Ltd, photo by Robert Yin; **202 bottom** © Periplus Editions (HK) Pte Ltd, photo by Robert Yin; **203 top** © Tupungato/Dreamstime.com; **204 bottom** © Thiti Tangjitsangiem/Dreamstime.com; **206 bottom** © Periplus Editions (HK) Pte Ltd, photo by Robert Yin; **207 top** © John Becker; **207 bottom** © Periplus Editions (HK) Pte Ltd, photo by Gary Bell; **208 bottom** © Don Mammoser/Shutterstock.com; **209 top** © Easy Divers Koh Samui; **210 top** © Easy Divers Koh Samui; **211 bottom** © ihab/Thinkstock.com; **213 top** © Searobin Dive Center; **213 bottom** © Soren Egeberg/Dreamstime.com; **214 bottom** © Scubaball/Dreamstime.com; **217 bottom** © Dudarev Mikhail/Shutterstock.com

Other titles of interest from Tuttle Publishing

ISBN: 978-0-8048-4474-1

ISBN: 978-0-8048-4224-2

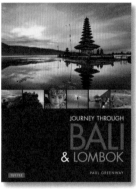

ISBN 978-0-8048-4386-7

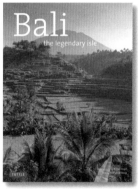

ISBN: 978-0-8048-4397-3

ISBN 978-0-8048-4211-2

ISBN: 978-0-8048-4212-9

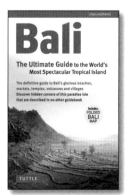

ISBN: 978-0-8048-4206-8